NORTHERN SPIRITS

Northern Spirits

John Watson, George Grant, and Charles Taylor – Appropriations of Hegelian Political Thought

ROBERT C. SIBLEY

McGill-Queen's University Press
Montreal & Kingston · London · Ithaca

© McGill-Queen's University Press 2008
ISBN 978-0-7735-3269-4 (cloth)
ISBN 978-0-7735-3303-5 (paper)

Legal deposit first quarter 2008
Bibliothèque nationale du Québec

Printed in Canada on acid-free paper that is 100% ancient forest free
(100% post-consumer recycled), processed chlorine free.

McGill-Queen's University Press acknowledges the support of the Canada
Council for the Arts for our publishing program. We also acknowledge the
financial support of the Government of Canada through the Book Publishing
Industry Development Program (BPIDP) for our publishing activities.

Library and Archives Canada Cataloguing in Publication

Sibley, Robert C. (Robert Cameron), 1951–
    Northern spirits: John Watson, George Grant, and Charles Taylor:
    appropriations of Hegelian political thought / Robert C. Sibley.

Includes bibliographical references
ISBN 978-0-7735-3269-4 (cloth)
ISBN 978-0-7735-3303-5 (pbk)

1. Watson, John, 1847–1939 – Political and social views. 2. Grant,
George, 1918–1988 – Political and social views. 3. Taylor, Charles, 1931–
– Political and social views. 4. Hegel, Georg Wilhelm Friedrich,
1770–1831. 5. Political science – Canada. 6. Canada – Politics and
government – Philosophy. I. Title.

B982.S52 2008   320.0971   C2007-906958-4

This book was typeset by Interscript in 10/13 Baskerville.

This essay is dedicated to my wife, Margret Kopala.
Her constancy, encouragement, and wisdom ensured its completion.

Contents

Acknowledgments

I incurred many debts in writing this essay. In particular, I wish to thank Brian McKillop, who provided the right book and the right idea at the right time; Peter Emberley, from whom I learned so much; Waller Newell, a superb teacher and a gracious friend; and Jack Healy, who introduced me to George Grant. My greatest debt, however, is to Tom Darby, who supervised my doctoral dissertation. He not only introduced me to political philosophy, but gave me his friendship. I am grateful and honoured.

I should also like to express my gratitude to colleagues at the *Ottawa Citizen*, management and staff, for helping to make it possible for me to combine my work as a journalist with my scholarly interests. Finally, my thanks to Judith Turnbull, whose editing greatly improved the material, and to Sharon Burnett for her timely help on the index.

NORTHERN SPIRITS

Spirit in Canada

Hegel did not have much to say about Canada. In fact, Canada is rarely mentioned in his writings, and then only in passing. There is a reference in the posthumous *Lectures on the Philosophy of World History*. In a comment on the War of 1812, Hegel says that the inability of Americans to conquer the Canadian colonies was due to their poor organisation. But looking to the future, he says Canada and Mexico "present no serious threat" to the United States. This will serve the United States well because, unlike most European countries, it will not need to maintain a large standing army to ward off threats of invasion. Such a situation might make the United States the "country of the future, and its world-historical importance has yet to be revealed in the ages which lie ahead."[1] And that, it seems, is the only thought the German philosopher ever gave to colonial Canada.

Canadians, on the other hand, have given much thought to Hegel. As John Burbidge notes, Canadians have often "found Hegel's thought a basis for understanding society and religion, thought and reality."[2] Some have argued that proportionately "Canada may produce more original work on Hegel than any other nation."[3] Indeed, it is arguable that Hegel's thought has been as fully articulated in Canada as it has been in the United States, if not more so. Because of the country's traditions and historical circumstances certain Hegelian principles have sunk deep into Canadian political thought. This interest in Hegel dates to the mid-nineteenth century. While Hegelian thought made its first impression in the United States with the arrival of German immigrants who became known as the St Louis Hegelians, Hegel was introduced into Canada through Scottish immigrants who imbibed the thought of the Scottish Enlightenment.[4] As Leslie Armour writes, "In the hundred years after 1850 the mainstream of philosophy in English-speaking Canada was more often than not Hegelian."[5]

   Philosophers live as long as their ideas continue to attract debate. If Hegel remains alive for Canadian thinkers, what is it about his ideas that still attracts so much discussion? Philosophic ideas almost inevitably emerge in response to social and political conflicts and crises. Plato and Aristotle established Greek philosophy to find those ideas that could respond to the crisis of the Athenian *polis*. Kant's thought reflected the tensions of an eighteenth-century German society divided by religious and ethnic differences, and a geography that saw Germans scattered among many other ethnic groups. Hegel's famous statement in *Philosophy of Right* that the Owl of Minerva flies only at twilight implies that philosophy comes into its own in times of change or when a particular way of life is disappearing. Which is to say, people turn to philosophy in times of change and uncertainty, when historical shifts erode and transform past traditions and practices. Canadian thinkers by and large reflect this psychology. As Leslie Armour and Elizabeth Trott say, "We needed ideas that were capable of spanning spaces and which could link sub-cultures which, because of their distribution, tended to grow in significantly different ways."[6]

   Arguably, Hegel's political philosophy appeals to the Canadian mind because it offers ways by which complex, pluralistic societies can use political systems, legal institutions, and social policies to mitigate or counterbalance those forces that threaten to tear them apart. Canadian thinkers – including my three representative Hegelians, John Watson, George Grant, and Charles Taylor – turned to Hegel to help them comprehend the tensions of Canada's existence. Hegelian concepts offered theoretical tools for working out how different groups might be united politically regardless of their seemingly irresolvable differences. In a country such as Canada, with its ethnically and linguistically diverse population, vast geography, and historical domination by imperial powers, a philosophy that might reconcile this diversity even as it respected diversity was valuable in that it helped to account for the nature of the country and, hence, to respond intelligibly to that which threatened its existence. As Elizabeth Trott observes, "The Hegelian dialectic has offered a way of understanding the relative success of the uneasy and fragile existence of Canada."[7] Canadians were attracted to Hegel by his "argument for the essential unity and interconnectedness of things: philosophy and science, thought and nature, reason and experience."[8]

   Hegel, in other words, appeals to Canadian theorists because he provides a dynamic vision of a political and social order that attempts to reconcile what seemingly cannot be reconciled. Watson, for example, devotes much of his political philosophy to questioning the proper purpose of the state and the proper relationship between the individual and the state.

Grant was concerned with the survival of the Canadian nation-state, seeing its demise as the consequence of the Hegelian progressivist consciousness that, when combined with excessive individualism, proves corrosive to healthy social and political traditions. Taylor devotes much of his thought to questions of civil society and how to reconcile the diverse elements of the Canadian state to help diverse cultural communities survive.

Such employment of Hegelian principles stands in contrast to the more romantic tendencies of American thinkers. Where American Hegelians link Hegel's concepts of progress and freedom to notions of manifest destiny, Canadian Hegelians tend to emphasise the communitarian side of Hegel – that is, the Hegel who was concerned with the harmonisation of individual freedom and the communal existence of human beings. Francis Fukuyama, for example, draws on Hegel's notion of historical progress to conclude that, with the collapse of communism, the ideological evolution of mankind has come to its end. With the fall of the Soviet empire, he argues, the historical process that had seen the rise of feudalism, monarchism, fascism, communism, and liberalism has come to its conclusion. Democratic practices and free markets such as those embodied in the United States have triumphed over all competing systems as the best way to organise human affairs. The kind of liberal democracy practised in the United States is the final form of human government and is destined to transform the globe into a likeness of itself.[9]

This triumphalist appropriation of Hegel can also be detected in the nineteenth-century St Louis school of American Hegelians. Intellectuals such as Denton J. Snider and William Torrey Harris were attracted to Hegel's social and political philosophy by, in part, its apparent capacity to reconcile the individual and the community and serve to countervail British empiricism. Snider links Hegel to American manifest destiny in a 1904 book, *Modern European Philosophy*, in which he argues that Hegel fails to fully comprehend the potential of the United States to become a modern state in spite of its unsophisticated and undeveloped people. Nor, Snider argues, does the German philosopher recognise the nation's capacity to create even more free states as it expanded westward. Nevertheless, Snider anticipates Fukuyama when he borrows from Hegel to describe the United States as the embodiment of the most recent form of World Spirit: "The odyssey of the Hegelian World Spirit is clear – the United States has already arrived on the scene, bearing in its political structure the principle destined to become the *Begriff* of all future political reality."[10] This point will become more evident when John Watson's thought is compared with that of some of his contemporaries in the United States.

Canadian Hegelians tend to be less absolutist – and less triumphalist – than their American counterparts. Tom Darby, for example, critiques Fukuyama's thesis, arguing that "his total picture of the end of history is distorted" in its assumption that "liberalism has won out," and that his sketch of the post-Soviet New World is overly optimistic in its triumphalism.[11] This is an argument that George Grant also considers – and denounces. Both John Watson and Charles Taylor are drawn to Hegel because Hegel provides a theoretical framework that encourages people to recognise diversity and allow particular cultures to develop and retain their distinctive features, but, at the same time, encourages them to look for ways to coexist in a single state. This idea of an integrated yet diverse society can be seen at the concrete level, so the argument goes, in such nation-building institutions as Canada's welfare and health care systems, its telecommunications policies, its public broadcasting system, its national unemployment insurance and pension plans, and even its nation-spanning highways and railways. Some argue that such institutional accommodations make Canadians, as a whole, unconscious Hegelians.[12] Canadians seem to have grasped intuitively, if not reflectively, that it is the unending regional and ethnic tensions of their political existence and the constant continentalist temptation that makes Canada the kind of state it is, for good or ill.

The theme of crisis and survival runs like a bright red thread through the tapestry of Canadian historiography and political theory. Numerous scholars point to a deep-seated uncertainty about Canada's political survival as an independent and united state on the northern half of the North American continent.[13] This uncertainty about the country's survival – and about what is necessary to ensure its survival – is the consequence of various historical experiences and the constant recasting of responses to those experiences. Canadian political history, according to this argument, reflects the clash of conflicting forces: "a struggle to build a nation in the face of stern geographic difficulties;"[14] the pull of external powers such as Britain and the United States; and the abiding tensions of a culturally diverse population. The most crucial fact about Canada, it has been said, and what makes Canada's survival so problematic, is the question of English-French relations – "two nations warring in the bosom of a single state," to quote Lord Durham's famous phrase. Some, of course, have argued that any permanent reconciliation of these differences is impossible and that the Canadian political order is a mistake of history.[15]

Regardless of whether Canada's political existence ultimately proves to be a "mistake," it is reasonable to suggest that it is the tension of and doubts about Canada's political existence, along with the endless conflicts borne of that tension, that inform what it means to be Canadian. Canadians, in Leslie Armour's words, "have never really been able to conceptualize Canada as a simple cultural unity and have had to think in terms of plurality, but, more importantly, that the tensions in this plurality have always been endemic to it."[16] In response to this tension, Canadians have tried to maintain a kind of dynamic balance in the country's political existence by various means, including offsetting one party's dominance at the federal level with the election of other political parties at the provincial level. We have tried to mitigate regional tensions with the countervailing attractions of federal institutions and national policies. We have attempted to compensate for the divisions fostered by a polyethnic society with a "rational pluralism"[17] that has produced ideas such as multiculturalism and, arguably, an emphasis on "peace, order and good government." Add to these dynamic circumstances the reality of dwelling in "a state of more or less permanent constitutional crisis"[18] and we have a constant pressing need to think through what these existential realities might mean for Canada's social and political future, or, indeed, whether it has a future.

Canada emerged in the age of nation building. The nineteenth century saw the formation of a number of nation-states – Germany, Italy, and Australia, for example – as part of a worldwide movement for national unification. Canadian Confederation was part of this movement. But Canada's situation was somewhat different, particularly in comparison to another "new society" on the North American continent, the United States. The American founders, guided by the principles of the Enlightenment, sought to create an ideal national type that would apply to all citizens regardless of their ethnic or linguistic background. The Americans thought it possible to establish a new national identity that would be, broadly speaking, culturally and ideologically homogeneous. Newcomers were expected to cast off their European ideas of society and adopt a new set of ideas – the American way of life.[19] However, Canada, according to one widely accepted view, consisted of two fragment societies, each of which had its own values, traditions, and language. One was French-speaking, Catholic, and, by and large, agrarian; the other was English-speaking, Protestant, commercially minded, and conservatively liberal in its view of society.[20]

Given Canada's different societies and cultures, it proved difficult to find agreement on fundamentals. Historically, the creation of an overarching national identity – such as that espoused by the Canada Firsters in the late 1800s – in which all Canadians could see a reflection of themselves, has been impossible. Canadians' historical preoccupation has been with catering to differences, not similarities. Canadians have focused on fostering a

state that was sufficiently unified, not on instilling a binding national my-
thology. They have sought ideas that would allow culturally disparate
groups to coexist more or less peaceably. It is debatable as to which nation, Canada or the United States, will prove to be more stable (and sustainable) in the long run, but there is no denying that Canada lacks an
ideal national type because there is no overarching national "faith" that
all Canadians would willingly profess in common. As Barry Cooper points
out, the central Canadian myth of the "survival of the garrison" has little
imaginative claim on western Canadians: "[T]he West is not a trans-
planted imaginative Ontario garrison."[21]

What French- and English-speakers shared was their retention of ties
with a transatlantic culture – imperial Britain in the case of English-
speakers and Catholic France in the case of the French. Paradoxically,
then, the single element the two fragment societies shared was one that
precluded them from achieving a consensus on the fundamentals for a second new society in North America, a Canadian way of life, if you will. Confederation reflected the creation of a political entity that owed its birth to
the concerns of both fragment societies to preserve their respective cultures. Certainly, there was some consensus among the two groups, but it
was not derived from a particular culture or a set of theoretical principles.
Rather it was a pragmatic consensus that recognised and even encouraged
diversity. George-Étienne Cartier expressed this view when, in supporting
the idea of Confederation, he argued that nations had to be formed "by
the agglomeration of communities having kindred interests and sympathies."[22] The idea that different races could be unified was, in Cartier's
view, utopian and impossible. Central to the interests and sympathies of
these two European founding fragments was the view that conformity to a
single national identity, a national faith, was not possible. Ever since, Canada's political history has been characterised by the never-ending need, for
the sake of political unity and independence from the United States, to
accommodate differences and to avoid imposing cultural uniformity.
Canadian society was to be based not on a celebration of individual freedom – "life, liberty and the pursuit of happiness," in the words of the American constitution – but rather on "peace, order and good government."
Canada's federation, in short, was not to be glued together by a nation-
binding myth but by law and institutions.

The question of Canada's existence provides an overarching *leitmotif* for
this essay. The establishment and maintenance of the Canadian political
community have been achieved in the face of various conflicting forces, both
internal and external. The interrelated factors of geography, economics,

and politics; of different traditions, religions, and languages; of conflicting claims for national unity and regional autonomy; of communitarian impulses clashing with individualistic aspirations – all these have informed Canadian political experience. And the general thrust of this political tale has been, and continues to be, to accommodate and reconcile as best as possible the divergent stresses and strains created by historical experience.[23] This historical situation has made Canadian political thinkers realise the importance of maintaining political and social institutions that preserve and reflect the dynamic balance of the country. Hegel's political philosophy has been helpful in providing the theoretical means for this effort. Hegel reveals a way of rationally mediating the tensions and conflicts that are inevitable in the Canadian balancing act. When Hegel posits the notion of the identity of identity and non-identity, the key word for Canadian political theorists is the conjunction *and*, which implies the function of both linking and separating. That is to say, Canada's Hegelians see the necessity for both a pulling away *and* a coming together, a need for disunity amidst unity. Leslie Armour and Elizabeth Trott express this view in suggesting that there is a kind of "philosophical federalism" at work among Canadian thinkers, "a natural inclination to find out why one's neighbour thinks differently rather than to find out how to show him up as an idiot."[24]

By way of contrast, Hegel's American and, to some extent, British interpreters tend to collapse the non-identity side of the equation into identity. Generally speaking, they take differences and collapse them into a new identity that incorporates identity and non-identity. This is evident in Fukuyama's end-of-history triumphalism, as well as in Snider's sentiments regarding American manifest destiny. But it is also seen in the thought of F.H. Bradley and Bernard Bosanquet, who tend to subsume the individual in the state. Similarly, Josiah Royce, the American Hegelian, in adapting Hegel's principle of reconciliation, replaced the Hegelian Absolute with a community united by a common understanding of and feeling toward the world suitable for the newly minted American nation. Royce also reflected the greater tendency of Americans to read Hegel psychologically (as distinct from socially), which is perhaps indicative of the American concern for individual self-fulfilment. Such an approach tends to place less emphasis on the dynamic of the Hegelian dialectic, downplaying that there is inevitably a reaction against any apparent "moment" of equilibrium. But it is this dynamic aspect of the dialectic that Canadian theorists find particularly fascinating and useful. The Canadians seem to see identity and non-identity as two forces or entities that function in a kind of yin-yang relationship; paradoxically, that which keeps these forces apart is that which keeps them together. Canadian Hegelians take the attitude that every *push* to overcome disunity and to create unity results in opposition or disunity. Conversely, every *pull* that generates differences or diversity similarly turns into its opposite and generates forces that seek greater unity. This phenomenon can arguably be seen in Canada's history. When the forces of regionalism become too strong, Canadians offset them with a stronger federal government; when the federal government becomes too overbearing, regional pressures grow more insistent.[25]

Hegel's system building reflects historical circumstances that Canada's nineteenth-century nation builders would have found familiar. In Hegel's time, Germany was not yet a nation. The German-speaking people of nineteenth-century Europe were divided from one another by religion, ethnic origin, and a geography that left them scattered among Czechs, Slovaks, Poles, and the French. In the late 1700s and early 1800s, German states were fragmented by quasi-feudal institutions that sought to maintain local identities and traditions at the expense of German unity. Hegel both applauded and castigated the collectivism and corporatism of the Holy Roman Empire. He endorsed the French Revolution's ideals and the rationalisation of Europe under Napoleon, but turned away in horror from the Terror and Napoleon's destructiveness.[26]

Hegel's political philosophy demonstrates a theoretical effort to mediate the conflicts of geography, religion, ethnicity, and language that divided nineteenth-century Germans. Or, put another way, Hegel's thought reflects an attempt to work through the conundrums of identity and freedom to address the problematic questions of the relationship between the individual and the community, between freedom and collectivity. Hegel's theoretical elaborations on social and political institutions and practical philosophy continue to make his thought relevant to contemporary concerns regarding issues of community, national identity, group identity, and individual rights. Hegel's theories on modern institutions – the family, corporations, and the state, for example – consider the problematic nature of the relationship between freedom and community with a view to reconciling both egalitarian and collectivist impulses. Hegel was, thus, among the first to consider the inherent conflicts and tensions of the institutions, practices, and historical forces that have shaped modern society.[27]

Canadian thinkers, too, have sought concepts and ideas that would unite Canada's diverse peoples and regions even while respecting those forces that promote difference and diversity. As emphasised above, Hegel provides a theoretical framework that encourages people to recognise diversity and allow cultures to maintain and develop their distinctive features. And it is this aspect of Hegel's thought that makes it so attractive to Canadian theorists, including my representative Hegelians, each of whom found in the German philosopher a theoretical language that provided them with a philosophic model by means of which they could articulate their concerns regarding Canada's situation. Which is to say, their efforts to find solutions to the problems of the Canadian political community were informed, in part at least, by their appropriations of certain elements in Hegel's thought – from his project of reconciliation and his view of the state and its relationship to the individual to his understanding of the relationship between freedom and community and his concept of the master-slave dialectic as the engine of history.

My essay attempts to track some movements of Hegelian philosophy in Canadian political thought, or, if you will, the movement of Spirit in the Canadian mind. I use this trope bearing in mind the etymology of the word *spirit*.[28] As a noun, *spirit* comes from the Latin *spiritus*, which is derived from the verb *spirare*, to breathe. The Latin is a translation of the Greek word for breath, *pneuma*. In the Augustan period, *spiritus* referred to the breath or soul of life, that which gives life to the physical organism. It also had connotations of courage and vigour. In Hegel's time, Spirit, or *Geist*, referred to the highest mode of existence or the principle of life. In this sense, Spirit is something dynamic, having to do with purpose and what is that *is*. A phenomenology of Spirit is an account of why things are the way they are and not otherwise.[29]

My essay is written in this spirit. The question to which the essay is a response is twofold. First, how have Canadian thinkers employed Hegel to address their concerns about the questions of their time – the influence of technology, the problems of multiculturalism, the implications of globalisation, the lure of continentalism, and, more recently, the renewed debate on empire in the Age of Terror? And second, is there anything in their appropriations of Hegel that Canadian thinkers can still draw on to address the problematic nature of Canada's existence in the twenty-first century? In effect, following Hegel, I am inquiring into the animating principles of the Canadian state, the modes of existence that Canadian theorists have detected in attempting to respond to the tensions and uncertainties of Canada's political existence. I am in good company. To read Watson, Grant, and Taylor is to see Hegelian thought alive and acting in the present, not as some dead philosophical artefact of the past. There is an abiding sense in all three that Spirit is at work in the here and now, permeating everyday life and the larger events of the world. To track the movement of this Spirit as it relates to the phenomenon of Canada is to discover the changing concepts and understandings about this country, our shifting sense of what it means to be Canadian and what our purposes are – if any – as a nation.

PART ONE

Hegel and the Spirit of Reconciliation

1

Reconciliation, Freedom, and the State

Iris Murdoch once remarked that knowing what scares a philosopher offers insight into his deepest aspirations: "It is always a significant question to ask about any philosopher: what is he afraid of?"[1] The observation certainly applies to Hegel. He applauded the French Revolution in its initial stages as a legitimate assertion of human freedom, but turned away in horror when the pursuit of unlimited freedom became a justification for Robespierre's Terror.[2] "The fanaticism of freedom, put into the hands of the people, became terrible,"[3] he writes.

Hegel's fear of disorder is evident in the preface of his 1807 book *Phenomenology of Spirit,* where he refers to the early nineteenth century as "a birth-time and a period of transition to a new era." The world that once seemed stable and permanent is "dissolving bit by bit." This dissolution is unsettling and full of foreboding. Yet beneath this shaky surface is an ordered, coherent, and intelligible whole. If we could comprehend this whole, we would see, as in a sudden burst of sunlight in a darkened cave, "the features of the new world." The coming-to-be of this new world will be a time of upheaval. But once this new world, this Spirit, is comprehended and actualised in its fullness, then, says Hegel, our sense of disorder will be overcome at the personal, political, and metaphysical levels.[4] Even earlier, though, in the introduction to an 1801 essay, Hegel says that philosophy comes on the scene in times of need, when the harmony of existence is fragmented by the mind's awareness of antinomies in its understanding of reality, when people no longer have faith in their gods, when man is alienated from the natural world, when the individual no longer identifies with his community. As he states, "Dichotomy is the source of *the need of philosophy*."[5]

Given the aims of my essay, a full exegesis of Hegel's philosophic enterprise is not necessary. My purposes require only a brief summary of key

Hegelian concepts – as distinct from a detailed analysis or commentary – to provide the necessary philosophic context for my discussion of the thought of Watson, Grant, and Taylor. With this narrow purpose in mind, I have employed the notion of Hegel's "project of reconciliation"[6] as the over-arching conceptual structure within which to summarise those aspects of his political thought applicable to my needs. I do so for two reasons. First, whether Hegel is interpreted as a revolutionary, a reactionary, a free-market liberal, a communitarian, a conservative, an atheist, or a Christian meta-physician, there is little dispute that at the core of his philosophic enter-prise is the effort to reconcile the disorders of modern life – social, political, and spiritual. Second, the notion of reconciliation fits well with the concerns of my essay. The idea of a project of reconciliation offers a way to understand why Hegel continues to have considerable resonance in Canadian political thought. As I hope to demonstrate, it is not unreason-able to claim that the theme of reconciliation resides at the centre of Cana-dian political philosophy. Thus, the concept of reconciliation provides a structuring metaphor that allows me to deploy Hegel's thought in relation to the various Canadian appropriations of that thought. Or, put differently, Hegel's project of reconciliation provides a convenient lens through which to track my "northern spirits."

Reconciliation, or *Vershönung*, is Hegel's term for the process of supersed-ing the antinomies of existence, the sense of being alienated from the natu-ral and social worlds in which one exists. In this process of reconciliation, the diremptions, or sense of separation and dividedness, that individuals ex-perience in terms of their self-comprehension are surmounted, as well as the divisions they experience between themselves and the social world. Rec-onciliation is that experiential condition in which consciousness knows itself to be at home both with itself and with others, including the "other" that is the whole.[7] While Hegel never made the concept of reconciliation an ex-plicit topic in his philosophy, it is clearly central to his thought.[8] Of course, for Hegel, the essential means for this reconciliation is philosophy. By means of reason, philosophy seeks to reconcile the individual not only to what exists, but also to the *real*, the *actual*, or *das Wirkliche*, that informs exist-ence. From his early essay *Differenzschrift* through to *Philosophy of Right*, Hegel holds that the need for philosophy emerges in times "of cultural conflict and intellectual disillusionment, where there is a perceived disunity be-tween human ideals and human reality."[9] And "'philosophy is the reconcili-ation following upon the disintegration of the real world.'"[10]

This theme of reconciliation resides at the core Hegel's *Phenomenology of Spirit*.[11] The book explores various strategies that human consciousness has used in attempting to overcome the antinomies of existence. Hegel shows all these strategies of thought to be attempts at reconciliation – whether in the form of a master who asserts his self-certainty by dominating another, the stoic's flight into solitude in order to escape suffering, the attempted escape of the sceptic who seeks release from the world's claims by denying reality, or the unhappy consciousness of the religious dogmatist who projects an ultimate justification of human existence into a realm beyond time. Inevitably, these ways of escape are insufficient because they cannot maintain a concrete sense of reconciliation amidst the divisions they inevitably promote.[12] It is because of the seeming impossibility of overcoming the tensions and discord of human life that Hegel describes the development of human consciousness, in its quest for self-realisation and some ultimate justification for human suffering, as "the pathway of doubt" or "the way of despair."[13] At the same time, Hegel shows that the way of despair actually promotes the effort to seek reconciliation. It is the tension of existence itself – the apparent incoherence between consciousness and reality, the existential experience of alienation – that engenders the dialectical project of reconciliation.

The centrality of the concept of reconciliation for Hegel becomes apparent when the word's meaning in German is more fully understood. Reconciliation, or *Versöhnung*, has deeper philosophical implications than those generally associated with its English translation. *Versöhnung* possesses a more active and positive connotation than the English *reconciliation*, with its connotations of quietism, resignation, or reluctant acceptance. *Versöhnung* has none of these suggestions of submission, surrender, or acquiescence. Rather, *Versöhnung* involves a sense of affirmation and a process of transformation. This process is to be understood as an overcoming of conflict, division, and alienation that leads, in the end, to an experience of harmony, unity, and friendship or love.[14] Regarded in this light, the concept of reconciliation provides a framework for understanding Hegel's tale of Spirit's development as presented in the *Phenomenology*. As Tom Darby describes this tale, an entity, a consciousness, experiences the presence of another entity or consciousness. Initially, the relationship between the two entities is harmonious because they are barely aware of each other and seldom encounter each other. Eventually, though, their awareness of each other sharpens. The result is conflict. And with that conflict history begins. History ends when after aeons of conflict, reconciliation is achieved as each and every consciousness recognises all other consciousnesses and is reconciled to them. In the *Phenomenology*, Hegel works through the endlessly repeating historical moments of order, disorder, and reordering in

narrating the story of Spirit-in-the-world as it develops from a state of immediate awareness and unreflective consciousness to one of complete
self-consciousness and absolute knowledge, or wisdom.[15]

For my purposes, the essential point is that there is an abiding dialectical quality to the experience of conflict or alienation and reconciliation.
Each consciousness is necessary to the other consciousness. As Michael
Hardimon says, "[T]he experience of alienation is directed toward the
ideal of reconciliation, and the ideal of reconciliation is contained within
the experience of alienation."[16] At the centre of Hegel's phenomenology
of consciousness resides an understanding of alienation, or *Entfremdung*, that
is both the opposite of and the pre-supposition for Spirit's self-actualisation
in all its various forms. Philosophy uncovers the forms of disorder in an attempt to reconcile the antinomies of human life: reason and irrationality,
freedom and necessity, self and other, and thought and action, or philosophy and politics.

The *Phenomenology*, while focused on the struggles of the individual consciousness to resolve the tension between itself and reality, does not ignore
the need to reconcile the antinomy of the individual and the community,
or, to use Hegel's language, the opposition between Subjective and Objective Spirit. One of the most crucial forms in which this reconciliation of
subject and object, of self and world, must occur is that of the integration
of the individual and the community so that each achieves its particular fulfilment. "The reconciling Yea, in which the two 'Is' let go their opposed existence, is the *existence* of the 'I' which has expanded into a duality, and
therein remains identical with itself, and, in its complete externalisation
and opposite, possesses the certainty of itself."[17] This statement encapsulates Hegel's notion that individuals come to know themselves through an
external world – which includes other individuals – that is other to them.
This reconciliation amounts to the identity of self and other, or, in Hegel's
terms, the identity of identity and non-identity. Hegel's most concrete
application of the abstract notion of reconciliation occurs in *Philosophy of
Right* when he applies the concept to the tension between the individual
and the community. He extends the concept to the social and political
spheres with a view to harmonising the relationship between the individual
and society, as well as to unifying the individual's fragmented consciousness. To the degree philosophy provides people with the ability to perceive
the actual world as rational, "to recognize reason as the rose in the cross of
the present," they achieve a reconciliation that allows them to harmonise
their desire for meaningfulness and intelligibility with the reality of the

world in which they live. We are reconciled and at home in the world when we know it, still more so when we comprehend it.[18]

Hegelian political philosophy thus seeks to comprehend and resolve the tensions of modern life. These divisions are characterised by the conflict between the claims of the communal ethical life, or *Sittlichkeit*, which Hegel sees as characteristic of the Greek *polis*, and the modern principles of individual freedom that informed Protestant Christianity and the French Revolution. This makes the essential political problem a matter of determining the proper relationship between the community and the individual. Ultimately, for Hegel, the state provides the reconciliation of thought and being, individual and community, theory and practice.[19]

2

Spirit and *Sittlichkeit*

Spirit, or *Geist*, is the concept that overarches Hegel's philosophic enterprise.[20] Hegel reveals the concept's importance in a typically abstruse passage: "That the True is actual only as system, or that Substance is essentially Subject, is expressed in the representation of the Absolute as *Spirit* – the most sublime Notion (or Concept) and the one which belongs to the modern age and religion. The Spiritual alone is the *actual*; it is essence, or that which has *being in itself*; it is that which *relates itself to itself* and is determinate, *it is other-being* and *being-for-itself*, and in this determinateness, or in its self-externality, abides within itself; in other words, it is *in and for itself*."[21]

Spirit, in other words, is both subject *and* object, an internal activity that appears as something finite, determinate, and actualised in the empirical world when it externalises or alienates itself. Yet in its external appearance, it objectification, Spirit also relates back to itself because of its abiding self-consciousness, which sets the stage for further external manifestations and inner transformations. In this manner, Spirit develops as a process. This process begins out of inner necessity and unfolds over time to reveal Spirit's inherent meaning in the world as made present in its concrete manifestations. Spirit does not transcend or go beyond its own process because it *is* the process itself. Spirit *is* the interconnected and ongoing process of disorder and order, of alienation and reconciliation, of subjective and objective moments, as well as the forms of consciousness that emerge in this process to enable consciousness to understand its own actions in the world. Hegel does not identify Spirit with any individual knower, any particular "I," because he regards the single individual, or the autonomous self, as an abstract universal. The particular I, or ego, is simply any I until it exists in some social or political context and thus acquires its personality and individuality. And for Hegel individuality is only possible in relation to an other. Only in relationships with others does the individual properly conceived, the particular I, emerge from the abstraction of universality.[22] This concern for the nature of the individual in relation to the community figures prominently in the thinking of both Watson and Taylor, albeit in different ways.

In Hegel's view, our sense of being an I, an individual, reflects the power of consciousness to construct abstract meanings and thereby understand the nature of the objects it encounters in concrete experience.[23] If, as Hegel maintains, consciousness is what *is*, and what *is*, is Spirit, then Spirit is consciousness, which is the enfolding of thought and being. This symbiosis of thought and being is revealed historically as consciousness develops to higher levels of self-awareness until it achieves complete self-consciousness. Or, as Michael Allen Gillespie explains, history reveals Spirit's recovery of itself in the concrete, in-this-world manifestations of self-consciousness. This process of Spirit's recollection is self-generating in that consciousness bears within itself the power of what Hegel calls the negative. The development of consciousness, the dialectic of Spirit, proceeds through struggle and strife, through disorder and division. This is because negation is rooted not only in the individual subject, or consciousness-as-Spirit, but also in the object of thought. But this content of thought is always in the process of being recast and transformed by Spirit. Thus, consciousness, or Spirit, "as thetic, antithetic, antinomious, and dialectical is the source of the motion of history."[24]

But because consciousness is self-reflexive, it is also the ground of its own unity. As the source of historical movement, consciousness seeks to become self-conscious. This desire, according to Hegelian science, is the ground for the reconciliation of the antinomies – thought and being, subject and object, freedom and necessity, individual and community. In other words, consciousness is the source of both its alienation from the world and its potential for reconciliation. Inasmuch as humans are the embodiment of Spirit, then their concrete history as expressed through religion, cultural and political institutions, artistic enterprises, and social communities reflects the unfolding of Spirit-in-the-world. History, in short, is "the self-movement of consciousness."[25] As I shall discuss later, George Grant found this notion morally offensive and politically frightening.

Hegel argues there is an order to history that emerges from the end toward which history moves. This end is freedom. The events of history reflect the realisation in consciousness, and the subsequent embodiment in the concrete world, of self-determined and self-motivated Spirit, which is the Idea of freedom. History, then, is the progressive self-realisation and self-actualisation of freedom. Historical events are essentially the events of Spirit's myriad appearances in the world after emerging out of nature as consciousness. Since humans are the most spiritual or freest of natural beings, history amounts to the progressive emergence over time of human freedom and, eventually, at the end of history, of the complete realisation of freedom, conceived as the reconciliation of the antinomies of reason and nature, thought and being. Such is the *telos* of history.[26] Again, this is a concept that Grant came to denounce.

Hegel defines freedom in terms of self-direction. In his analysis of will in *Philosophy of Right*, Hegel seeks to determine what is necessary for the will to achieve its freedom. He asserts two basic ingredients for freedom: achieving one's ends and acting voluntarily. The notion of freedom as voluntary follows Kant's idea of autonomy, that is, obey only those laws you impose on yourself. This "positive" definition of freedom as self-directed stands in contrast to the idea of individuals being directed by what originates outside themselves, including desires that may be based on or shaped by language, cultural background, or historical circumstances.[27] As I shall discuss later, Hegel's notion of freedom is somewhat at odds with Charles Taylor's notion of the expressivist identity of freedom and Taylor's idea that individual authenticity is rooted in communal attachment.

Hegel's definition of freedom as self-directed also echoes the concept of negative freedom – that is, freedom *from* coercion or the absence of interference. We do not want to be imposed on against our will because we want our lives to reflect our will. And we want our will to express our true selves. Hegel, however, insists that the freedom to do as we please, to act arbitrarily, is not true freedom.[28] Satisfying unreflective desires is not genuine freedom because those desires may derive from cultural and social conditions that do not reflect our rational will. Genuine freedom is not simply a matter of the capacity to satisfy desire, but an activity that fully realises reason: "The absolute goal ... of free mind is to make its freedom its object, that is, to make freedom objective as much in the sense that freedom shall be the rational system of mind."[29] Hegel's idea of freedom, while influenced by the Kantian idea of autonomy, is also a response to Fichte's notion of absolute self-sufficiency. Taylor, as I shall argue, misconstrues this Fichtean presence as a flaw in Hegel's social philosophy by failing to acknowledge Hegel's critique of Fichte's notion of freedom.

In *The Science of Ethics*, Fichte states that "the final end of my activity is absolute freedom, absolute independence of nature."[30] Hegel objects to this idea, arguing that Fichte's concept of right, which he derives from his definition of freedom, requires an ethical and political order in which individuals would have to restrict their freedom to allow for the freedom of others. Such an idea of right is flawed, according to Hegel, because it implies that relationships with others are a restriction on freedom rather than an enhancement. He defines the flaw in Fichte's idea of freedom this way: "In a community with others ... freedom must be *surrendered* in order to make possible the freedom of all rational beings living in community. Conversely, the community is a condition of freedom. So freedom must suspend itself in order to be freedom. This again makes it clear that freedom is here something merely negative, namely, absolute indeterminedness ... If the community of rational beings were essentially a limitation of true freedom, the community would be in and for itself the supreme tyrant."[31] According to Hegel, such a view presupposes an "infinite sphere of freedom," as Fichte says, that exists prior to communal existence, a condition of freedom that is limited by the presence of others. From this ontological assumption Fichte sees the forms of ethical life, including the state, as repressive of this original condition of freedom because they are tantamount to an external coercive power. The community creates hostility in the individual rather than the realisation that the community is the necessary condition for freedom. As Hegel says, individuals in Fichte's state "maintain a cold attitude of negativity as regards one another, the confinement becomes closer and the bonds more stringent as time goes on, instead of the state being regarded as representing the realisation of freedom."[32]

To be sure, Fichte acknowledges that men have their freedom only in the community. Nonetheless, he maintains that the community is a restriction on the self-positing "I" and that, in the end, the "I" can only regard the "we" as a limitation on its freedom, not as its self-realisation. In other words, the identity of the "I" cannot be completely authenticated in and through the "we." Because of this, the "I" remains a finite will, not an absolutely infinite will as Fichte requires. Hegel, however, regards Fichte's thinking on this point as flawed because he "was unable to grasp the concept of infinity or Spirit, i.e., of identity in difference."[33] According to Hegel, the essential problem with Fichte's concept of freedom is its Kantian presumption of a separation of morality and nature, and the consequent conclusion that the two cannot be reconciled through moral action.[34] Hegel shares Fichte's notion that to be moral is to be rational and to be rational is to be free, but he questions Fichte's confinement of rational morality to the thought of the individual and his rejection of its possible embodiment in social and political institutions. Such a restriction on the conception of morality implies an absolute separation of thought and being, and, thus, no possibility of a genuine reconciliation between the individual and the community. In effect, the external world remains an unrealisable idea of freedom for Fichte. Freedom exists only as concept, but not in reality. Only through the transformation of nature, the "not-I," into morality, or "I," is the unity of thought and being possible. This is problematic for Hegel. In confronting the not-I, I become aware of its otherness. But I am constrained against my will in terms of my own self-determinations. In a world where I am surrounded by others, I am required to recognise all the not-Is, the others, in order to realise my self-identity and, hence, my freedom. But this, as Steven Smith observes, is "an essentially infinite and thus impossible moral task."[35] I eventually realise that I can never have complete moral freedom. I am always a slave to that which is other to myself. But this implies that my freedom can be achieved only in and through society. Moral duty and the moral law thus acquire an intersubjective dimension for Fichte. However, this implies a limit on my freedom in that my freedom is dependent on the recognition of others. I can only be myself if others agree to let me be myself. I must recognise all others and hope they recognise me, too. How can that be genuine freedom? How can I be free on the basis of my own self-determinations rather than on some subjective element related to satisfying the expectations of others?

Hegel's response to this Fichtean quandary is the concept of *Sittlichkeit*, or ethical life, in which the "ought" has been overcome, and freedom and duty are identical. For Hegel, as Allen Wood explains, "social institutions and our duties within them are not hindrances on freedom but in fact actualizations of freedom, when the content of those institutions is rational and the performance of our duties is a vehicle for our self-actualization."[36] While Hegel draws his concept of freedom from Kant's notion of autonomy and Fichte's conception of self-sufficiency, he argues against what he sees as their inadequate understanding of the relationship between the self and the other. In particular, Fichte cannot realise genuine freedom – the absolutely infinite will that allows for autonomous activity and fully actualises reason – because he lacks the concept of Spirit, which, for Hegel, undergirds ethical life. As Ken Foldes states, "To solve the problem of realizing an absolutely infinite will one must first solve the problem of conceiving a relationship with the other which does not restrict but rather guarantees my freedom; where the other is regarded neither as sheer limit nor negation of myself … Only through such a relation with the other can an infinite will be realized."[37]

Charles Taylor interprets this view of Spirit and *Sittlichkeit* as suggesting that Hegel's reconciliation of the individual and the community requires that the self master the other and make the other its own. And this means, according to Taylor, that Hegel's conception of the relationship between Spirit and ethical life promotes excessive unity. For this reason, Taylor questions whether the concept of *Sittlichkeit* is a suitable model for political community, because, in his view, it makes no allowance for unresolvable differences.[38] I shall consider Taylor's argument in more detail later. It perhaps suffices for now to suggest that Hegel's notion of *Sittlichkeit* is more nuanced, that Taylor attributes to Hegel what he should confine to Fichte. This can be demonstrated by considering Hegel's idea of community and what might be called the dynamic of recognition essential to that idea.

The basis of Hegel's concept of ethical life is the idea of humans as self-conscious beings who actualise themselves in their highest potential through participation in and identity with a community. Hegel's master-slave dialectic in *Phenomenology of Spirit* offers his most famous discussion of how self-consciousness develops. Self-consciousness begins with the individual's initial effort to make certain of his existence by engaging what is other to himself, and concludes with his knowledge that what is needed for self-certainty is self-consciousness, which is available only in and through the recognition of another self-consciousness.[39] For Hegel, then, having to distinguish myself from the other is not a limit on my self, as Fichte argues, but rather an expression of my self. Which is to say, the other is not a restriction on my freedom, but a requirement for its actualisation. Freedom consists of "being with oneself *in* an other."[40] As Hegel says, "In duty the individual acquires his substantive freedom."[41]

The acquisition of freedom begins in the first stage of self-consciousness's development with a sensory encounter with external nature, an encounter with an alien entity. In this encounter, the consciousness of proto-man seeks to show its independence from the other (and, thus, the dependence of the other) by destroying it, or negating it, to use Hegel's word. Thus, the initial experience of self-consciousness in its encounter with the other is essentially negative. Nonetheless, this initial encounter reveals the first principle of the dynamic of recognition. Proto-man seeks to be reconciled with the other by negating it in some fashion. This produces a kind of freedom in that it reveals the disappearance of the other, thereby reinforcing a sense of presence, of being alive, in the remaining individual consciousness. However, this effort by the proto-individual consciousness to negate the external world, to consume it and take it into the self, is frustrating because there is too much world. The external world cannot be completely dominated and consumed. Nature defeats proto-consciousness with its overwhelming abundance. Repeated attempts to negate nature merely tell proto-man that far from being independent of the world, he is dependent on it. In fact, proto-man discovers that unless he negates (or eats) some portion of the other (nature), he will die.[42]

But the biggest psychological shift for the individual consciousness occurs when it encounters an *other* that is not passive, that struggles against being negated. The ensuing conflict, in which both proto-consciousnesses try to claim their freedom by negating the other, results in each recognising the other as an other. And here, according to Hegel, is the beginning of human history. The willingness of proto-man to risk the death of his *animal* body in a fight for an *idea*, for some abstract notion of prestige, is the seed of society. This fight for domination over an other who also desires recognition, the effort to determine who is master and who is slave, not only sets history going, but provides for the genesis of community and the freedom available in a particular community. Most important, the effort of self-consciousness to negate the other and, by means of that negation, to assert its own self or identity "reveals self-consciousness as that which must relate itself to another being."[43] And that implies, in Alexandre Kojève's words, that "the human being is formed only in terms of a Desire directed toward another Desire, that is – finally – in terms of a desire for recognition ... It is only by being 'recognized' by another, by many others or – in the extreme – by all others, that a human being is really human, for himself as well as for others."[44] This leads logically to the claim that Kojève makes on behalf of Hegel: "Man can only be truly 'satisfied,' history can only end, in and through the formation of a Society, of a State, in which the strictly particular, personal, individual value of each is recognised as such ... by *all*."[45]

For Hegel, then, the historical development of individual self-consciousness comes about through the continued opportunities for recognition provided by the various forms of *Sittlichkeit* – the family, civil society, and the rational state. In the latter, self-consciousness attains the fullest possible political realisation. In the community and its social and political arrangements, individuals are to be free – that is, self-satisfied in their determinations – because they see in those arrangements the achievement of their own highest rational aspirations. As Robert Wallace explains, for Hegel, the family, like the state, extends "the individual's ability to be with herself in what is other than her"[46] – that is to say, these institutions extend freedom. Hegel's master-slave struggle marks the beginning of a process by which self-consciousness moves from an original condition of unself-conscious immediacy in which thought and will are unified, to a position in which, after its encounter with the otherness of the world, self-consciousness retreats from its original immediacy to a moment of reflection, or what Hegel calls a moment of *Entzweiung*, or bifurcation. Over the course of history, with the development of community, various efforts are made to heal the rift between thought and being. But for Hegel this reconciliation occurs only at the higher level of right or law. *Sittlichkeit*, or ethical life, reveals freedom in its actuality.[47]

A similar shift in consciousness occurs within ethical life itself through the development of the "Idea," or Spirit. Free will, Hegel says, requires embodiment. This embodied will is sustained by "things" or external objects. But as a self-consciousness whose substantive purpose is the realisation of its will, self-consciousness acquires its initial embodiment of freedom through the possession of *Eigentum*, or property – the sphere of formal and abstract right.[48] The initial freedom of immediate unreflective existence is not permanently satisfying. Self-consciousness in its subjectivity imagines fulfilling its desire to be free. In this psychological state, self-consciousness is focused on its own intentions without regard to the external world. It imagines the world in its own image, but that is all it is, an imagined world. Self-consciousness can only actualise its freedom in concrete existence. Hence, for Hegel, the sphere of morality is only an abstract moment in the development of *Sittlichkeit*.[49]

The form of community that best provides freedom is ethical life. Ethical life is the community's self-consciousness as expressed in the consciousnesses of its individual members, the perception on the part of individuals that the community is not alien to them but rather reflects their universal purposes. Ethical life is Spirit, or self-conscious freedom, in its objective existence, "the concept of freedom developed into the existing world and the nature of self-consciousness."[50] But as Robert Wallace argues, ethical life, too, reflects a pattern of development. First, there is the natural life of the family in which self-consciousness is united by love and feeling. As the individual consciousness matures in its reflexive capacity, this primary bond is loosened. The individual then encounters a civil society in which individuals relate to one another as independent actors linked by reciprocal needs. For Hegel, this is the sphere of contract, the realm where associations, groups, and corporations emerge as members endeavour to express their social identity and sense of belonging. The final political reconciliation of self-consciousnesses occurs at the level of the state – the stage of ethical life and Spirit that, according to Hegel, provides the unity of autonomous individuality and universal substantiality. For Hegel, as Wallace notes, the state's task "is to protect its citizens and promote their welfare, by protecting the family and guiding civil society, but also to 'bring all of this back to the life of the universal substance,' which sets limits to these subordinate spheres, within it."[51] It is worth quoting Hegel in full on this point because his claim regarding the ideal relationship between the individual and the state is of considerable interest to Watson, Grant, and Taylor: "The state exists immediately in custom, mediately in individual self-consciousness, knowledge, and activity, while self-consciousness in virtue of its sentiment toward the state finds in the state, as its essence and the end and product of its activity, its substantive freedom ... The state is absolutely rational inasmuch as it is the actuality of the substantial will which it possesses in the particular self-consciousness once that consciousness has been raised to consciousness of its universality."[52]

With the concept of *Sittlichkeit*, then, Hegel's project achieves the theoretical reconciliation of the tensions between the autonomous freedom desired by modern individuals and the individuals' concomitant desire to overcome their alienation from the world and from others, their desire to belong to something that transcends themselves. Hegel's concept of *Sittlichkeit*, derived from his notion of recognition, promotes the view that freedom is not simply a matter of abstract rights, the avoidance of restraints or doing as you wish. *Sittlichkeit* is a matter of being able to *belong* to the community *in* and *through* mediations and institutions that you have freely chosen. In responding to the abstract formalism of Kant and Fichte, Hegel attempts to show that the supposedly fragmenting and alienating tendencies of modern freedom are due to an inadequate comprehension of the subjective moment of willing. His solution, as Vasanthi Srinivasan says, "is to illuminate the objective moment of freedom so that the will's embodiment in concrete laws and institutions becomes transparent to modern self-consciousness."[53] And for Hegel, it is the state, as the embodiment of Objective Spirit, that is both the source and product of modern freedom.

3

The Dialectic of Self and State

Hegel has often been criticised for fetishising the state. Such criticism misses his concern for individual freedom. Hegelian individuals are deeply political. They are not only self-interested competitors in the marketplace, but also willing participants in an overarching political order. The state, as the manifestation of Objective Spirit, is an organic totality that includes the government, other institutions, and the social culture. The state provides the arena where, under the rule of law, reconciliation is sought between the universal and the particular, the community and the individual. The rational state can bring humans to consciousness of their freedom. Concomitantly, in seeking to satisfy their rational desires, individuals further the development of the state and contribute to the unfolding of freedom, thereby fulfilling history's purpose. Hegel's state thus reveals the process of history as the working out of the reconciliation of the subjective freedom of the individual and the objective freedom of the organised political order.[54]

Hegel's concept of the state as a means for mediating conflicts between individuals or groups has obvious similarities to the Hobbesian notion of the covenant by which men submit to the sovereign's overarching authority for the sake of mutual survival. But Hegel goes beyond Hobbes's contractarian solution. In his view, the Hobbesian commonwealth does not overcome the asymmetrical domination that characterised the initial master-slave relationship in that it makes the state the dominant partner in the relationship. This sets up the state or community as an external power that hovers over the individual.[55]

According to Hegel, individuals find in the state their essence – that is, their substantive freedom. The state is that entity in and through which individuals actualise in concrete terms the desire for recognition that motives their struggle for freedom. In *Philosophy of Right*, Hegel says that the

state cannot be based on a social contract: "The intrusion of this contractual relation ... into the relation between the individual and the State, has
been productive of the greatest confusion in both constitutional law and
public life."[56] The idea of a social contract between the individual and the
state is illusory because it implies an element of choice where, in fact, there
is none. The state is "an entity whose authority transcends anything that
might have been conferred on it by contractual choice."[57] Indeed, Hegel
presents the state as a person, both in the sense of having legal rights and
obligations and in the moral sense. The state formulates plans of action,
justifies those actions, and assumes responsibility for them. To repeat a
statement from Hegel cited above, "the state is the actuality of the ethical
Idea ... The state exists immediately in custom, mediately in individual self-
consciousness, knowledge, and activity, while self-consciousness in virtue of
its sentiment toward the state finds in the state, as its essence and the end
and product of its activity, its substantive freedom."[58]

But if the state embodies the idea of a free individual life as the end of
human desire, then, like any individual, the state cannot be treated as a
means, but only as an end in itself. Its survival is not debatable. And it is
because the state has an enduring identity as an ethical entity that it is
distinguishable from civil society and cannot be regarded as a partner in
a contract. In fact, Hegel warns against identifying civil society with the
state: "If the state is confused with civil society, and if its specific end is
laid down as the security and protection of property and personal freedom, then the interest of the individuals as such becomes the ultimate
end of their association, and it follows that membership of the state is
something optional."[59]

Hegel's point, says Roger Scruton, is that the contractarian model con-
fuses distinctions between state and civil society by taking an instrumental
and utilitarian view of the state and its institutions. Such a position treats
the ties of citizenship and sovereignty as relations of interest and,
thereby, undermines that which gives civil association its ethical weight –
the overarching authority of political order. Scruton points out that one
of the more significant developments in modern political science has
been the emergence of political systems that do the opposite of what
Hegel argues against. Rather than dissolving the state in some provisional
order of civil society, these systems undermine civil society by means of a
coercive state. In the coercive state, the distinctions between state and society are lost because the legal institutions, social associations, and cultural
arrangements that provide the basis of civil society have been effectively
absorbed into the state. The result is totalitarian government that is not

subject to the corrective influences of civil society because it places itself as an impersonal entity that is above the law through which it seeks to impose itself on society.[60]

Patchen Markell extends this idea in arguing that Hegel's account of ethical life, particularly as it culminates in the state, provides a corrective to the initial asymmetrical relationship between the master and the slave in which the latter concedes its dependence on the former. In the Hegelian state, both self-consciousnesses mutually acknowledge their interrelationship by recognising themselves as members of a political community.[61]

It is this shift to intersubjectivity that allows Hegel to avoid Taylor's charge of promoting excessive unity because Hegel replaces modern atomism with intersubjective relatedness. As Robert Williams writes, "Hegel does not collapse the other into the same, mediation into self-mediation." For Hegel, "consciousness is not a disembodied, foundational, wordless subjectivity. Rather, consciousness is embodied, situated and equiprimordial with other subjects and the life-world. Consequently, subjectivity is actually intersubjectivity, and requires intersubjective mediation. This mediation is not reducible to dialectical self-mediation."[62] Or, put differently, Spirit is a social subject. *Geist* does not exist as a subject opposed to an alien object, a Kantian transcendental ego abstracted from the world. Spirit-as-freedom is an I that is a we and a we that is an I.

Hegel's notion of the completion of the individual *and* the state in their relationship to each other needs to be emphasised, particularly in light of communitarian interpretations of ethical life that tend to give greater emphasis to the communal side of the equation. As Vasanthi Srinivasan observes, while Hegel regards the state as embodying the reconciliation of the individual and the collective, he is not implying some sort of undifferentiated collectivity. That would mean a reversion to pre-modern substantiality. Rather, he sees the state as accomplishing the actualisation of freedom, maintaining the universal within the particularity of civil society. The reconciliation of the self and the other that Hegel seeks takes into account the actions of individuals and groups within society; it is not a unity imposed from on high.[63]

Hegel clearly regards the state as more than a neutral instrument whose restrictions on individual freedom are accepted for the sake of peace, order and good government. As Adam Krob says, the Hegelian state is an aggregate of social and institutional arrangements that enables people to discover their authentic individuality in relationships with others. It is through the participation of individuals in the Spirit of the state in its various "moments" that the focus of their morality progresses from that of personal self-interest to that of the community as a whole. Individuals transcend themselves and contribute to the good of the community in which they satisfy their requirement for freedom and, at the same time, their longing to belong to something greater than themselves. Individuals' self-conscious participation in the life of the state enables them to develop what it means to be a rational human. At the same time, the state achieves its own actualization through the actions of its members.[64]

Hence, for Hegel, the modern constitutional state and the principles of individual freedom go hand in hand. Each is necessary to the other. In its Ideal[65] form, the modern liberal democratic state, with its recognition of intrinsic human rights and its capacity to provide people with a necessary sense of belonging, enables citizens to assert those rights and freedoms that reflect the truest purposes of human life. Concurrently, it unites these separate individuals with the common good and the fulfilment that comes from belonging to a community. This Ideal is the synthesis of the particular and the universal. If there is a single passage in *Philosophy of Right* that makes this notion explicit, it is this one:

> The state is the actuality of concrete freedom. But concrete freedom consists in this, that personal individuality and its particular interests not only achieve their complete development and gain explicit recognition for their right (as they do in the sphere of the family and civil society), but, for one thing, they also pass over of *their own accord* into the interest of the universal ... The principle of modern states has prodigious strength and depth because it allows the principle of subjectivity to progress to its culmination in the extreme of self-subsistent personal particularity, and yet at the same time brings it back to the substantive unity and so maintains this unity in the principle of subjectivity itself.[66]

Hegel certainly seeks to overcome the disorders of modern individualism and the resulting detachment of rights from communal duties or belongingness. But he cannot be accused of promoting excessive unity or coercive collectivism to achieve this end. Indeed, by Hegel's criteria, the state loses legitimacy – and is no longer rational – if it does not protect individual freedom. Hegel makes this abundantly clear in *Philosophy of Right*: "The basis of right is, in general, mind [Spirit]; its precise place and point of origin is the will. The will is free, so that freedom is both the substance of right and its goal, while the system of right is the realm of freedom made actual, the world of mind brought forth out of itself like a second nature."[67] In this fashion, Hegel challenges the idea of regarding the individual as prior to society – that is, as an autonomous self detached from history and tradition. The idea of an utterly free and autonomous self is an empty abstraction. The free individual exists in and through the arrangements of *Sittlichkeit*. The individual and the community (or state) require each other to actualise Spirit. Freedom and belonging are concomitant. Substantive freedom is *actualised* only in community, while the true end of the community or the state is *actualised* only to the degree it engenders individual freedom. Neither achieves its end without the fulfilment of the other: "The state is the political unity with which one identifies and understands common action while maintaining individual and communal moral space."[68]

Hegel is especially cautious about trying to create the immediacy of belonging between the individual and the community that he regards as characteristic of the ancient *polis*. As Vasanthi Srinivasan remarks, Hegel recognizes that long-established social customs and traditions do not always produce self-conscious participation in community life. While Hegel wants to see the modern constitutional state regain a semblance of the ancient immediacy of belonging, says Srinivasan, he does not want that sense of belonging to be based on a substantive account of the good. Instead, he seeks to mediate the relationship of the individual and the community through the objective manifestations of subjective freedom. The immediacy of a substantive identification with the community is characteristic of pre-modern communities, but this kind of immediate identity disappeared with Christian subjectivity. Such unreflective communal attachments are not necessarily available to moderns. Hegel is therefore cautious about the potential excesses of civil society and aware of its potential for undermining individual freedom. Civil society reflects the achievements of modernity as well as its dangers; that is, civil society upholds the primacy of individual freedom against traditions of the pre-modern world that tended to suppress the individual. But civil society can also be divided and fragmented by the proliferation of excessive demands to belong, by demands for too much recognition. That is why Hegel emphasises the necessity of trust among individuals as the foundation for both civil society and the constitutional state, seeing "the potential for community *within* modern freedom without recourse to authentic identity," as Srinivasan puts it. "In his notion of ethical life … Hegel shows that modern freedom is not simply about abstract rights but about forging solidarity in and through concrete norms and institutions."[69]

Trust is rooted in a sense of confidence that we will be treated fairly by the other, whether this other is an individual, the community at large, or the state.[70] This concept of trust is both the means and the end of *Sittlichkeit* and, hence, a form of reconciliation. Consider, for example, Hegel's ideas regarding the corporation. For Hegel, the corporation is more that a collection of commercial interests or a bureaucratic administrative organisation. Rather, it links disparate aspects of ethical life – the family, civil society, and the state. The corporation prevents individual freedom from descending into endless competition for power by attaching individual recognition to the pride an individual feels in his avocation and participation in society.[71] Such trust is grounded in the individual's awareness of the rightness, or rationality, of the institutions and arrangements of the state. For example, Hegel refers to sentiments such as patriotism as "a product of the institutions subsisting in the state, since rationality is *actually* present in the state, while action in conformity with these institutions gives rationality its practical proof." Hegel regards such sentiments as evidence of trust – "the consciousness that my interest, both substantive and particular, is contained and preserved in another's (i.e. in the state's) interest and end ... In this way, this very other is immediately not an other in my eyes, and in being conscious of this fact, I am free."[72] Thus, while Hegel recognises the linkage between freedom and abstract rights, he maintains that substantive freedom is embodied in community relationships. Such a position has obvious affinities with contemporary communitarian claims that we are always embedded in a particular cultural or community milieu. Hegel shares the communitarians' concerns about the excesses of individualism, but he insists that the way to establish rights is through a more Ideal understanding of freedom. Rather than imposed notions of the good of the community or the attainment of authentic identity, the constitutional state and the rule of law, along with the trust-engendering associations of ethical life, should be the focus of communitarian concern. The excesses of individualism are mitigated not by replacing a politics of rights with a politics of communal good, but by recovering Spirit within the institutions and political arrangements that protect individual rights.[73]

Hegel is also careful to explain that the relationship of the individual and the state is dialectical. Each needs the other to further the Spirit of the other. There must be reciprocity in obligations between the state and the individual. The individual is duty-bound to sustain the goods of the state, both for his own sake and that of others. But the community, and the institutions through which it expresses its purposes, is also obliged to sustain the freedom of the individual. If freedom is an individual's essence, as Hegel asserts, then only to the degree the state furthers this freedom is it rational and, thus, owed the individual's support. Conversely, individuals achieve their highest fulfilment and freedom in their dutiful affirmation of the state. They recognize the state as the objective embodiment of their highest purposes. They recognise who and what they are – their most universal, or free, selves – in the actions of the state. They find substantive freedom in the bonds of family, through the economic and social interactions of the workplace and marketplace, and through their participation in the political life of the state. They come to see themselves not as alienated, but as participants in an enterprise that provides them with transcendent meaning. In this way, through habit and education, individuals perceive the symbiotic nature of their relationship to the community. In Hegel's words, "The right of individuals to be subjectively destined to freedom is fulfilled when they belong to an actual ethical order, because their conviction of their freedom finds its truth in such an objective order."[74] Ethical life, therefore, is the means by which individuals reconcile their subjective wills with the universal will of the community, and come to understand the community as enabling the fulfilment of their freedom. By this argument, Hegel's community, particularly in the form of the rational state, uses individuals' obligations to further them in their freedom.

To be sure, Hegel at times appears to subordinate the individual to the community. He refers to the individual having a "supreme duty to be a member of the state."[75] He even seems to suggest that the community is indifferent to the individual's existence, referring, for instance, to the ethical order as "a circle of necessity" whose moments "regulate the life of individuals."[76] But Hegel also declares that it is only in and through individuals that these powers become actualised. This suggests that Hegel is concerned with articulating and establishing some kind *separation* from the community for the individual in order to ensure that the individual is not completely identified with the community *all the time*. He does this in the section on morality in *Philosophy of Right* where he works through the problematic nature of the individual's relationship to the community. The realm of morality is that psychological arena in which individuals determine within themselves the right or wrong of conflicting claims of abstract right. This moral realm is not necessarily identified with ethical life because it is where individuals set their subjective will against the communal will.[77] Does Hegel think there is ever a moment when it is right for individuals to set their subjective will against that of the community? Certainly, Hegel argues for the most part that the will of a rational individual should accord with the community in that each recognises the other. Yet Hegel finds in Socrates' defiance of his fellow Athenians the penultimate example of an instance when an individual's inner sense of right must be asserted against the community, when subjective will supersedes communal will. This happens when individuals look within themselves and determine that what they recognise as right and good cannot be satisfied in society. And how might this occur? In the "pure certainty of oneself alone" that occurs when self-consciousness "evaporates into itself the whole determinate character of right, duty, and existence, as it remains both the power to judge, to determine from within itself alone, what is good in respect of any content." And when might this occur?

> When the existing world of freedom has become faithless to the will of better men, that will fails to find itself in the duties there recognised and must try to find in the ideal world of the inner life alone the harmony which actuality has lost.[78]

> It is only in times when the world of actuality is hollow, Spiritless, and unstable, that an individual may be allowed to flee from actuality in his inner life. Socrates lived at the time of the ruin of the Athenian democracy. His thought vaporised the world around him and he withdrew into himself to search there for the right and the good.[79]

Hegel would agree with the communitarians about the importance of membership in a family. And he would accept that the attachment to the state cannot be reduced merely to the satisfaction of individual desires or the assertion of rights. But he would disagree with communitarians, too, because what he values in family membership or in being a citizen of a state is how those roles enhance the individual's freedom, not whether they promote authentic identity. In the above quotations, Hegel is referring to Socrates and saying that Socrates' moral freedom takes precedence over the community. In this case, Hegel describes an individual who possesses a sense of identity that *transcends* the community. Athens failed in its obligation to enhance Socrates' freedom by not acting as a *rational* state. Such an example implies that Hegel sees the various forms of *Sittlichkeit* as inseparable from the individual's freedom, but not the totality of freedom. But for Hegel, this means, as Srinivasan notes, that the satisfaction of the desire to belong must be institutional rather than cultural because what is at stake in the relationship between the individual and the community is freedom, not cultural or national identity.[80]

This issue – and the Socratic model from which it emerges – is central to my essay. John Watson uses Plato's description of Socrates' situation as a controlling trope to elucidate his understanding of the relationship between the individual and the state. Charles Taylor's communitarian take on Hegel is flawed by his misapprehension of Hegel's interpretation of Socrates' predicament. Hegel, in his interpretation of Socrates' situation, reveals that his concern for reconciling the individual and the community is not primarily about identity or a sense of belongingness, but first and foremost about individual freedom. While Hegel acknowledges the problems of atomistic individualism and the importance of communal belongingness, his deeper concern is with establishing a system of rights or law that enhances individual self-determination. The project of reconciliation does not allow for dissolving all differences in communal identification.

Philosophy of Right makes it clear that for Hegel the will to freedom is embodied in legal rights and political practices and institutions. Individuals find themselves living within certain institutions – the family, the market, civil society, the constitutional order, the state – that can be shown to be "right," or rational, to the degree they embody the principle of freedom. All these institutions of modern society *extend* the individual's ability *to be an I in conditions of otherness*. Through the rational state, individuals can be what they most essentially are – free beings. Hegel's primary political concern, then, is with strengthening the constitutional order to protect the rule of law and the concrete associations and institutions that engender freedom.

On this final point let me turn to considering how my three Canadian Hegelians manifest Spirit.

PART TWO

John Watson and the Spirit of Empire

4

Idealism and Imperialism

Toward the end of the nineteenth century, Otto von Bismarck, the Prussian leader who forged the German Empire, remarked that the most important thing to know about the twentieth century was that Americans spoke English. The point was obvious: an alliance between the British Empire and the United States, the world's largest English-speaking states, would create the most powerful political entity on the planet. Bismarck's remarks proved prescient. When he died on 31 July 1898, the Spanish-American War was coming to an end, delivering the last remnants of the Spanish Empire to the newly emergent American empire.

Others made similar observations – Rudyard Kipling, English imperialist Alfred Milner, Winston Churchill, and Theodore Roosevelt.[1] But the sentiment expressed in Bismarck's words was also given careful consideration in Canada, a country born of the clash of empires, a country whose political destiny was, it seems, linked to the fate of those empires.[2] In the late nineteenth century, men such as George Monro Grant, George Robert Parkin, and, later, Stephen Leacock, Andrew Macphail, and James Cappon, all of whom described themselves as Canadian nationalists and British imperialists, wondered at Canada's future on a continent dominated by the United States. Some spoke of a grand alliance of the English-speaking people.

Parkin, the one-time headmaster of Upper Canada College in Toronto and a self-described evangelist of empire, wanted the United States and the British Empire to come together in a union to overcome the "bifurcation of Anglo-Saxon national life" caused by the American Rebellion of 1776. He envisioned a new world order in which Britons (which, of course, included Canadians) and Americans worked together to fulfil their providential mission of spreading the spiritual and material benefits of "Anglo-Saxon civilisation" around the world.[3] George Monro Grant, the principal of Queen's University from 1877 to 1902, also saw Canada's great mission to be that of healing the rift within the Anglo-Saxon nation – that is, to reconcile Britain and her wayward offspring, the United States: "No greater boon can be conferred on the race than the healing of [the] schism of [1776]. That is the work that Canada is appointed by its position and history to do. We are to build up a North American Dominion, permeated with the principles of righteousness, worthy to be the living link, the permanent bond of union, between Britain and the United States."[4]

Neither of these Canadian imperialists was anti-American. Their political dreams of Anglo-Saxon unity reflected concern about Canada's future as an independent state. They believed Canada was in danger of being absorbed into the United States, first economically and then politically. And it was this perceived threat of American continentalism that made the question of Canada's relationship to the British Empire one of the major political questions at the turn of the twentieth century. For the imperialists, the issue of whether Canada became part of a united empire or followed some other political destiny was "the greatest political question of the hour."[5] The imperialists warned that unless Canadians attached themselves to the empire and what it ideally represented, the United States would inevitably absorb them. Canada was too small a country to act alone on the global stage. Nor could a "Little Canada," as some disparagingly referred to the idea of a Canada detached from its British connection, provide the spiritual scope to satisfy the highest aspirations of its best citizens. Only through membership in the empire, sharing in both the benefits and responsibilities of imperial citizenship, would Canadians overcome their colonial mentality and attain true greatness as a nation.

It is probably impossible to establish a definitive cause-and-effect link between the enthusiasm for the British Empire among English-speaking Canadians at the turn of the last century and the philosophic Idealism that dominated the dominion's intellectual life at the time.[6] Nonetheless, there is little doubt that the imperialist sentiments of many prominent Canadian nationalists were indebted to Idealist philosophy, and in particular to the Objective or Speculative Idealism of John Watson.[7] In the history of Canadian philosophy, Objective Idealism[8] dominated the half-century from 1872 to 1922, achieving its stature "chiefly through the labours of John Watson."[9] But even beyond Canada, Watson was recognised as one of the leading exponents of Objective Idealism in the Anglo-Saxon world.[10] Within Canada, though, Watson's influence was considerable, touching everything from the formation of the United Church of Canada and the reform of the federal civil service to the development of educational policy and school curricula.[11] Those who listened to Watson during his long career would also have "heard much that could serve to give the argument for an increased imperial connection much philosophical substance."[12]

Watson's linkage of imperialism and Idealism received its most explicit statement in the one book he devoted to political philosophy, *The State in Peace and War*, published in 1919. It is Watson's most direct response to the political questions that dominated his time, particularly in the wake of the First World War. It is also his most overtly Hegelian work. Watson's thought, some scholars argue, should be understood primarily as a reaction to the religious climate of his time, the crisis of faith precipitated by evolutionary science and the higher criticism.[13] Certainly, religion plays a central role in Watson's work, but the political dimension of his thought is not simply an adjunct to his theological concerns. Like Hegel, Watson believes that religion shares the stage with other products of human consciousness, including art, philosophy, and politics. In *The State in Peace and War*, Watson considers, among other issues, the philosophical relationship between Idealism and imperialism, and provides, ultimately, a theoretical basis for promoting Canada's role within the British Empire. He sees the British Empire offering a political order that would reconcile the aspirations of individual nations with the requirements and responsibilities of citizenship in a larger political community. This vision of an empire in which Canada would play a dynamic world historical role is sustained by a philosophic Idealism that, for Watson, provides an intelligible response to the social and political uncertainties generated by the First World War. Watson's Idealism, in turn, is drawn from Hegelian thought. Hegel provided Watson with the theoretical means to address questions regarding the relationship of the individual and the state, notions of power and reason, and even evolution and progress that had suddenly become problematic as a result of the war experience.

Carl Berger has argued that imperialism was a form of Canadian nationalism. Men such as Grant, Parkin, Leacock, and Macphail were imperialists because they saw in the British Empire the means to check the forces of a materialist ethos that threatened to overwhelm the values and traditions necessary to a properly functioning and humanly fulfilling social and political order. They saw the empire as the embodiment of a spiritual mission to spread the benefits of Christian civilisation around the globe. Canadians, as imperial citizens, would find true freedom and attain true nationhood in this enterprise. The movement for imperial unity was both a reflection of Canadians' desire to preserve traditional values and an expression of their new-found sense of power about themselves and their place in the world.[14] Stephen Leacock, for example, writing on the eve of the 1907 Imperial Conference, voiced this Idealist aspect of imperialism when he urged the conference delegates to "[f]ind for us something other than mere colonial stagnation, something other than independence, nobler than annexation, greater in purpose than a Little Canada. Find us a way. Build us a plan that shall make us, in hope at least, an Empire Permanent and Indivisible ... We cannot in Canada continue as we are. We must become something greater or something infinitely less."[15]

This notion of empire was highly influential. In 1889 the Imperial Federation League included about a quarter of the members of Parliament.[16] Prime Minister Wilfrid Laurier's imperial preference tariffs of 1897 revealed the influence of imperialist sentiments on the Canadian government's commercial policy. This influence was also felt at the military level when Laurier, under pressure from English-speaking Canada, sidestepped traditional French Canadian isolationism and agreed to dispatch Canadian troops to the Boer War in 1899. The imperial question dominated the political agenda again in 1909 during the so-called naval scare. Canadian imperialists contended that the rapid expansion of German naval power was a threat to British supremacy at sea; it was time, they said, for Canada to help Britain by shouldering some of the costs for maintaining the fleet upon which Canada's own security depended.

While this notion of empire may be discredited for some today,[17] Canadian nationalists of a century ago saw the British Empire as a bulwark against the alien political tradition of the American republic. They regarded the rising power of the United States with trepidation and looked to the British Empire as a counterbalancing force. The empire, they argued, offered "the greatest secular instrument for good in the world."[18] With its worldwide sweep, the empire could ensure the progress of the human race through the dissemination of civilised standards. Canada's great privilege was to participate in such a noble venture. By means of imperial membership, Canada could fill its potential as a great nation in the world. In this way, "the imperial idea became at once a popular enthusiasm and a reasoned political and ethical philosophy."[19] As Berger notes, reinforcing the notion of an Idealist dimension to Canadian imperialism, "all the imperialists identified imperialism with an extension of Canadian freedom and her rise to nationhood."[20] James Cappon, a colleague of Watson's at Queen's University, offers a representative example of this view in arguing that the British Empire "represents an ideal of high import for the future of civilisation, the attempt to assemble in a higher unity even than that of nationality the forces which maintain and advance the white man's ideals

of civilisation, his sense of justice, his constitutional freedom, his respect
for law and order, his humanity. It is an attempt to transcend the evils of
nationality ... without impairing the vigour which the national consciousness gives to a people ... To reconcile the principle of Imperial unity with
freedom of national development for all parts capable of using such freedom is the ideal of the British Empire."[21]

Of course, this imperial Ideal was only one facet of the Spirit of the
times. The political thought of the late nineteenth and early twentieth centuries, in Canada and elsewhere in the English-speaking world, reflected
an age of transition, a world undergoing both destruction and construc-
tion at numerous levels. One well-known writer of the period, Arnold
Haultain, captures this sense of crisis in an article that is highly revealing of
the spiritual and psychological state of mind of a thoughtful person contemplating what direction the last century of the millennium might take. It
is worth quoting him at length, even if only to appreciate how familiar his
words are a century later:

> The nineteenth century seems to have brought us to the edge of a preci-
> pice, and to have left us there gazing wistfully into outer space. That
> rather smug era led us to believe that we stood on *terra firma* whence ...
> we might bridge any chasm that presented. It was a scientific century,
> and – so it seems to us now – rather a myopic one. Given matter and
> motion; given a collection of atoms and a law of evolution ... it con-
> structed you a cosmos. But things have changed ... Materialism, we be-
> gin to think ... does not explain everything. The terra firma is not as
> solid as it looked, and we see before us a *terra incognita* without any foot-
> hold from which to bridge what appears to be an unconscionable length
> of span ... [This is] an age that finds no anchorage in materialism, yet is
> afraid to drift; an age which feels that the nineteenth century solution of
> the world-problem was inadequate, yet that is too far removed from the
> solutions offered by the eighteenth century to derive much comfort
> from them; an age which sees that it must find a solution for itself, but
> has no data for the task, and as yet can do little more than stand shiver-
> ing timorously at the brink.[22]

Faced with such a crisis, Canadian intellectuals, like their counterparts in
the United States and Britain, had to rethink their concepts of social and
political order. The result was "a frantic search for an ideal, a new world
view which explained the nature of man and his place in the universe."[23]
Idealism filled that requirement for some.

Idealist philosophy appeared first in Britain in the 1870s and then in Canada in the 1880s. The Idealism that informed Canadian intellectual life in the decades before the First World War can be seen as an effort to retain traditional Christianity's moral authority and its monistic worldview against the challenge presented by empirical science. Idealism seemed to restore the validity of the Christian faith with its claim that reality was essentially spiritual. It offered a substantive response to those who viewed the social, political, and economic realms of human activity in strictly materialistic or utilitarian terms and, from the Idealist perspective, who sought to reduce human relationships to the formulae of social Darwinism.[24]

At the core of Idealist thought is the notion of the unity of the whole, the idea that all entities are merely differentiated aspects of one systematic and rationally ordered whole. Translated into political terms, Idealism suggests that a "wholesome" political order expresses the collective will of a community composed of members who recognise that their fulfilment is bound up in their interconnectedness. In this regard, while it might be impossible to demonstrate a causal connection between imperialist nationalism and philosophical Idealism, there seems little room to doubt that the thinking in wholes characteristic of Idealists was compatible with the belief of Canadian imperialists that Canada's national identity was tied to the political question of empire.[25] Indeed, individuals such as James Cappon tried to convince those whom he described as philosophical liberals that their Kantian longing for universal peace could be better served through the "new and greater political units of our time," that is, through empire.[26] This compatibility between Idealism and imperialism is amply illustrated in Watson's writings. For example, near the conclusion of *The State in Peace and War*, Watson addresses the question of international relations in the post–First World War era. His views are premised on the claim that the British Empire is "the only thoroughly successful experiment in international government that the world has ever seen." Using distinctly Hegelian language, Watson attributes the empire's success to its "combining the freedom of the separate organs with the unity of the whole."[27]

It is this concern with the relationship of parts and wholes that is most distinctly Hegelian about Watson's thought.[28] Borrowed from Hegel, the fundamental idea of Watson's philosophical system is the "internal relationship of all entities."[29] The concept of reality as rational, of the universe as reasonable and therefore knowable, and of nature as essentially spiritual provided the foundation of his thinking. On the basis of this metaphysic, Watson, like Hegel, perceives a linkage between man's religious experience, his social life, and his political orders. And it is from this metaphysical position that

Watson derives his moral and political theory. In asserting the essential rationality of reality, of what is, Watson argues for the immanence of reason in human affairs, including in man's social and constitutional orders. And he follows Hegel in maintaining that the inherent rationality of constitutional orders underpins the moral purpose of politics as it is manifested in the various institutions of civil society.

For Watson, consciousness involves the awareness of the order of reality that all humans share. However, this awareness is individuated by the fact that individuals' experience of that order is variously manifested. Hence, there is always a tension in the relationship between self and other, the individual and the community (and even between one state and other states, presumably). Watson's fundamental philosophical concern is to show how the relationship between the two entities is one of mutual interdependence and that to recognise this truth and act on it is to achieve the only reconciliation available between the individual and the community (or between states). His arguments on this score are subtle and nuanced. He does not see the state (or society) as taking precedent over the individual; he is not the complete communitarian as some scholars suggest.[30] On the other hand, neither does he promote subjectivist individualism. These distinctions point up the essential problem in Watson's political philosophy – what he calls "the problem of uniting public authority with individual freedom."[31]

Watson's basic methodology in addressing this political concern is to compare and contrast his views with those of other philosophers. This Hegelian approach is readily apparent in *The State in Peace and War*. The book begins with Periclean Athens and the thought of Plato and Aristotle and works through the Stoics and the Epicureans and the political philosophies of the Middle Ages until it reaches the modern period, starting with Machiavelli, Hobbes, and Locke through to Kant, Hegel, Bentham, Mill, and Spencer. Watson concludes with commentaries on Nietzsche, Haeckel, and Treitschke. Behind this historical method is Watson's acceptance of the Hegelian notion that reason develops and evolves in and through historical experience. In this regard, as an entry point into Watson's fundamental political question, it is appropriate to consider the historical experience that occasioned his venture into political philosophy, namely the First World War.

5

Watson's Political Problem:
The Individual and the State

The destructiveness of the First World War shattered the reputation of
Hegelian Idealism, particularly its notion of reason manifesting itself in
historical events and in the existence of an ordering intelligence.[32] By
1919, the Idealist view of the state, along with liberal political economy,
was under siege.[33] If there is one thinker who best exemplifies this hostility
toward the Hegelian view of the state, it is the English philosopher L.T.
Hobhouse. Toward the end of 1918, with the First World War having
ended in an armistice, Hobhouse published a study of theories of the state,
The Metaphysical Theory of the State. In a dedication to his son, a Royal Air
Force officer killed in France, he writes: "In the bombing of London I had
just witnessed the visible and tangible outcome of a false and wicked doctrine," the "Hegelian theory of the god-state." Hegel, in Hobhouse's view,
was the intellectual source of German militarism, a proponent of absolutist
state power over the individual, a belief whose "most faithful exponent[s]"
had been Idealists such as Bernard Bosanquet.[34]

Watson, like Hobhouse, regards the First World War as a conflict between competing ideas about the state. However, in *The State in Peace and
War*, Watson defends the Hegelian view of the state. He argues that, for
Hegel, the state was not an instrument of coercive force, but "the highest
expression of the reasonable will, the will which aims at the general good
of the whole." The state as a whole is "the custodian of the conditions under which a given people manifests its ideal ends."[35]

These contrasting views are significant. Hobhouse's harsh view of Hegel
may no longer be credible – Hegelian philosophy is no longer identified
with "the philosophy of modern totalitarianism," as Karl Popper once put
it[36] – but during the first half of the twentieth century, Hegel was out of
favour in scholarly circles, particularly among British intellectuals. Hegel

was held responsible not only for providing the philosophical underpin-
nings of German militarism, but also for subordinating individual and
social relations to the interests of the state. Watson disputes this judgment,
arguing that Hegelian Idealism, properly understood, provides a theoretical reconciliation of the individual and the state eminently suitable to
liberal-democratic orders.

The contrast between Hobhouse (and other critics of Hegel) and Watson
can thus be understood as a conflict between different ideas of what constitutes the proper relationship between the individual and the state.
Watson's views on this topic are similar to those offered by the British
Idealists T.H. Green, Bernard Bosanquet, and Edward Caird, under whom
Watson studied. But rather than simply recasting their thought, Watson
prefers to elucidate his Idealist philosophy through a historical study of political thought from ancient Greece to his own time. Such a method follows
Hegel's historicist approach to philosophy, but at a philosophic level, it
also reflects the Hegelian concept of *Aufhebung*, or sublation.[37] Like Hegel,
Watson sees the movement of reason manifesting itself through developments wrought by historical experience that incorporate past events, including the philosophic thought of the past, into a new whole.

Philosophic "moments" in history embody the understanding of the essential intelligibility underlying the order of reality, and this understanding is available to a particular thinker at any particular moment in time.
This historical approach to philosophy allows Watson to compare and
contrast the past with the present and thus distinguish what is true and
universal from what is not. This method is similar to Hegel's in the early
section of the *Phenomenology* in which the inadequacies of past modes of
thought about reality are exposed and sublated into higher modes of consciousness. In following Hegel's method, Watson demonstrates that the
truth of Idealism resides in its capacity to show that the various historical
understandings of reality as revealed by empirical thought, while valid
within certain limits, cannot be regarded as conclusive.[38] When one considers the various ideas about the relationship between the individual and
the state offered by past philosophers – everyone from Plato and Aristotle
to the Stoics, Aquinas, Machiavelli, Hobbes, Rousseau, and even Spencer
and Nietzsche – the overarching point Watson makes is seen to be de-
monstrably Hegelian: the history of philosophy reveals how the inability
to reconcile freedom and duty in the political community is due to the experiential limitations of human consciousness at any particular historical
moment and, hence, to the incomplete comprehension of the rationality
of the whole.

But what does Watson mean by *individual* and *community*? He rejects the dualism of atomised individualism put forward by the empiricists and positivists as simplistic and a distortion of reality. At the same time, though, he criticises the conceptual inadequacies of Rousseau's and Kant's notions of the individual. Behind Watson's political thought, then, is a fundamental concern for the problematic nature of individual identity and the relationship between self and other. To be sure, Watson's thought on this matter is embedded in a complex conceptual system that he worked out over the course of his philosophic career. He argues, for example, against the atomised individualism of the positivists and empiricists, rejects the materialist determinism of the evolutionists, opposes the contractualism of Rousseau and Kant, rejects the supposedly unitarian political system put forward in Plato's *Republic*, and, finally, refutes the idea of a universal world government.[39] Nevertheless, Watson's work includes key emblematic statements, and even particular paragraphs and sentences, that encapsulate the Idealist themes in his political and social thought: (1) How is modern individuality possible? (2) What is the function of civil society in terms of individual freedom and moral obligations? (3) Is there a tension between moral autonomy and social unity and purposiveness? (4) Can the purposes of the state be reconciled with those of the individual?

The questions regarding the proper relationship between the individual and the state emerge almost immediately in *The State in Peace and War* when Watson, referring to Pericles' funeral oration, defines the fundamental political problem to be that of "uniting public authority with individual freedom."[40] Watson provides the answer to his own questions almost immediately, albeit in an esoteric manner. The core themes of Watson's political philosophy can be extracted from his commentary on two Socratic dialogues, the *Apology* and the *Crito*, that follow his statement about the fundamental political problem with which he is concerned. This commentary contains, in a highly condensed form, his basic political philosophy, and the remainder of his book is, in large measure, a working out of the permutations and ramifications of his confrontation with these dialogues.

Watson sees Socrates' defence of himself during his trial and the reasoning behind his subsequent refusal to flee the Athenians' death sentence as paradigmatic in regard to Socrates' basic political question – the relationship between the individual and the community. Furthermore, the statement with which Watson concludes his commentaries on the two dialogues neatly summarises his concept of the proper relationship between the individual and society. The burden of these two dialogues, Watson states, is this: "Disobey the law when a higher impersonal law would otherwise be violated;

obey the law where only one's own individual interest will be adversely affected."[41] Watson argues that the *Apology* is "indirectly a discussion of the problem [of] how far the individual is under obligation to obey the law of the state." The question in *Crito*, on the other hand, is "whether it is permissible to act contrary to a higher law, and so violate one's conscience."[42]

Nearly thirty years earlier, in the 1898 edition of *An Outline of Philosophy*, Watson indirectly alludes to these two dialogues in a chapter on moral philosophy. In a statement that evokes the figure of Socrates described in the 1918 book, Watson says that an individual must learn to set aside his individualistic inclinations and see himself as an "organ of the community." To do so is "the only way to be moral." And it is only from this moral position that the individual may justifiably criticize his community. In Watson's words, "He may criticize, and seek to improve the community, but his criticism must rest upon a recognition of the principle that the individual has no right to oppose himself to the community on the ground of inclination."[43] The statement is revealing. Not only does it establish a particular notion of the social good, but it also provides the basis upon which one can criticise society.[44]

Watson follows Hegel in arguing that the historical development of the Ideal of political community parallels the Ideal development of the moral individual. The Ideal of the individual, already latent in the Greek *polis*, has developed in modern times to the point where it has become the grounding principle of all civilised forms of political community. No longer is it permissible to identify morality with the customs and laws of a particular community, class, or group. Morality, Watson asserts, "must rest upon the wider basis of humanity."[45] These comparisons underscore the consistency in Watson's thought, but more important, they contain in compact form the major political concepts with which Watson was concerned, namely individual freedom, the nature and function of the state, and the relationship between the two.

Watson's theory of the state is tied to his notion of the development of reason in history. Like Hegel, he sees the development of reason reflected in the dominating political order of the times. This view is evident in the preface to *The State in Peace and War*, in which Watson outlines his intention to describe how the idea of the state has developed from the time of Plato and Aristotle, through to the Roman Empire and the Middle Ages, until, finally, in the modern nation-state, with its notions of sovereignty, contract, and a political system of checks and balances, we see the emergence of a concept of the state "as existing for the establishment of the external conditions under which the highest human life may be carried on."[46]

In describing the development of the idea of the state, Watson articulates a conception of the state as one of "inseparable relation." The state, he says, is "a community of rational beings not externally bound together but organically connected."[47] In an argument that echoes Hegel's critique of Fichte, Watson says that unless this view of the state is accepted – that is, the idea that individuals are their own end only to the degree that they possess a social consciousness – we are forced to accept the contractarian conception of the state as an external power, an agency of force, whose main function is to keep individuals from interfering with one another's rights. For Watson, though, such a conception of the state means there can be no real reconciliation of the individual and the community, no substantive identity of freedom and duty.

Watson implicitly articulates his quest for a principle of reconciliation for society with his citation of Thucydides' account of Pericles' funeral oration. Pericles refers to Athens as the singular political community that had achieved a balance between public and private lives and, most importantly, between public duty and private freedom. Watson's purposes in beginning his defence of Idealist political philosophy with Pericles' funeral oration are not only thematic but also rhetorical. By beginning with Pericles, Watson not only consciously links his time to that of the ancient Greeks, but also links the First World War to the Peloponnesian War. Such a linkage implies that the war between Britain and Germany parallels the conflict between Athens and Sparta. More deeply, at the philosophical level, it implies a correlation between British and Athenian democracy and German and Spartan militarism. By implication, then, Watson suggests that Hegelian Idealism offers a defence of British democratic principles and does not, as critics such as Hobhouse would have it, threaten the destruction of those principles.[48]

Watson regards Pericles' funeral oration as one of the most comprehensive statements ever made about the relationship between the citizen and the community. It expresses the fundamental political problem to be one of "uniting public authority with individual freedom." For the Athenians of Pericles' time, the *polis* was both the protector of citizens' freedoms and the promoter of citizens' highest potential. In this regard, Athens achieved the two main goods of political community: it was "pervaded by a single mind, and it allow[ed] free play to the capacities of the individual."[49] The Athenians solved what Watson's contemporary Bernard Bosanquet referred to as the paradox of self-government – that is, the condition of obeying the rules of the political community while at the same time obeying oneself.[50]

In this regard, it is understandable why Watson devotes the single largest section of *The State in Peace and War* to an examination of Greek political thought, particularly that of Plato and Aristotle. The question of how reconciliation between the citizen – or, in modern terminology, the individual – and the community could be achieved is central to both philosophers' political thought: "The problem of politics is to bind men together in a free and orderly community."[51] Hence, by looking through the prism of Watson's reading of *Apology* and *Crito*, we can see how Plato and Aristotle help Watson deliver his Hegelian response to his fundamental political concern.

For Plato and Aristotle, Watson argues, the freedom of the citizen and the fulfilment of the philosophic life are possible only in a political community. Political duty does not necessarily mean a curtailment or restriction on the citizen. At the core of Plato's and Aristotle's political thought is the claim that obligation is the condition for freedom. Both assume that the city-state is the necessary condition for the highest life. Only in and through the *polis* are citizens able to distinguish between their real and their apparent purposes. This, in turn, implies a relationship between the community and the freedom of the citizen. As Watson observes, the Platonic question "What is a good man?" is intrinsically tied to the question "What is the good state?"[52] Because the *polis* is the necessary condition for the best life, the study of politics is inseparable from morality; that is, political philosophy is inherently linked to moral philosophy.

Watson compares this view with that of the Sophists and Cynics, who, rather than seeing the *polis* as the necessary condition for moral freedom, regarded it in a utilitarian manner. Political obligation is merely a contract for maintaining peace among citizens, each one of whom is bent on satisfying his selfish interests. Political community, according to this theory, reflects the surrender of some portion of freedom in order to secure selfish interests. There can be no true reconciliation of the citizen and the community for the Cynics and the Sophists.[53] By setting Plato's and Aristotle's Idealist views against the materialist claims of the Cynics and the Sophists, Watson establishes a framework for his own theorising. He aligns his Idealist stance with what today is called a communitarian view of politics, setting it against a more contractarian point of view, which he sees as reflecting a materialistic and egocentric worldview. Watson attributes this materialist metaphysic to thinkers such as Thomas Hobbes, John Locke, John Stuart Mill, and Herbert Spencer, whom he describes as descendants of the Greek Sophists and Cynics. It is on this claim that Watson takes his stand against social contractarianism. The mistake the contractarians make, he argues, is to conceive of individuals as having a nature separate from the community. For Watson, there can be no concept of the individual apart from the community: "The principle of society is present in individuals, and without it they would not be themselves or rational."[54] Outside the community there is no freedom, only animal existence.

Watson places his own Idealist position within the metaphysical camp of Plato and Aristotle, in which "the freedom of the individual was shown to be compatible with the authority of society."[55] According to Watson, Plato articulates the problematic nature of the tensions between the citizen and the *polis* in the dialogues *Apology* and *Crito*. In the *Apology*, Plato asserts that the community has no right to retard by force a citizen's efforts to develop himself to his highest potential. The citizen is in the right to assert his own conscience as the final authority if he possesses a higher truth than that put forward by the community in its claim to authority. In the *Crito*, however, Plato balances the principle of freedom against the principle of communal duty. With Socrates' refusal to flee Athens in order to escape death, Plato is saying that the authority of the *polis* supersedes the claims of the citizen when the citizen is acting solely for personal, self-interested ends. Unless the citizen is acting on the basis of a transcendent principle, the authority of the community must prevail. Thus, in Watson's view, Plato articulates the view that the citizen is capable of realising his highest potential only within a community, only in relation to others. As such, the community needs to be organised in such a way as to allow for the development of that potential.[56]

To say this, though, is to claim knowledge of what it is to be most fully human – to know, in other words, the nature of reality. For Plato, the one person capable of knowing "what is," is the philosopher. But only a few are capable of being philosophers; thus, only a few are able to experience the rational order of the whole. Or, put differently, only a few are capable of being free and of pursuing the best life. Furthermore, while Plato permits a certain class differentiation within the city, he denies any differentiation within the classes themselves. Watson objects to this because such a political order imposes a basic separation between those who govern (the public authority) and those who are governed (the mass of citizens). Such a distinction, he says, degrades both. The governed are denied the opportunity to participate in government and thereby to gain greater awareness of their rational ends, while the governing class are removed from the valuable self-knowledge to be gained by participating in everyday life. Plato's hierarchical society denies people the opportunity to fulfil their true potential as human beings, which means that there can be no real reconciliation between individuals and the community.[57]

For Watson, the individual's true potential resides in his capacity for reason. But to be a reasoning human being requires being able to share in the life of the community. Reason, in other words, is manifested in the dialectical relationship between the individual and the community. In Watson's view, Plato's account of reason holds that reason is the preserve of the governing class and is imposed on the unreasoning masses. Reason functions only in the external ordering of the *polis*, not in the citizens' identification of their inner life with the external realm established by public authority. Behind this notion of the *polis* is Plato's "conception of a special race" that, because it possesses reason, is entitled to rule. Such a claim "denies that reason is a universal possession."[58] And, for Watson, that exposes the essential flaw in Plato's political theory. Plato was unable to conceive of a political order beyond the Greek *polis* in which the highest forms of reason could be present in others besides the members of a small elite ruling class.[59]

Watson, in keeping with his intention to link Periclean Athens to his own times, makes a similar claim against the rulers of nineteenth-century Germany. Under the regime of Frederick William the Third, democratic and national movements toward unity and liberty were stifled and the majority of people were refused even moderate rights for many years. The state was conceived of as vastly superior to the individual, as a political entity to which the individual owed obedience. This suppression of individual rights and the notion of an absolutist state were contributing factors in the rise of German militarism in the late nineteenth century that led to the First World War, says Watson, who faults the philosophies of Treitschke and Nietzsche on this score.[60]

Watson's point in tying his criticism of Plato's concept of political order to his criticism of nineteenth-century German thinkers is to defend his own argument that the state is an organic entity in which all members must actively participate if the state is to remain united and, equally important, if its individual members are to realise their highest potential as reasoning beings. Watson takes his guidance on this issue directly from Hegel's *Philosophy of Right*. Defending Hegel against those who accuse him of fomenting German militarism and statism, Watson says that Hegel saw the state as "an organism in which life is continually streaming from the centre to the extremities and back from the extremities to the centre." The unity of the state is maintained, not by force or the imposed order of a ruling class, but, in Hegel's words, by "'the deep-seated feeling of order which is possessed by all.'"[61] To be sure, Watson notes, this Hegelian conception of the state is implicit in Plato's own description of the best *polis*: "The State must be not only organic, but every member in it must take an active share in all its concerns, unless we are to have a conflict of classes and a consequent weakening of the body politic."[62] Nevertheless, Plato failed to conceive of a political system in which philosophic reasoning was possible for more than an elite few. Lacking the modern historical sensibility, Plato did not account for the possibility that political orders could grow and change with the evolution of human consciousness. Plato's political theory rests on what Watson sees as the untenable assumption that the city can be made virtuous by the alteration of external conditions. Plato's effort to identify the citizen and the community fails because it "takes away that intense consciousness of personality that is the condition of the higher life. He who has no self cannot be unselfish."[63]

Watson's interpretation of Plato on this point can be questioned. In his commentary on *Apology* and *Crito*, Watson clearly describes Socrates as subsuming his self-interest to the city and seeing himself as an organ of the community while, in another context, asserting a personal priority because of his allegiance to the demands of conscience. This suggests that Plato did, in fact, allow for a certain differentiation between the citizen and the community, acknowledging that the interests of some citizens could at times supersede those of the community. Watson seems to have missed some nuances in his own interpretation of Plato, turning instead to Aristotle to provide the corrective to Plato's promotion of excessive unity. Aristotle, says Watson, recognises that while man is fundamentally a political animal and the political community is rooted in private life, no community can achieve the kind of unity or complete organisation that is necessary in the household. In this way, Aristotle vindicates the idea of property as the bedrock of moral life and the family as the necessary, if insufficient, precondition for political community. Nonetheless, the political community is essential if citizens are to achieve their highest potential. This, in turn, suggests a mutual interdependence between the two. The *polis* is logically prior to the citizen – the city, after all, exists before the existence of all but those who founded it – but the *polis* owes its reason for existing, its end or purpose, to the needs of citizens, including the satisfaction of higher needs. In Aristotle, then, Watson discerns the most crucial element of classical Greek political philosophy: the essential principle that the development of man's inherent intellectual and moral virtues – the reasoned life, in short – is made possible "by the concentrated activity of various minds all working towards a common end,"[64] which is to say, in a political community.

Both Plato and Aristotle understand that reason is the standard by which politics is to be judged and fulfilled. They recognise that "the real bond of the State is therefore reason ... [because] it is reason that binds men

together by teaching them to understand one another."[65] The rational life
enables each citizen to develop his capacities to the fullest without the unwarranted interference of others. It is this capacity for a rational life that
the ancients understand as freedom. To recognise by means of reason that
my self-interest is broadly identical to the interests of the community as a
whole is to align my will with that of the community. My freedom is therefore identical to my duty. The philosophic life is not possible if I indulge
only my self-centred desires; my freedom, which is the life of reason, is obtained in obeying laws that I recognise as reflecting my capacity for reason.

For Watson, though, Plato's and Aristotle's understanding of the relationship between the citizen and the community remains flawed because
both see the penultimate purpose of the *polis* as that of securing the possibility of the best life, which, of course, is the life of philosophy. But only a few
are capable of being philosophers, which means that Plato and Aristotle promote a political community whose ultimate purpose is to allow a few to enjoy the life of the mind. Those who lack the highest capacities of reason
exist to allow a few to fulfil their potential. The "main body of the people"
are "instruments for the production of the highest results in the person of
a few privileged citizens."[66] Watson objects to this aspect of Plato's and
Aristotle's political thought, concluding that while they demonstrate how
the individual's freedom can be compatible with the authority of the community, they fail to recognise that the capacity for reason is latent in all
people and, hence, that all people deserve equal treatment in the community and an equal opportunity to participate in the political arrangements
of that community. Or, put differently, we all possess the potential to develop those virtues that constitute our freedom, which means that there is
a general, rational law binding on all of us.[67]

Such a claim about the evolution of reason underscores how Watson, following Hegel, thought that reason develops historically. The philosophical
concepts of the past are not frozen in time. They reflect understandings of
reality at particular historical moments and provide the means to a more
comprehensive understanding of the relationship between the individual
and the community.

The development of political theory from the fundamental idea of Plato
and Aristotle that the State exists for the production of the best life,
through the long and troubled period of the Roman Empire and the
Middle Ages, is a continuous development, in which one element after
another obtains prominence, until we reach the period of the modern
Nation-State, in which the ideas of check and balance, of a law of nature,

of absolute sovereignty of contract and utility form stepping stones to
the clear and simple conception of the State as existing for the establishment of the external conditions under which the highest human life
may be carried on.[68]

And, for Watson, the study of these historical moments allows the philosopher to distinguish those ideas and patterns of human conduct that are
true and universal from those that are false and transitory.

6

Watson's History of Universal Reason

John Watson credits the Stoics with enlarging the notion of reason to make it universal. He traces this development to the collapse of the ancient *polis* and the subsequent establishment of the Macedonian Empire under Alexander the Great and, later, the creation of the Roman Empire. Stoicism provided the theoretical bedrock for Roman law. The empires of the ancient world forced people to look beyond the narrow confines of the *polis* and to rethink their understanding of the relationship between the citizen and the community. But the centralising nature of imperial rule excluded masses of people from the kind of participation in political life that would satisfy their longing for community. The vastness of the empires required a new understanding of the self-conscious citizen that had been central to Plato and Aristotle. If citizens could no longer seek fulfilment in the moral and religious life of their city, where were they to find meaning and purpose in life?

The Stoics and the Epicureans attempted to conceptualize a new understanding of human nature that would account for the experience of imperial politics. With the empire's borders having obliterated ancient boundaries and the ultimate political power residing in the hands of a single man, the emperor, the Stoics argued that citizens could turn away from political life and still find fulfilment through their identity with "the great State of the World,"[69] which was comprised of both political (or moral) and religious life. This aspiration was sustained by the idea of man's fundamental homogeneity regardless of different customs and traditions. Individuals might be excluded from participating in the political life of their city, but they can still conceive of themselves as part of the greater whole because any particular political order reflects the rational order of the world. While individuals might be alienated from the political order, they still know that their life has meaning because they, like all other people, are subject to the laws of reason manifested throughout the universe. And since all people possess the same fundamental rational nature, it could be asserted, as the Stoics claimed, that what is reasonable for one is reasonable for all. In this manner, Stoicism, with its notion that all men are essentially free and equal because they share the same rational nature, became the basis for natural law theory as it was practised in Roman jurisprudence and eventually throughout the Western world, providing "a system of universal legislation that has formed the starting-point for the jurisprudence of all civilised peoples."[70]

The Stoics' law of reason also prepared the way for the positive universal religion of Christianity and its claim that beyond all worldly differences people are equal in the eyes of Heaven. With this claim, according to Watson, Stoicism promoted a fundamental shift in human self-comprehension that helped bridge the political transition from the *polis* to the nation-state. Moreover, it embedded the seedling notion of a world-state in the consciousness of the West. This notion of the world-state is crucial in Watson's political thought, and I shall return to it later in discussing his theoretical support for imperialism. In the meantime, it is necessary to look at some of his arguments now because they have a bearing on his views of how the modern nation-state came to be.

Watson's discussion of Stoicism recalls Hegel's argument in *Phenomenology of Spirit* regarding the development of stoical consciousness whereby the individual, whether master or slave, retreats into an inner life in response to external domination and necessity.[71] At this stage of consciousness, the inner life attempts to stand as a bulwark against a hostile and frustrating outer world. In effect, though, consciousness seeks to retreat from a fearful, alienating world to some refuge in the mind. This abstract universal, as Hegel calls it, manifests itself at the political level in a relationship between the individual and the state that is considerably different from that of the Greek *polis*. Under the Roman Empire, the Greek notion of the public citizen working for the good of the community with which he identified his interests largely disappeared. It was replaced by the notion of the citizen as a private person who did not give much regard to communal concerns outside his own particular interests. The interests of the whole were thus placed in the hands of the emperor and the bureaucracy that served him. As a result, the citizen was reduced to an atomistic self disconnected from the public life of his community. The citizen of the Greek *polis* saw his universal self in the institutions and monuments of his city. But the imperial citizen, restricted from participating in the political life of the empire in any substantive way comparable to that of the Emperor, was at a loss to find a public mode of conduct that could satisfy his need to belong to the wider community. In Watson's words, "The appropriation of all political functions by the Roman Empire naturally shut out the individual from any direct political relations, and this forced him back upon himself."[72]

Hegel is disturbingly clear on what this means, namely the effective alienation of most citizens from the political life of their community.[73] While Watson offers only a gloss on Hegel's analysis, his description of the Roman Empire indicates that he adopted Hegel's analysis as his own. For example, in an argument that has considerable bearing on his moral support for imperialism, Watson points out that under the empire anything like an independent political life disappeared in the conquered peoples. An emperor who gathered all power in his own hands retarded other possibilities of political development. The result was that the Stoic conception of a law of reason in which all men are free and equal as citizens of the world had no substantive influence on imperial affairs, since in practice only the singular will of the emperor made law.[74]

Watson concludes that the Stoic concept of a universal reason possessed naturally by all men – which therefore made all men fundamentally equal – was inadequate because it found no concrete expression in the real world. The Stoics mistakenly thought the highest ideals of an individual need not be tied to the concrete realities of daily life. They conceived of an ideal abstract self but ignored Aristotle's insight that man is also a political being. The Stoic ideal implied a political order in which all are equal – a world-state, in other words. The problem was that such a world-state was unachievable. The Stoics thus effectively alienated individuals from the bonds of community that provide the substance of concrete life.

Nonetheless, Watson recognises that the Stoics provided a powerful transformative idea. Stoic thought helped give birth to a consciousness amenable to the emergence of Christianity. The Christian principle of the equality of individuals in the eyes of God is similar to the Stoic notion of natural equality. Where the Stoics had rooted the law of reason in the rational order of the cosmos, the Christians grounded natural law in a supernatural being. In this way, Stoicism provided a conceptual bridge between the ancient *polis* and the modern nation-state by establishing the nascent idea of a world-state that could realise itself through the organisation of the various nation-states.

Watson describes how, from the fall of the Roman Empire to the emergence of the British Empire, the idea of the nation-state worked itself out over the course of the Middle Ages, and he argues that it was through the

medieval monarchical orders that the Stoics' abstract universal was actualised. The medieval world provided a corrective principle to overcome the
alienation between the citizen and the political order that had characterized the Roman Empire. It was generally held that a monarch's authority
was derived from God, and while this divine authority was needed to maintain order in this world, the political function of the monarch was "to
maintain justice, to suppress vice and crime, and to maintain the Catholic
faith."[75] Such an understanding of the monarch's secular purposes implies
a particular relationship between ruler and ruled, between sovereign and
subject. This relationship required people to obey the ruler. However, the
ruler was obliged to maintain the conditions necessary for his people's
well-being. Implicit in this relationship is the notion that the subject – or a
group of subjects such as an assembly of the people – was the ultimate
source of political legitimacy. The subject had natural rights that could not
be reduced or impaired by the ruler or a prince. Indeed, the fundamental
legitimising purpose of the sovereign was to protect the subject.

Watson argues that this feudal conception of the relationship between
sovereign and subject re-established the ancient concept of the *polis* as the
highest form of community, albeit in a different form. This is reflected in
the exaltation of the sovereign as the sole representative of the common
interests and common life of the community. Out of this notion grew the
idea that princely power was the single power standing above the subject,
commanding his loyalty in return for protection. This idea in turn gave
birth during the medieval era to the notion of the state as the overarching
authority, the single power, standing above the individual. As Watson puts
it, "the origin of the State is to be found in a contract of subjection made
between the People and the Ruler." This idea prepared the way for the
subordination of the church during the fourteenth and fifteenth centuries
and eventually developed to the point where "all subordinate power was to
be delegated by the sovereign power, the State," which acted in the interests of the whole.[76]

Watson's argument closely follows Hegel's on the development of the
state. In *The Philosophy of History*, Hegel writes that the development of
monarchies out of the feudal order resulted in the rise of a supreme authority whose dominion embraced all – a political power so-called whose
subjects enjoyed an equality of rights and in which the will of the individual
was subordinated to that common interest that underlay the whole. Hegel
concludes that this arrangement of power set the stage for the coming-
to-be of nation-states in that the necessary condition for the establishment
of monarchies was the emergence of particular nationalities.[77]

In a similar argument, Watson says that with the development of the idea of the sovereign state, political speculation about the growth of nation-states began again. Thus, medieval thought "prepared the weapons for that combat between the Sovereign State and the Sovereign Individual which fills the subsequent centuries."[78] According to Watson, Thomas Aquinas is able to reconcile the state and the individual by reconciling church and state. Aquinas accepts Aristotle's description of man as a political animal and of politics as a natural expression of what it means to be human. Aquinas also holds that it is in and through the community that the individual is able to attain the good life. For Aquinas, every political community requires a ruler whose chief function is to establish those laws that provide for the continuance of the community. Which is to say, the ruler's obligation is to provide those conditions by which the members of a community can seek the good life, understood in its Christian context to mean obeying God's will. Since the ruler is the medium of God's will, it is the duty of every subject to obey the ruler because to do so is God's will. And since the church has jurisdiction over the interpretation of divine law and embodies the "unity of faith" that overarches all particular states, it is right and proper that the church should require Christians to "obey their earthly rulers, because such obedience is essential to the order and stability of society."[79]

Here again Watson draws on the paradigmatic model of Socrates' relationship to the Athenian *polis* described in *Apology* and *Crito*. Just as Socrates justifies his disobedience of the communal will by appealing to a higher spiritual authority, so too does the church allow the communicant to claim a spiritual loyalty that transcends the political order. At the same time, though, echoing the rationale Socrates articulates in *Crito* to explain why he has to accept the authority of the city, Aquinas says that it is the obligation of subjects to obey the earthly authority when what is at issue is not a matter of transcendent conscience. Aquinas, therefore, establishes a unifying bond between sacred and profane powers. Each is necessary to the other in the sense that only through their mutual interaction is it possible for people to satisfy their best purposes. The church requires the existence of profane power because without it there would be no means by which to direct people toward God's will. Conversely, without the sacred, rulers would have no end or purpose beyond the pursuit of power. In Watson's view, then, Aquinas's thought reflects Hegel's concept of *Aufhebung* (and, arguably, *List der Vernunft*, the cunning of reason) in that he reconciles the apparent dichotomy of the sacred and profane realms in such a way that their opposition is overcome without the sacrifice of their necessary distinctiveness.

The Aquinian moment of a reconciliation of heaven and earth, of natural law and positive law, was short-lived. The clash between the sacred and the profane was renewed after Aquinas's death. This time, however, the strength of the national monarchies overcame the efforts of a weakened church to maintain the medieval doctrine of the unity of faith under the dominion of a single emperor. By the end of the fifteenth century, this imperial idea could not be sustained. With the growth of cities and the expansion of trade and commerce, along with the schism in the church, the national idea came to dominate people's minds.[80] For Watson, what is theoretically important in these historical developments is how the abstracted notion of the imperial idea represented by the Holy Roman Empire, with its Christian conception of the equality of all individuals, was to be made concrete through the development of nation-states that would embody the awareness of the value of diverse, if subordinate, forms of human organisation. The development of the nation-state reconciles, in principle, the universal ideal of human equality and freedom with the ancient idea that the political community should provide the conditions necessary for the citizen's quest for the good life.[81]

Watson credits Niccolo Machiavelli with being the first political theorist to comprehend the significance of the church's waning influence and to announce the nascent nation-state as its replacement. Machiavelli sees that the notion of a political empire co-extensive with the Christian faith is an empty abstraction. He recognises the commingling of nationalism and monarchy in the wake of the Holy Roman Empire's fragmentation. The resulting disorder prompts him to ask how a strong, united, and efficient authority could be established. His answer is to abandon the idea of natural law as the guide in political science. Because the idea of a political empire co-extensive with Christian Europe is no longer feasible, order can only be restored to Italy if a strong-willed prince makes himself master of the separate regions and leads them in a fight against the domination of foreign powers. Hence, according to Watson, Machiavelli articulates a new, modern spirit that would eventually see the nation-state become the prevailing form of political order in the West.[82]

Machiavelli also detaches politics from ethics, political virtue from moral virtue, by teaching the radical lesson that sound political order depends on the capacity of the ruler to do what is necessary to maintain the state, even if this use of power means acting contrary to traditional morality. All that counts is maintaining the sovereignty of the state, by whatever means necessary. Watson acknowledges that there is a distinction between individual morality and the morality of a ruler who is acting to ensure the survival of the state. As representatives of the state, rulers sometimes have to use modes of action that would earn the individual condemnation. But in comments that have considerable implications for his philosophic support for imperialism, Watson is careful to say that the state, and the ruler who represents the state, cannot be completely absolved of all moral responsibility. In a rebuttal to Machiavelli's amorality, Watson argues that the morality of a ruler's acts has to be judged in terms of the effect those acts have "upon the whole spiritual life of the nation."[83] The actions of a state, like the actions of an individual in his dealings with his community, are to be judged on the basis of their consequences.

In making this argument, Watson is again extending the lessons he extracted from *Apology* and *Crito*. As previously discussed, the former dialogue asks how the citizen's obligation to the community is to be determined, while the latter asserts that a citizen may not set his will against the community on the basis of self-interest. Watson's resolution to the conundrum of the dialogues is this: you can set yourself over the community when obedience to the communal authority violates an impersonal transcendent law, but you must obey the community's laws when your conduct is solely self-interested. Watson applies the same criteria to his analysis of Machiavelli's political ethics, concluding that no state should conduct itself solely at the expense of other states "as if the real interest of one nation were necessarily in antagonism to the interests of all other nations." To act this way is contrary to "the higher interests of the State" because it ignores the reality that all states, like all individuals, are enmeshed in relationships with each other.[84]

Watson is essentially saying that Machiavelli's reaction to the abstractness of the medieval imperial idea goes too far in the other direction. Machiavelli abandons the concept of a more universal humanity in favour of safety and order in a particular state, thus ignoring the need to maintain a balance between the universal and the particular. Machiavelli may argue that only by means of a ruler's authority is it possible to preserve a particular state's existence and secure the freedom of its citizens, but in Watson's view, the real consequence is to inflate the power of the ruler and open the door to tyranny. As in Roman times, the interests of the nation-state become bound up with the interests of a single person who may or may not act out of self-interest. Stated another way, the interests of the one are potentially at odds with the greater good of the many. Machiavelli's political theory implies that the individual takes precedence over the community, the particular comes before the whole, and morality is at odds with law. Machiavelli, in short, fails to reconcile the individual and the community.

Watson's moral philosophy, informed by an organic conception of relations between the individual and the other, cannot accept this tension of law and morality. His objections emerge most clearly in his criticism of the social contract theories of Hobbes, Rousseau, and Kant, none of whom finds a definitive way to reconcile the individual and the public authority.

7

The State in Question:
Hobbes, Rousseau, and Hegel

According to Watson, the basic political problem after Machiavelli lay in establishing the legitimacy of the nation-state. Watson's devotes four chapters of *The State in Peace and War* to this subject, considering the thought of Thomas Hobbes, James Locke, Jean-Jacques Rousseau, James and John Stuart Mill, and Herbert Spencer, among others. While he acknowledges the differences among these thinkers, he argues that they share a materialist metaphysic at odds with his own Idealist view. This materialist metaphysic produces political philosophies that are fundamentally utilitarian and posit a social contract by which individuals are to be kept orderly by the state's threat of force.

Watson's harshest criticism of this materialist ethos is directed against Spencer. Like the pre-modern Sophists, Spencer sees the relationship between the state and the individual as one of perpetual tension, a condition where "what is gained by the State is lost by the individual, and what is gained by the individual is gained at the expense of the State."[85] Watson traces the modern promotion of this idea of an enduring tension between the community and the individual to Hobbes. Hobbes, he says, thinks that individuals can be adjusted to the community if absolute power is contracted to a sovereign, or leviathan, who alone can mediate among conflicting interests: "A contract or pact is made by which individuals hand over their power to some individual or individuals, who henceforth act with the combined power of all individuals."[86] Watson says that this view is based on the assumption that, prior to this imagined contract, people enjoyed natural rights that preceded the establishment of a community and were surrendered only in order that they might better secure their individual interests, satisfy their desire for recognition, and avoid violent death. He thinks that this claim divorces rights from duties and imposes an unbridgeable barrier between the community and the individual. Watson draws from Spinoza to argue that rights are tied to the existence of community: "There can be no right which does not flow from the consciousness of a common interest on the part of the members of a society, since a right implies recognition by the common will."[87] Hobbes's political philosophy is flawed by his metaphysical assumption that the individual exists apart from or precedes the community in some state of nature.

Watson makes a similar argument regarding Rousseau. Like Hobbes, Rousseau asserts the primacy of the individual while, at the same time, seeking a political process in which conflicts between and among individuals are subject to an overarching authority. That authority is the state, which, for Rousseau, is the objective expression of the collective general will. Within the political order, the people are sovereign, and through the agency of the government, which applies the general will, they express their sovereignty. Watson regards such a claim as theoretically inadequate, arguing that if an individual is originally free, as Rousseau claims, then obviously some freedom is lost in his submitting to an association involving others, but if association with others increases his security and goods, then, at least on the material level, he is freer than in the non-social environment of a state of nature. Rousseau, Watson argues, would have each person hand over his natural freedom to the general will only to receive that freedom back in the form of a social or moral freedom that reflects the individual's rational identity with the greater good of the whole. Watson perceives a flaw in this idea: implicit in the notion that the social contract requires the individual to identify with the whole is the corollary idea that the individual who does not attain this identity can be forced to obey the general will. Citing Rousseau's *Social Contract*, Watson says that this "means nothing less than that he will be forced to be free."[88] This in turn implies that the state, as the vehicle through which the general will is manifested, is ultimately based on coercion and the threat of force. Under such conditions, Watson questions how a genuine reconciliation of the individual and the state can be effected.

Watson summarises social contract theory along the following lines. The creation of a contract establishing the sovereign power requires agents who are naturally free and rational, and able to agree among themselves to give up some natural freedom in exchange for the safety and protection afforded by a political community. Such an agreement implies that individuals possess an autonomous existence prior to establishing a political order but choose to surrender some of their autonomy for the sake of security or

social freedom. It also implies that those who do not accept the social contract, who do not willingly subsume their particular will to the general will,
can be subjected to state or community coercion. For Watson, however, the
idea that an individual can be "forced to be free" is morally incoherent. He
refers to the French Revolution to make his point. The revolutionists forgot that freedom, and the possibilities of self-development that go with it,
cannot be imposed from the outside. Thus, the French Revolution demonstrates the potential dangers of social contractarianism: "Beginning in a
protest against tyranny, the Revolution ended in a ruthless attempt to
'force other nations to be free,' an attempt which ignored the principle,
that the freedom of a people, like the freedom of an individual, cannot be
secured by any form of external compulsion."[89]

Such a statement has obvious implications for Watson's ideas about the
purposes of imperialism, and I shall return to this issue when I consider his
views on empire. In the meantime, I note that Watson regards Rousseau's
contractarianism as inadequate in terms of its effectiveness in reconciling
the individual and the community. To be sure, Rousseau, like Plato and
Aristotle, understands that political community is founded on more than a
contract, that community is intrinsically linked to the development of individuals as rational and moral beings. Indeed, Rousseau sees the civil state
as the embodiment of moral freedom. His famous phrase "Man is born
free and everywhere is in chains" should not be regarded as a criticism of
political society. Rousseau recognises, says Watson, that civil liberty is distinct from natural liberty and that the law is possible only in a lawful community. The question for Rousseau is how to establish an association that
can defend and protect civil society while, at the same time, allowing the
members of that society to be free unto themselves even as they obey the
will of the community. His answer is the concept of the general will, understood as those expressions of the common good that form the basis of law-
making and political decision-making. This general will can be manifested
in an open assembly where all citizens can make their voices heard and
thus form the general will.

Watson, however, knows that the idea of direct democracy is not only impractical in a modern nation-state, but also raises the prospect of majoritarian tyranny: "The general will is not the mere sum of individual wills ... but
the will of all in so far as the common good is its object: and law is its expression, but only in so far as it is what it ought to be."[90] In other words,
the general will is not simply the consensus of a majority; rather, it reveals
the degree to which the actions of the political community as a whole accord with the underlying order of reality. Rousseau, however, is not always

careful to distinguish between the general will and the will of all. Hence, Watson argues, what is best for the good of the whole "is by no means manifest to every citizen in his ordinary mind; his real will must be revealed to him."[91]

With this argument Watson again invokes the lessons of *Apology* and *Crito*. The former dialogue, it will be recalled, seeks to determine how the individual's obligation to the community is to be determined; the latter maintains that individuals cannot set their wills against the community out of self-interest. Watson reiterates this dictum in his critique of Rousseau. He suggests that Rousseau's occasional identification of the general will and the will of all results from his failure to distinguish among individuals manifesting their true freedom on the basis of right will – a higher impersonal law – and those who act on the basis of uncomprehending self-interest or private will. The idea of a general will cannot be sustained because the metaphysical basis of social contract theory – the rational individual apart from a community – precludes such a possibility. While Watson endorses Rousseau's linkage of civil freedom and the general will, he does not think Rousseau's understanding of the true nature of these concepts is adequate. Rousseau holds to the fallacy that man can be free (and rational) apart from society, whereas for Watson, it is only in society that man has any substantive freedom.[92]

Rousseau, Watson concludes, believes that social or civil freedom emerges from the repression of natural freedom. Rousseau may argue that civil society embodies a moral freedom that, because it reflects the individual's higher or rational self, is not merely the renunciation of natural freedom, but in Watson's view, this still assumes that natural man is at odds with man as a political being.[93] While Rousseau may insist on the priority of the individual, he, like Hobbes, continues to argue for a sovereign power that imposes limits on the individual. Thus, in Watson's view, Rousseau, like Hobbes and Plato, is guilty of wanting too much unity and, therefore, contractarianism fails to reconcile the individual and the community.

Indeed, for Watson, the underlying assumption of social contract theory is that isolated individuals are ends unto themselves. Only the willing acceptance of all to enter into a reciprocal relationship is the basis for the state. But Watson, following Kant, argues that just as a husband and wife are joined in a relationship that points to ends beyond those of self-interest, so too are the members of a political community bound up in an inseparable relationship that exists apart from any contract and goes beyond their own self-centred desires. "It may be expressed by saying that it is the relation of a community of rational beings not externally bound together but organically connected."[94] Watson concludes that so long as we fail to grasp this organic connection with one another, we are forced to accept the idea that the only thing that holds humans together, the only basis for political community, is force.

For Watson, though, this view violates man's essential social nature. Only through social relations do individuals realise their qualities as rational beings. A penultimate passage summarising Watson's rationale for rejecting social contract theory recalls his commentary on Plato's *Crito*: briefly, that the individual possesses his highest humanity when he acts on the basis of motives that subordinate his self-interest – that is, when he acts as a social being. The commentary is worth quoting in full:

> Only in society have men any rights, and rights are justified because they
> are the necessary conditions of the moral life. Morality is not the willing
> of the individual nature, but the willing of the social nature. If we
> separate morality from society, and suppose it to be a law by which the
> individual is an end to himself, it is not possible to go beyond the ab-
> stract rule to do one's duty for its own sake, and such a rule gives no
> guarantee, of any specific duty whatever. Morality is essentially social,
> and the institutions of the State can be justified only as essential to the
> development of this social morality.[95]

There are also echoes of *Crito*'s higher self as the standard of moral conduct in Watson's notion of the nation-state as formally perfect. He argues that the modern nation-state is, in principle, potentially capable of accommodating all that the individual could reasonably want in political life: "In truth, the State is not the result of any self-surrender of an original position, but the recognition that such an opposition is one-sided and abstract. The State is neither a despotism, forcing individuals to submit to its commands, nor is it an arbitrary agreement of individuals to protect their personal rights by making concessions to others; it is the recognition and realisation of the essentially indivisible nature of the consciousness of self and the consciousness of other selves."[96]

Hegel, says Watson, is the one modern thinker able to convincingly refute contractarian political theory in favour of an organic conception of community. Hegel shows how to overcome the atomistic assumptions of the social contractarians and, in this overcoming, provides the deepest insight into the nature of the modern nation-state. As Watson writes in an 1894 essay, Hegel's "general conception of society and the state seems to me to be, in its grand outlines, a remarkable synthesis of the just claims of the individual and the universal."[97] While Hegel accepts Rousseau's and Kant's fundamental principle of moral freedom, or the free will, as the distinctive quality of man, he sees their conception of human freedom as flawed by its abstractness. In particular, the defect in Kant's thought is to conceive of morality and individual rights as somehow in opposition.

Watson echoes Hegel in arguing that, for Kant, morality is conceived of as willing duty for duty's sake. As such it is "perfectly empty" in that it remains a universal or general law that can never be realised outwardly. Kant's claim regarding individual rights effectively isolates the individual from others because it conceives of the individual as an end in himself. This leads to a purely subjective view of morality and to an abstract and negative view of rights. If morality is understood to be willing duty for duty's sake, it becomes impossible to actualise in any substantive external manner because the individual can never go beyond the empty general law to do his duty. According to Watson, the individual cannot *see* his duty in the world. His duty remains something abstracted from his concrete existence. If human freedom is purely subjective and has no outward expression that does not require the surrender of its autonomy to some degree, then, as far as Kant is concerned, individual rights exist only at the behest of the community. This means, according to Watson, that rights are imposed externally by the state, which is to imply that the state's fundamental function is to maintain the atomised individual in his isolation from others.[98]

For Hegel, Watson says, this Kantian notion of rights belonging to individuals in their isolation leads to the idea of the state as an external or alien power whose chief function is to keep individuals from harming one another. In attempting to surmount the Kantian antinomy, Watson writes, Hegel seeks to overcome the opposition between morality and rights by showing that freedom involves the "outward realisation of what is inwardly demanded by reason" and that the state and society are the arena in which this reconciliation takes place. Human freedom loses its abstractedness and becomes concrete or actualised by externalising itself in a system of law and institutional order. Watson sees this notion of human freedom made concrete, or true individuality, as being embodied in Hegel's notion of *Sittlichkeit*. In Hegel's ethical system, "the inwardness of morality and the mere externality of law are reconciled."[99] Thus, according to Watson, Hegel's political philosophy "is really an attempt to unite the two ideas of freedom or self-determination, and organic or spiritual unity."[100] Hegel's vehicle for this reconciliation of the subjective and the objective is the state.

This Hegelian concept of political order echoes Plato and Aristotle in terms of achieving an identity between private persons and public authority, but Watson also believes that Hegel's thought goes beyond that of the Greeks. Hegel accepts the ancient understanding that the political community must be an objective and concrete manifestation of the inner will of the people. But he also asserts that the political community has to embody this inner will through more than custom and tradition. The modern state, while retaining the sense of community of the ancient *polis*, must also reflect modern subjectivity. Hegel conceives of the state not as the product of a contract among autonomous and isolated individuals, but rather as an organic expression of individuals' rational identification with their community, an identification rooted in the fundamental social nature of humans. With his concept of *Sittlichkeit*, Watson says, "Hegel removes the last vestige of the false theory that the State is based upon contract, making its foundation to rest upon the true principle of the common will, as distinguished from the mere sum of individual wills."[101]

Watson adopts Hegel's organic conception of the state and rejects the notion that identifies the state with the power of the majority to impose its will and force others to be free. No one can be made free by force, Watson says, concluding that "it is not any number of separate individuals, choosing to make a pact with one another that justifies the existence of the State. The real justification is to be found in the social nature of man ... The whole complex organisation of society gets its justification from its fitness to realise man's essential nature, and different political constitutions must be judged by this standard."[102] The state, in other words, cannot be an arrangement for controlling individuals or have its chief function be that of keeping individuals from interfering with the freedom or rights of others. Rather, the state is the highest expression of human freedom as manifested through the objective institutions that make up the state – family, property, civil society, the courts, the government, the constitution – and it operates by the free assent of the individuals to those institutions.

Perhaps the single most comprehensive statement demonstrating Watson's appropriation of Hegel's political thought regarding the Ideal relationship between the individual and the community comes in a passage at the beginning of the tenth chapter of *The State in Peace and War*. The passage follows Watson's philosophical history of the various concepts of political community, up to the modern nation-state. It is worth quoting in full because, as I shall discuss later, it lends theoretical weight to his Idealist view of empire.

As the ultimate object of society is the development of the best life, each individual must recognise the rights of his neighbour to as free development as that which he claims for himself. The justification of this claim is not any fictitious "right of nature," but the just claim that without freedom to live his own life under recognised external conditions, he is not capable of contributing his share to the common good. A man has rights that are recognised by society, but they are not made right by legislation, as Bentham held, but are recognised because they are essential to the development of the common good. The possession of rights and their recognition by society are not two different things, but the same thing; for, as the individual claims rights in virtue of his being an organ of the common good, so the State recognises his rights on the ground that they are required for the realisation of the highest good of all. The State, we may say, is under obligation to secure to the individual his rights, and any State that fails to do so ceases to fulfil its essential function.[103]

For Watson, then, the state does not exist as some sovereign entity that rules over other community institutions such as churches, volunteer organisations, or even other governmental organisations. The state is the net that holds all these other entities together. It holds them together not because of some absolute superiority over other organisations, but because it is the ultimate means by which these organisations can be harmonised so as not to interfere with one another. The state is the Ideal of reconciliation made real.

Thus, as far as Watson is concerned, the Hegelian conception of the state provides a modern answer to the central question of his political thought: What is the proper relationship between the citizen and the community? The modern state, grounded in the notion of popular sovereignty, provides individuals with the opportunity to develop their full human potential through their participation in the community. The individual, in turn, identifies with the state because he recognises in its laws and institutions the embodiment of his own rational will. The question asked in *Apology* – To what degree must the citizen obey the laws of the community? – is also answered: The modern state, so far as it manifests the rational will of the whole, does not impose laws on the individual that are contrary to the rational will of the individual. Similarly, the question posed in *Crito* – Can the citizen oppose his conscience to the will of the community? – becomes moot, theoretically at least, because the individual's conscience, his subjective freedom, is reconciled to the objective laws of the state. In sum, Hegel resolves the problem Watson traces to Pericles: how to unite public authority with private freedom.

But how does this reconciliation of freedom and duty, morality and law, manifest or actualise itself? What are the particulars of Watson's conception of the relationship between the individual and the community? My discussion so far suggests that, for Watson, the existence of community is the necessary if insufficient condition for the emergence of self-consciousness or individuality and, equally, the full development of that individuality is the fundamental purpose of community. Other commentators have not interpreted Watson this way. He is generally thought to give priority to the community over the individual. Leslie Armour says that Watson "constantly makes the point that community comes before individuality."[104] Frederick Hoffner, however, thinks that Watson gives priority to the individual over the community: "For Watson, the problems of political society were not a case of protecting the individual from the unified purposes of the state but of transforming the unified purposes of the state into the service of the individuals."[105] I agree with Hoffner on this issue. But I also think that Watson's position is more nuanced. For Watson, the question of the proper ordering of the relationship between the individual and the community is not simply a question of which takes priority or precedence, but rather is a matter of symbiosis and reciprocity.

Watson himself lends weight to such an interpretation in *The State in Peace and War*. Drawing from Hegel's understanding of the emergence of self-consciousness, Watson argues that to know oneself psychologically as an individual, different and separate from other individuals, one must first become aware of others distinct from oneself. But an awareness of one's difference from others is possible only if one recognises one's relationship to them – that is, if one is conscious of the underlying unity that makes possible the discernment of difference. As Watson puts it – in an obvious appropriation of Hegel – "Identity is necessary to difference."[106] The recognition of a relationship between self and other, and the sense of community born from this recognition, are only possible if one is already self-conscious. Self-consciousness, in short, is co-present with community.

Perhaps the best way to grapple with this argument is to consider Watson's critique of "atomism" and his theory of relative sovereignty. Not only does Watson's analysis of atomism underscore his opposition to contractarianism, but it also highlights the distinctiveness of his Hegelian response to the purposes of the modern nation-state and, as I shall show later, his hopes for the British Empire. Furthermore, as we shall see in Part 4, Watson's argument foreshadows Charles Taylor's own criticism of atomistic individualism, although Watson comes to a different conclusion than Taylor about how atomism can be overcome.

8

Watson's Theory of Relative Sovereignty

Watson does seem at first glance to grant the community priority over the individual in arguing that the individual is incapable of realising his higher potential outside a community, regardless of how inadequate that community may be in actualising the universal principle of reason. In his 1895 book *An Outline of Philosophy*, Watson states that "the true good of the individual" is identical to "the consciousness of a social good." "What holds human beings together in society is this idea of a good higher than merely individual good. Every form of social organisation rests upon this tacit recognition of a higher good that is realised in the union of oneself with others ... It is still true that only in identifying himself with a social good can the individual realise himself."[107]

However, in *The State in Peace and War*, Watson makes a more subtle argument, pointing out that if self-consciousness is relative to the consciousness of other selves and if the development of this self-consciousness is possible only in contrast to other selves, then there is an abiding tension in the relationship between the individual and the community. In self-consciousness we become aware of the rational order of reality. Self-consciousness is thereby unifying – not, as Kant would have it, separative. At the same time, though, we also become aware that this order is manifested, however inadequately, in other objects, including other human beings. It is impossible to have one without the other. But this means that a fundamental tension exists in the relationship between self and other because the individual and the community can never be absolutely identified. Furthermore, to attempt to forcefully bring about the complete identity of the individual and the community, or, for that matter, the complete identity of different groups within a state, is to fail to recognise the true ends of each. In an analysis of rights that echoes his commentary on *Apology* and *Crito*, Watson seems to suggest that the individual, as an "organ of the common good,"[108] has a duty to criticise the community in an effort to improve it if it falls short of its true purposes.

What does this mean in terms of Watson's hope to achieve reconciliation between the individual and the political order within which the individual discovers himself? Basically, Watson follows his Socratic model, asserting that criticism of a particular social or political order, and hence the effort to change that order for the better, are justified when those demanding change do so on the basis of principles that transcend their own self-interest – that is to say, when they act in accordance with the principles of right reason. There can be no notion of the individual acting on the basis that his interest takes precedence over the community's. Watson does not believe that individual rights come before the good of the community as a whole. But neither does he espouse the supremacy of the state or the community over the individual. Near the end of *The State in Peace and War*, in an allusion to the Socratic model with which he began the book, Watson reiterates his core thematic concern about the individual's relationship to the state when he says that it is right for individuals to resist the law if that law does not express the common or rational good. "The conscience of the individual may be higher than the law of the state."[109]

This notion of a kind of dynamic tension between the individual and the community is at the core of Watson's theory of relative sovereignty. The best way to approach this theory is indirectly, through a consideration of Watson's concerns about atomism. In Watson's thought, there is no possibility either of the individual having priority or supremacy over the community, or of the community, in any of its forms, including the state, having supremacy over the individual. For Watson, the community in all its forms is the functioning differentiation of individuals. It is in this individuation that we experience our freedom, which Watson defines as the condition of being able to fully express this process of individuation. In seeking your own individuation, however, reason dictates that you recognise the right of others to do the same, since that which makes others different is, like your own uniqueness, the ground of their freedom. In this way, reason fosters the awareness of a common good among individuals that can, by means of the state and its myriad institutions, further the freedom and the sense of belonging of all. In this schema, the purpose of the state becomes the safeguarding of the individual's freedom through a system of rights that ultimately is of benefit to the state, or the whole.

Watson outlines his view of rights in the tenth chapter of *The State in Peace and War*, "System of Rights." He argues that man has rights that are recognised by society but are not made rights by the state's laws; rather they are recognised as rights because they are crucial to the development of the common good. The notion of natural rights is, he says, a fiction. Rights are not something the individual possesses but modes of recognition by others of the realms of freedom available for the best possible development of that person. Rights, including property rights, are not intended to protect the individual from an alienating society; they exist through others' recognition. This implies, of course, that the individual needs the community, or the state, in order to be free.[110]

According to Watson, this vital relationship between the individual and the state, and the system of rights it engenders, are undermined in the atomistic politics promoted by a mechanistic utilitarian view of the world in which individuals are regarded as separate from and independent of one another. Politics, by this view, is an imposition on our original freedom. But Watson argues that such a utilitarian understanding of politics threatens the state and, ultimately, the freedom of individuals, because in reality the state is, or should be, the preserver of freedom. The problem with atomistic, utilitarian accounts of individual rights is that they undercut the moral basis of rights by seeing them as a matter of satisfying individual egos. Such a notion of rights, Watson argues, is an insufficient basis for communal obligation: "There is nothing to compel individuals to enter into a contract, and therefore nothing to explain why it should be made. To reduce the contract to an expedient for attaining a larger amount of happiness, does not explain why any man should be under obligation to assent to the contract, if he thinks he would obtain more satisfaction by purely individual initiative. And if all men should take this view, as according to the theory, they might, what becomes of society and the State?"[111] Watson argues instead for an ethical conception of politics in which the state is obliged to protect the rights of individuals. Indeed, he says that any state that fails to secure the rights of its members "ceases to fulfil its essential function."[112] The state that does not assure its citizens' freedom loses its legitimacy.

Watson contrasts his ethical understanding of the state with that of individualist thinkers such as Herbert Spencer, who was much influenced by Darwinian evolutionary theory. Spencer regards society as analogous to a living organism whose component "cells" are engaged in the struggle to survive against all other "physiological units." Since the social organism, unlike the natural organism, has no central consciousness, there can be no suggestion that the cells might exist for the sake of the whole. Rather, the whole exists to serve the parts. Translated politically, Spencer's biological analogy implies that the state exists to serve the individual's ends. But Spencer, according to Watson, saw the relationship between the individual and the community or state in fundamentally antagonistic terms. "There is such an opposition between the individual and the State that what is gained by the State is lost by the individual."[113]

According to Watson, this atomistic view of political and social relations leads to the idea that the individual is utterly independent of other selves. Moreover, it implies that communal relations and political life are unnatural, albeit necessary. This tension, or alienation, between the individual and the community is dangerous for political order and social cohesion. Watson agrees with Hegel that the division of powers among various political, social, and economic organisations and institutions could provide strength and cohesion to the state. But he also sees that it could create the appearance of the state as merely the aggregate of individuals fighting for their self-interest. In an argument that echoes his criticism of Machiavelli, Watson says that such a condition can leave individuals psychologically fragmented, forced to act different roles, depending on the realm or institution in which they find themselves, and leading private lives at odds with their public lives. We may want individual, social, and political morality to be one and inseparable, says Watson, "but the complexity of modern life is so great, and the various forms of organisation so many and distinct, that often a man will act in different spheres in ways quite inconsistent with one another. The man who in private life is considerate and unselfish may in his public life display all the rancour and bitterness of faction; he may practically deny that the nation should be guided by the same principles of morality as are binding on the individual."[114]

Watson is concerned that this fragmentation of the individual undermines the integrity of the state. If self-interest becomes the dominant motive in public life, politics degenerates as public figures come to regard their particular interests as identical to those of the state. When this happens, the possibility of rational politics is lost and the bonds of community unravel as each individual asserts his self-interest without regard for the ends of the state as a whole. This is the logical consequence of Spencer's refusal to grant any interference with the absolute rights of the individual: "His doctrine, if logically developed, would lead to the conclusion that the State has no function whatsoever"[115] beyond a modest role as an arbitrator of disputes.

Watson sets those who advocate absolute state sovereignty, such as Nietzsche, Haeckel, and Treitschke, at the other end of the spectrum.[116] These German thinkers, Watson says, distort Hegel's thought by ignoring his insistence on the state's rational grounding and replacing that substance with power. Hegel believes in the absoluteness of the state in the sense that it provides the final political authority in relation to its own citizens, as well as in dealings with foreign states. However, the other three Germans ignore Hegel's declaration that will – not force – is what binds the disparate elements of the state together. Nor does Hegel regard the state as the instrument of conquest and domination. For Hegel, the continuation of politics is not war, but art, philosophy, and religion, all of which are made possible because the state provides the necessary conditions for their respective activities. According to Watson, it is philosophically impossible for Hegel to advocate world dominion for some particular state. A philosopher who is an exponent of free will (which is also the moral will) cannot at the same time advocate an absolutist doctrine in which the state has no limits to its self-interest.[117]

The post-Hegelian philosophers strip Hegel's thought of its spiritual substance and replace it with a materialist element. This substitution of will by power led to the rise of German militarism, according to Watson. He sees this substitution reflected in the perversions of Nietzsche's thought: "[H]is worship of power has been eagerly caught up by the new Germany which came to self-consciousness after 1870" with a mission "to 'carry heroism into knowledge and to wage war for the sake of ideas.'"[118] Watson sees state absolutism as the other side of sovereign individualism. The former abstracts the state from the individuals of which it is composed, effectively severing it from reason and making the state an end in itself. The latter abstracts the individual from his community and makes the atomised individual an end unto himself. Thus, we have two abstract theories of the relationship between the individual and the community that are impossible to reconcile.

Watson, as I have discussed, sees the underlying assumption of social contract theory to be that isolated individuals regard themselves as ends unto themselves. He argues, however, that members of a political community are bound up in an inseparable relationship that exists apart from any contract and goes beyond their self-centred desires. This relationship, he says, "may be expressed by saying that it is the relation of a community of rational beings not externally bound together but organically connected."[119] Unless we acknowledge this organic connection, we are forced to accept the idea that, ultimately, the only thing that holds humans together, the only basis for community, is force. Watson, of course, cannot accept this, and his response to this tension between the individual and the community is his theory of relative sovereignty. In an adaptation of Hegel's concept of *Sittlichkeit,* Watson argues that there must be demarcated spheres in which the individual is sovereign in some and the state or community in others. The question is: What is the principle of demarcation? It has been suggested that Watson does not make this principle entirely clear.[120] Perhaps so, but by drawing on Watson's paradigmatic model of Socrates, we can discern the principle underlying Watson's concept of relative sovereignty.

Watson does not accept the idea that the state's existence can be justified if it is merely an aggregate of individuals agreeing to a contract with one another. The state's justification resides in the essential social nature of man, and man's freedom and individuality consists of the concrete realisation of this social nature. The organisation of society obtains its justification from its capacity to realise man's essential nature, and according to Watson, different constitutional orders must be judged by this standard. The absolutist state must be condemned not only because it is unsuitable for realising man's nature, but also because it does not grant the individual adequate scope to determine his life as he sees fit. This same objection also applies to any attempt to subordinate those institutional and organisational forms through which the individual's life is best realised. This does not mean that any particular form of organisation, whether a trade union, a corporation, or even a religious institution, can be absolutely independent of the state. While social institutions must be able to manage their own affairs, none can act against the good of the community as a whole. As Watson puts it, "The principle of the enlightened state is to grant freedom of action to all legitimate forms of organisation within its boundaries, but it cannot surrender its ultimate power of harmonising differences without ceasing to be a state."[121]

What is the basis for determining when the state can intervene in other institutions of society? Watson's answer again draws on Pericles' funeral oration and its definition of the essential political problem ("uniting public authority with individual freedom"), as well as on his own paradigmatic response to this problem in his commentary on *Apology* and *Crito.* The former dialogue amounts to a discussion of the individual's obligations to the state, while the latter considers the integrity of individual conscience in the face of community demands. To recall Watson's penultimate moral judgment: the individual is entitled to disobey the law when a higher impersonal law would otherwise be violated, but he is obliged to obey the law when it is solely a matter of his self-interest. Watson's theory of relative sovereignty reflects this criterion for determining the Ideal relationship of the individual and the state.

Watson says the state should not intervene in the conduct of other organisations when to do so would offend its own nature – that is, when it would be undermining its essential function as the promoter of the best interests and rights of the individual. This obviously makes the state a moral agent, albeit an indirect one. To be sure, the state is not in the business of directly promoting morality. The state can intervene in the affairs of an individual or organisation only when it is defending a higher impersonal law for the good of the whole – that is to say, when it is acting on the basis of the rational will. Watson offers the example of the relationship between church and state. While the state can legitimately play a role in harmonising conflicts of authority among different civil organisations, it must not interfere with the private beliefs of its citizens except insofar as an ecclesiastical body attempts to impose its creed by force or if the beliefs it promulgates are inimical to the good of the whole. Because it serves as a central regulative body, "the state has a right to see that the internal organisation of either church or civil association shall not be inconsistent with the organisation of society at large." For the state to fail in this function would be to allow a church or a corporation to "subvert the end and purpose for which political institutions exist."[122]

With this example Watson distinguishes between absolute and relative sovereignty. The former, he says, is incompatible with the independent actions of another entity. The latter, however, is only incompatible with a certain kind of activity. A body may have supreme power within its own sphere but also be subject to power beyond that sphere. Whether the church, the family, a corporation, or a trade union, each is beyond interference by the state insofar as it has certain recognised spheres of operation with which the state cannot legitimately interfere.

Watson contrasts his own views with those espoused by Harold Laski in his 1917 book *Studies in the Problem of Sovereignty*. Laski asserts that Hegel's concept of the state points to a monistic unity of power in which society is subordinate to an "all-embracing one, the State." In such a monistic society, Laski says, "what the state ordains begins to possess for you a special moral sanction superior in authority to the claim of group or individual." The individual is required to surrender his personality to the state's demands, to make his will identical to that of the collective. Laski, like Watson, uses the example of the relations between church and state to illustrate his concerns about sovereignty. Unlike Watson, however, Laski sees the modern church as being "compelled to seek the protection of its liberties lest it become no more than the religious department of an otherwise secular organisation."[123] Laski's point is that the state cannot be all-embracing of society without undermining the role and purposes of other social organisations. Watson challenges this argument with his theory of relative sovereignty, defending an Idealist conception of the state in which state power does not interfere with the internal organisation of the church (or any other civil association) unless the church acts outside its proper sphere. What makes the state sovereign over all other entities is that, first, its authority encompasses all citizens, and second, it possesses the final authority for harmonising relations between individuals and organisations within society.

Behind this concept of the state is Watson's Idealist claim that sovereign power is not identical to government but rests upon the will of citizens as a whole, or, more precisely, on their rational will, which, as he notes, is not necessarily identical to the will of the whole. This rational will is not expressed in one particular institution, but in all institutions. Nevertheless, the state is the singular institution charged with protecting the rights of individuals from the unwarranted interference of other subordinate institutions. The state is not absolutely supreme in the sense of having the power to override or encompass all other institutions; rather, it possesses relative sovereignty in that its central function is to ensure that all other institutions have the freedom to manage their own affairs without interference from others.[124] And, as Watson's Socratic model suggests, the state's – or the government's – legitimacy can be challenged to the degree that it fails to reflect the rational will of the whole.

Watson's theory of relative sovereignty is his answer to the problem of maintaining a proper relationship between the individual and the community or state, of reconciling freedom and duty. For Watson, the Idealist state honours and promotes individual autonomy and social pluralism while at the time safeguarding the need of individuals to belong to a community. Watson rejects Laski's view of the state as another social organisation, arguing that such an understanding ignores the crucial harmonising function of the state that other institutions do not possess. Watson concedes that Laski is right to be concerned about an absolutist state in which all individuals and organisations are subordinate to government and possess no real independence. But under the theory of relative sovereignty, the state has supremacy only in relation to that of other institutions. Through its government function, the state is the ultimate legal authority, but its power is (or should be) dedicated and limited to its own sphere – to guaranteeing the rights of individuals and harmonising the conflicts among individuals or other institutions. All other social entities enjoy their own relative sovereignty so long as they do not violate the sovereignty of others. The state may be said to include all of a society's institutions, but this does not grant it any absolute right to determine the actions of subordinate institutions. By Idealist standards, any state that attempts this has failed to be a proper state. As Watson concludes: "Freedom of life to citizens to form what associations they please, and to construct rules for their own guidance, is implied in the whole conception of the State as the organisation by which the best life is realised. It is by the free action of various subordinate forms of association that progress is made possible in the community, and the function of the State is not to dictate to those institutions their action or to impede its exercise, but to aid them in every way compatible with their harmony with one another and with itself."[125]

In this statement, Watson's appropriation of Hegel's emphasis on the reconciliatory function of the state is readily evident. Watson concedes that Hegel grants the state and the bureaucracy more power than Britons, Americans, and (perhaps) Canadians would find comfortable, but he does so only because he sees the state as "essential to the realisation of the good will."[126] This argument may seem similar to Spencer's notion that society exists for the benefit of its members, but it must be remembered that, for Watson, the individual's self-development ultimately redounds to the betterment of the community, since it is only in the community that the individual's development is possible. For Watson, freedom – the capacity to develop one's reason – is the freedom to achieve an identity with the whole, whether at the political or the metaphysical level. And the good of the whole is attainable only by securing the good of the individuals who make up the whole. Thus, Watson's views on the state as reflected in his theory of relative sovereignty stand in contrast to the views of both those who emphasise the autonomy of the individual and those who fear the power of the state. Where Kant and Rousseau assert their perspectives on the state in terms of the social contract, Watson holds that Hegel's concept of *Sittlichkeit* demonstrates the inadequacy of social contract theory. Similarly, Laski and other critics of state monism, who see Hegel as at least partly responsible for German militarism and the promotion of state absolutism, have, according to Watson, confused the Idealist conception of the state with an absolutist idea of the state.[127]

To draw out the nuances of Watson's theory, it is worthwhile to compare his thought more directly with that of his contemporaries, particularly other Idealists influenced by Hegel. For example, the British Idealist T.H. Green questions how Hegel's notion of the state as the basis of individual development can be reconciled with the experience of an "untaught and underfed denizen of a London yard with gin shops on the right and left."[128] Green suggests that Hegel is being "seriously misleading" about the state, given the abundance of historical evidence showing how "the requirements of the State have so largely arisen out of force directed by selfish motives,"[129] and when the only reason individuals obey the state is out of fear. In Green's judgment, Hegel's notion of freedom as embodied in the state does not seem to fit the realities of society as it is or as it could be. For Green, in other words, Hegel's conception of the state as the embodiment of the common good is too benign and even naive.

Bernard Bosanquet, another British Idealist, takes a more positive view of the Hegelian state. In a direct response to Green's argument, Bosanquet argues that the psychology reflected in Hegel's concept of *Sittlichkeit* reveals how individuals, even though they may not consciously concern themselves with abstract notions of the common good, nonetheless express this common good to the degree that they conduct themselves as law-abiding citizens, treat others with fairness, respect the property rights of others, and expect others to respect their "belongings." Even an ordinary labourer is aware in some fashion that his well-being depends on a degree of commonality between himself and others. Thus, says Bosanquet, "it is not true that either the feeling or the insight which constitute a consciousness of a common good are wanting to the everyday life of an average citizen in a modern State."[130] In this regard, the state constitutes "the entire hierarchy of institutions by which life is determined." The family, the trade union, the corporation, the church, and the university – all are included in the state "not as the mere collection of the growths of the country, but as the structure which gives life and meaning to the political whole."[131]

Watson's account of the Ideal relationship between the state and the individual – and the proper role of the state in this relationship – is clearly closer to Bosanquet's thought than to Green's. Yet, as Leslie Armour and Elizabeth Trott note, Watson is "substantially less conservative" than Bosanquet.[132] This suggests that there are facets to Watson's political thought that require further consideration. In particular, I want to demonstrate that Watson comes down on the side of the individual more than the British Idealists do, or, for that matter, the American Idealists.[133]

9

Watson contra the British and American Hegelians

Watson's metaphysics, it will be recalled, asserts that the individual's real or Ideal nature is that of self-conscious, active reason. Ideally, this metaphysic manifests politically as the individual's real will reflected in the rational or general will of the community. It follows from this metaphysical position that if the individual acts in a way contrary to the rational will, then the community is justified in imposing its will on the individual insofar as the communal will itself reflects the individual's rational will, if the individual only realised it. The state can legitimately interfere with the individual's life, including requiring the individual to obey the law, when such interference serves the rational will, because it is that rational will with which the individual seeks to identify himself in striving for his truest nature, even if he does not know it.[134]

However, Watson is careful to point out that while the will of the whole of the citizenry should be the basis of state action, that does not mean that the absolute agreement of citizens is the only condition for realising the general will. Watson argues that the concept of the rational will also provides the means for justifiably opposing the state, particularly absolutist government. While an absolute ruler may believe he is acting for the good of the whole, such absolutism is contrary to the fundamental character of individuals as rational and social beings. Individuals cannot be forced to act, even if such action is promoted with the best of intentions, because what is imposed by the state has the character of force and not will.

Such an argument implies that the individual can legitimately resist a state that interferes with the development of his truest self when such interference is, at the same time, contrary to the good of the whole – that is, contrary to the rational will of which the individual is a part. This is a tricky point. Watson is saying that so long as the individual's will reflects the rational will, the state is in the wrong if its actions interfere with the self-development of the individual when that self-development is, or would be, good for the community. A state that interferes with an individual's ability to identify himself more closely with the rational will is acting contrary to the rational will that it is supposed to represent and is therefore failing in its essential role. And that grants individuals the right to criticise the state and, if necessary, oppose it through rebellion. Watson is explicit on this point: rebellion is permissible if "the conscience of the rebels is really better than that which is embodied in the existing State."[135]

How would you truly know whether the rebels' conscience is better than that of those who govern the state? Or, for that matter, how would you judge whether the state's position is more rational than that of the rebels? Watson does not answer these questions directly – and perhaps they are impossible questions to answer with any certainty – but I suggest that his Socratic template provides a standard for judgment: *Disobey the law when a higher impersonal law would otherwise be violated; obey the law where only one's own individual interest will be adversely affected.* For Watson, that "higher impersonal law" is the rational will. So long as the individual knows with utter certitude that his actions reflect the rational will better than those of the state do, then he may be entitled to rebel against the state. This does not mean that Watson is granting the individual priority over the state. Rather, Watson is saying that the individual is expressing the rational will that the state should embody and, in so doing, the individual effectively acknowledges an identity between himself and the state.

Such an interpretation of Watson's thought provides a credible response to those of his contemporaries who accuse Hegelian Idealism of providing insufficient scope for legitimate disagreement and conflict in society, particularly in regard to the state's coercive power.[136] Watson's insistence that those who wish to criticise the state or engage in rebellion must be certain that their morality transcends that articulated by the state, provides a standard of judgment that puts the onus on critics of Idealism to offer a coherent alternative to the Idealist position. Such an assertion supports Armour and Trott's claim that Watson is less conservative than, say, Bosanquet.

To be sure, in the ninth chapter of *The State in Peace and War,* in which he analyses the modern state, Watson defends Bosanquet's argument that all society is under the final control of the state and that it is the state that gives meaning to the political whole. This defence is made in the context of a response to critics such as Deslisle Burns, Bertrand Russell, and G.D.H. Cole, who had attacked Idealism – and Bosanquet, in particular – for its theoretical inadequacies regarding international relations. Cole, for example, argued that Idealists like Bosanquet had followed Hegel in reifying the state to the point where they identified the state with society. The result was a failure to appreciate the diversity and plurality in society; in effect, the Idealists expected too much unity from the state. The same applied to Idealist notions of international relations. The Idealists made the mistake of regarding states as unified actors, when, in reality, international relations among states were conducted among diverse people and organisations. In modern society, Cole argued, state power was not exercised exclusively between two sovereign (and rational) wills, but also involved myriad individual and group interests.[137]

Drawing on his theory of relative sovereignty, Watson rejects the idea that Idealism fails to account for social diversity. The Idealist state promotes diversity by having as its fundamental purpose the self-development of individual citizens. What sets the Idealist state apart, however, is that unlike any other organisation its powers encompass all citizens. Watson turns the tables on critics like Cole by arguing that they are guilty of reducing the state to the government, of mistaking the part for the whole. Government, Watson says, is merely the organ through which the state endeavours to harmonise the various organisations of society. Critics incorrectly assert an antagonism between the state and society when, in fact, they are referring to tensions between government and non-government organisations. "The State, however, we contend, is not the Government, but the whole system of organisations by which the general will is realised."[138] On this point, Watson approvingly quotes Bosanquet's definition of the state as that entity "which gives life and meaning to the political whole." By this definition, the state encompasses all the associations of society through which the general will is expressed, but cannot itself be identified with any one association, including government. Moreover, as Bosanquet's definition implies, it is the institutions of society that affect the power of government and thereby promote the general will. It is not a case of the state being opposed to the plurality of society, but rather of society providing the vehicle for giving life to the state, which, in turn, functions to sustain the diversity and plurality that gives life to society. What Watson is claiming, in effect, is the reconciliation of freedom and obligation, of civil liberty and the general will, in and through the state. With this assertion, Watson defends Bosanquet, who, he says, clearly points out the importance of subordinate institutions to the vitality of society and, ultimately, the state. Bosanquet's critics fail to catch his distinction between the state and government. While governments might act antagonistically toward individuals, the Idealist vision of the state still holds out the possibility of a harmonious community.[139]

Nevertheless, regardless of how much Watson might defend Bosanquet, there are differences between the British and the Canadian theorists. Watson, I suggest, gives greater priority to the individual than may at first appear, given his communitarian concerns. He does not follow Bosanquet in granting the community primacy.[140] Rather, Watson's position is much closer to that of his mentor and teacher, Edward Caird. Both Caird and Watson are reluctant to look at political and social problems through a dualist lens, sharing instead a "theory of interactivity" by which they understand the relationship between the individual and the community. Caird posits "a principle of unity in all seemingly opposed ideas, concepts and theories."[141] Such a principle is similar to Watson's notion of the internal relationship of all entities, which is reflected in his theory of relative sovereignty. Like Caird, Watson opposes the simplistic tendency to theorize on the basis of dichotomous positions: individual versus community, state versus society, rich versus poor. Both trace this dualistic fashion to the discoveries of nineteenth-century science, especially Darwinian evolutionary theories, which were often interpreted as pitting the individual against nature. Watson and Caird prefer to interpret evolutionary theory as promoting reconciliation, arguing that "the idea of organic evolution" is "leading us away from the 'falsehood of extremes.'"[142] This shared metaphysical perspective is echoed in their respective political theories.

Caird argues that the idea of evolution as a "reconciling idea" posits a political order that seeks "the utmost development of individual capacity, the utmost development of individual independence," while at the same time promoting "a close interdependence and connection of all individuals with each other." In this view, a "truly organic society" of self-respecting and self-governing citizens requires simultaneously both differentiation and integration. "Division without such union is on the way to death by disintegration; unity without such independence is on the way to death by paralysis."[143]

Watson captures this unity-within-diversity aspect of Caird's thinking in two commentaries on his mentor.[144] Caird, Watson argues, seeks to overcome the Kantian diremptions whether at the metaphysical, epistemological, or political level. And Hegel is Caird's guide, of course, providing the British Idealist with a philosophic perspective that regards the antithesis of materialism and spiritualism as relative rather than absolute opposites. Indeed, Watson credits Caird with being the first to detect in Hegel the notion of reconciliation. "What Caird finds in Hegel is, therefore, in the first place, a principle of reconciliation, which had not been detected, or at least not clearly detected by any previous thinker."[145] This principle of reconciliation is reflected in Caird's political philosophy. The state is not merely an aggregate of individuals, but the expression of man's fundamental nature, a nature that is most fulfilled in and through a life of reason, which is freedom. But while reason is inherent in man, it can only be realised in "a State that allows free play to individuals, while yet it suppresses all that is recognized as contrary to reason."[146] For Caird, then, the principle of reconciliation demonstrates the interdependence of the individual and the community.

Watson, too, sees the relationship of the individual and the community as symbiotic. Idealism starts from the principle "that the good of the individual is identical with the good of the community."[147] This means that there can be no claim regarding the state's superiority to the individual because the state itself constitutes the functioning differentiation of its members, and it is this capacity for individuation that establishes the individual's freedom. Such individuation is no threat to the state because the freedom it entails allows the individual to recognise that his "best mind," his Ideal self, identifies with the state and therefore wishes to maintain it. Thus, both Watson's theory of relative sovereignty and Caird's theory of interactivity see the proper relationship between the individual and the community as one entailing the mutual reinforcement of their respective ends.

How does this understanding compare to Bosanquet's? Near the end of *The Philosophical Theory of the State*, Bosanquet considers the basis on which the state can be criticised. In its proper form, he writes, "the state exists to promote good life, and what it does cannot be morally indifferent." But, at the same time, the state's actions cannot be identified with the deeds of its agents or morally judged in the same way as private actions. This is so because the state's actions are always "public acts, and it cannot, as a State, act within the relations of private life in which organised morality exists." That is to say, the state cannot be expected to act according to the same moral standards as those which bear on private life. In fact, since the state is the "supreme community," it is itself "the guardian of the whole moral world and not a factor within an organised moral world."[148] If agents of the state, acting as the public authority, act corruptly for their own private interests, this reflects the failure of their private morality, not any immorality on the part of the state as the expression of the general will. The moral incoherence of politicians and bureaucrats is a personal failing and does not reflect the failure or inadequacy of the whole community. The closest Bosanquet comes to imagining a state's public immorality is when he discusses a situation in which the organs that act on behalf of the state behave in ways that exhibit "a narrow, selfish or brutal conception of the interests of the state as a whole, in which, so far as can be judged, public opinion at the time agrees." In such circumstances, the state may be "acting immorally, i.e. in contravention of its main duty to sustain the conditions of as much good life as possible." But even in this case Bosanquet argues that the state, as the organ of the public good, has "simply been defrauded by those who spoke in its name."[149]

Bosanquet's point seems to be that the immorality of those who represent the state does not provide grounds for assuming some inadequacy on the part of the state. States cannot be judged by standards of private conduct. This seems to make sense; after all, an individual can behave badly in his personal life, but admirably as a citizen, or vice versa. Being a good citizen is not the same as being a good friend or family member. But are the two spheres so antithetical, as Bosanquet seems to imply? Bosanquet's own theory of the state would seem to suggest not. The state, he says, should not be regarded as an entity separate from other forms of social life, but as the overarching framework within which rational social life is possible.

> The State, as thus conceived, is not merely the political fabric ...
> [I]t includes the entire hierarchy of institutions by which life is determined, from the family to the trade, and from the trade to the Church and the University. It includes all of them, not as the mere collection of the growths of the country, but as the structure which gives life and meaning to the political whole, while receiving from it mutual adjustment ... The State, it might be said, is thus the operative criticism of all institutions – the modification and adjustment by which they are capable of playing a rational part in the object of human will. And criticism, in this sense, is the life of institutions.[150]

The overarching nature of the state is also brought out in Bosanquet's reference to the state's possessing "the only recognised and justified force."[151] Bosanquet is referring to more than physical coercion; he is also referring to the forces of law, routine, organisation, tradition, and custom. Without this power the state would be unable to harmonise the competing claims of individuals and groups. And it is this complex of institutional arrangements that reflects the rational or general will. Thus, our real will is our will to be citizens, and we actualise this will, and attain our individual freedom, by adapting ourselves to the institutions of our society. Like Rousseau, Bosanquet holds that the individual who subordinates his immediate desires – or actual will – to the discipline of societal institutions attains his real or rational will.

For Bosanquet, then, force is inherent in the state, although it need not be identical to physical force. Citizens can govern themselves to the degree they accept the authority of their social institutions and fulfil their social responsibilities. Self-government is the necessary criterion for rational life and the manifestation of human freedom. Yet given this, how can an agent of the state, as a citizen, reject private morality in his public functions? The logic of Bosanquet's theory of the state implies a close identity between morality and citizenship. Watson, however, finds it difficult to reconcile Bosanquet's statement that the state is the supreme community with his theory of the state as the expression of rational wills, especially if the British Idealist maintains that there is no linkage between the state and private life. How can the state have a duty to maintain the conditions for individual moral development if it is not in some sense a factor in the larger moral world? If the state cannot be criticised on moral grounds, then all that seems left to question is whether the state and its agents are efficient in carrying out their functions, moral or otherwise. On this view, though, it does not matter if we are talking about a tyrannical state or a constitutional state, so long at it is administratively efficient.[152]

This point brings me back to Bosanquet's "vexed question" about criticising the state: Are the public and private spheres so separate, as Bosanquet seems to imply?[153] It is on this question that Watson takes issue with Bosanquet, revealing, as Frederick Hoffner suggests, Watson's distance from any of the more absolutist inclinations of British Hegelianism.[154] "By a curious process," Watson writes, Bosanquet "seems to take all the responsibility from the State and to impose it upon its agents."[155] Watson does not think that the state, as the reflection of public will, can so easily evade responsibility for its actions. Certainly, as I noted in considering Watson's views on Machiavelli, Watson acknowledges a distinction between individual morality and the morality of a ruler acting in the interests of the survival of the state. Those who represent the state sometimes have to use modes of action that would earn the individual condemnation. But Watson also says that state representatives cannot be absolved of all moral responsibility. The morality of their actions can be judged in light of their effect on the nation's spiritual life. When agents of the state act immorally, they do so in contradiction of the true or rational will of the state. If these actions are not seen as being due to the rational, or the public, will, then no one can be held responsible. And if immoral actions by agents of the state do not reflect the rational will of the state, then responsibility lies elsewhere. If they are actions of the government, which, as an organ of the state, expresses the actual will of the citizenry, then "it must be held that the really

responsible agents are the people and not the immediate agents."[156]
Hence, for Watson, there is no easy distinction between the private actions
of individuals and the public actions of the state. The state has moral obligations even though its actions are of necessity different from those of private individuals. Therefore, it must be held to be an organised institution,
one that cannot justify immoral actions – breaches of faith, fraud, violence,
or cruelty – by claiming a distinction from the individual citizen.[157]

This argument highlights Watson's symbiotic conception of the relationship between the individual and the state, and distinguishes his thinking
from that of British Hegelians such as Bosanquet. By absolving individual
citizens of responsibility for their government's behaviour, Bosanquet effectively grants the state priority over the individual. Indeed, he seems to
absolve the state of the kind of moral conduct expected of citizens, which
means, in effect, that individuals do not have the right to act against the
state when it acts immorally or in contradiction to the rational will.[158] In
this light, Watson shows greater concern than Bosanquet for the autonomy
of individuals in terms of the relationship between the state and its citizens,
particularly in emphasising the responsibility citizens have to monitor the
morality of the state. Watson grants individuals the obligation to criticise
and even oppose the state if its actions are contrary to the rational will.
Bosanquet tends to express a closer identification between the individual
and the state; for instance, he writes, "The State is the fly-wheel of our life.
Its system is constantly reminding us of duties."[159] Watson, however, as his
theory of relative sovereignty implies, avoids such an absolutist inclination
with his understanding of the symbiotic relationship of the individual and
the community. While he accepts Bosanquet's notion of an overarching
unity in the state, he also subscribes to the view that the rational will of the
state relies on a balance between the individual's self-development and the
social character of individuality. There is no sense in Watson's thought, as
there is in Bosanquet's, of a "final primacy to the community."[160] For all
his defence of Bosanquet, Watson is less of a communitarian than other
British Idealists. Indeed, in some ways, he shares a greater affinity with
American Hegelianism.

The American Idealists, like the British, see the individual defined by his
membership in the community, which consists of an ever-widening circle,
from family and friends to the state. Yet they also place a greater emphasis
on the importance of individual fulfilment. The St Louis Hegelians, for example, appropriated Hegel's organic conception of individuality and self-
activity to argue that people are free and morally responsible to the degree
their actions are self-prescribed and rational. Thus, true individuality can

be found within the system of internal relations that makes up the whole of society. Other American Hegelians employed Hegel's concepts of freedom and the state, along with his master-slave dialectic and philosophy of history, to argue that the emergence of the United States was a historical world event. Even the American Civil War was seen by the St Louis Hegelians as a manifestation of the development of World Spirit, a dialectical clash between principle and the law out of which would emerge a better country. Hegel's principles of dialectical relation, his concept of reconciliation, and his notion that all antagonisms are provisional were adopted by these intellectuals as a rationale for comprehending the chaos of disunion, war, and reconstruction.[161]

William Goetzmann observes that nineteenth-century American intellectuals saw in Hegel's philosophy a way of thinking that allowed them to come to terms with and even direct their dynamic and expanding country. "Virtually every event in nineteenth-century America could be fitted into the ongoing dialectic and the unfolding process of the concrete universal." Hegelianism was "a philosophy of unbounded optimism born out of a virtually infinite series of desperate situations, and it thrived on clashes and confrontations." This made it the ideal philosophy for a country continually confronted by expanding boundaries and an ever-increasing population. Hegel's thought provided a way of thinking that amounted to "a kind of Manifest Destiny of the Mind, aiming always towards the formation of the greater community."[162] At the level of politics, too, American Hegelians subscribed to Hegel's concern that the state's unity must be "concrete," that is, organically whole in both preserving and vivifying the individual parts. Men such as J.B. Stallo and August Willich "brought out, directly or indirectly, the liberal element in his [Hegel's] political philosophy."[163]

The American philosopher who can most usefully be compared to Watson is Josiah Royce, generally acknowledged as the greatest systematic philosopher the United States has produced.[164] He, like Watson, is deeply influenced by Hegel. The two men also share interests in metaphysics, epistemology, and religion. In 1897 Watson and Royce debated each other in a series of lectures on Christianity and Idealism before the Philosophical Union of the University of California at Berkeley.[165] Finally, they share similar political concerns. Like Watson, Royce is concerned with the relationship of the individual and the community, particularly in the face of the disintegrative tendencies of atomistic individualism. And it is against these fragmenting forces – "the modern revolt against moral tradition" and "the restless spirit of our reforming age," as he puts it – that Royce offers his theory of community in his 1908 book, *The Philosophy of Loyalty*.[166] The book has been described as Royce's "version of a world unified and redeemed."[167]

At the core of Royce's theory of community is the concept of *loyalty*. By ← this term, Royce does not mean to suggest any of the negative connotations we might apply to it today – militarism, political oppression, or blind obedience, for example. For him, loyalty means what we might define as authenticity and commitment – that is, an intensely personal sense of ethical obligation. As Royce uses the term, loyalty entails the "willing and practical and thoroughgoing devotion of a person to a cause." He insists that the best and most fulfilling life is one in which the individual devotes himself to a cause that binds him with others. The moral imperative for the individual is always to maximise his loyalty to the community.[168] Such a concept, with its absolutist tendencies, has obvious practical implications in promoting a unified society, one that, as Leslie Armour points out, went well with "the melting-pot thesis then popular in the United States."[169]

Behind this concept of loyalty or commitment is Royce's insistence that the life of a fully developed individual, the person who exemplifies loyalty, is lived in the dialectic between the private and the social spheres. Our individuation depends not only on the struggle to fulfil some self-chosen life plan, but also on our capacity for self-sacrifice. Royce insists that to achieve complete self-fulfilment, the individual, through his free choice of a cause, must renounce his selfishness, his self-interest. Only by recognising one's selfishness can one see the emptiness of egoism and renounce it.[170]

According to Royce, it is the idea of commitment to a cause that awakens an individual to his social nature and satisfies his sense of belonging by uniting him with others who serve the same cause. At the same time, though, this commitment also fosters a person's sense of freedom because he is aware that his choice of a cause is made of his own volition. In effect, loyalties create community – families, corporations, unions, armies, and nations – in which individuals are able to simultaneously preserve and surrender their individuality. Commitment to a cause unifies individuals with their community but still allows them to retain their freedom by virtue of their voluntary decision to serve the cause.

Watson expresses something similar in *The State in Peace and War* when, in his critique of Plato's promotion of excessive unity in the *polis*, he says that the "intense consciousness of personality" is the necessary if insufficient condition for higher consciousness. "He who has no self cannot be unselfish."[171] Royce's concern for loyalty and social commitment also shares Watson's concern about the proper relationship between the individual and the community, especially as reflected in Watson's paradigmatic reference to Socrates. How do you decide where your loyalties reside – with the individual conscience or the authority of the state? How do you know that the cause to which you have committed yourself is a good one? And what happens if you have conflicting loyalties? Royce acknowledges such questions: "Loyalty is a good for the loyal man; but it may be mischievous for those whom the cause assails. Conflicting loyalties may be general social disturbances; and the fact that loyalty is good for the loyal does not of itself decide whose cause is right when various causes stand opposed to one another."[172] He also sees the irony of a situation in which conflicting appeals to loyalty serve the concept itself: "Where such a conflict occurs, the best, namely loyalty, is used as an instrument in order to encompass the worst, namely the destruction of loyalty."[173]

Royce's response to these concerns, his attempt to furnish further criteria for determining the worthiness of the individual's cause and avoid a clash of loyalties, is the principle of *loyalty to loyalty*. The individual satisfies his loyalty or commitment only if that loyalty can avoid being destroyed by the loyalties of others. In choosing his cause, then, the individual ought to choose the cause that is most likely to further the loyalties of, and satisfy the self-realisation of, other members of his community. Ultimately, Royce "specifies the cause of universal loyalty as the highest and most general cause the moral agent can and ought to serve."[174]

But how is this universal loyalty to be concretely served? Royce acknowledges that by virtue of the individual's nature and social embeddedness, the individual belongs to a family, a community, a state, and humanity. Initially, the individual must choose his cause or causes; these causes must satisfy the individual's whole self, aspects of which will no doubt involve conflicting loyalties. In the end, though, these competing causes can form one cause "only in so far as they constitute an entire system of causes." And it is on this point that Royce, sounding much like Watson, touches the bedrock of his concept of universal loyalty: "My loyalty will be subject, therefore, to the ancient difficulty regarding the one and the many." Unless loyalty is "one in its ultimate aim," there can be no overarching universal principle of loyalty that will do justice to the varied instincts and myriad social interests of the individual.[175]

Royce offers no easy resolution of this problem. To avoid a charge of empty formalism, he offers the notions of *decisiveness* and *fidelity*. In the face of ignorance about the future, the individual simply has to decide on a cause and course of action that furthers loyalty itself. This decisiveness also requires fidelity to the cause. The only justification for abandoning a cause is when the cause involves being disloyal to universal loyalty. To abandon a cause unjustly is to destroy an individual unity of purpose. But given the complexity of human life and the relative ignorance in which individuals exist, how is the individual to know with any reasonable confidence that his choice of loyalties is worthy? Peter Fuss addresses this question in defining Royce's concept of loyalty as a "doctrine of right conduct" in that it imposes on the individual certain social obligations while at the same time maintaining that those obligations are freely chosen. Royce's loyal man submits to the authority of his community as to an "institutionalized social cause," and he does so freely because such a choice conforms to his own natural impulses, capacities, and needs.[176]

Royce, then, like other Idealists, seems to offer a way to harmonise the good of the individual with good of the community as a whole. Nevertheless, the question remains: What kind of guidance or standard does Royce's concept offer for choosing rightly? Fuss describes Royce's doctrine as unsatisfactory, particularly with regard to providing practical criteria for determining the relative worthiness of conflicting causes that demand loyalty. He argues that employing the principle of loyalty to loyalty is of little help in arbitrating either the rightness of the individual's choices or the worthiness of the causes he chooses. In the former case, the principle of universal loyalty is supposed to serve as a criterion of subjective rightness, whereas in the latter application, the principle is intended to function as a criterion for objective rightness.[177] Supposedly, in evaluating his loyalty to a chosen cause, the individual asks himself whether his loyalty coincides with, or is not purposely harmful to, the loyalties of others. Obviously, this is a difficult thing to know. Faced with two equally worthy, if conflicting, causes, and unable to ascertain the consequences of his choice, the individual simply cannot know which cause best serves universal loyalty. So how does he decide?

Royce's notions of decisiveness and fidelity are of little help. Presumably, the individual undertakes a thorough examination of his conscience (much as, say, Socrates did) and determines that he is serving his cause decisively and faithfully and that he has done everything he can to make sure his cause is morally right. By this account, the individual's conduct is subjectively right and, to that extent, morally worthy. But Royce's principle of loyalty to loyalty is more problematic. Fuss observes that Royce's philosophy of loyalty wraps traditional conceptions of conscience – benevolence, justice, courtesy, honesty, patriotism, and even good manners – into a single package. The concept of loyalty systematises these virtues and customs, organising the individual's conscience into something more than a cluster of dictates and formal imperatives. Almost by definition, then, loyalty offers a theoretical restoration of the institution of the family. As well, the concept can be applied to efforts to maintain social harmony between, say, the rich and the poor, labour and corporations, and even church and state. In this regard, Fuss argues, the concept of loyalty serves to preserve social stability in a time of social fragmentation.

However, despite all this effort to provide for individual self-realisation by means of loyalty to the wider community and its institutions, Royce cannot quite find the link between self and other, the concrete example that provides a standard for judging right action from wrong action. Universal loyalty may aim at the overarching social harmony of all loyalties, but given that the consequences of even morally worthwhile actions are often unknowable, the principle of loyalty to loyalty, as Fuss states, is not only "highly abstract," but comes nowhere near providing "the dependable criterion of the objective worthiness of causes" that Royce would want.[178]

Watson, I suggest, succeeds where Royce fails. To be sure, Watson echoes Royce in many of his social concerns, and his notion of duty parallels Royce's concept of loyalty in terms of their respective purposes. Yet duty, according to Watson, "implies the identification of the subject with a universal end in which the true self may be realised," and "freedom is the capacity ... of this self-identification."[179] In the union of oneself with others, we experience the freedom available to us as human beings. Duty is freedom not because it negates desire or self-interest, but because it transforms desire into a higher end that leads to realising the true nature of the self. To grasp the concept of duty-as-freedom is to realise the universal through the particular, to comprehend the identity between the willing of the law and the willing of the self.[180] In this regard, Watson provides the missing element to Royce's moral code, the principle that gives substance to Royce's empty formalism, the formula for deciding how to decide between two conflicting loyalties.

I refer, of course, to the Socratic template Watson derived from the *Apology* and *Crito*. Applying Watson's standard, the Roycean individual faced with two worthy, if conflicting, loyalties should base his choice on whether it violates a higher impersonal law or whether it mainly furthers his self-interest. With such a template, Watson's Hegelianism, when compared to that of either Royce or Bosanquet, is distinctly less absolutist. Watson is more easily able to accept the dialectical interdependence of the individual and society. This position is sustained by his understanding of reason as something that develops historically. By complementing his theory of history with a developmental epistemology, Watson is able to place a greater emphasis on individuality and history than can either Bosanquet or Royce, who tend to given priority to community. While Watson regards community as crucial, he also insists that the fulfilment of community lies in its capacity to promote individual freedom. It is in this way that Watson's recognition of the symbiotic relationship of the individual and the community is distinctly different from the triumphalism of the St Louis Hegelians or the melting-pot psychology of Royce. As Leslie Armour says, "Watson understood that people did not stand still to be absorbed into the Absolute – rather, they wanted to express themselves in a plurality that would exhibit all the richness the Absolute might contain."[181] The absolute, in short, is expressed pluralistically.

There is thus a distinction between the American and the Canadian Hegelians, a difference that underscores the distinctiveness of Watson's political thought. For Watson, community, or unity, emerges from a plurality of perspectives. That does not mean that the individual has priority over the community, rather that the community cannot claim priority over the individual. Freedom, says Watson, is that condition in which one can individuate oneself and not be regarded as an entity identical to some overarching organisation. At the same time, this free individual also recognises the freedom of others, since their individuation is the necessary condition for his freedom. The individual, like Socrates in the *Apology*, can take as his authority the law of his own reason. But again like Socrates in the *Crito*, the individual must also recognise that the outward laws and institutions of his community are embodiments, however imperfect, of that same rational order. Moral intelligence and freedom depend upon the capacity of the individual consciousness to discern the identity between his own reason and that of the community and, in doing so, to feel himself constrained by his reason to submit to the public authority of the community. And he can accept his duty because he sees that the laws of the community, while imperfectly expressed, are an expression of his own rational self. To further the rational will is to further one's freedom.

By comparison, where Royce wants the individual to achieve self-realisation through what amounts to a renunciation of the self before some overarching loyalty and Bosanquet seeks the individual's ultimate identification with the state, Watson tries to find a balance that reconciles (but does not eliminate) the tensions between the individual and the community. Watson opposes both those who emphasise the individual at the expense of the state and those who set the state above the individual. His Hegelianism amounts to a reconciliation or balancing of 'absolute' opposites, the articulation of a kind of pluralism that "is the expression of an underlying unity."[182]

Watson extends this notion of reconciliation to relations among states. Just as the state must not hamper the individuation of its citizens, so too must there be no attempt to eliminate differences between states. States are differentiations of the organic unity of man as a whole. This means "the good of one state cannot be separated from the good of another." Hence, the Ideal rational relation of states is cooperative, not antagonistic. And the purpose of any system of states is to protect the independence and individuality of its members. "No State," says Watson, "can surrender its autonomy without ceasing to be a State."[183]

This view comes through in Watson's opposition to the kind of statism promoted in Germany before and during the First World War.[184] Yet, in the wake of Germany's defeat in 1918, Watson was equally opposed to the notions of world government that were then fashionable. For him, the independence of each state is necessary for the good of humanity as a whole, since each state has its "special mission."[185] Such a claim has obvious implications with regard to his support for the British Empire. Indeed, Watson's Idealist notion of international relations is best reflected in his support of empire.

10

Watson's Imperial Spirit

Watson does not accept the idea of a world-state, or any other notion of world government, that would erase the differences between nations and cultures. Certainly, a world-state based on the combination of variously differentiated states is a "possible ideal," but a "world-state which abolishes all the differences of race and nationality and individuality is an empty ideal."[186] For Watson, the true Ideal of international affairs is the uniting of love of country with devotion to the rational development of humanity as a whole. How, though, does Watson's support for cultural and political autonomy accord with his support for British imperialism? The answer to that question emerges through a consideration of Watson's appropriation of Hegel's master-slave dialectic and how in that dialectic man's inner diremption and the tension between self and other are overcome.

Watson's use of the dialectic is allusive and indirect. His most overt reference to the master-slave dialectic is in his 1895 book *Outline of Philosophy*, where he concludes his analysis of Kant's "kingdom of ends" and the notion that morality requires individuals to conceive of themselves as members of a social organism. The passage in question, quoted in full below, is a highly compacted summary of Watson's essential political teaching on the proper relationship of the individual and the community. His choice of words calls to mind his frequent allusions to the two Socratic dialogues of the *Apology* and the *Crito* and the basic question of his political thought: How can public authority and individual inclination be reconciled? Watson's Idealist view of empire can be extracted from this passage: "In purely savage life it [moral consciousness] takes the form of submission from terror to a superior force. But even in this imperfect form, there is implied the recognition of a law superior to the caprice of individuals. For, in submitting to one who is superior to himself in courage and contempt of life, the savage recognises that there is something higher than his merely individual self. Thus there arises some sort of social order."[187]

In Watson's view, the history of the development of consciousness reveals that morality has emerged from "the ever clearer consciousness of the unity of each with all."[188] This does not mean that Watson's Idealism blinds him to the abuses of empire. Like it or not, the development of consciousness has meant the use of violence, the conquest of some people by other others, the forced submission of "savages" to a superior civilisation. Watson, to repeat, acknowledges that the "purely savage life" submits out of "terror" to a "superior force." But out of this "there arises some sort of social order.[189] Such language pales in comparison to Hegel's graphic description of the Terror of Death at the hands of the master.[190] Nonetheless, Watson does not ignore the ugly realities of Spirit's development: "The first contact of the civilised trader with the savage races has often led to the most deplorable results; the natives have been robbed, corrupted by opium, murdered in cold blood and sold as slaves."[191]

Watson also insists, however, on the equal truth that out of this conquest, and implicit in it, has come the further development of freedom and hence the development of a higher moral and social order. He argues that even in submitting to a greater power, the "savage" – by which he simply means a being lacking higher self-conscious development – implicitly acknowledges and accepts the superiority of his conqueror's civilisation. Some will undoubtedly accuse Watson of advocating an end-justifies-the-means view of imperialism, but that is to misinterpret his argument. Watson, like other Idealists of his time, including Caird and Bosanquet, condemned Britain's conduct in the Boer War. Even the Idealists' severest liberal critics acknowledged that "there was a right kind of imperialism which entailed a responsible and sustained effort to prepare indigenous peoples for self-government."[192] Watson's Idealism, in this regard, is not promoting empire for the sake of conquest or material gain, although he does not deny that this is how most men see it. Watson sees in the submission of the savage an implicit recognition of a principle of order that transcends the savage and, at a deep psychological level, the longing for the knowledge of that order. For Watson, the beginning of morality requires the awareness and acceptance of a principle that is higher than one's self-interest. This higher principle, the law of reason, is supposed to be embodied in the master or superior civilisation. Thus, Watson effectively extracts the ethical substance of imperialism from Hegel's master-slave dialectic.

To be sure, Watson also recognises that the problem with the master – and by extension, the superior civilisation – is that while he is in possession of a higher Ideal of himself, he does not necessarily understand himself as a moralising agent who needs to act on the basis of reason. The master can too easily fail to recognise that it is only to the degree that he embodies a principle higher than his own self-interest, a higher impersonal law, that his use of power is justified and his authority legitimated. Rulership over others is only justified if the rulers exercise their authority for a good that transcends their own desires. Unless the master is consciously acting on the basis of a higher good, he has no legitimate authority. And the savage, Watson seems to suggest, submits only because he can see that the master is exercising his authority under the guidance of a higher principle, not on the basis of caprice and selfishness.

Watson's notion of moral leadership on the part of those with power and authority certainly accords with the early twentieth-century Idealist view of imperialism that cast the British Empire as an agent for developing the spiritual potential of mankind, including that of the savages. Watson, like many British Idealists, believes that whatever one's view on how Britain had acquired its empire, there was no way it could retreat from the moral responsibilities of protecting its subject peoples. The hope for the Idealists is that "out of the chaos was emerging a more human and responsible attitude to native peoples."[193] Imperial rule is acceptable so long as the power and authority of the empire builders is aimed beyond the satisfaction of their own interests. This is the basic position Watson takes in *The State in Peace and War* when he discusses international relations in the post–First World War era. He is well aware of the exploitation and violence that inaugurated the British Empire, but nevertheless believes in the effort, as Caird puts it, "to make our government tend to the good of the governed, and to open to the governed all the privileges of their governors."[194] For Watson, the British Empire came closest to this mandate. It was, he says, the only successful experiment in international government because it fulfilled the fundamental political concern of reconciling individual peoples in an imperial community. Or, to recast Watson's basic political motto: the empire succeeded in "combining the freedom of the separate organs with the unity of the whole."[195]

The British Empire also exemplified Watson's theory of relative sovereignty at the international level. The members of the empire were differentiations of the organic whole that is mankind, and the purpose of each member state was "to secure the best conditions of life for its citizens in harmony with and limited by the universal principles of morality."[196] In the same way that there must be differentiation among individuals in a particular state if the good of the whole society is to be achieved, there is a need at the international level for independent nations with different cultures. Each state, Watson argues, has as its particular task the development of its particular form of civilisation. Watson does not support the idea of a universal or absolutist world-state, or any expansion of internationalism that seeks to suppress patriotism. He specifically rejects Bertrand Russell's proposal for an international authority that would see people shed their patriotism and surrender national sovereignty. This rejection reflects Watson's concern for a balance between national and international interests that is similar to his desire to find a balance between the individual and the community. While rejecting a parochial nationalism, he recognises the idea of internationalism as a utopian abstraction: "The union of the love of country with devotion to the cause of humanity is the true ideal, and neither a selfish patriotism nor a vague humanitarianism that leads to nothing but neglect of the duty that lies nearest."[197] Watson advocates that one should act imperially, think locally.

The British Empire is Watson's model for the reconciliation of the national and the international. He supports the autonomy of nation-states and cultures, but nevertheless argues for the legitimacy of imperialism on the grounds that a civilisation with a more developed rational consciousness can exercise political authority over a less developed state so long as that authority is wielded for the good of that state's citizens. Idealism, with its emphasis on citizenship, duty, and patriotism, as well as its exhortation that one must take responsibility for the world's weaker or less civilised members, provides the moral foundations for the kind of imperialism that sees empire as less an economic and military enterprise and more an agent for the development of mankind's higher spiritual potential. Watson responds to those who see imperialism in a less favourable light by putting forward the Idealist caveat that an empire is justified if it is a force for civilisation, which, for Watson, meant the increasing development of the moral consciousness. "[T]he only justification for the rule of a superior over an inferior people is that the former should regard as its special task the elevation of the latter to its own level ... There is no justification for the rule of a foreign government which does not seek to promote civilisation, liberty and progress in the subject people, and does not take the necessary steps to fit them for self-government."[198] In other words, there is a "right" imperialism and a "wrong" imperialism.

As far as Watson is concerned, there is no denying the reality of imperialism in world affairs, and that necessitates a response more intelligent than denunciation. Instead of merely condemning imperialism, he argues that the empire should be consciously directed toward the goal of preparing subject people for self-government and the rational comprehension of their inherent freedom. Furthermore, lifting a colonised people to a higher level of consciousness does not require the destruction of their culture. In a statement that conforms with his idea that each culture, each state, has its mission, Watson says that the better elements in the subject society must be fostered. Moreover, the imperial nation should not expect to maintain a permanent rule over the colony. It is the duty of the imperial power to raise the self-consciousness of colonial citizens. To repeat, it must "take the necessary steps to fit them for self-government."[199]

Watson uses British rule in India as an example of relatively enlightened imperial rule, of one civilisation trying to lift another to a higher level of rational development. But he also applies this standard of recognition to the Allies' treatment of postwar Germany. While Watson may reject the criticism levelled against Hegelians by the likes of Hobhouse and Russell, he echoes their condemnations of states that act immorally. In *The State in Peace and War*, Watson decries states that lower the standard of human morality by engaging in torture, using poison gas, or targeting civilians during war. He does not at this point specifically name which states he has in mind, but given the context of his comments, there is little doubt that he is thinking of Germany.[200] However, Watson does not let the Allied states off the hook. On the issue of German war reparations, he applies the same moral standard. To impose heavy reparations on German would only confirm the view that Allied war aims were motivated by commercial self-interest. In a prescient warning, Watson says that harsh reparations would only stir the racial pride of the German people and serve to perpetuate their militarism and "prepare for the next war."[201]

Sustaining Watson's argument against reparations is his teleological view of human reason and the historical development of the rational will. Germany may be guilty of starting the Great War, but it is also a state with legitimate interests in the world. German militarism would not be overcome through the economic suppression, or diminishment, of the German state, but only through the recognition and acceptance of the German nation as a part of the community of states. With this argument – an argument, I suggest, that has certain similarities to contemporary notions of nation building, foreign aid, international development, and Third World debt relief – Watson makes concrete his notion of rights as applied at the international level: that is, rights are not a property we possess inherently, but a form of recognition by others of the spheres of freedom needed for full self-development, whether as an individual or a nation-state.[202]

Watson sees this notion of relations reflected, however imperfectly, in the British Empire and the relations between Great Britain and the dominions. The empire represents a "form of government ... founded on principles which appeal to the highest political ideals." In a statement that echoes his theory of relative sovereignty, Watson judges the empire's "remarkable success" to be based on "combining the freedom of the separate organs with the unity of the whole."[203] He concludes that within the empire there exists the greatest possible freedom for the self-development of each member state, and the greatest possible sense of belonging to a community of common sentiment and common ideals. The evidence for this, Watson argues, is the loyalty that the dominions showed to Great Britain during the First World War. These self-governing colonies were free of Britain's dictation, but freely chose to do their part in furthering the success of the empire as a whole.[204] Thus, for Watson, the empire as a whole expresses a rational will that is embodied in the various forms of the different member states. Or, put another way, the imperial arrangement provides a credible response at the international level to that essential political problem – uniting public authority with individual freedom.

Drawing on Hegel's master-slave dialectic and the logic of negation and sublation, Watson perceives that imperialism is not necessarily morally offensive despite its origins and abuses. So long as imperialism is ultimately devoted to the service of an Ideal morality, to creating the conditions by which member states can conduct themselves in ways that transcend self-interest, then it is morally justifiable. It is "entirely immoral" for states to use other states as mere instruments for satisfying their own desires, Watson says. Especially in the case of "races inferior in civilisation," the only justification for ruling them is to "rule them entirely with the end in view of gradually making it possible for them to lift themselves to a higher plane."[205] For Watson, the British Empire served this Ideal end.

> This group of groups has thus shown by a brilliant example what may be effected when the outlook is that of free men, attached by the bond of common descent and common or at least similar institutions, and all performing their part in furthering the success of the whole. We have in this modern State an almost perfect example of the unity in diversity which we have already seen to be necessary in a single nation. The common will is the hidden spring of this community of nations, a will which is manifested in each and yet is necessary to the harmony of the whole. Here we have the real general will present in its degree in every one of the co-operating groups.[206]

Watson's understanding of the questions Plato raised in *Apology* and *Crito* can again be discerned. Rational empires are based on the recognition of a greater good to be realised in the union of oneself with others.

At the centre of Watson's political philosophy, then, is the idea of a moral community grounded in the universality of human reason. Such a community, with its emphasis on reasoned authority and organic unity, would provide stability and coherence in times of transformative social change, while sustaining faith in progress. Watson does not assume that this rational will can be achieved any time soon, or that the end of history is approaching. Like Hegel, he never forgets that there is a great difference between the actual and the real will. Still, like all Idealists, he sees history as a process by which individuals and their communities gradually develop a greater awareness of and identity with the underlying spiritual order of existence. For Watson, history shows that the development of the rational will best occurs in a well-organised state composed of institutions through which individuals enjoy the freedom necessary for their self-development. Just as Pericles regards the "great impediment to action" to be "the want of that knowledge which is gained by discussion preparatory to action,"[207] Watson sees the institutions of empire – democratic governance, a system of rights and laws, parliamentary debate, to name a few – as the means for promoting the self-criticism and self-correction needed to develop the common good. Contrary to those who see Idealist philosophy as too abstract, or as providing unwarranted support for the established order, Watson sees it providing the reflection necessary for choosing actions that would be in accordance with the rational will.

Watson employs Hegel's concept of *Sittlichkeit* to argue that a rational and moral state (or rational and moral empire) is grounded in the recognition that the freedom of all and respect for the state's or community's traditions are embodiments of universal reason. The deeper problem of the modern political order is not so much a matter of protecting the individual (or the individual state) from an absolutist state (or system of states), but a matter of making the state serve individuals in their rational freedom. In a time of social change, it is imperative that the interdependence of individuals (and states) be recognised for the good of the whole. "It is only by mutual dependence upon each other that the best powers of men are called forth into exercise. Wide-spread industry tends to eliminate purely self-referent interests, by bringing men into intimate relations with each other, it generates that mutual trust and confidence which result in a healthy tone of public morality ... The seeming sacrifice of independence is really the condition of the only independence that is worth having."[208]

That last sentence might serve as Watson's theoretical justification of imperial order. As an Idealist, he sees empire providing the reconciliation of freedom and duty that allows a community to stand against the disintegrative forces that threatened its civilisation. With such a claim Watson anticipates many of the communitarian arguments against the supposed fragmentary tendencies of individualistic liberalism, including those of George Grant and Charles Taylor.

PART THREE

George Grant and the Spirit of Tyranny

Canada's "Fate" and
the Worship of History

George Grant is often credited with awakening Canadians from their nationalist slumbers. The publication of *Lament for a Nation* in 1965, it is said, sparked an intense period of nationalism. Spurred by Grant, Canadians began to reflect on what made Canada worth preserving. Out of this reflection came various political, economic, social, and even artistic responses to foster national identity and sovereignty.[1] This claim is at odds with Grant's consistent denial of nationalistic motives on his part and his explicit statement in *Lament* about "the impossibility of Canada." As he recounts in the book, Grant saw the 1963 election defeat of John Diefenbaker's Conservatives at the hands of the Liberal establishment as a concrete demonstration of the unwillingness of Canadians to maintain a sovereign nation independent of the United States. Even in later years, while acknowledging the "traces of care" shown by Pierre Trudeau's nationalist policies, Grant maintained that "below the surface the movement toward integration continues" because of "our position in the empire."[2]

I have no intention of debating whether Grant's claim about Canada's "disappearance" is correct in any practical sense, especially when the issue remains undetermined. My interest lies with the seeming paradox of Grant's status as "a father of Canadian nationalism,"[3] given his insistence that he was not trying to promote the nationalist cause. As he put it in 1985, "Because people quite rightly want finite hopes, people have read a little book I wrote (*Lament for a Nation*) wrongly. I was talking about the 'end' of Canadian nationalism. I was saying that this is over and people read it as if I was making an appeal for Canadian nationalism. I think that is just nonsense. I think they just read it wrongly."[4]

Grant seems straightforward about why Canada has come to an end: the principles upon which the country was founded have given way to those of the American republic. These American principles promote social and political arrangements that make particular cultures and nations like Canada redundant. And because Canadians on the whole believe that the principles of modernity are right and proper, they have little reason to maintain an authentic and independent political existence. In ascribing to the goods of modernity exemplified by the American way of life, Canadians effectively surrendered those characteristics that once distinguished Canada from the United States and gave it a reason for being. Hence, Grant concludes that Canada is impossible as a sovereign nation-state because of the "character of the modern age."[5]

How can the disappearance of Canada be attributed to the character of the modern age? The question brings forward the central concern of this part of my essay – how Grant's linkage of modernity with Canada's political fate is bound up with his philosophic relationship to Hegel. The German's influence on Grant is well known. So too is Grant's "turn" from Hegel. However, there has been insufficient consideration given to the connection between Grant's Hegelianism, both in its initial appeal and its later repudiation, and Grant's claim about the impossibility of Canada. I argue that Grant's lament is bound up with his interpretation of and response to the thinker he once described as "the greatest of all philosophers."[6]

In the 1959 edition of *Philosophy in the Mass Age*, Grant praises Hegel as the one philosopher who has been able to synthesise classical reason, Christian theology, and modern freedom. Hegel, he says, reconciles the concept of modern man as an autonomous, history-making being with the account of pre-modern man as a being who dwelt under the dispensation of an eternal, divinely given natural law. This optimistic appraisal of Hegel did not last long. Grant eventually recognised that it was impossible to bring together classical natural law and the modern ontological notion of time as the history created by men free to make of themselves what they will. Grant's turn from Hegel and liberal progressivism has been called his "era of retractions,"[7] that period when, under the influence of such thinkers as Leo Strauss, Jacques Ellul, Friedrich Nietzsche, Martin Heidegger, and Simone Weil, Grant reconsidered his attachments to the modern project.

Seven years after the initial publication of *Philosophy in the Mass Age*, Grant had undergone an intellectual conversion. In an introduction to the 1966 second edition of the book, Grant wrote: "I came to the conclusion that Hegel was not correct in his claim to have taken the truth of antique thought and synthesised it with the modern to produce a higher (and perhaps highest) truth; that on many of the most important political matters Plato's teaching is truer than Hegel's. Particularly, I have come to the conclusion that Plato's account of what constitutes human excellence and the possibility of its realisation in the world is more valid than that of Hegel."[8] However, despite Grant's disavowal, Hegel continued to have an abiding influence on his thought, providing him with the theoretical tools to account for the character of the modern world. Grant implies as much when, in his 1966 repudiation of Hegel, he says it is difficult for anyone who ascribes to "the Western Christian doctrine of providence to avoid reaching the conclusion that Hegel has understood the implications of that doctrine better than any other thinker."[9]

This comment demonstrates that Grant continued to regard Hegelian philosophy as the fullest expression of modernity. Therefore, it can be argued that Grant's subsequent thought constitutes an ongoing reappraisal of Hegel in light of what he regards as the failings of the modern project, especially as it is manifested in North American society. Even in rejecting Hegel, Grant could not excise the German's influence in any absolute sense because he maintains throughout his work the truth of the Hegelian account of modernity.[10] Hence, Grant's turn from Hegel should be interpreted not so much as a rejection of Hegel but as a shift in consciousness on Grant's part akin to the psychology reflected in Hegel's concept of *Aufhebung* – a conversion of consciousness that incorporates and sublates a previous mode of consciousness. The question therefore becomes this: What is it about Hegel's thought that Grant cannot abide even though he recognises that it provides the most comprehensive account of the modern condition? Answering this question penetrates to the heart of Grant's judgment about the impossibility of Canada.

Grant was often criticised for his pessimism about modernity, particularly in regard to Canada's political future. *Lament for a Nation*, for instance, was attacked as an indulgence in Loyalist nostalgia, a "panic remembrance" of Athens and Jerusalem.[11] More generally, while praised for revealing the nihilism of modernity and the "destruction of man's inner life in a technological society,"[12] he was accused of having no adequate response to the modern crisis, of failing to offer a constructive alternative to modernity.[13] Such criticism fails to comprehend Grant's philosophic ground. Those who expect Grant to provide a systematic countervail to modernity arguably demonstrate their ascription to the assumptions of modernity. They miss what is arguably *the* ground of his thought: the vast distance between necessity and goodness. Grant does not share the modern historicist assumption that historical events lead inevitably to the betterment of humankind. In rejecting this view, Grant sets himself against the prevailing liberal faith in progress. As he puts it in a revealing statement, "To partake even dimly in the riches of Athens or Jerusalem should be to know that one is outside the public realm of the age of progress."[14]

This statement suggests that, for Grant, the fate of Canada has implications beyond any narrow parochial concern for Canada's fate as a sovereign state. Indeed, Grant sees Canada's disappearance as a moral question bound up with the character of modernity. In this regard, those who criticise Grant for his pessimism are in a certain sense right, but for the wrong reasons. Grant is certainly pessimistic about modernity, but then he is not a "modern." He is a Platonist within Christianity. His consciousness is pre-modern at its deepest philosophical level. Grant regards himself as a witness to modern nihilism, implying as much when he says, "the Western world might well be a failure."[15]

Grant often states that the most pressing need in the modern world is to bring together in the same thought the truth of classical reason and modern technological thinking.[16] His philosophic career reflects this attempt. Early in his career, Grant believed that Hegelian philosophy provided him with the means to achieve this unity of thought and that this philosophic reconciliation would provide the theoretical basis for the continuation of Canada as a genuinely sovereign political community. But he eventually recognised that Hegel's synthesis is impossible. It is impossible to reconcile the metaphysical assumptions underlying pre-modern philosophy with the ontological assumptions on which modern thought is based. Either the classical assumption of a natural order of which humans are part is true, or it is not; either the modern assumption of an unordered universe subject to human ordering is true, or it is not.

Given this, any substantive understanding of Grant's political thought requires comprehending the philosophical and theological concepts that inform his politics. The disappearance of a particular nation-state such as Canada might be necessary under the imperatives of modernity, but Canada's disappearance – or that of any particular political community – might not necessarily serve the "good." From this position, Grant's insistence on the distance between necessity and goodness is both a repudiation of Hegel and a moral judgment regarding the modern project. It is this rejection of the modern, or Hegelian, synthesis and many of its concrete manifestations that underlies Grant's judgment on Canada. In this regard, Grant's thought as a whole constitutes a continuous reassessment of Hegel's thought, a constant reconsideration that opens us to a deeper understanding of what Grant means by the impossibility of Canada.

I have already noted the long-standing interest in Hegel on the part of Canadian theorists and scholars, and how certain Hegelian ideas have sunk deep roots into Canadian political culture because of this country's political and geographical circumstances. These thinkers are attracted to a philosophy that seeks to reconcile the kinds of tension engendered by these circumstances. Hegel appears to provide a theoretical framework that allows diverse cultures to maintain and develop their distinctive features even while uniting in a single political order. Grant's initial employment of Hegelian ideas seems to reflect this attitude. Given his concern with Canada's independence on a continent dominated by the United States, what may have contributed to Hegel's appeal for Grant was the German philosopher's understanding of how pluralistic societies can use legal and political systems and institutions to mitigate those forces that threaten to tear them apart. In *Philosophy of Right*, for example, Hegel argues that modern societies are to be understood by reference to the fundamental concepts that guide them, and that the modern state seeks to enable citizens to assert those rights and freedoms that reflect the truest purposes of human life and, at the same time, reconcile them so as to uphold the common good.[17] Grant asserts a similar sentiment in *Lament* when he says that "a society only articulates itself as a nation through some common intention among its people."[18] Thus, Canada exists as a nation-state so long as it holds to the essential idea on which it was founded: "an inchoate desire to build, in these cold and forbidding regions, a society with a greater sense of order and restraint than freedom-loving republicanism would allow."[19]

Grant's initial appropriation of Hegel clearly stands in sharp contrast to that of American thinkers, who, as I have previously discussed, tend to interpret Hegelian concepts in a triumphalist manner. Francis Fukuyama's end-of-history thesis in the wake of communism's collapse is a case in point. Grant, as I shall show, eventually comes to the conclusion that this triumphalist appropriation of Hegel is the one that has the most meaning for the modern world, at least in the sense that the technological society of North America is the most complete embodiment of Hegel's thought. However, before considering what it is about the Hegelian project that Grant cannot accept, I need to address what specifically Grant laments.

In his essay "Canadian Fate and Imperialism," Grant states that "man cannot help but imitate in action his vision of the nature of things."[20] And if that vision is at odds with the reality of the given world – which, for Grant, is subject to a divine order – then men's lives will be violent, chaotic, and without meaning. For Grant, statecraft requires soulcraft. If the latter lacks harmony, then so too does the former. This is Grant's concern as a *political* philosopher. As a philosopher, Grant seeks to reawaken for himself and for others the *eros* of the soul in its pursuit of the good. But as a political philosopher Grant knows, as Plato knew, that the *idea of the good* can only be known in the quotidian routines of life. Grant makes this point when he says that only in loving our own – our families and friends, our neighbourhoods, cities, and countries – is it possible to experience that which is beyond calculable reason and will-to-power, and gain some insight into what it means to "not be one's own." In the knowledge of such experience, we are vouchsafed a glimpse beyond the cave. "Love of the good is man's highest end, but it is of the nature of things that we come to know and to love what is good by first meeting it in that which is our own – this particular body, this family, these friends, this woman, this part of the world, this set of traditions, this country, this civilisation."[21] In other words, only through the everyday realities and particularities of the material world is knowledge of a transcendent good possible.

Grant's lament for Canada's disappearance is grounded in this idea of loving one's own. The words *one's own* is Grant's shorthand phrase for alluding to the psychological and spiritual homelessness of modern technological society. In the modern project, one's rootedness or particularity – culture, class, nation, traditions – is denied a uniqueness or meaning apart from its function in and value to the overall productive task of society. But without one's own there can be no experience or knowledge of what it means to be not one's own. And without this latter experience, the former is meaningless. Such a view draws on classical thought in which the private realm – such as the household and the family – is regarded as the necessary, if insufficient, condition for the establishment of a worthy public or political realm. But it also echoes the classical philosophers' concerns about the importance of the private realm, such as the family, being prior to and an essential prerequisite for the political realm. Politics, as Aristotle argues, may be the arena where the means and ends of society are debated, but in order to enter this debate, humans must remain rooted in a private realm that satisfies their requirement for the necessities of life, including the psychological necessity of love and intimacy. This grounding in the private realm prepares the citizen to enter and survive the common or public realm.

Grant says as much in "Canadian Fate and Imperialism" when he writes: "It is true that no particularism can adequately incarnate the good. But is it not also true that only through some particular roots, however partial, can human beings first grasp what is good and it is the juice of such roots which for most men sustain their partaking in a more universal good."[22]

Technological society, according to Grant, erodes this prerequisite private realm and, in doing so, undermines the public or political realm. At the individual level, the subordination of the private realm to the productive and administrative requirements of a technological order has meant that the formation of individual character, the attempt to manifest the good in one's daily life, is sacrificed to the imperatives of technological efficiency. Even one's thought becomes an object for the distortions of technologically oriented psychotherapies and sociological adjustment practices. Something similar happens at the political level. The particularity of Canada is submerged beneath the imperatives of modernity as expressed in its dominant doctrines, namely modern liberalism and technology.[23] As Ian Angus writes, "Standardisation of culture by technology requires that all that is one's own be pressed into the service of empire."[24] In such a situation, Grant argues, love of one's own becomes even more necessary if one is to possess any vision of the good. Only through loving particular things are we able to hold to any idea of a good that is not simply a surrender of one's own to the demands and imperatives of technological development.

This concern is at the heart of *Lament for a Nation* where Grant contemplates the tensions between differing Canadian loyalties and how the forces (and temptations) of economic and cultural integration tend to extinguish the particularities of Canada. On the surface, *Lament* relates the story of how Progressive Conservative prime minister John Diefenbaker and his cabinet colleague Howard Green attempted to maintain Canadian sovereignty against the connivance of Lester Pearson and the Liberal Party, and how the Conservatives, under attack by Canada's pro-American corporate and bureaucratic elites, lost the debate on stationing American nuclear warheads on Canadian soil. Grant's anger was directed against those who conspired to bring about the downfall of the Diefenbaker government in 1963 for selfish and parochial ends, particularly the Liberal establishment and the Canadian business elite. Not that Grant was fond of or even admired Diefenbaker. He was explicit in saying that "[n]othing in Diefenbaker's ministry was as noble as his leaving of it."[25] Yet Grant saw Diefenbaker's fate as symbolic of the weakness of Canadian conservatism in countering the pull of American culture and economic prosperity. The fall of the Diefenbaker regime highlighted Canada as a microcosm of mankind's confrontation with the technological forces that were transforming the world.[26] As Peter Emberley puts it, "Lying behind the immediate decisions arising from our status within the [American] empire is the deeper question of the fate of any particularity in the technological age."[27]

What was it that Grant tried to hold on to as his own? Why, and in what way, did he realise it was impossible to do so? How did he respond to this existential situation in a way that was itself not tantamount to partaking of the technological liberal imperative? The first question is essential in gaining a purchase on Grant's thought. Grant saw in Diefenbaker a form of nationalism and a sense of conservatism that were similar to his own. Twenty years before the publication of *Lament for a Nation*, Grant had written a number of political pamphlets that more or less reflected beliefs traceable to both of his grandfathers, one of whom, George Monro Grant, was influenced by John Watson and the other of whom, Sir George Parkin, was an ardent promoter of the British Empire.[28]

Grant's conservatism should not be misconstrued. He was not hostile to change or even to technology.[29] Nor did he indulge in nostalgia for the past. Grant's conservatism is not reactionary or revisionist. Rather, it reflects a particular understanding of the relationship between the individual and the community. It is akin, I argue, to Hegel's conservatism. To recall, Hegel holds that while the modern state embodies the unity of individuals, it is not an undifferentiated collectivity as was the case in some premodern political orders. The freedom that the individual achieves in the modern state reflects the view that personal individuality and particular interests attain their fullest development within the community. At the same time, though, individuals freely accede to the universal interest, recognising it as their own rational will and taking "it as their end and aim and are active in its pursuit."[30] This is essentially John Watson's position, too, as I have discussed.

Grant, as I have noted, holds that nations or communities are to be understood by reference to the fundamental ideas or intentions that guide them.[31] Following this notion, Grant's political thought is rooted in the belief that "a nation (or state or political system) is a partnership that is to be understood primarily or fundamentally by understanding the purposes of the partners in forming the partnership."[32] Individuals enjoy their freedom as citizens not solely in satisfying their egocentric or materialist desires, but also in recognizing that their best interests are linked to the community and that they are most free and fulfilled when there is a reconciliation of individual desire and communal purpose. Grant's conservatism is thus grounded in the assumption of an overarching good – in this case, the good of Canada as a sovereign nation-state able to exist so long as it holds to the intentions for which it was founded.

The order that Grant seeks to conserve, the tradition he believes essential to Canada's sovereign existence, is the order that was shared by the country's founding political cultures, the British Empire Loyalists of English Canada and the *ultramontane* Catholics of French Canada. For Grant, the Canada Act of 1791, which divided Canada into two colonial provinces and met the demands of the English-speaking Loyalists for their own legislative assembly, was the primal constitutional document. It, along with the constitutional arrangements of the nineteenth century, expressed the determination of both the French and the British not to be absorbed by the American republic. Both linguistic groups realised that they would not be able to preserve their cultures on their own. Only together did they have a chance, only if their diversity was made into unity. Grant writes about the French Canadians' motives for joining Confederation: "The French Canadians had entered Confederation not to protect the rights of the individual but the rights of a nation."[33] This rejection of American republicanism, together with the individualistic ethos that went with it, is central to Grant's understanding of the *idea* that gives Canada its reason for being. So long as that idea holds, particularly among the ruling elites, then Canada is possible. And it is this possibility, this good, that Grant loves as his own.

Grant admires French Canadian nationalism and its insistence on maintaining a French nation in the heart of North America. He sees it as a bulwark against the press of the modern project. But to remain independent, Canada also has to be British. As he writes in *Lament*, "Growing up in Ontario the generation of the 1920s took it for granted that they belonged to a nation. The character of the country was self-evident. To say it was British was not to deny it was North American. To be a Canadian was to be a unique species of North American."[34] Grant's conservative concern for the preservation of a Canadian national identity embedded in its British heritage is most revealingly stated in some of his few direct reflections on Canadian foreign policy. The titles of two of his writings published in 1945 pose two questions: "Have We a Canadian Nation?"[35] and *The Empire, Yes or No?*[36]

In the first, he argues that nationalism at its most positive "embodied in an individual culture ... unique contributions to the world." In the particularity of a nation, "the colour and glory of life are not found in uniformity but in diversity."[37] However, unlike European countries that had had centuries to see the slow and organic maturation of their cultures, Canadians have had to create their culture around "certain conscious ideas."[38] For Grant, the essential or primal Canadian idea was the conscious decision to avoid a revolutionary severing of our links to Britain. To cut these ties, to consciously abandon our founding traditions, opens us to the revolutionary principles of the United States. Canada, says Grant, "will only continue to exist as long as we represent something individual and special in ourselves ... If we don't have that belief in our own way of life, if we don't continue to practice these [conservative] values, we will soon cease to be a nation. If we cut ourselves off from our roots, we will die. We always have the alternative to being Canadian – we can become American."[39]

In his understanding of the conservative ideas that hold Canada together, Grant emphasises the reconciliation of individual freedom and social order. Canadians share with Americans a belief in the individual's inalienable rights, but Canadians differ in their regard for the need to maintain social harmony. Canadians want their freedom, but not so much freedom that it threatens the pattern of social order. "Our inherent conservatism said order and self-discipline are a natural concomitant of freedom."[40] On this point, Grant sounds distinctly Hegelian.[41] One of Hegel's key concerns in *Philosophy of Right* is to synthesise the negative freedom of modern liberalism and the positive freedom of ancient republican thought regarding the identity of the individual and the community. Freedom and duty go hand in hand. Freedom is impossible without the corresponding recognition of duty because our rights are claims that others must recognise if they are to be effective. Hence, the fundamental purpose of the modern state is the reconciliation of individuality and universality. Hegel seeks a balance that avoids the extremes of atomistic individualism or coercive collectivism: "The state is the actuality of concrete freedom. But concrete freedom consists in this, that personal individuality and its particular interests not only achieve their complete development and gain explicit recognition for their right (as they do in the sphere of the family and civil society) but, for one thing, they also pass over of their own accord into the interest of the universal."[42]

Grant, in an argument foreshadowing his concerns about technology corroding the relationship of the individual and the community, writes that the great problem facing Canadians at the end of the Second World War was how they were going to organise themselves efficiently as required by industrial society – Grant would later use the phrase *technological society* – without sacrificing individual freedom. With its conservative heritage, Canada was uniquely positioned – "the compromise between the individualism of the U.S.A. and the extreme social order of the U.S.S.R.,"[43] as Grant puts it – to maintain this balance. It was smaller than the United States, and lacking the obligations and impulsions of superpower politics, it could better address the problems of democracy in an industrial society. And Canada was able to maintain this independent compromise of freedom and order because of its stature in the British Empire. On this issue,

Grant's sentiments are little different than those of either his maternal grandfather, George Parkin, the international promoter of imperial federation and evangelist of empire, or his paternal grandfather, George Monro Grant. Both men shared the ideal of Canada and the other dominions linking with Britain to oversee a globe-spanning empire dedicated to civilising the world.[44]

The sentiments of the elder Grant certainly find an echo in his grandson's thought. This suggests, perhaps, an indirect Hegelian influence on the younger Grant through the medium of his grandfather, who, as head of Queen's University in the later decades of the nineteenth century, was on intimate terms with John Watson and deeply influenced by him.[45] Grant's biographer, William Christian, notes that "G.M. Grant's influence on his grandson was strong but indirect; it came through the curriculum and the other structures of the institution he had formed."[46] And those structures were imbued with a "Queen's spirit" that was in large measure shaped by Watson's Hegelian Idealism.[47] Grant, it might be said, was an unconscious Hegelian even before he encountered Hegel.

This is reflected in Grant's attitude toward the turn-of-the-century Idealism of his forefathers, who identified Protestantism and liberalism and regarded the Empire as a force for progress. "It was quite hard for me to leave the progressive liberalism of the nineteenth century because of the second war."[48] This lingering attachment to Idealist liberalism is evident in Grant's other 1945 work, *The Empire, Yes or No?* Here he expresses optimism about the development of a new world order. As far as Grant is concerned, those who spoke against the British connection because of some notion about Canada's so-called colonial status were being mendacious. They were also dangerous. In a world that threatened to divide into two power blocs, the British Empire would be the power to counterbalance them. Behind the naive demands for independence from Britain was an implicit ascription to the ideas of the American Revolution, which, in Grant's view, promoted political decisions that would eventually subordinate Canada to the United States. This subordination, Grant predicts, would be most evident in Canadian foreign affairs and defence policies. *Lament for a Nation* is Grant's testament to the consequences of "thinking" American.

Like John Watson,[49] Grant advocates a special role for Canada as a member of the British Commonwealth. Because Canada was both a North American nation and a member of the world-spanning Commonwealth, it could play an influential role in ensuring that the United States took its "proper place" in world affairs. With the world seemingly divided into "the two immense continental empires of the U.S.A. and the U.S.S.R., and the maritime empire of Great Britain," there was considerable danger of continental regionalism. Grant sees the Commonwealth as a potential counterweight to regional isolationism. With its decentralisation, its diverse cultures, and its need to act cooperatively, the Commonwealth was "an ideal the world must strive for."[50] Moreover, Grant, again like Watson, regards Canada's membership in the British Empire (or Commonwealth) as a means to ensure its own sovereignty and independence of action in world affairs, as well as to promote world peace. As he writes:

> Cut off from the British nations, as an independent country, we would have little alternative but to join the South American nations in the hemispheric Empire of the U.S.A. And as part of that we would be strengthening the power of the U.S.A. to retire into isolation. We would be abetting its ability to establish an anti-Russian block. We would be increasing the chance for an American-Soviet conflict. On the other hand, as a member of the Commonwealth, we would be doing the exact opposite. Friendly to the U.S.A., we would still not be her satellite. By our world-wide interests, we would, as her chief neighbour, be pulling her out of continental isolation and toward effective commitments to a world order.[51]

Like Watson and his grandfathers, Grant also sees a high moral calling in Canada's Commonwealth membership. In an enunciation of the triumphalist Hegelian world-state that he would later repudiate, Grant argues that Canada's aim "must be the upward climb of mankind into a perfect and effective world government."[52] With its particular traditions and circumstances, Canada provided a balance between the extreme atomistic freedom of the United States and the extreme communitarianism of the Soviet Union. Or, to put it another way, Grant regards Canada's continued existence as both a political and a philosophical issue. In a statement with which neither Hegel nor Watson would disagree, he says: "[I]t is important that this continent should have this diversity of social philosophy. The great question of the modern world is going to be to what extent, and within the complicated patterns of industrialized civilisation, freedom and authority can be truly integrated."[53] Grant, like Watson, sees Canada embodying an idea, the fate of which may be a harbinger of the fate of the West. Thus, in a most Hegelian manner, Grant makes Canada's existence a civilisational – and hence philosophical – concern.

Despite the public optimism of his 1945 writings, however, Grant in private was not so hopeful. Letters he wrote at about this time show a growing pessimism about the future, particularly with regard to the impact of industrialisation on the traditions that had sustained Canadians as a whole and as individuals. "I am now somehow suddenly scared," he wrote to his sister in early 1945. "At the moment, this colossal, material change of industrialism has been too much for our great tradition (really a remarkably thin veneer) of personal responsibility, the dignity of the individual."[54] Grant's hope for a new world order along these lines was broken by the Truman Doctrine and its division of the world into two power blocs. With the outbreak of the Cold War, Grant largely fell silent on explicit political matters regarding Canada's status as a sovereign nation – until the 1965 publication of *Lament for a Nation*.

In this book, Grant details the coming to pass of what he had feared twenty years earlier – Canada's *de facto* absorption into an American empire. Grant chastises the surrender of Canada's liberal elites to the Americans during the defence crisis of 1962 and 1963. He singles out the bureaucratic mandarins, including those in External Affairs, who, he says, "were the instruments of a policy that left Canada a satellite internationally."[55] Against this, he contrasts the loyalty of John Diefenbaker, who, whatever his faults and failings, held to the idea that while Canada was an ally of the United States, it was also an independent nation and need not take its marching orders from the White House. Diefenbaker learned differently, of course. His government was defeated in the 1963 election and replaced with that of Lester Pearson, who quickly acceded to the American demands.

Behind Diefenbaker's electoral defeat, Grant sees the defeat of Canadian nationalism at the hands of a business, cultural, and political elite more concerned with profit and power than nationhood. "The economic self-seekers had never been the ones to care about Canada as a nation."[56] But behind this obeisance to economic self-interest, Grant sees an even deeper deprival. Canada, he argues, had been founded with the deliberate intention of creating an alternative, conservative political order on the North American continent. The betrayal of Diefenbaker's government by the country's elite revealed that those in positions of power no longer cared to maintain the old idea of Canada, that Canada's elites no longer embodied the Spirit that once served to sustain the country's sovereign existence. Thus, when Grant declares "the impossibility of Canada," he means that Canadians have abandoned their founding intention to preserve themselves as politically and culturally separate from the United

States. Canadians, unconsciously or not, wanted to be part of the more dynamic southern republic. Canada ceased to be a nation not because its formal political existence had come to an end, but because the idea that had
provided its meaning and purposiveness was no longer seen to be worth
preserving. The church walls still stood, but the spirit was gone. The Canadian elite gave its loyalty to economic well-being instead of to Canada's sovereignty as a nation. And as far as Grant is concerned, to be satisfied with
hedonistic consumption as a way of life is to be a creature of technique and
utilitarian liberalism.[57]

At the core of *Lament for a Nation*, then, is the claim that conservatism,
particularly that expressed in the Loyalist tradition in Canada, had reached
its historical end point. Even socialism could not save Canada, since it
shared the progressivist, pro-technological assumptions of liberalism. Grant
understands that the essence of contemporary liberalism is the identification of freedom and technology. Modern secular man believes that his
freedom requires control of the world and that this is to be accomplished
through the application of technology.[58] But for Grant it was this kind of
thinking that contributed to the impossibility of Canada.

After the publication of his collection of essays, *Technology and Empire*, in
1969, Grant seems to have stepped away from nationalist issues, at least in
a direct way, or, more accurately perhaps, his understanding of Canada's
fate shifted to another level. Grant came to see Canada's crisis of identity
not only as a problem for Canadians, but as a symptom of a larger crisis facing all North Americans. Canada's disappearance was bound up with what
had happened to the spirit of Western Christendom in the modern age.
And for Grant, it was Hegel who most comprehensively grasped the fate of
this spirit.

Grant's thought in the late 1950s and early 1960s has been described as
"reluctant Hegelianism."[59] Grant, it is said, "was deeply engaged with the
thinker who had brought the concept of time as history into western thought,
G.W.F. Hegel,"[60] and through him, he acquired a set of theoretical tools that
could account for the character of the modern technological world. But in
the seven years between the publication of the first edition of *Philosophy in the
Mass Age* and the publication of a second edition in 1966, Grant shifted from
a hesitant acceptance of Hegel's historicism to a seemingly outright rejection
of it. Yet, even after this rejection, Hegel's indirect influence remained considerable.[61] In this regard, Grant's repudiation of Hegel presents us with a
crucial interpretative problem in our attempt to comprehend his political
philosophy, particularly since, despite Grant's rejection of the Hegelian synthesis, Hegel continued to influence his thought.

Grant confirms the importance of this influence in a 1966 review of Jacques Ellul's *The Technological Society,* writing that Hegel had grasped with "greater clarity" than anyone else how the modern West had come to be.[62] But even in his direct recantation of Hegel, Grant admits it is difficult for anyone who ascribes to "the Western Christian doctrine of providence to avoid reaching the conclusion that Hegel has understood the implications of that doctrine better than any other thinker."[63] He does not say what exactly he means by the "Western Christian doctrine of providence" or what it is about this doctrine that Hegel saw better than others. But three years later, in *Technology and Empire,* Grant makes an oblique reference to his early Hegelianism when he criticises his 1963 essay "Religion and the State." He says that he had continued to regard Hegel as the greatest of all philosophers for the longest time simply because he himself "could not face the fact that we are living at the end of western Christianity."[64]

Grant's confrontation with Hegel begins in *Philosophy in the Mass Age* when he claims that history is a problem for the moral philosopher who seeks to know which actions are right and which are wrong: "The historical situation of the West, and of Canadians in particular, calls for the frankest and most critical look at the principles of right in which we put our trust."[65] Thus, Grant makes history a core concern in his thought. He shows how history displaced the ancient understanding of nature as the overarching concept by which man understands the world. History, says Grant, is the key theoretical concept by which moderns understand themselves. Historicism posits the claim that our knowledge of the world is to be understood only through historical movement. History for Grant is "*the* idea, the central theoretical and practical idea of our age."[66] To understand history is to penetrate to the heart of modernity. Or, as Grant states, "'History' is one of the key words in which English-speaking people now express what they think they are and what they think the world to be ... Therefore, if we desire to understand our own understanding of ourselves, it is well to think about this word which has come to have such a unique connotation amongst us."[67]

Grant presents arguments on historicism throughout his writings. In *Technology and Empire,* he writes: "The dominant tendency of the western world has been to divide history from nature and to consider history as dynamic and nature controllable as externality."[68] Again, in *English-Speaking Justice,* Grant links liberal notions of justice with the historicist denial of classical natural justice that claimed that man was "directed to a highest good under which all goods were known in a hierarchy of subordination and superordination."[69] The modern lowering of standards of justice to the convenience of the social contract was the result of man's abstractedness from nature and his acceptance of historical and moral relativism. Likewise, in *Technology and Justice*, Grant identifies historicism with the kind of scientific positivism that produced a technological civilisation that denied all meanings beyond those man created for himself through his mastery and domination of nature, including human nature.[70] In the 1969 lecture series *Time As History*, he contrasts the modern notion of time as history with the pre-modern idea of time as a reflection of eternity. Not only does the word *history* refer to the study of the past, it is "also used to denote a certain kind of reality – human existing." Both meanings – the study of the past and an ascribed reality – are interconnected: the past is scrutinised in the belief that "man is essentially an historical being and that ... the riddle of what he is may be unfolded in those studies."[71] Modern man believes that he is understandable in terms of his historical development in time.

Grant contrasts historicist consciousness with ancient consciousness.[72] Historicism, he says, regards the world as a constant flow of unique and irreversible events that have to be dominated and controlled by means of the human will. Ancient consciousness, on the other hand, considers time "as the moving image of an unmoving eternity and in which the passing events of life only have meaning as they lead men to the unchanging reality of God."[73] Grant, of course, sides with the ancients and rejects historicism. He cannot agree that man is ultimately knowable as a historical being, and much of his philosophic career was devoted to countering this notion. In particular, his effort to understand the significance of historicism reflects his confrontation with Hegel, who, for Grant, was the great exemplar of historicist thinking. What turned Grant from his initial acceptance of Hegel's notion of historical development was his recognition that it carried too much of the positivist idea of progress as the ultimate aim of man and, worse, made even evil a purposive good. Such a claim ignores the idea of man's existence having a given highest purpose or good that transcends time or history. According to Grant, Hegel's identification of necessity with goodness ultimately means that history is the judgment of those possessed with the power to impose their will. For Grant, to make history "the final court of appeal" for man's meanings is tantamount to "worshipping force."[74]

Grant's repudiation of historicism – and Hegel – is stated most clearly in the final chapter of *Lament for a Nation*:

I must dissociate myself from a common philosophic assumption. I do not identify necessity and goodness. This identification is widely assumed during an age of progress. Those who worship "evolution" or "history" consider that what must come in the future will be "higher," "more developed," "better," "freer" than what has been in the past. This identification is also common among those who worship God according to Moses or the Gospels. They identify necessity and good within the rubric of providence. From the assumption that God's purposes are unfolded in historical events, one may be led to view history as an ever-fuller manifestation of good.[75]

Against this historicist perspective, Grant sets Plato and classical philosophy. The ancients distinguished between eternity, the good, and necessity, the realm of becoming that remains distinct from the good even while participating in it. Only by maintaining this distinction between necessity and good can we retain the distinction between good and evil. Grant, however, sees in Hegelian thought the erasure of this distinction. By identifying progress and providence, Hegel reduces all that is "other" to human subjectivity – that is, to historical development – and human willpower. The otherness of God that allows man to maintain a concept of goodness separate from and not subject to his history-making is lost.

In his turn from Hegel, Grant had come to see the concept of progress and the ideology of liberalism as containing a destructive element that militates against their worth. No longer could he share his forefathers' view of human development. No longer could he accept the Watsonian melding of Christian ethics and liberal Hegelianism. No longer could he share the Idealist optimism regarding human perfectibility. What was it that changed his mind? And, more important, how was his mind changed?

12

Hegel's Theology of Glory

According to Plato's *Republic*, the sanction of the gods is necessary to build a just city. Hence, Socrates demonstrates his piety to the goddess on a visit to Piraeus even before he begins laying the rhetorical bricks of his city in speech. And when Socrates and Adeimantus start to construct their city, they immediately agree that such a city requires that even speech about the gods – theology, in other words – must obey the laws of the city for the sake of justice.[76] But what if the city becomes decadent? What if its citizens turn away from the eternal and the divine? Must theology then bow to a regime that creates unholy orders or advocates non-theological principles? No, not necessarily. In the decadent city, those who speak about the gods engage in negative theology – that is, in speech about what God is not.[77] Negative theology, or *via negativa*, offers individuals a glimpse through the darkling glass of the light beyond, illuminates a temporal world that has lost its astonishment and wonder at the mystery of existence. That said, negative theology is not the dominant form of Christian speech, especially in the Protestant tradition. Christianity has been dominated by biblical theology, that is, by reflection on God as manifested in revelation. Negative theology, while acknowledging biblical theology, focuses on the limitations of temporal existence in an effort to disassociate those limitations from men's claims to possess knowledge of the eternal and from their use of that knowledge to satisfy selfish desires. In this way, negative theology seeks to place limits on man's doing and making by pointing out the tension between the temporal and the transcendent and thereby offering the possibility of the experience of the divine.[78]

This negative approach is reflected in Grant's rejection of the modern project and in his turn from Hegel as the exemplar of that project. Throughout his post-*Lament* writings, Grant is engaged in one way or another in negative theology.[79] He does not always directly address those things that are most important to him. And about those things to which he initially appears to speak directly, Grant is more indirect in his speech than might be expected. Grant's critique of technology seeks to reawaken an awareness of the connection between thought and love, reason and reve- lation, philosophy and charity. As he once said, "Those who care about charity must care about communication, and to communicate requires sys- tematic thought."[80] At the core of Grant's *via negativa*, then, is the need to comprehend technology, because to know technology is to know ourselves. But to know ourselves requires knowledge of the tension that abides within the Western theological tradition. Grant defines this tension as the conse- quence of the two distinct theological languages that have dominated Western civilisation: the "theology of glory," as presented in rationalist in- terpretations of biblical revelation, and the "theology of the Cross," which holds that the divine is not ultimately scrutable to reason.[81]

The scattered nature of Grant's writings, as Harris Athanasiadis ob- serves, makes it easy to miss the centrality of theology in his thinking. Nonetheless, certain aspects of the theological tradition served to orient and even structure Grant's thought, particularly in his confrontation with Hegel and the modern project.[82] Grant is especially clear in his claim that certain Christian theological traditions were instrumental in shaping mo- dernity. One of his most comprehensive statements on this subject is in *Technology and Justice*:

[I]t seems true that western Christianity simplified the divine love by identifying it too closely with immanent power in the world. Both Protes- tants and Catholics became triumphalist by failing to recognise the dis- tance between the order of good and the order of necessity. So they became exclusivist and imperialist, arrogant and dynamic. They now face the results of that failure.

Modern scientists, by placing before us their seamless web of necessity and chance, which excludes the loveable, may help to reteach us the truth about the distance which separates the orders of good and neces- sity ... Christianity had prepared the soil of rationalism from which modern science came, and its discoveries showed that the Christian God was dead. That formula gets close to the truth of western history, but is nevertheless not true. The web of necessity which the modern paradigm of knowledge lays before us does not tell us that God is dead, but reminds us of what western Christianity seemed to forget in its moment of pride: how powerful is the necessity which love must cross.[83]

In short, moderns have replaced the theology of the Cross with a secular theology of glory that has taken the form of faith in historical progress.

The phrases *theology of the Cross* and the *theology of glory*, and the distinction between them, come from Martin Luther, of course, and provide a touchstone to much of Grant's thinking in both his early and late writings. Grant heard in Luther's words "The theologian of glory says that evil is good and good evil; the theologian of the Cross says the thing is as it is" a primal tension in the modern Hegelian project.[84] In an essay originally written in 1947, "Two Theological Languages," Grant sides with the theology of the Cross, criticising "rational theology" – or the theology of glory – for too easily identifying necessity with goodness. According to Joan O'Donovan, Grant regards such thinking as implicitly affirming that "good is evil and evil is good – rather than the very different affirmation that the thing is as it is."[85] Nearly forty years later, in *Technology and Justice*, Grant repeats, in almost identical wording, his objection to Western theological thinking, arguing that claiming to have knowledge of providence leads one to assert that "evil is good and good is evil, and so lose what is essential to any love of truth – namely the continual recognition that the world is as it is."[86]

Implicit in Grant's distinction regarding the two theologies is the view that there is an infinite distance between man and God. Hence, necessity and goodness are infinitely distanced from each other. This makes the modern historicist project, with its doctrine of progress, essentially a secularised form of Christianity's theology of glory. Modernity and technology attempt to collapse necessity and the good by conceiving the good as immanent within history. This modern theology of glory receives its most profound philosophical expression in Hegel's thought. To regard history as the progressive unfolding of goodness under the impetus of the "cunning of reason" is to secularise divine providence. And the bringing together of providence and progress is tantamount to the worship of force, says Grant, because, as history shows, force is the principal means of historical change.[87] For Grant, though, it is increasingly difficult to perceive a rational purpose in history, given the state of the contemporary world. What remains, he says, borrowing from Nietzsche, is the "finality of becoming."[88] This view, however, reveals the onset of a destructive nihilism that undermines even the weak transcendence of a future historical good. Modern nihilism breaks down any definable moral limit to human action. Everything, including nation-states, is open to technological manipulation. Even the tendency to worship force, implicit in the doctrine of progress, is no longer subject to any theoretical restraints. "The last men and the nihilists are everywhere in North America."[89]

The destructiveness of nihilism is the focus of much of Grant's negative theology. In bringing out the corrosive consequences of nihilism on traditional principles of thought and action, Grant seeks to reveal the darkness of modernity, a darkness that has obscured and corrupted the Christian revelation. This strategy echoes that of Blaise Pascal, whose apology for Christianity assumes that only in revealing the inadequacy of traditional Christian thought can people be open to its saving truths. Grant attempts something similar in his analysis of modernity. Embedded in his negative critique of technological society is a positive, if silent, affirmation of an alternative to nihilism and Hegelian rationalism. Grant's negative theology, his rejection of a theology of glory, both contains and embodies his metaphysical alternative, as well as his epistemological and pedagogical challenges, to modernity. Grant seeks to bring his readers to a remembrance of those animating experiences of eternity by which men once defined their purposes and meanings, and by which they once knew the limits of their acts. He seeks to remind us of the deprivals of modernity in the hope of reawakening in us a consciousness of the divine. In this regard, Grant's thought can be regarded as embodying the world of God-space, of time as eternity, over and against the modern historicist – and Hegelian – understanding that reflects the world of man-space, or time as history. In thinking through the dispossessions of modernity, Grant articulates what God is not, and in doing so, negatively demonstrates the great distance between necessity and the good.

Grant claims no originality in adopting this standard. His guide was Simone Weil, who best articulated the experiential ground of his negative theology. Her thought was "the great teaching concerning the eternal in this era." She showed him "what it is to hold Christ and Plato together."[90] Which is to say, Weil offered Grant a way to hold classical philosophy and biblical revelation together as a unity. It is beyond the scope of this essay to offer a comprehensive discussion of Weil's influence on Grant.[91] Nevertheless, it is worth noting some parallels between Grant and Weil, particularly those that offer some insight into his turn from Hegel.

Perhaps the most striking parallel between Weil and Grant is their respective conversionary experiences. In 1942, after contracting tuberculosis, twenty-four-year-old George Grant "deserted" from the Merchant Marine and went into the English countryside to work on a farm. One day, he relates, "I went to work at five o'clock in the morning on a bicycle. I got off the bicycle to open a gate and when I got back on I accepted God."[92] With that sentence, describing a simple act of getting off and on a bicycle, an action that took at most a few seconds, Grant provides his only public account of an experience that saints and mystics recount as the height of human experience. For one brief moment, Grant was graced with the knowledge that beyond time and space, beyond the temporal realm, there is eternal order. It was an experience that he acknowledges as the most important in his life, and the truth of which he never doubted. Perhaps it was this experience that enables Grant to accept Weil's experience of Christ: "When she says Christ visited her, came down to her, I have to believe her. I have to know that it did happen."[93]

Grant offers only the most general statement on what his own experience meant to him personally: "If I try to put it into words, I would say it is the recognition that I am not my own."[94] He was more forthcoming about what the experience meant philosophically and politically, saying that it provided him with the experiential ground for his rejection of the modern project and, arguably, of Hegel. As he put it, "[I]f modern liberalism is the affirmation that our essence is our freedom, then this experience was the denial of that definition, before the fact that we are not our own."[95] Indeed, for Grant, the modern notion of individualism is deeply flawed because it diminishes or even denies the sovereignty of the divine, resulting in a distorted understanding of reality.

Grant apparently first encountered Weil's writings in 1950. In the late 1950s, his reading of Leo Strauss would provide him with much of the theoretical structure for an understanding of his dissatisfaction with modernity, but it was his earlier encounter with Weil that confirmed his experiential insight and, arguably, made him more amenable to Strauss's critique of Hegel and the modern project. What Grant learned from Weil can be boiled down to a single core idea – the idea of a limit to human freedom, individuality, and willing. Grant encapsulates this idea in *Philosophy in the Mass Age* in asking, "Is there anything that we should never do under any circumstances to another human being?"[96]

Following Weil, Grant accepts the idea of "limit" as the idea of God, and with it the notion that there are things that humans are not free to will and cannot know, especially the essential inscrutability of providence. To suggest that there is a limit to or a restraint on human freedom is, of course, to assert a distinctly anti-modern understanding of human being. Modernity posits freedom as its most essential principle and denies limits to human willing. In receiving this idea of limit from Weil, Grant discovered how he could step outside the Hegelian circle. This makes Grant's conversionary experience essential to understanding his rejection of Hegel. Weil confirmed his experience in showing him the infinite distance between man's will and God: on his own, man cannot ascend to God; God must take up man to Himself in the act of grace.[97]

This points up another parallel between Weil and Grant. If necessity is distinctly other than good, then it is devoid of existential purpose and meaning without the good. And this in turn means that to see God as intervening in the realm of necessity for some particular end is to identify God and eternity with time and history and, in the modern context, to link progress and providence. Weil and Grant reject interpretations of divine providence that would identify necessity and goodness. "I must ... reject these Western interpretations of providence," says Grant. "Belief is blasphemy if it rests on any easy identification of necessity and good ... It must be possible within the doctrine of providence to distinguish between the necessity of certain happenings and their goodness."[98] Likewise, Weil says, "the ridiculous conception of Providence as being a personal and particular intervention on the part of God for certain particular ends is incompatible with true faith."[99] For Grant and Weil, then, God is not in history. In creating the world, God has, as Weil puts it, "withdrawn Himself, permitting a part of Being to be other than God."[100]

How, then, is one to link Being and being, eternity and time? How does one experience the perfect in the realm of the imperfect? For Weil and, following her, Grant, one way is through loving contemplation of the beauty of the world. Since the world is the result of a "divine renunciation"[101] in which God set limits and, thereby, created necessity, then what connects eternity and time is the act of love and the beauty that was the product of that act of love. Love and beauty are mediations and remembrances that unite the realm of necessity and the realm of the good without in any way mixing them. To be sensible to the beauty of the realm of necessity, to love what is as it is, is to partake in some measure of the good.[102]

But if Weil's vision of the good helped Grant comprehend the inadequacies of modernity, it also enabled him to come to grips with the concept of the theology of the Cross in a way "that brought Plato and Christ, philosophy and faith, together."[103] Which is to say, Weil helped Grant to ground his philosophy in theology rather than in Hegelian historicism. This emerges most explicitly in Grant's comparison of the theology of the Cross with the theology of glory. As noted above, the importance of these two concepts to Grant's thinking about modernity is evident in his essay "Two Theological Languages." Theology, Grant argues, is born of the encounter between time and eternity. As such, theology is an attempt to work out in a particular time and place the truths of eternity. To do this intelligibly, theology must consider the distinction between the language of rational theology and biblical theology. According to Grant, Plato and Aristotle engaged in rational theology, with reason and desire being central concepts. Our truest desire is that to which we are turned by our natures; reason gives us the idea of human fulfilment in the concept of the good, although reason can become a slave to the passions. Human freedom, according to rational theology, refers to the acceptance of human limitation in the recognition of reality as it is; that is, the height of human reason is attunement to the natural order. As Grant puts it, "Freedom is recognition, affirmation and acceptance of necessity."[104]

Indeed, Grant argues that the language of biblical theology is expressed in ethical terms – guilt, sin, responsibility, remorse, disobedience, and rebellion – and points to the idea of the individual's responsibility for his conduct within the order of reality. In this language, *freedom* does not refer to the capacity of reason to discern the truth, but to something given to humans regardless of their capacity for reason. Biblical theology posits that freedom is given apart from reason and, that being so, has nothing to do with the intelligible recognition and acceptance of necessity. Rather, biblical freedom is unknowable or, in Grant's words, "the unfathomable and irrational – an abyss into which our reasons are swallowed up."[105] This distinction has significant implications, both philosophical and political, for Grant. As Sheila Grant observes, Grant's attempt to grapple with the seemingly irreconcilable tensions between rational and biblical theology marked "the beginning of his distrust of rational philosophies of history"[106] – in other words, of Hegelian philosophy. In rational theology, freedom or self-perfection is attained through our own efforts, our own intellectual ability. In the language of biblical theology, freedom is experienced, if at all, as a fathomless mystery, dependent upon what is unexplainable or even irrational. Certainly, Grant criticises the language of biblical theology for its rejection of reason, objecting to the idea of an experiential faith that does not attempt to give a rational account of itself. At the same time, though, he says that only biblical theology is able to demonstrate the mystery of man's primary freedom of responsibility or charity. Only biblical theology comprehends why, even without reason, humans act with moral regard toward one another or why, if they do not, against any rational argument they feel guilt and remorse.

Grant's dilemma, then, entails attempting to speak or reconcile the two languages into an authentic theology. How can he reconcile his intellect's need for rational comprehension with his experiential awareness of the primary freedom of morality? Each theological language has its particular weaknesses. Rational theology tends to "disregard the problem of evil or trivialize it,"[107] Grant says. It is best to refer to mysteries when confronting evil simply because the problem is not one about which anything intelligibly

comprehensive can be said. Rational theology demonstrates a kind of pur-
blind shallowness in its inability to grasp the more confounding elements of
existence. Rational theology cannot answer the ultimate metaphysical questions of why anything exists rather than nothing, why a being of infinite
goodness allows evil, why a being of infinite mind would create finite mind.
Rational theology, in other words, posits a connection between the finite
and the infinite but is unable to account for that connection. By contrast,
biblical theology posits a mysterious distance between man and God, an infinite gap between necessity and goodness. Grant says that this disconnection
underscores the fundamental mystery of human responsibility and morality
and, as such, requires a necessary agnosticism in our attempts to understand
evil. Without that agnosticism, he says, without an acknowledgment of the
distance between necessity and the good, we are in danger in our confrontations with evil of asserting that "good is evil and evil is good – rather than the
very different that the thing is as it is."[108] While biblical theology may lean
toward irrationalism, rational theology tends to sidestep the reality of evil.

Like Hegel (and, it should be noted, like Watson), Grant wants to reconcile the two languages – reason and revelation. Such reconciliation would
not only respond to the deepest problems of reason, but would confront the
dilemmas of contemporary technological society. It would also reconcile
the individual and the community in the most profound sense of satisfying
the desire for freedom while, at the same time, assuaging the need to belong to something that transcends the limitations of the self. Yet, nearly four
decades after writing "Two Theological Languages," Grant was no closer to
his goal. The languages of reason and revelation remained far apart for
him, as a 1988 addendum to the essay makes clear. Grant writes that the
central task of thought still requires an awareness of the "tension between
what comes to us from Athens and what from Jerusalem," or, as he prefers,
"what comes to us from Socrates and from Christ."[109] In this regard, "Two
Theological Languages" has to be viewed as one of Grant's most essential
writings when it comes to understanding his turn from Hegel.

Indeed, Sheila Grant suggests that Grant's first serious confrontation
with Hegelian thought is implied in the reference he makes in the original
1947 essay to Martin Luther's twenty-first thesis of the Heidelberg disputation and the distinction between the theology of the Cross and the theology of glory.[110] And Grant's notebooks from the mid- to late 1950s also
demonstrate his preoccupation with and ambivalence toward Hegel. Notebook 4, in particular, contains numerous references either to Hegel himself or to Hegelian scholars, including Alexandre Kojève, Jean Hyppolite,
Walter Kaufman, and Herbert Marcuse. The notes allude to Grant's concern

about the relationship, if any, between Hegel's cunning of reason and the mystery of biblical theology. At one point, Grant says that Hegel "could grasp the mystical world, but he did not grasp it anymore than negative theology had been able to do."[111] Elsewhere in the notebook, Grant discusses the relationship of reason and the problem of evil, saying, "Hegel is simply brilliant on good and evil (and) freedom and reason in the old metaphysics."[112] However, perhaps Grant's ultimate statement on the relationship of reason and the question of evil is one in which he refers to his colleague from Dalhousie University, the Hegelian scholar James Doull: "Though I would agree with James that Hegel is right to say that the philosopher is only concerned with reconciliation in thought, he must, – *qua* philosopher – take into his thought, and not forget, that he is not in truth reconciled."[113]

At the time he was making these notes, Grant was apparently working on a book on acceptance and evil. In a section discussing Isaiah Berlin's remarks about the dangers of philosophies of history, he writes, in an obvious reference to Hegel, that philosophies of history "prevent those who believe them from seeing the facts as they have been." The result is "a blurring of the evident facts of cruelty, pain and oppression" until, gradually, good and evil actions are no longer seen distinctly for what they are, but "both must be interpreted as leading to some good." In this way, Grant concludes, "evil is gradually turned into good."[114] He also challenges himself never to accept such a philosophy of history, writing in Notebook 4, "The great question is history and you, G.P.G., have been continually right to refuse to interpret history in rational terms as so many do – see this and don't give it up."[115] Twenty-five years later, Grant reiterated the concerns of his younger self: "What was always the thorn which kept me from accepting Hegel was those remarks in the philosophy of history, about wars being the winds which stir up the stagnant pools. That is the idea that good can come out of bad in a way that we can understand."[116]

In other words, by Grant's view, Hegelian philosophy – and the modern project – expresses a theology of glory – or rational theology – that trivialises evil and makes God identical to the aims and purposes of human history. Hegel asserts rational theology's claim to make providence scrutable, to know the mind of God. Hegel posits an immanent eschatology in which Spirit is made concrete in time, the result of which is history's actualisation of Spirit as freedom. Hegel's philosophy attempts to unify freedom, necessity, and the good "through progressive reflection on the rational 'wholes' of history."[117] For Grant, though, such a philosophy amounts to the secularisation of the Christian idea of history as the working out of the providential process of salvation that leads to the Kingdom of God, resulting in the immanent idea of history as progress in which man creates his own utopian kingdom on Earth. Grant rejects this recasting of the Christian doctrine of providence, seeing it as tantamount to identifying not only freedom with necessity, but also good with evil. It is worth quoting Grant at length on this point because doing so reveals how he sees the seeds of modernity embedded in Christianity:

It may appear that the spirit of the modern world is the very antithesis of the religious, rooted as it is in the idea of progress rather than the idea of law, and emphasizing man's trust in his own ability to make the world rather than his trust in God. But what must be insisted is that the very spirit of progress takes its form and depends for its origin on the Judeo-Christian idea of history … [In] its moral connotations there is nothing more important to its understanding than to recognize how the Christian idea of history as the divinely ordained process of salvation, culminating in the Kingdom of God, passes over into the idea of history as progress, culminating in the Kingdom of Man; how Christianity's orienting of time to a future made by the will of God becomes the futuristic spirit of progress in which events are shaped by the will of man.[118]

Grant recognises, of course, that the Reformation idea of freedom exemplified by Luther offers a concept for mediating between providential and progressivist histories. But he points out that this idea is central to Hegel's thought in that it was the German philosopher who most comprehensively understood how the modern experience of freedom emerged first in the Reformation's religious thinking. This is a subtle point and needs elaboration because it highlights Grant's understanding of the "mistake" of Christianity that is so central to his turn from Hegel.

13

The "Mistake" of Christianity

Reformation thinkers such as Martin Luther maintain that we cannot ultimately know either ourselves or God even though our essential desire is to
have such knowledge. We cannot accept our own mortality – our fallen-
ness, as it were – and instead seek to save ourselves through our thoughts
and actions rather than surrender to the reality of our finitude and embeddedness in this world. So we create God according to our subjective image
and assume our will is His. Or, to put it differently, we mistake historical
freedom for biblical freedom. For Luther, though, and Grant following
him, we cannot know God through our finite images or rituals, and to
attempt to do so is to proclaim a theology of glory.[119] As Grant writes in
Philosophy in the Mass Age, appropriating Luther, "no man should find his
proper rest in any natural images."[120]

According to Grant, this theology of glory was reflected in the thought of
the pre-Reformation scholastics. The theology that emerged from St Thomas
Aquinas's synthesis of Aristotelian natural law and the Christian conception of the God of history is of a moral God who punishes sinners and
rewards the faithful. This theology asserts that, given his capacity for reason, man possesses the ability to better himself. Man can move in some
measure toward the good and earn God's grace. Human will and human
reason have a role in human salvation. But if man is capable of some
movement toward the good through his own efforts, then, presumably,
God's will can be manifested in the finite images created by man's
thoughts and actions in the world. God's will and man's will can to some
extent be reconciled in the perfecting of individual and collective life in
history.[121] But to link God's will and man's will in this fashion is, says
Grant, to obscure the distance between necessity and goodness. It is to assert that knowledge of providence is within human possibility. And that,

in Grant's view, is a fundamental attribute of Hegel's philosophy of history and the reason it amounts to a theology of glory.

But if Hegel recognises that the modern idea of freedom arose first with Luther in the Reformation, how was Luther's theology of the Cross, and its insistence on the inscrutability of God's will, transformed into a theology of glory? Grant answers this way: the Reformation's denial of reason's capacity to know God, its rejection of mediating finite images of thought and ritual, opened up the idea of infinite freedom by arguing that there need be no mediation between the individual and God. Luther's rejection of "finite images" standing between man and God is, dialectically, an assertion of unlimited freedom. As Grant writes in *Philosophy in the Mass Age*, Luther's theology of the Cross "is more than simply protest, because it asserts that the principle of freedom must be regulative of any future theory of practice. It is more than negative in that the idea of freedom is the affirmation that the human spirit cannot be limited by any determinations."[122] While the Reformers may have initially intended only to assert freedom within the religious sphere, such an idea could not be confined to that sphere. Indeed, according to Grant, Luther's theology of the Cross was transformed into the secular theology of glory that we refer to as technology.[123] Luther's Protestantism, in its rejection of Aristotelian scholasticism, ultimately "led too many Protestants to a false denigration of reason."[124]

Adopting Martin Luther's terms, Grant describes Hegelian philosophy and its doctrine of progress as a theology of glory that exalts human will and makes the realm of necessity, or history, and not the good, or eternity (or nature), the arena for man's redemption. A theology of glory regards historical events as manifestations of divine will, setting up the idea that such events are unique and irreversible because their meaning is derived from God's will. This, in turn, tends to exalt human will and implies that action must be future-directed in that humans have their fulfilment not in the present but in the future.[125] In Grant's view, this conflation of necessity and goodness received its fullest expression in Hegel's notion of world history as the unfolding of reason: "*Die Weltgeschichte ist das Weltgericht*," or "World History is the world's judgement."[126] Such a notion is anathema to Grant: "Hegel makes God's providence scrutable, and that is a teaching which offended me then and now at the deepest level."[127] Hegel, in other words, identifies progress and providence. And that, in Grant's view, is to call evil good and good evil. Thus, Hegelian historicism casts the future as necessarily better than the past, effectively justifying suffering as necessary for the sake of progress.[128]

What this also suggests to Grant is that biblical religion has a causal connection to the emergence of modern historical progressivist consciousness.

He traces the historicist mindset to the Jewish prophetic religion of the Old Testament in which events in time were regarded as manifestations of God's will, pointing to some final redemptive act of God to which all events in time were leading, such that to participate in these events was to partake of God's overarching purpose.[129] "It was the Jews who discovered the very idea of history. More than anything else, what has made Western culture so dynamic is its impregnation with the Judaeo-Christian idea that history is the divinely ordained process of man's salvation."[130] The culmination of this vision of time was the Incarnation, the singular event that, for Christians, made history, or time, the realm in which man's eternal salvation was worked out, the realm in which good ultimately overcomes evil.

Grant regards this Christian teleology as biblical theology's most radical departure from the ancient religion of natural law – and the most difficult obstacle in any attempt to reconcile Greek rational theology and Christian biblical theology. The medieval synthesis of the two theologies culminated in Thomism, but that was breaking down by the fifteenth century. Besides, the medieval attempt to reconcile these two traditions and unify them around the doctrine of the Trinity was, according to Grant, never a successful synthesis. Against this background, the Reformation marked the revitalisation of the biblical religion of history, albeit with a corollary diminishment of the natural law tradition of Greek philosophy. And the last half-millennium has seen Christianity's salvational history succumb to the secular religion of progress, in which man's salvation is worked out in time by means of modern science or technology. As Grant concludes, "[T]he moment of technical mastery comes out of the same science which gives us the historical sense."[131]

Thus, Grant links Luther's theology of the Cross with the secularised theology of glory manifested in the external freedom of contemporary technological society. The Enlightenment thinkers turned the spiritual freedom sought in Reformation theology into worldly freedom. In Hegel's words, "This is the essence of the Reformation: Man is in his very nature destined to be free."[132] Luther posited an inner freedom that rejected the ostensibly oppressive mediations of Catholicism's finite images in defining the individual's relationship to God. But, according to Grant, in doing so Luther effectively undermined the moral and spiritual foundations of the medieval institutions that had traditionally mediated time and eternity.[133] Obviously, Luther did not intend to destroy the institutional supports for man's spiritual life. Yet, as Grant acknowledges, the conscious intentions behind our actions often acquire a historical meaning much different from that conceived at the time of the event: "To accept the difference between intended action and the meaning of events is to have insisted that historical explanation only completes itself within philosophy."[134] So, in the modern world, the *meaning* of Luther's actions is a vision of freedom utterly detached from the divine, a worldly freedom that aims at the complete satisfaction of subjective desire, a freedom that, paradoxically, requires greater control and manipulation of nature, including human nature.[135]

Grant's appropriation of Hegel's philosophy of history is readily evident in these arguments. But so, too, is his discomfort with that philosophy. While Grant follows Hegel's understanding of the Reformation and the subjectivisation of the idea of freedom in the Enlightenment, he is uncertain about the consequences of this dialectic of freedom. He voices this uncertainty in a key passage in *Philosophy in the Mass Age*: "The question thoughtful people must ask themselves is whether the progressive spirit is going to hold within itself any conception of spiritual law and freedom; or whether our history-making spirit will degenerate into a rudderless desire for domination on the part of our elites, and aimless pleasure seeking among the masses. Can the achievements of the age of progress be placed at the service of a human freedom that finds itself completed and not denied by a spiritual order?"[136] Simone Weil may have taught Grant the idea of limit, but she also informed his question. Grant is asking whether moderns, in their claim to freedom, have forgotten eternity. Do we any longer acknowledge the necessity of limits in our history-making and nature-dominating actions? Is there anything that we must never do under any circumstances?

Grant responds to such questions in *Philosophy in the Mass Age* and *Time As History* by comparing the consciousness of modern society with that of the ancient world. His purpose is to highlight the unquestioned assumptions of modernity. Drawing on Mircea Eliade, Grant describes how, in pre-modern consciousness, events in time have significance only insofar as man is a participant in an overarching and unchanging cosmos. Temporal events reflect the eternal order. Human meaning and purpose are not to be found in the making of history, but rather in the capacity of humans to comprehend and thereby participate in divinely given archetypal patterns. Even justice is grounded in a perception of divine order, and laws were mirrors of eternal law, a conception of transcendent order that informs the Western natural law tradition. And individuals are free to the degree that they are able to use their faculty of reason to comprehend and thereby participate in the order of the cosmos and the natural limits it imposes.[137] Grant finds this mythological consciousness reflected in Plato, who perceived time "as the moving image of eternity" and passing events as meaningful only "as they lead men to the unchanging reality of God."[138]

Modern historical consciousness conceives a different understanding of freedom, a freedom based on its rejection of the ancient cosmology. Where the ancients believed that man achieved his greatest fulfilment through a reasoned comprehension of and obedience to the cosmic order, moderns regard freedom as a reflection of their ability to impose their will on a world devoid of any intrinsic meaning or teleological purpose. This modern understanding of freedom is sustained and promoted by a consciousness that sees "time as a series of unique and irreversible events. Human freedom depends on man's ability to shape events according to his subjective desires. Historical consciousness requires us to regard the world as the arena of "limitless possibilities of men for action in space and time."[139] Where ancient man saw himself as a participant in the cosmos and at home in the world despite its sufferings, modern man sees himself as an alien who must master the world and remake it as a home. As Robert Meynell succinctly states, in the pre-modern world "the cosmos moved us; we did not move the cosmos."[140]

Grant is clearly disturbed at the thought that Judaism and Christianity are at least partly responsible for shattering the ancient mythic consciousness and giving birth to modern alienated consciousness.[141] That concern is reflected in his turn from Hegel and modern philosophy. Hegel, in his notion of the cunning of reason, attempts to reconcile the divergent ideas of man as the maker of history and as the perceiver of an order to which he is subject. Grant's rejection of Hegel amounts to a rejection of the concept of *Aufhebung* – or preservation and transcendence – at the centre of the Hegelian system. With this rejection, Grant detaches himself from the dominant Hegelian tradition in Canadian thought, particularly that of John Watson, whose appropriation of Hegel's thought reconciled Christian morality, liberal progressivism, and imperialism.[142]

Despite this rejection, Grant still accepts the Hegelian argument that "time as history" emerged out of Judaism's incorporation into early Christianity. Theologians from Augustine to Thomas Aquinas continually attempted to synthesise biblical theology and Greek transcendent rationality, combining Judaism's notions of a personal god who intervenes in human events with the Greek notion of a timeless god to produce the god of project and reform. As Grant puts it, "The idea of human freedom merges with Judaeo-Christian hope and produces the idea of progress. For a humanism arising in a Christian setting was bound to be quite different from one which had arisen from the archaic religious cultures ... It was a humanism that put science and technology at its centre, as the means of redemption."[143] The Incarnation made historical events absolutely important, lending weight to the sense that history can be the arena for man's redemption and salvation. However, to think this is to believe that time is not "the moving image of eternity," but rather the realm in which good overcomes evil.

From this perspective, particular events can be interpreted as manifestations of divine will, which sets up the idea that each event is unique and irreversible because its meaning is derived from divine will. This, in turn, tends to exalt human will because it makes human consciousness the sensorium in and through which God's will is manifested. And this implies that human action must be future-directed in that actions have their fulfilment not in the present but in the future. Hence comes the notion of historical progress and, arguably, ideas about human development and perfection. As Grant writes in *Time As History*, "[T]ime was raised up by redemption in time, and the future by the exaltation of the *eschaton*."[144] And this, Grant writes in his essay "Faith and the Multiversity," was the essential mistake of Western Christianity: it "simplified divine love by identifying it too closely with immanent power in the world."[145] Which is to say, Christianity in the West became triumphalist because the historicist consciousness that informed and sustained it denied the infinite distance between necessity and good. The Reformation contained the seeds of its own demise because the idea of infinite freedom opened the door for unending criticism of religious traditions and an immanentisation of redemption and salvation. The Enlightenment's scientific-rationalist critique of Christian traditions undermined the doctrines of natural law and divine providence, replacing those traditions with immanent secularised versions. In short, the modern project transformed natural law and providence into rights and a faith in progress, Christianity became liberalism, and liberalism becomes imperialistic.[146] In other words, says Grant, the mistakes of early Christian leaders produced a "procrustean triumphalist Christianity" that led Western Christianity "to go out into the world, thinking it could do anything to other civilizations, and which was even more terrible when ... it had become secularized Christianity."[147] No wonder Grant regards Augustine as a key source for the "great errors"[148] that produced triumphalist Christianity and its secularisation in technological society.

Grant came to this conclusion, at least in part, through his reading of Philip Sherrard's 1959 book *The Greek East and the Latin West*. The book was important to Grant because he thought it took him to the root of the modern West and helped him account for the character of modernity and how it had come to be.[149] Essentially, Sherrard attempts to explain the "rationalising spirit [that] led to the break-up of the medieval Christian ethos and the formation of modern Western society and culture."[150] He traces this phenomenon to the schism between Eastern and Western Christianity caused by the conflict over the doctrinal addition to the Creed of the *Filioque* clause on the nature of God, which received papal approval in 1014. Sherrard argues that behind this conflict was a clash in metaphysical views traceable to the difference between the thought of Plato and Aristotle.

According to Sherrard, Aristotle's thought amounts to an exteriorisation and rationalisation of Plato's thinking. Plato's metaphysics conceives of the whole in dualistic terms; that is, form and matter stand in contrast to each other, although not absolutely. In the Platonic view, sensible existence results from the interdependence and interaction of form and formless matter. While these two principles may appear to be opposed, they are not, for two reasons. First, "form" – Plato's demiurge – is not the overarching reality; it is a determination of that reality, the good, which transcends all formal characteristics. And, second, "formless matter" is not the substance out of which things are made; it is something that precedes the sensible thing that comes to be because it participates in the undetermined reality from which form itself emerges. Thus, both form and matter possess a meaningfulness that does not depend on their relationship to each other, or on whether one is subordinate to the other. Each has its value because each has its origins "in that supreme reality in which their apparent opposition or duality is transcended and absorbed."[151] Plato's "Ideas" are not merely transcendent or Ideal in relation to the world of sensible objects that they determine; they are immanent within those objects. Life is linked to the divine source of its creation because of its intelligible nature, which participates in that which transcends it.[152] As Sherrard puts it, "The creature possesses its own intelligible nature through actual participation in the creative cause which brought it into being."[153]

Aristotle exteriorises Plato's metaphysics by denying the objective reality of this divine source and asserting a sharp distinction between form and matter. Where Plato maintains a relative dualism between form and matter, Aristotle's exteriorisation asserts an absolute dualism. "In effect, Aristotle was unable to visualize the existence of such forms apart from their sensible objects. This, in its turn, had its counterpart in his inability to visualize a creative principle, not merely of sensible objects, but of their creative forms themselves." This means, says Sherrard, that there is "no direct relationship" between Aristotle's supreme principle, the First Mover, and the forms that exist as material objects in the sensible world. Nor do these sensible objects participate in some transcendent principle, even though they may long to do so. Thus, matter must be regarded as utterly disconnected from any divine source. In Sherrard's words, "[T]here is an absolute, and not merely relative, dualism between form and formless matter."[154] In other words, for Aristotle, the sensible world is the only intelligible world.

This difference between the thinking of Plato and Aristotle has profound implications. Plato asserts that man's highest purpose is contemplating and participating in the transcendent realities of the cosmos. This is possible through philosophy, conceived of as "an initiatory process likened by Plato to a kind of dying and spiritual rebirth"[155] that surpasses all individual and natural limitations. This philosophic experience brings with it an awareness of a transcendent order in which man may participate. Man's awareness of this order demonstrates that he possesses faculties that allow him to participate in a transcendent reality. One faculty is reason, which achieves its knowledge through observing the sensible world, while the other is "divine intellect," which can gain knowledge of transcendent reality through initiation and illumination.[156]

Aristotle, however, denies the existence of any knowable objective reality apart from the world of sensible objects. This means that it is impossible to experience something that is *beyond* this world because there is no supernatural reality to be intuited. There is no beyond to the material world, nothing transcending human consciousness. To assert this, though, is to make the mind of man the highest order and the life of reason his highest purpose. Moreover, this strictly worldly purpose is conceived within a worldview that sees the external world in terms of an absolute dualism between the rational and the irrational, mind and matter. In such a worldview, the method of reasoning shifts to a deductive and analytic practice and away from the Platonic method of the inductive and intuitive.[157]

Sherrard goes on to argue that this Aristotelian mode of thought was taken over by the Romans, who employed it to master nature and organise their society to satisfy human purposes. "Rome was to succeed, where Greece had failed, in extending the rational order over the whole imperial world."[158] And it was this Roman mind that informed the Christian church. The early church fathers were influenced by the mystical and contemplative tradition of Plato, but when Christianity became the official religion of the empire it forced the exteriorisation of the faith, turning Christianity into an imperial religion.[159] The church had to involve itself in the running of the world, and as the Platonic mode of thought was ill-suited to secular affairs, the church turned to those modes of thought better able to assert power and control. In the first place, since the true end of man could only be achieved in and through the church, everybody within the imperial state had to be made Christian. It was easier to accomplish this by taking the "exterior" approach of Mosaic law and Aristotelian empiricism than by taking the "interior" or metaphysical approach of Christ's revelation.[160]

Sherrard describes how these different modes of thought played out in the *Filioque* schism over the doctrine of God, and how this schism shaped the future of the West. Influenced by Plato, the Greek East maintained the transcendence of God, or the good, in a way that the Latin West, influenced by Aristotle, did not. Essentially – and this is the essence of what Grant took from Sherrard – the Eastern church remained closer to the Gospels, or biblical theology, and Platonic contemplative philosophy by claiming that both the Son and the Holy Spirit proceeded from the Father alone. For the Eastern church, the Christian revelation demonstrated that the essence of God was ultimately unknowable in that it transcended all human knowledge and experience. God's existence or being could only be known to humans through the mediation of the Trinity. This mediation sustained God's unknowability and thereby kept the divine from the claims of human reason without denying that God was immanent in the world and the ground of being. God was both immanent (the Trinity) and transcendent (the unknowable essence). Man could be opened to the divine through experience of the beauty of the world and the deification of Christ, but there remained a final mystery beyond man's rationalisations.[161]

The Western church, on the other hand, sought to overcome the paradox of God's immanence-transcendence by blurring the distinction between God's essence and being, and it did this by identifying God with being itself. "What Western theologians tended increasingly to stress," says Sherrard, "was the idea of the *Summum Ens*, of the absolute One in whom no distinctions of any kind may be admitted."[162] This identification of God with being meant that while the theologians of the Latin West could still speak of God's unknowability, the substance of that claim had become more shallow. The insertion of the *Filioque* clause – the claim that the Spirit proceeds from the Father *and* the Son – "was a further attempt to circumscribe the mystery in and transcendence of God."[163] God, in short, was rationalised a little more, made more subject to man's subjective purposes. This doctrinal development, as Athanasiadis remarks, when combined with an Aristotelian denial of transcendental ideas and an emphasis on human reason, encouraged a kind of speculative rationality that promoted the theology of glory of the West over and above the negative and more Platonic theological tradition of the East.[164] This not only had consequences for the development of the Catholic Church, encouraging a greater concern for worldly influence, Sherrard argues, but also contributed to the spread of a rational spirit in the West that links thinkers such as Augustine and Aquinas to Descartes and Hegel.[165]

Sherrard also finds a link between the Latin West's emphasis on rationality and will in the shaping of historical events, particularly after the rediscovery of Aristotle's thought in the twelfth century, and the subsequent emergence of modern science and technology.[166] While the *Filioque* clause was consistent with Augustine's thought, it encouraged later theologians, particularly Aquinas, to claim greater powers for reason in man's attempt to know God's will. Luther and Calvin might have rejected the mediations and impositions of Catholicism, but they, too, accepted the proposition of God's intelligibility and the idea that nature is subject to human will. Francis Bacon and René Descartes took the rationalising spirit even further, although in doing so they effectively reduced reason to being an instrument by which man shapes the world to suit his desires. No longer is reason the means by which man participates in the divine order and perceives the good of the whole. Thus, between the rationalising spirit of Western theology and the influence of a world-focused Aristotelian thought, Western Christianity was provided with an increasingly powerful method of rationally knowing and shaping the world to suit man's will.[167]

Sherrard's influence on Grant should be readily apparent. This Western assertion of the supremacy of human reason and the distinction between Platonic and Aristotelian modes of thought clearly informed Grant's understanding of Hegelian philosophy, providing him with a deeper comprehension of the tangled sources of the modern technological project. What was at stake for Grant in the *Filioque* controversy was "nothing less than the nature of God and the question of how far reason could go in understanding the divine."[168] Sherrard's arguments about Eastern Christianity's notion of an unknowable God were, for Grant, closer to a theology of the Cross that sees God's absence in the world as safely beyond human reason.[169] Understanding this enabled him to perceive the mistake of Christianity to be its complicity in producing modernity's theology of glory.

Nowhere, Grant argues in *Philosophy in the Mass Age*, has the theology of glory manifested itself more vigorously than in the progressivist liberal societies of North America. It is because North Americans have no history before the age of progress that the modern project holds dominion over them. Yet, Grant also links this faith in progress to Protestant Christianity, arguing that there is something within Protestant theology that provided the seedbed for technological society. Thus, Grant detects a deep paradox in modernity as it is experienced in North America: Protestant theology fostered the modern secular spirit not because it reflected more of a biblical theology than Catholicism did, but because it was less reliant on rational theology. So the question becomes, What is the connection between Protestantism – or North American morality, as Grant puts it – and an age of progress that seems bent of producing an aimless, hedonistic society? And how is it that the age of progress continues to hold within it particular notions of Christian morality, notably charity and equality, that seem to clash with the triumphalism of its rationalist, history-making spirit? Answering such questions entails a closer look at Grant's thinking about North American society.

14

The "Fate" of North America

According to Grant, North American mass society epitomises modernity's history-making consciousness. Lacking any history prior to the age of progress, North America incarnates more than any other society the values and principles of progressivism, including a largely unquestioned subscription to mass production and its techniques, standardised consumption and education, and hedonistic entertainment. This makes North America "the most complete political incarnation of the modern consciousness of freedom ... the true heir of the Reformation spirit."[170]

Grant identifies two basic characteristics of North America's mass society. First, a scientific-technological epistemology and the attempt to apply that theory of knowledge to the domination of nature, including human nature. Second, the use by an economic and political elite of various institutions and structures to extend this control such that even the elite is subjected to technology's dominion. Under the sway of modern epistemology even reason comes to be an instrument to satisfy subjective purposes. Man's innate capacity for reason becomes part of the apparatus for enclosing him in an ever-tightening circle.[171] In an argument demonstrating his turn away from the liberal progressivist optimism of his forefathers, Grant asserts that it is an illusion of liberalism to think that individuals have any substantive freedom under the sway of technological dominance. Genuine freedom – the inner freedom originally espoused by Protestantism – is compromised and subject to the imperatives of mass society. "Every instrument of mass culture is a pressure alienating the individual from himself as a free being."[172] Nowhere, Grant argues, does this technological encirclement hold greater sway than in the United States, making that country the centre of the modern project. The United States is inherently imperialistic because it is technological in the deepest ontological sense, Grant says.

This imperialist intention does not necessarily express itself through colonies and territorial conquest; rather, it reveals itself through the imperatives of a technological society that gives priority to market forces, techniques of efficiency and mass culture, and, nowadays, continental security.

How does Grant see this technological imperialism reflected in the necessity of Canada's disappearance, and how is that disappearance related to his confrontation with Hegel? Answering this question requires a brief return to *Lament for a Nation*. To recall, *Lament* is on the surface the tale of how John Diefenbaker's Progressive Conservative government came under attack from Canada's political, corporate, and bureaucratic elite. It tells the story of how a national debate about stationing American nuclear warheads on Canadian soil turned into a conspiracy by Canada's liberal establishment and business elite to defeat Diefenbaker in the 1963 election. Grant had little admiration for Diefenbaker – before the defence crisis, as I have noted, he "saw nothing in [Diefenbaker's] favour"[173] – but he regarded his electoral defeat as evidence of the impossibility of a genuinely sovereign Canada and, by extension, as evidence of "the fate of any particularity in the technological age."[174]

Grant saw in Diefenbaker an expression of conservatism akin to his own. This conservatism should not be misconstrued. As I have previously noted, Grant was not an anti-technology Luddite.[175] Rather, Grant's conservatism required maintaining connections to the older institutional orders and social traditions inherited from Britain. So long as those connections and the traditions embedded in them held sway in Canadian society, particularly among the dominant elite, then Canada was possible. The fall of Diefenbaker's government at the hands of a liberal-minded elite revealed how tenuous these ties had become among the elite, especially in English-speaking Canada. The elite welcomed the influence of the United States, an influence that was expanding continent-wide through the growth of corporate capitalism. Expansion brought wealth, and thus it was in the interests of Canada's ruling classes to attach themselves to the forces of continentalism, which in the Canadian context "is a catch phrase that signifies the loss of identity, sovereignty and distinctness."[176] Or, as Grant puts it, "[t]he impossibility of conservatism in our era is the impossibility of Canada. As Canadians we attempted a ridiculous task in trying to build a conservative nation in the age of progress."[177]

Grant may fault the elites for their betrayals, but he recognises that the deeper sources of Canada's disappearance reside in the modern ontology. "The confused strivings of politicians, businessmen and civil servants cannot alone account for Canada's collapse. This stems from the very character of the modern era." Even if the bureaucrats and politicians had been more loyal, they could not have long withstood the imperatives of the modern project. A conservative Canada is impossible because "the aspirations of progress have made Canada redundant."[178] Grant traces Canada's redundancy to the religious faith of North America's first European settlers. Protestantism, with its reliance on biblical theology as its ground of meaning, may once have accorded with the experience of North America's pioneering communities, he argues, but in a mass society it is no longer able to claim the minds of many people.

Grant sees the Western tradition rooted in two primals: reason and love, thought and charity, or, if you will, reason and revelation. Following Weil, Grant gives primacy to "the magistery of revelation."[179] Reason, or philosophy, is the means by which love – the obedient giving away of oneself, the attention to otherness, as Grant puts it – comprehends itself. But for Grant, contemplation is always subservient to charity. He sees remnants of this hierarchy of activities in modern society with its emphasis on equality and human rights. Behind modern ethical ideals is a morality rooted in the universalism of Christian love. Grant thus posits a connection between technology – understood as the attempt to overcome chance (or nature) – intended to improve the human condition and Christian notions of love and charity. Technology is not simply oriented to freeing humans from nature, an expression of will and hubristic dominance; it is also an expression of charity. The technological enterprise, he says, "was undertaken partly in the name of that charity which was held as the height in one of those ancient systems of meaning."[180] Yet, as previously noted, Grant also links certain destructive elements of secular modernity to Christianity.

Such an understanding of the primals of modernity reflects Hegel's concepts of negation and sublation, *Negativität* and *Aufhebung*, in which something and its other engage in a dialectical process that sees something negated by its other without whatever distinguishes the two being lost. The other contains or sublates the idea of what it negates and is thereby transformed. For example, Protestantism negates Catholicism, but Protestantism is not simply non-Catholic; it contains elements of the tradition that it negated. Likewise, modern North American society reflects the sublation of elements of pre-modern traditions that it negated in coming to be what it is.

In an essay in his 1969 book *Technology and Empire,* "In Defence of North America," Grant observes that while North America's dominant society has its roots in European civilisation, it nonetheless lacks the contemplative tradition of Europe that goes back to ancient Greece and Rome. He attributes this lack to North America's primal experience of Calvinist Protestantism.

This type of Christianity tends to foster the idea that nature is subordinate to human will. Behind this attitude is a deep connection between Protestantism and empirical science. Historically, Protestantism and science have been bound together by their mutual rejection of Greek natural, or rational, theology and the medieval ascription to Aristotelian teleology. Modern science claimed that the Aristotelian tradition interferes with man's ability to see the world objectively. Protestant theology, on the other hand, taught that natural theology "led men away from fundamental reliance on Christian revelation."[181] Such a theology, Grant argues, "encouraged men to avoid the surd mystery of evil by claiming that final purpose could be argued from the world. Such mitigation led men away from the only true illumination of that mystery, the crucifixion apprehended in faith as a divine humiliation."[182] In other words, Protestantism led men away from loving contemplation of the world and encouraged them to see the world as something to be mastered according to their will.

According to Grant, the Calvinist doctrine of will served to compensate for the absence of natural theology and the liturgical comforts of Catholicism's finite images. This was particularly the case for the Puritan settlers who confronted a harsh and alien land. Left alone to face the unknowable will of God, the Puritans sought reassurance of divine favour in mastering nature and solving the practical problems of life. "This will had to be sought and served not through our contemplations but directly through our practice. From the solitude and uncertainty of that position came the responsibility which could find no rest."[183] The result was a restlessness to master the land for the sake of survival and to prove oneself worthy of God's favour. The problem, though, says Grant, was that this wilful restlessness eventually produced a society with little sense of inwardness or regard for reflection. With the waning of the Christian faith and its lingering moral restraints, what we have is a society of administrators, technicians, and consumers who try to satisfy themselves with ever more complex technological trinkets and a morality made up of banal slogans about values and progress. "All society's members, from the corporate executive to the union member, the farmer, and the university administrator, accepted mastery over nature as their common religion."[184]

Grant was much influenced in this judgment by Max Weber's *The Protestant Ethic and the Spirit of Capitalism*.[185] Weber, too, emphasised the Calvinist effort to find assurance of salvation through practical endeavour. The Puritans held that knowledge of God was ultimately hidden in mystery even though the fate of each individual was laid up in eternity. This combination of God's absolute transcendence and the sense of the individual's distance from God had the psychological consequence of encouraging individuals to regard worldly achievement as a sign of God's favour. Individual success embodied God's glory. In North America, this work in the world took the form of capitalist free enterprise. Through the self-disciplined accumulation of capital – a practice that Weber called "systematic worldly asceticism"[186] – the individual could simulate his salvation, since wealth and success were evidence of divine favour.

Grant certainly recognises the influence of Calvinist Protestantism in shaping North American society. What puzzles him is how Calvinism's worldly asceticism, its attempt to manifest the kingdom of God in earthly good works, was reduced to secularised hedonism. How did the desire to obey God's will and self-disciplined practicality descend into individualistic narcissism? Or, to ask the question in another way, how were the principles of inward freedom and individuality that came to North America with the Puritans reduced to an egocentrism that regards freedom as merely the capacity to satisfy material desires? Grant finds the answer in Protestant theology's denigration of reason and the European contemplative tradition.

In coming to North America, European settlers were confronted with a seemingly indomitable land. To survive, let alone prosper, they required intense will, an abiding pragmatism, and a strong focus on the practical. These early settlers had little time for contemplation. At the same time, North America's Puritan settlers espoused a biblical faith that posits a God who acts in history and wants men to act in such a way as to manifest His will. Where Greek thought emphasised contemplative reason, biblical thought focused on acting in the world, reworking it in conformity with what was assumed to be God's will.[187] Or, to put it differently, where Plato practised a natural theology that saw the finite as participating in the infinite, biblical theology gave greater independence to the finite in relation to the infinite. It was this later ontology that informed the practices of Calvinist Protestantism. "Protestantism, with its renewed emphasis on the simply biblical, brought into the western world a fresh interest in action through its intense desire to shape the world to God's purposes." The early Calvinist Puritan settlers felt called upon "to act so as to bring in God's kingdom on earth."[188]

Given this historical backdrop, Grant concludes that North American society is not solely a product of liberal progressivism but has one of its sources in the reformist spirit of Protestantism. Indeed, he argues that the hedonism and materialism that now dominate North American society have their roots in Protestant theology's emphasis on charity. "The idea of freedom as the ability to change the world, exists in our minds as dependent in part upon an attenuated altruism – the last remnant of the Protestant vision of the Kingdom of God on earth – and in part upon a growing self-centred hedonism."[189] But contemporary society, under the sway of technology's imperatives and cut off from the contemplative tradition and its sense of transcendence, has come to regard its ability to change the world to suit its technologically induced desires as an end in itself. The Calvinist faith in God's loving will on which North American society was founded has faded, and with it have gone the traditional restraints on human thought and action. As a society, we have transferred our loyalties from the transcendent to the immanent, transferred our faith from the promise of the beyond to a faith in technology and our ability to transform the world according to our will. Thus, Grant traces North America's fate to the primal experience of Protestant theology's denial of the classical tradition of contemplative reason. This leaves North Americans susceptible to the world-mastering tendencies of modern science and the instrumental notion of human rationality embodied in technology.

In *Philosophy in the Mass Age*, Grant points out that modern rationality is grounded in a conception of "knowing" and "making" that is radically different from that of pre-modern traditions. Modern technological society can dominate human and non-human nature in a variety of ways – through the technical manipulation of things, the rationalisation of economic activity, the bureaucratic objectification of labour, the pacification of people by means of entertainment, and the management of people through the application of behavioural techniques. Each of these modes of domination inhibits people from assessing their lives in moral terms; that is, people are unable to examine their lives in terms of a transcendent standard of the good.[190]

In evoking the Platonic concept of the good, Grant argues for "that rational reassessment of life which I call moral philosophy."[191] Modern Western society has lost this pre-modern tradition of transcendent rationality. In this tradition, reason is a way of approaching the truth of reality as a whole, not an instrument for the control and manipulation of reality according to human desires. Transcendent reason is how we discover the meaning of our lives and make that meaning our own. The world is not of human making or willing, but one with which we must harmoniously abide in order to know our proper ends.[192]

By contrast, modern rationality is a tool for the control of nature, including human nature. As far as Grant is concerned, instrumental rationality and mass technological society are both the products of and the producers of each other. This concept of instrumental rationality arose out of a paradigm of knowledge that reflects the modern experience of man as a historical being. Out of this conception of historical self-consciousness has come the belief that the world's meaningfulness, and our knowledge of that meaning, depends on man's will. But for Grant, knowing and making are in their modern form a species of willing, and it is this coming together of knowing and making, of reasoning and will, that is the fundamental characteristic of modern rationality. Modern rationality is grounded in the notion that the world is "a field of objects that can be known in their workings through the 'creative' acts of reasoning and experimenting by the thinking subject who stands over them." And such a stance, Grant argues, is "a stance of will."[193]

Grant describes this stance of will, this welding of knowing and making, as a consequence and reflection of historicism. Historical man gives meaning to the world through the wilful imposition of a worldview that is brought forth to fulfil a predetermined conception of what is good for all. But this good is defined only in terms of what man is more and more able to control; that is, modern good is defined by wilful mastery. The meaning that modern man finds in the world by mastering the world is not the same meaning that pre-modern man found through contemplation of the cosmos as it appeared to him. The modern actualisation of meaning is to set forth a world according to the self-determinations of a will to power. Meaning and purpose in the modern consciousness are dependent on the ability to control existence so that good can be created out of the manipulation of things. To know the *use* of things is to know their *value*. Thus, modern knowing, in Grant's terms, is the instrumental ordering of objects as means to ends that reside solely in our subjective and creative willing. Meaning is created through the *making* of what it is that we *know*. Modernity, then, for Grant, is a project of reason-as-will, of instrumental rationality, in which man summons nature-as-object before him and forces from it its reasons for being what it is as an object. And modern man believes, in principle at least, that everything can be or should be controlled (and, hence, known) through rational calculation.[194]

Grant contrasts this with the pre-modern natural law tradition in which nature was the paradigm within which all standards of morality and justice, good and evil, purpose and meaning, were thought and acted. There was a perceived order to the universe, and it was because this order appeared to be beyond complete human understanding that it could be used as the standard against which man could judge his knowledge and actions. Historical man has traded the external standard of nature for an internal standard of his own willed creation. Moderns no longer accept the natural definitions of reality; rather they define what is real in terms of their own will and freedom. "The belief in the mastering of knowledge of human and non-human beings arose together in the very way we conceive our humanity as an Archimedean freedom outside nature, so that we can creatively will to shape the world to our values."[195]

North American liberal society embodies this form of rationality. While liberalism promotes equality and progress and happiness for all, at its core is an epistemological ascription to the instrumental rationality of science and technology, both of which have made plain, in Grant's view, that "reason is only an instrument and cannot teach us how it is best to live."[196] Indeed, Grant argues that liberal politics has become largely instrumental in that its goal is a conception of happiness that has been shrunk to fit a consumer society. Modern liberalism, penetrated by the instrumental rationality of science and technology, reduces freedom to the satisfaction of unreflective desires. The consequence of this is the reduction of politics to the administration of desire.[197]

Grant's understanding of politics-as-administrative rule also owes a great deal to Max Weber.[198] Not only did Weber show Grant how deeply Calvinist Protestantism had influenced North American society, but Weber also helped him understand the influence of modern rationalism on liberal society. Weber sees the Western world's special peculiarity for expanding rationalisation throughout modern life in the increasing prominence of *formal* rationality over *substantive* rationality. The latter is a matter of values, of norms or ends that cannot in themselves be judged for logical consistency and efficiency. The former refers to matters of fact, to the calculation of means and procedures and rules of conduct. According to Weber, the social structures of Western society – political institutions, legal and bureaucratic administrations – are, in the main, formally rational because they hold to the concepts of objectivity and rely on formal rules and procedures for determining standards of conduct. They are also formally rational because they employ calculative techniques that emphasise efficiency and control over nature, including human nature, and require specialised knowledge of those techniques for their proper functioning.[199]

Weber argues that, with formal rationality, ends and means are conflated. The *end* in terms of which modern life is rationalised – maximum calculability and efficiency, for example – is transformed into a generalised *means* that effectively determines the substantive *ends* being pursued. Where traditional pre-modern societies once restricted the possibilities of rational means by given substantive ends – the contemplation of Plato's good or the Christian faith in God's revelation, for instance – modern societies judge their ends or purposes on the basis of the means for achieving self-chosen goals. These goals are themselves regarded as legitimate only insofar as they fit the rationalist norm of calculation and efficiency. Thus, under formal rationality, the means become the ends; and the ends become the means. The ancient standards of human conduct that had been imposed by substantive rationality are no longer legitimate under the criteria of formal rationality.

Weber sees the extremes of formal rationality reflected in the bureaucratisation of modern industrial society and the emergence of rule-bound social structures dominated by an instrumental approach to human relationships. He raises the spectre that as capitalism advances, it places an increasing emphasis on the imperatives of efficiency as the way to bring means and ends closer. The result, he predicts, would see the value and worth of social relations more and more determined by how well they fit the calculative regimen imposed by an increasingly bureaucratic and technologically oriented world. In other words, the *end* of any social action would be judged as worthy by the availability of rational *means* to achieve that *end*. Weber fears that this conflation of *means* and *ends* would produce a "'new iron cage of serfdom.'" Notions of value-oriented action would be "suffocated by the almighty bureaucratic structures and by the tightly knit networks of formal-rational laws and regulations, against which the individual would no longer stand any chance at all."[200]

Grant shares Weber's concern. He sees North American society increasingly penetrated by the instrumental rationality of science and technology. In particular, he sees politics "increasingly replaced by administration."[201] But how exactly is the rationalisation of the world manifested in the political and social realities of North American society, including Canada? This is a crucial question in that it brings Grant's understanding of the necessity of Canada's disappearance into sharper focus and reinforces how that disappearance is related to Grant's confrontation with Hegel. To answer the question, however, entails looking at Grant's prime example of rationalised politics, or politics-as-administration – his consideration of the political thought and practices of Pierre Trudeau, whom Grant regards as the quintessential Hegelian liberal.

15

Trudeau and the Betrayals
of the Bureaucrats

In *Philosophy of Right*, Hegel promotes the state's civil servants as a universal class dedicated to the service of the whole. The civil service integrates the particular and the universal, providing the basis of a workable constitutional state and the configuration of a proper relationship between the individual and the community. For Grant, though, the public service is more problematic. Grant sees the Hegelian Ideal as neither possible nor, ultimately, desirable. The idea of a universal class capable of transcending its own self-interest and functioning for the good of the state as a whole fails in the face of reality. For Grant, Hegel's universal class leads to the iron-cage bureaucracy envisioned by Max Weber. His evidence for such a conclusion can be found in his critique of Canada's political, bureaucratic, and corporate elites. Indeed, the villains in Grant's tale of Canada's disappearance include these elites.

Grant acknowledges that no modern state can function without considerable authority being placed in the hands of the civil service. Ideally, the bureaucracy operates as a countervail to those forces that threaten political and social disintegration. To the degree Canadian politicians use the civil service skilfully, it can balance the "anti-national forces" of the corporate elites.[202] But that is not what happened with Diefenbaker's government. Diefenbaker failed to gain the respect of the federal bureaucracy and thus neutralised its efficacy as a counterbalance to the forces arrayed against Canadian sovereignty. And during the defence crisis of 1962 and 1963, the Diefenbaker government did not receive loyalty from the civil service.

Grant attributes the bureaucrats' betrayal of Diefenbaker, in part at least, to the waning of British traditions in Canadian life. "The best civil servants were devoted to the British account of their function and the conception of a sovereign Canadian nation."[203] But among Canada's liberal

elites, the British connection was seen as a retardant to Canadian sovereignty. The defence crisis revealed how tenuous this connection had become among these elites. While Diefenbaker continued to accept the
British connection as a substantive part of Canada's political culture, much
of the English-speaking corporate elite no longer felt such a tie. They welcomed the growing influence of the United States, an influence that was
expanding continent-wide through the growth of corporate capitalism. Expansion brought wealth, and it was in the interests of Canada's ruling
classes, in both the private and public spheres, to attach themselves to the
forces of homogenisation and continentalism.

It is easy to understand why for the sake of profit Canada's corporatists
and capitalists were willing to forego the country's independence. "No
small country can depend for its existence on the loyalty of its capitalists."[204]
In an "uncertain nation" such as Canada, "the civil service is perhaps the
essential instrument by which nationhood is preserved." So why, Grant
asks, were Canada's public servants so amenable to being "more and more
representative of a western empire rather than civil servants of a particular
nation-state?"[205] Grant's answer is obviously influenced by his understanding of how modern rationality has replaced genuine politics with politics-
as-administrative rule, or, more precisely perhaps, with the politics of
efficiency and technique. To be sure, the betrayals of the bureaucrats – or, in
Grant's words, their "confused strivings" – cannot alone account for
Canada's disappearance. "The aspirations of progress have made Canada redundant."[206] Yet, if the strivings of people reflect the aspirations (and assumptions) of their times, and if those aspirations have led to Canada's
disappearance, then, presumably, those strivings can be held to account.
And as far as Grant is concerned, if there is one politician whose aspirations
epitomise liberal, rationalised administrative politics, whose "confused strivings" made Canada less possible as a sovereign nation, it is Pierre Trudeau.

Ramsay Cook, writing in the early 1970s, remarked that "the two most
important Canadian intellectuals of the past twenty years" were Pierre
Trudeau and George Grant.[207] Both raise questions about the predomi-
nant traditions of their country within the context of a modern technological society. From their respective liberal and conservative perspectives,
they ask fundamental questions about Canada in the context of a globalised, technological world. Trudeau embodies the liberal progressive vision.
He believes that the use of technological rationality is the key to preserving
Canada's independence, and that through the techniques of rational planning, Canada, with its rationally chosen federalist structure, will provide a
model for the rest of the world to emulate, an example for the emerging

Third World nations of the efficacy of liberal democratisation. Grant, on the other hand, argues that the increasing penetration of technological thinking threatens the political and cultural institutions that once sustained Canada's independence as a sovereign state. Technology and the kind of instrumental rationalism it reflects undermines the reasons for Canada's existence. Cook sums up these differing views this way: "Trudeau, the liberal, believes that technology can be controlled for man's benefit; Grant, the conservative, believes that technique already controls man."[208]

Trudeau certainly places considerable importance on rational decision-making, whether domestically or in foreign policy.[209] He wants reason and rationality to be the guiding principles of governance. A federal system, he writes, is "a product of reason in politics."[210] Tacked on to this faith in reason and rationality is a faith in science and technology as the means to perfect the world. For Trudeau, it has been said, "reason is associated with science, automation, cybernetics, technology and international economics while emotionalism is associated with Trudeau's great ideological enemy – nationalism."[211] In fact, Trudeau advocates a "cybernetic revolution" in which "the political tools of the future will be designed and appraised by more rational standards" than currently applied in Canada. These tools "will be made up of advanced technology and scientific investigation, as applied to the fields of law, economics, social psychology, international affairs and other areas of human relations,"[212] to overcome the irrational elements of politics.

Trudeau's well-known anti-nationalism and his support for the concept of federalism also reflect his view that politics should be rational. Nationalistic governments, he writes, tend to be intolerant, discriminatory, and, ultimately, totalitarian. In advanced societies, Trudeau argues, nationalism should become as obsolete as the divine right of kings. "The title of the state to govern and the extent of its authority will be conditional upon rational justification; a people's consensus based on reason will supply the cohesive force that societies require; and politics both within and without the state will follow a much more functional approach to the problems of government."[213] Canada, says Trudeau, must not be narrowly nationalistic in its efforts to retain its sovereignty. As a democratic federal state, Canada should "serve as a mentor" to those other nations in the world wracked by the plague of nationalist disturbances. He refers in this regard to his travels to Indonesia in 1955 and to Ghana two years later, where, he says, the oppression of the people and the promotion of war were justified by the leaders as necessary to protect national sovereignty. Canada's cooperative federalism "could become a brilliant prototype for the moulding of tomorrow's civilisation."[214]

Interestingly, the views espoused by Trudeau as a mature man stand in sharp contrast to those he had as a young man. According to one biography, Trudeau promoted a xenophobic, anti-Semitic Catholic nationalism well into his twenties.[215] But as an adult, after having left Quebec to be schooled at Harvard University and the London School of Economics, he declared nationalism to be the enemy.

To the extent that these statements reflect Trudeau's mature political thinking, they demonstrate his essential ascription to the principles of Enlightenment rationality. Trudeau holds to the idea of individual freedom as the pre-eminent good for personal self-fulfilment. He conceives of the state, and, by extension, the international system of states, as a servant to its citizens. In a sketch of his intellectual development in his memoirs, Trudeau recounts that as a young man studying at the London School of Economics, he wanted to develop a theory of the state, "wanted to know the roots of power," of "how governments work and why people obey." He asked himself the penultimate political question: "Does the ultimate authority lie in the state or in the human individual?"[216] Trudeau's answer is a far cry from that of the young man who wanted a "revolution that will be Catholic, French and Laurentian."[217] But then his memoirs make no mention of his once anti-liberal views. Instead, Trudeau takes his answer from that most liberal of political theorists, T.H. Green, the nineteenth-century British Hegelian. From Green, he learned that "the focal point [of political power] was not the state, but the individual – the individual seen as a person integrated into society, which is to say, endowed with fundamental rights and essential liberties, but also with responsibilities."[218]

Trudeau claimed that this basic philosophy would inform all his future political decisions. And for him, the paramount political concern was always individual freedom, not something as irrational as communal identity. Trudeau's notion of freedom is clearly connected to his ideas about reason.[219] If so, what we have then is the following Trudeauvian – and Hegelian – formula: federalism is the political order best suited to harmonising reason and freedom. The function of the state is to provide the conditions that will best allow individuals the freedom to satisfy their aspirations. These aspirations, in turn, are to be shaped by reason and rationality. In short, reason makes us free. Why else would Trudeau insist on "cold, unemotional rationality" in politics or that politics must be "a pure product of reason"?[220]

Such a worldview is essentially Hegelian,[221] although, bearing in mind my discussion of Weberian rationalism, it is questionable whether Trudeau's understanding of reason is the same as Hegel's, much less Plato's, Grant's, or

Watson's. The problem is, as Grant argues, that Trudeau's formulations, taken to their logical extreme, leave little room in politics for such irrational-isms as love of country, patriotism, or loyalty to one's own, or even for belief in something that transcends the satisfaction of individual desires. Moreover, Trudeau's understanding of reason is essentially instrumentalist in its con-tention that human will could bestride technology and engineer it to useful ends, including that of preserving Canadian federalism. Grant, I suggest, would argue that the inevitable result of Trudeau's identification of reason with freedom is a theology of glory, a progressivist notion that humans can create a perfect world by means of technologically efficient politics.

Grant never did a theoretical analysis of Trudeau's thought as a whole, but his writings contain scattered critiques of Trudeau, both as a politician and as a political thinker. For example, Barry Cooper points out that in *Lament for a Nation* Grant spots the self-contradiction – and the fundamen-tal Hegelianism – of a 1964 essay in *Canadian Forum* to which Trudeau contributed. The essay, or manifesto, "An Appeal for Realism in Politics," argues for a new and revitalised federalism in terms of certain universal val-ues. It identifies Canada's survival as a sovereign state with that of the fu-ture international world order, declaring "the idea of a 'national state' [to be] obsolete." While ostensibly not wanting Canada to be integrated into "another geographical entity," the essay acknowledges such an eventuality might "conform to the natural course of the world's evolution."[222] More important, though, Canada, as a federalist state, can be at the forefront of the movement toward a universal world-state system.

> The most valid trends today are toward a more enlightened humanism, toward various forms of political, social and economic universalism. Canada is a reproduction on a smaller and simpler scale of this universal phenomenon. The challenge is for a number of ethnic groups to learn to live together. It is a modern challenge, meaningful and indicative of what can be expected from man. If Canadians cannot make a success of a country such as theirs, how can they contribute in any way to the elabo-ration of humanism, to the formulation of the international structures of tomorrow? To confess one's inability to make Canadian Confedera-tion work is, at this stage of history, to admit one's unworthiness to con-tribute to the universal order.[223]

Grant questions how Trudeau can logically assert his faith in Hegelian universalism while, at the same time, putting forward an argument for con-tinued existence of the particularity that is Canada. He writes: "The faith in universalism makes it accurate to call the authors liberal. But how can a faith in universalism go with a desire for the continuance of Canada? The belief in Canada's continued existence has always appealed against universalism. It appealed to particularity against the wider loyalty of the continent. If universalism is the most 'valid modern trend,' then is it not right for Canadians to welcome our integration into the [American] empire?"[224] In other words, if one is a universalist, why try to maintain any particularity? If Canadian nationalism is irrational and impedes liberal progressive principles, then surely such nationalism is obsolete.

Grant finds another contradiction in the manifesto. Its authors deplore the victimisation of Indians, Metis, Doukhobors, Orientals, Hutterites, and other dissidents from the norm, and demand protection for their cultures. But, Grant asks, how can Trudeau and the other authors espouse the idea of universal values to which all must accede, while, at the same time, arguing for the protection of particular cultures against universal principles? Whatever universal values may be, they can only be universal if everybody accepts them – that is, if everybody has the same worldview. One reason why people see things differently is that they reside in different cultures and partake of different traditions. But universal values imply a homogeneous culture in which everyone ascribes to the same values. Do the manifesto's authors not recognise this? Do they not see that "liberalism in its most inequivocal form (that is, untainted by memories of past traditions) includes not only the idea of universalism but also that of homogeneity?"[225] Observing that it was a Liberal prime minister who referred to democratic values when the Royal Canadian Mounted Police were sent against the Doukhobors, Grant, as Cooper says, argues that, instead of enhancing cultural diversity, liberalism tends to become violent when cultural differences become acute and present a political challenge.

Grant makes a similar argument about Trudeau's liberalism during the October Crisis of 1970, when the Liberals imposed the War Measures Act. Grant sees such a political action as another example of how modern liberalism was prepared to use force to overcome any resistance to its universalist claims. In his opposition to Quebec nationalism, Trudeau was undermining the basis of Canadian nationalism, leaving Canada even more susceptible to continentalist pressures. For Grant, the integration of French culture into the Canadian socio-economic structure was merely a way to help smooth Canada's integration into a continental empire. "It is obvious that any indigenous English-speaking Canadian society requires the help of Quebec. Yet how can this be advocated in a way that is not simply asking French-Canadians to be led along to their doom as a community? In other words are the French not best to be separatists in the face of the North American situation?" Grant warns against the "the powers of administrative rationality" that would see French culture submerged beneath a "homogenized English-speaking sea," arguing that Trudeau's invocation of rationality and his dislike of nationalism promote such a universalist project.[226] Trudeau, he said, sought to bring "the French-Canadian people fully into the mainstream of North American life. This desire to homogenize made him truly a modern liberal. He had no sympathy for the powerful desire of some sections of Québécois to continue to exist as a people."[227] Trudeau's talk of cybernetic politics, his internationalist outlook, and even his alterations to administrative structures in the name of rational planning – all partake of a worldview that identifies liberalism (or freedom) with technology (or efficiency). In the Canadian context, says Grant, such talk implies policies that further efforts to integrate Canada into the continental socio-economic system. In terms of changes to Canada's traditional parliamentary system, Trudeau's restructuring of the bureaucracy reflects the rising influence of a technocracy that sees administrative rule as the most efficient means of shaping society to fit the liberal mould and, hence, make Canadians' integration into the continental system an administrative success. Employing distinctly Weberian language, Grant concludes that "Mr. Trudeau combines plebiscitary appeal with acceptance of the assumptions of state capitalist 'rationality' ... Throughout his career his appeals have been to universalism, and universalism in a Canadian setting, means integration into a smoothly functioning continental system."[228]

Grant returns to this theme again when he criticises a 1976 speech Trudeau gave before the United States Congress on Canada's constitutional difficulties. Trudeau told the American politicians that the breakup of Canada would be "a crime against the history of humanity."[229] Such a statement, says Grant, seems attractive and worthy of any Canadian's support, but the phrase *history of humanity* implies something bigger than the political unit of Canada and sets up the notion that any step back from the bigness of humanity is a retrograde step. But if that is true, if the history of humanity demands bigger and bigger political units, then why should the end of Canada be a crime? Why should Canadians not welcome membership in the American empire? Trudeau's speech, Grant concludes, shows that the prime minister has adopted the liberal impulse of his predecessors that has resulted in Canada falling more and more under the sway of the United States: "As in the past with Pearson and King, the leader of the Liberal party talks about larger units in the attractive language of internationalism, but in fact what is implied are policies leading to imperial continental integration. This kind of language should make us hesitant about accepting Mr. Trudeau as the champion of our nationalism. We should doubt this plea not only because Mr. Trudeau is the leader of the party which has been the chief political instrument of continental integration for this country ... but also because Mr. Trudeau has always scorned nationalism as a retrograde force."[230] This scorn of nationalism is a necessary and basic part of Trudeau's political ideology, says Grant, because Trudeau's emphasis on rationality and cybernetic politics inevitably works against the retention of a Canadian national identity distinct from that of the United States.

As far as Grant is concerned, then, Trudeau contributes to the impossibility of Canada. Essentially, in Trudeau we have the identification of liberalism with the techniques of rational management, the consequence of which is the reduction of politics to administrative rule and elections that are little more than plebiscites over which set of technocrats will exercise power. And this, in Grant's view, makes Trudeau an exemplar of Hegelian rationalism. With his ascription to modern freedom as man's essence, his reliance on cybernetics and politics-as-engineering, and his identification of the Canadian national interest with that of a universalist world order, Trudeau offers ideas that act as a solvent to dilute the traditions that sustain Canadian sovereignty. For these reasons, Trudeau is an unwitting agent of the coming-to-be of what Grant, borrowing from Alexandre Kojève, the French Hegel interpreter, refers to as "the universal and homogeneous state."[231]

But Grant makes an even more subtle point about Trudeau and the impossibility of Canada. Borrowing again from Weber's notion of rationalisation as the "fate of our times"[232] and his concept of the charismatic leader, Grant links Trudeau's fate and that of Canada's. Fate, as the Greeks knew, is that which can never be overcome, and the fate of the classical hero was tragic in that he could never overcome contingency. However, in the modern world, contingency is what we try to overcome through the rationalisation of the world by the application of instrumental reason. As Grant recognises, this has been the essence of the modern project – to free man from contingency through rational science: "The building of the universal and homogeneous state by mastery [of the world] was the chief ideal of western liberal theory."[233] But in a world where contingency has been banished by bureaucratic rule and routine, it is the ironic fate of the charismatic leader to himself be rationalised and bureaucratised.

Grant also seems to have Weber in mind when he describes Trudeau as a plebiscitarian leader whose restructuring of the Canadian political system would "fulfil the needs of a society in which administrative rule is bolstered by plebiscites about personnel."[234] For all his belief in individual freedom, Trudeau was caught in the thick mesh of the rationalised world that threatens the very freedom it espouses. In terms of Canada's fate, Trudeau could do little to further Canada's independence, since the thinking behind his policies was predicated on concepts that ultimately deny the worth of maintaining Canadian sovereignty. To quote one of Grant's more well-known judgments: "Our culture floundered on the aspirations of the age of progress."[235]

This reality, says Grant, is also embodied in the administrative politics that increasingly shape the continent's integration. Despite the rhetoric of dispute between interest groups and political parties, or even between the Canadian and American governments, there is little substantive disagreement about the ends of politics. "There is almost no conflict in the western world as to what is the political good. The highest political good is thought by the vast majority to be the building of the technical society by the overcoming of chance, through the application of the natural and social sciences. The political only arises in disagreement about means."[236] But, for Grant, the loss of substantive politics as a practical activity – its reduction to techniques of administration – is also the loss of Canada. In a 1985 interview with David Cayley, Grant acknowledged that his lament for Canada's passing was, in Cayley's words, "as much a lament for the loss of politics" since they go hand in hand.[237]

Grant's thinking about Canada's impossibility cannot be adequately understood from psychological or sociological perspectives. To make such an attempt is to miss the philosophic dimension of his lament. For Grant, the impossibility of Canada as a sovereign nation-state in the North American continent is bound up with the impossibility of a meaningful conservative philosophy in the modern age. With no common political intention beyond the lure of material benefit, Canadians have given themselves over to the imperatives of technology. This ascription to the technological imperative has fated Canada to disappear. Indeed, all that's left is a country in name only, "a good place to live," to borrow Donald Creighton's phrase.[238] "Canada has ceased to be a nation," says Grant, "but its formal political existence will not end quickly. Our social and economic blending into the empire will continue apace, but political union will probably be delayed. Some international catastrophe or great shift of power might speed up this process."[239]

Grant regarded the free trade agreement between Canada and the United States in the 1980s as evidence of what he had forecast twenty years earlier – yet another move toward Canada's gradual integration into the American empire. But then such an integrative process was the fate of any particularity in the age of technology and there was little to stop it.[240] The price of our dependence on technology was surrender to "the process of universalisation and homogenisation."[241]

16

Philosophy, Tyranny,
and the "End" of Canada

Grant's understanding of Canada's political fate is captured in the phrase "the universal and homogeneous state,"[242] a phrase he appropriated from Alexandre Kojève. Kojève interpreted Hegel's philosophy to be a philosophy of time as history, and with this interpretation, he originated the now famous end-of-history thesis. Kojève sees the "end of history" to be consistent with the universal and homogeneous state. And this is why Grant sees the impossibility of Canada as the consequence of the coming-to-be of the universal and homogeneous state: conservative Canada disappears with the fulfilment of the Hegelian project.

Among the thinkers who brought Grant to this recognition was Leo Strauss. In particular, Grant's encounter with Strauss (and through him, Kojève) finally released him from the grip of Hegelian liberalism and, indeed, convinced him that a Hegelian future would be a tyranny. As Joan O'Donovan states, Grant's study of Strauss "caused him to abandon altogether his historical grounds for hope."[243] In this regard, Strauss's thought needs to be examined, if only briefly, to underscore how Grant's general acceptance of Strauss's analysis of modern philosophy and Grant's employment of that analysis provided him with the philosophical basis for his judgment regarding Canada's fate.

Philosophy, Strauss asserts, is the nothing more and nothing less than a search for the knowledge of the whole – God, man, and the world. Strauss accepts the ancient understanding that man's reason can gain knowledge of the whole and that it is this knowledge that constitutes human freedom: "Philosophy, in all its various forms, has always supposed that by unaided reason man is somehow capable of going beyond the given and finding a non-arbitrary standard against which to measure it, and that this possibility constitutes the essence of human freedom."[244] This understanding of philosophy contrasts with the modern assumption that reason is limited to empirical knowledge. This modernist reduction of reason is at the root of the modern devaluation of metaphysical knowledge. One result has been the modern distinction between facts and values. For moderns, knowledge of the world, if it is to be legitimate, must be grounded in facts, or empirical evidence. Moral claims – values, in other words – cannot be verified on this basis and are therefore beyond the purview of this delimited knowledge. Modern knowledge is value-free and morally neutral.[245]

Strauss, however, asserts that there is no such thing as value-neutral knowledge. All moral assertions are grounded in assumptions or truth claims, implicit or otherwise, regarding the whole, about what is that is. Strauss summarises his arguments about modern claims regarding knowledge in his essay "What Is Political Philosophy?" First, we cannot consider political phenomena without making value claims because it is impossible to know or do something without subjecting it to some evaluation. Second, the denial of value judgments assumes that values are not amenable to reason. Third, the claim that scientific, empirical knowledge is the highest form of knowledge implies the depreciation of classical knowledge. Finally, such positivist assumptions effectively translate into a historicist claim about knowledge, political or otherwise: "Historical understanding becomes the basis of a truly empirical science of society."[246]

Strauss traces the modern rejection of classical philosophy through a series of philosophic waves that began with a conscious turn by early moderns away from the transcendent morality of the Bible and the excellence demanded by classical ethics. This break resulted in a lowering of standards such that the satisfaction of man's own desires in the here-and-now became the highest end of human endeavour. Gone was the notion that man's truer or highest end is the contemplation of and attunement with a natural and eternal order. In effect, early modern thinkers cut God out of the moral equation by rejecting the need for a transcendent order as the standard to which man's ordering of the temporal world must conform. Modern thought proclaims man to be his own standard-setter and human reason as the sole source of truth and morality. Modern philosophy thus amounts to a deliberate denial of classical metaphysics.[247]

For the most part, Grant adopts Strauss's arguments regarding the breakdown of the pre-modern order. The first wave of this rejection began with Machiavelli, Hobbes, and Locke, who sought to "lower our goals" regarding the best regime in order to realise a regime that could preserve society and promote freedom. This entailed denying the idea that man is directed primarily toward the good. They hold instead that man is driven by the desire for self-preservation, and thus they effectively reduce the notion of a just order to a set of rights grounded in human nature. For the early moderns, a successful regime is one that preserves society by replacing virtue as the highest ideal with fear of violent death, the desire for glory, or even mere vanity and the comfort of property. In effect, the first wave of modernity replaced Christian charity as the height of social conduct with calculation and utilitarianism, and classical contemplation with manipulation and technique. It was, says Strauss, a "stupendous contraction of the horizon."[248]

The second wave of modernity included Rousseau and Hegel. They replaced human nature as a basis for political order with the concept of historical development. It is this wave of modernity that produced the doctrine of progress. In a sense, Rousseau marked a return to pre-modern thought in that he reinstated virtue as the height of purpose. However, it is a virtue that is innate to man and corrupted by society. Rousseau accepts the Hobbesian imperative of self-preservation, but unlike Hobbes, he regards the city as the arena of brutality. Man in the state of nature is naturally good. Man is corrupted only after accidentally becoming a historical and reasoning creature. Man is born free because his natural conscience is virtuous; only in society does he become unfree as his conscience is corrupted. His natural goodness can be restored, however, through the establishment of a properly ordered society. Which is to say, the individual can be made free because the general will of the community expresses the freedom and virtue of natural conscience. To accept the general will is to recover as much freedom as is available in history. At the same time, the freedom of the individual fosters the good of all. Strauss, however, argues that if society as a whole is to be the standard by which virtue is defined, then there can be no freedom beyond the regime, no transcendent good outside the political.[249] The personal is the political.

Hegel furthered this second wave by introducing the notion of the historical progress of freedom, a process that culminates in a universal and homogeneous state where all are equal because each recognises the other as free. This universal freedom is possible because all men as men are measured by their need for recognition, not by any transcendent standard. Hegel, says Strauss, constructs a political order that starts "from the untrue assumption that man as man is thinkable as a being that lacks awareness of sacred restraints or as a being that is guided by nothing but a desire for recognition."[250] But freedom through recognition is only possible because natural science and technology have made it increasingly possible for man to overcome nature and be freed from external contingency. "The brain which can transform the political matter soon learns to think of the transformation of every matter or of the conquest of nature."[251]

The third wave, represented by Nietzsche and Heidegger, was even more radical. Not only do they deny any notions of a transcendent order or a natural order, but their historicism lacks even Hegel's rational basis. While Hegel maintains a teleology, there is no teleology with Nietzsche and Heidegger. The wave is uncontrolled, with no end or purpose to achieve. All is unknowable, indeterminate, open to the manipulations of power and will. One consequence of this will to power, as Nietzsche points out, is the modern project's transvaluation of all values such that philosophers who once sought knowledge become power-wielding legislators and reformers, or what Nietzsche calls the "last men." But these last men no longer direct people to take their bearings from transcendent ends. Instead, they make virtue relative to the common good, or to what with Hegel becomes the end of history. The concern for modern thinkers – the new lower standard – is with how men live and not with the best life. This makes the reconciliation of philosophy (newly conceived) and politics more likely than under the ancient dispensation. Or, to express this reconciliation in Hegelian terms, the rational becomes the real and the real becomes the rational. Modern philosophy, then, has become the rationalisation of politics, the attempt to transform the wise men into social and political reformers.[252] Alexandre Kojève, the French Hegel exegete, advisor to the French government, and an early architect of the European Union, is perhaps a paradigmatic example of a last man. So, too, arguably, is Pierre Trudeau.

For Grant, Strauss's account shows that modernity has become nihilistic because of its disconnection from eternity. Grant follows Strauss in thinking that this denial of a purpose-giving eternal order carries in its wake the attempt to bring together thought and action by means of technology. Strauss sees this as modernity's fateful flaw: the bringing together of thought and action, philosophy and politics, by means of technique, the wilful application of instrumental reason to political realities that are not necessarily amenable to rationality. Philosophy is dangerous because it requires that everything be questioned. In politics, prudence requires that not everything can or even should be questioned, especially if violence is to be avoided. Rousseau is not responsible for the Terror of the French Revolution any more than Hegel and Nietzsche can be accused of promoting German militarism and Nazism. Yet their thought can be perverted by imprudent epigones. In this way, modern philosophy's nihilism contributes to modern totalitarianism. Indeed, as Allan Bloom once commented, "the particular horror of modern tyranny has been its alliance with perverted philosophy."[253]

Grant articulates his concerns on this topic in a 1963 essay, "Tyranny and Wisdom."[254] In this work, Grant offers an exposition of and commentary on a debate between Strauss and Kojève. Strauss raised he subject of this debate in his 1948 book *On Tyranny: An Interpretation of Xenophon's "Hiero,"* in which he argues that the Greek historian Xenophon (in his dialogue *Hiero*) shows a better understanding of the relationship between politics and philosophy than modern thinkers. The book contains Kojève's response to Strauss's argument and a rejoinder from Strauss to Kojève. Grant describes their debate as "the most important controversy in contemporary political philosophy."[255]

This is a large claim, but for Grant what is at stake is the validity of the modern project and what he perceives to be its ultimate end – the tyranny of a Hegelian universal and homogeneous state. "The argument that Canada, a local culture, must disappear can, therefore, be stated in three steps. First, men everywhere move ineluctably toward membership in the universal and homogeneous state. Second, Canadians live next to a society that is the heart of modernity. Third, nearly all Canadians think modernity is good, so nothing essential distinguishes Canadians from Americans."[256] Such a world-state, if realised, requires the effective end to Canada's political independence. The question for Grant is whether the loss of such a particularity is good. "If the best social order is the universal and homogeneous state, then the disappearance of Canada can be understood as a step toward that order. If the universal and homogeneous state would be a tyranny, then the disappearance of even this indigenous culture can be seen as the removal of a minor barrier on the road to that tyranny."[257]

The debate between Strauss and Kojève focuses on whether classical or modern philosophy provides the most adequate account of the relationship between politics and philosophy. At issue is whether the philosopher can claim a knowledge that transcends particular historical circumstances. Kojève contends that philosophical knowledge and, hence, political order are dependent on and determined by the historical process, the end of which brings into being the universal and homogeneous state. Grant accepts Strauss's refutation of Kojève's argument: the actualisation of the universal and homogeneous state would be a tyranny and not the culmination of man's historical struggle for recognition. Nevertheless, even in siding with Strauss, Grant acknowledges that Kojève's interpretation of Hegel's philosophy is "incomparably nearer the original" than that offered by the British Idealists.[258] The question for Grant, though, is which form of philosophy, the ancient or the modern, the transcendent or the historical, is best suited to human aspirations. Kojève's interpretation of Hegel is clearly "violent."[259] He casts Hegel as the first thinker to recognise the goal of human history as a striving for freedom by all individuals – freedom being defined as the satisfaction of one's desire for recognition by other equally free and desiring individuals. For Hegel, human history is not a senseless slaughterbench, but the unfolding over time of reason, or spirit-in-the-world. Reason's unfolding is accomplished through action and labour until it is actualised. With this self-conscious recognition of the aim of history, the end of history is, in theory, accomplished. Man-as-freedom can be actualised in the coming-to-be of the universal and homogeneous state in which all mankind shares the discourse of freedom and equality. However, philosophy also comes to an end because wisdom, or absolute knowledge and satisfaction of desire, has been achieved. Man at the end of history knows what is, was, and will be because he knows, in principle, the goal of history. In addition, he is satisfied, again in principle, because he is recognised as a free, unique, and equal citizen by all others in the state, who are also free, unique, and equal.[260]

The genesis of the world-state is, as I previously discussed, the dynamic of the master-slave dialectic. Hegel sees the beginnings of human society – the first stirring of self-consciousness – in proto-man's willingness to risk the death of his "animal" body for a mental construct, the abstract notion of "pure prestige." History begins when one individual desires that another recognise him. Since the other also wants recognition, the battle is engaged to determine which one will be master and which one will be slave. Without this fight about freedom, says Kojève, "there would never have been human beings on earth."[261] Thus, history begins with "the presence *and* absence of freedom in the world."[262] The master who wins the fight and gains the other's recognition achieves his freedom. The losing slave is denied positive recognition and, therefore, is not free. History amounts to the repetition of this original confrontation among all individuals. The cunning of reason propels man to struggle ceaselessly to resolve this conflict. The end of history amounts to a resolution of this long conflict in which all are free because all are recognised.[263]

Such a world-condition raises numerous issues. For example, for all to be free and equal means that there can be no substantial other. And this means that there can be no meaningful distinctions or particularities. Politically, the state will be the objective embodiment of man's subjective freedom. The universal and homogeneous state will thus manifest the union of universality and particularity.[264] Politics will also be a solely practical activity of administering to the world-state, while the task of post-historical philosophy amounts to merely the further elaboration of Hegelian principles. Politics and philosophy, as traditionally conceived, come to an end because there is nothing of substance to think about or do. Politics becomes administration; philosophy becomes ideology. Moreover, since there is nothing outside history, no "truth" that transcends man-as-historical-being, no external order to which man is subordinate and from which he can derive meaning, man as he has traditionally understood himself will come to an end.[265] The end of history and the end of philosophy bring about the "definitive annihilation of man" because "man himself no longer changes essentially [and] there is [no] reason to change the (true) principles, which are at the basis of his understanding of the world and himself. But all the rest can be preserved indefinitely; art, love, play, etc.; in short everything that makes man happy."[266] Which is to say, man's meanings and purposes are all self-created responses to his sense of time, or as Grant might put it, time is history.

Grant summarises Kojève's version of the West's philosophical development in "Tyranny and Wisdom," pointing out that Hegel's account of the Western tale hinges on the establishment of the universal and homogeneous state through the appropriation of elements of Greek and Christian thought.[267] The principle of a universal state was initiated by Alexander the Great, who created an empire in which membership depended not on common ethnic or geographic backgrounds, but on the common "essence" of members of a particular civilisation, which, in this case, was the Greek culture of reason. However, this universal state could not be homogeneous because it did not do away with class distinctions engendered by the fight between masters and slaves. The Greeks accepted the idea of a universal state because they understood men as having the same inherent nature. To the degree that men were members of a civilisation they shared this inherent nature and, thus, could be granted citizenship in the empire. Slaves and barbarians did not share this inherent nature. For the Greeks, there was a necessary differentiation of human beings whose natures shared little in common. Therefore, slaves and barbarians could not be granted equal status, and as a result, the empire could not be homogeneous.[268]

This differentiation of masters and slaves was overcome in the second stage of Western history under the influence of Semitic religions, particularly Christianity in the West, which, according to Kojève, provided the idea of homogeneity. In his essay "Tyranny and Wisdom," Grant pays close attention to Kojève's idea of homogeneity, describing it as "the idea of the *fundamental equality* of all who believe in a single God."[269] For Christians, there is no essential difference between humans. They are all equal because they share the same faith in the same God. Thus, says Kojève, the

Christian faith provides the means – the unity of faith – by which all natural or socially created distinctions between human beings can be overcome. Through a shared religious faith, Christianity negates the natural differences that divide human beings and, in the act of negation, synthesises their differing qualities into "a homogeneous unity not innate or given but freely created by 'conversion.'" The stage is thus set for the third stage of history, the coming together of the ideas of universality and homogeneity through the modern secular state.[270]

It is on this interpretation, and what he perceived to be the consequences of this coming together of the universal and homogeneous, that Grant turns from his early acceptance of Hegelian philosophy. Through his encounter with Strauss and Kojève, Grant sees that the establishment of the universal and homogeneous state as a political reality necessitates the de-divinization of the "Other" that is God. The universal and homogeneous state can only be established by the secularisation of the Christian ideal in favour of an anthropomorphic historicism that reinterprets Christian eschatological hopes for a perfected human community in a transcendent realm as a goal to be actualised in the material world.[271] But this can only be done, Grant argues, if philosophy takes its ground not from an ahistorical eternal order, but from an eternity that is "the totality of all historical epochs."[272]

But such a claim amounts to a theology of glory as far as Grant is concerned. To believe that philosophy is grounded in history and not in eternity is tantamount to making the emancipation of human desire the ultimate purpose of man's existence; that is, freedom is the escape from all limitations, moral or otherwise. But to escape divine restraints, to make history or necessity the judge of the goodness of world events is, ultimately, to worship force. This might be pleasant for those who have the preponderance of power on their side, but not for those who lack such power. As Grant writes with scathing bitterness, "The screams of the child can be justified by the achievements of history. How pleasant for the achievers, but how meaningless for the child."[273]

Grant abhors this moral nihilism. As an avowed Christian Platonist, he holds that historicist goals are not those for which humans are best fitted. Historicism assumes all thought to be historically bounded and therefore incapable of grasping anything eternal. But the consequence of such thinking, according to Grant, is historicism's inability to uphold any objective standards by which people can govern their actions and give meaning to their lives. The rejection of natural right, with its doctrine that individuals have a natural end that determines what is good for them, leads to a nihilism in which all principles become mere preferences, all horizons merely the opinion of the age. No truth has validity beyond its historical context, and no individual thinker can provide a truth that is universally true.[274] As a result, morality and ethics are whatever the dominant opinions or ideologies of the day determine them to be. But even these, following the logic of historical relativism, are finally unsupportable because historical man recognises that all his truths are inherently subjective. It is on this point that Grant, following Strauss, detects the worm at the heart of historicism. If historicism denies the possibility of any knowledge of the absolute, if it asserts the relativism of all standards, then, it too must be subject to its own claims.[275] Historicism, Strauss concludes, is guilty of dogmatism and arbitrariness.

For Grant, this means that the universal and homogeneous state, far from being the best social order, would, if actualised, result in a tyrannical order destructive of humans as conceived by classical philosophy. Grant follows Strauss's judgment on Kojève: "Modern political philosophy, which has substituted freedom for virtue, has as its chief ideal ... a social order which is destructive of humanity."[276] The universal and homogeneous state also means the end of philosophy, or, what is the same thing, the end of human excellence, since it is no longer acceptable to think that only a few are fitted for asking the most serious questions (never mind that there are no serious questions about human purposes to be asked at the end of history). For Kojève-Hegel, human satisfaction is grounded in historical recognition, or freedom and equality; for Grant-Strauss, human satisfaction is rooted in thought, in the contemplation of that which is unchanging. "Philosophy is the excellence of the soul," says Grant. "There cannot be philosophy in this sense unless there is an eternal and unchangeable order."[277]

But it is not only philosophy that comes to an end in the universal and homogeneous state. The lowering of horizons, the rejection of excellence, necessary to bringing about this end-state, also requires the denial of substantive distinctions among individuals, as well as among cultures and even nations. Thus, the end point of the Hegelian project means the end of the distinct political order that is Canada. Modern thought makes Canada impossible.

PART FOUR

Charles Taylor and the Spirit of Community

17

Recognition and the "Saving" of Modernity

Charles Taylor's studies on Hegel and the frequently Hegelian posture he employs in critiquing contemporary liberalism are well known. Taylor consistently promotes the lessons of Hegel's *Sittlichkeit*, arguing that a substantive, organic, historically grounded sense of community is more fulfilling to the individual than the abstract, atomistic, liberal *Moralität* that dominates Western societies. He follows Hegel in claiming that morality is dependent on and actualised within the community, asserting that the forms of *Moralität*, including rights-based, procedural liberalism, should be subservient to communal *Sittlichkeit*.[1] In Taylor's words: "The doctrine of *Sittlichkeit* is that morality reaches its completion in a community ... Because the realization of the Idea requires that man be part of a larger life in a society, moral life reaches its highest realization in *Sittlichkeit*. This highest realization is an achievement, of course, it is not present throughout history, and there are even periods where public life has been so emptied of spirit that *Moralität* expresses something higher. But the fulfilment of morality comes in a realized *Sittlichkeit*."[2]

Such a position unquestionably places Taylor on the communitarian side of the fence in the liberal-communitarian debate.[3] At the heart of this debate is concern on the part of the communitarians with the ostensible erosion of social and political existence, the decline of community. Communitarians argue that the modern project to free individuals from hierarchical and theocratic social and political structures has been almost too successful. "The dark side of individualism is a centring on the self, which both flattens and narrows our lives, makes them poorer in meaning, and less concerned with others or society."[4] Modern individuals are too concerned with their rights and insufficiently concerned with their duties toward others, their need for a sense of belonging, or what is necessary for them to be mature, integrated, social, and political beings.

Taylor shares the communitarian concern. He, too, discerns in the excesses of liberal individualism a focus on the self and a concomitant lack of awareness of concerns that transcend the individual, be they religious, political, or historical. Modern individualism, he says, "is by its very essence a solvent of community."[5] However, unlike some other communitarians, Taylor does not reject or completely oppose modern liberalism or, for that matter, the modern project. It would be wrong to place him with both feet in the anti-liberal camp. He appears to share liberal principles on social and egalitarian matters, and readily asserts traditional liberal notions regarding civil liberties and rights.[6] Indeed, while he agrees with much of the communitarian critique of liberalism and modernity, he argues that the chances of mitigating modernity's excesses are better sought within the forms of modern self-understanding than in any attempt to return to pre-modern or classical humanism. Much more than George Grant, Taylor believes there are ethically valuable concepts and theoretical resources within modern liberalism that are worth saving and restoring.[7] At the core of Taylor's project, as demonstrated in his 1989 book, *Sources of the Self*, is the notion that modernity has hidden moral sources that can provide reasonable responses to the reification of individualism and its attendant self-absorbed subjectivism. "The intention of this work was one of retrieval, an attempt to uncover buried goods through re-articulation – and thereby to make these sources again empower, to bring the air back again into the half-collapsed lungs of the spirit."[8]

Taylor's effort to find sources within the modern understanding that can compensate for the excesses of modernity has considerable affinity with Hegel's notion of *Aufhebung*, in which concepts are preserved even as they are overcome. In this regard, Taylor's thought constitutes an attempt to uncover – or, perhaps more accurately, to recover – the potential for belongingness within modernity. In attempting to recover community, Taylor draws upon various thinkers, including Hegel, Herder, and Rousseau. From these sources of modernity, Taylor extracts his claim that the modern ideal of freedom is bound up with and dependent upon an authentic reconciliation of the self and the other, the individual and the community. This ideal relationship is most comprehensively articulated in Taylor's concept of recognition and his expressivist theory of authentic identity. In his view, an authentic identity reconciles the individual and the community through forms of "recognition" that have the potential to satisfy both the individual's need to belong and his concomitant desire for freedom.

Taylor's thinking on this score finds its way into various aspects of his political philosophy: the nature of community; the affirmation of everyday life; a critique of procedural liberalism; the notion of dialogical society; and, finally, the concrete problem of Canada and Quebec nationalism. Bearing this in mind, I need to trace the philosophical sources of morality that Taylor believes to be embedded within modernity to show how, in retrieving those sources, he attempts to overcome, or sublate, what he regards as the malaise of modernity – excessive individualism, instrumental reason, and the consequent loss of genuine freedom, for example. Not every critic thinks Taylor succeeds. Some question how he can assert a quasi-Hegelian confidence in being able to find sources within modernity that can counter the excesses of modernity when he does not accept the ontological assumptions of Hegelian historicism. As John Dunn remarks, "[I]n the face of distressing choices [Taylor] is apt to cling tenaciously to both horns of the dilemma, refusing ... to let either of them go." Taylor, says Dunn, seems simultaneously attached to "the modern post-Romantic project of self-exploration" and the pre-modern project of situating individuals within an "objective order of natural and social value."9

Dunn has zeroed in on a central problem in Taylor's thought. Taylor's interpretations rest, on the one hand, on his historical approach to saving modern individuality and, on the other hand, on his intimation of a larger moral order that provides objective standards of judgment for determining the "good" of community. Considering Taylor's apparent rejection of the central thesis of Hegelian metaphysics – in brief, the cunning of reason – this suggests a tension within Taylor's thought as a whole. Taylor endorses Hegel's efforts to reconcile the individual and the community; indeed, his promotion of multiculturalism is rooted in the precepts of Hegelian idealism.10 But in the absence of his accepting Hegel's metaphysical attachment to an overarching rational order that embodies itself in history, there remains an abiding conundrum in Taylor's thinking that casts doubt on his efforts to find a basis for the reconciliation of the individual and the community. To be sure, Taylor is careful to note that his critique of atomised liberalism should not be construed as advocating a family-like community. Yet, considering the emphasis he gives cultural identity and language in his expressivist theory, it is questionable whether Taylor adequately avoids slipping even deeper into the subjectivism and relativism that he himself regards as one of the dangers of post-modern society. Does his desire to salvage the community from the ostensible excesses of atomistic liberalism have the latent potential to create greater dangers for both the individual and the community, including the Canadian community, than those he fears? As Janet Ajzenstat observes, it is "not always easy to see how substantive liberalism in Taylor's schema differs from the illiberal, closed regime."[11]

This observation raises a number of questions: (1) What does Taylor mean by recognition and his expressivist notion that the authentic human life is essentially dialogical? (2) Concomitantly, what is his understanding of the "recognised" and authentic individual within the context of a community? (3) Precisely how is the reconciliation of the individual and the community achieved, and in what political form does Taylor see this reconciliation transpiring? and (4) Is Taylor's reconciliation intelligible? or, put differently, Does Taylor's employment of Hegelian thought in his quest for substantive community satisfy the individual's desire for belonging but at the same time sidestep temptations toward the kind of illiberal, tribe-oriented communality that can lead to authoritarian or even totalitarian political orders?

Scholars have argued that concepts of identity and recognition provide the theoretical backdrop to numerous issues and events that have come to dominate the post–Cold War era – everything from Islamist terrorism and ethnic conflict to resurgent nationalism and regional secessionist movements. As Nancy Fraser observes, "[T]he 'struggle for recognition' is fast becoming the paradigmatic form of political conflict"[12] in the contemporary world. Taylor deploys Hegel's principle of recognition as a theoretical tool for addressing issues of identity and difference in pluralist, multicultural societies. Hegel's concept demonstrates that individual identity is at least partially shaped by the views of that individual held by others. And, for Taylor, Hegel's thinking on intersubjectivity highlights the moral injury that can be done to an individual by the characterisations of others. As Taylor says in a penultimate statement, "The thesis is that our identity is partly shaped by recognition or its absence, often by the *mis*recognition of others, and so a person or group of people can suffer real damage, real distortion, if the people or society around them mirror back to them a confining or demeaning or contemptible picture of themselves. Non-recognition or misrecognition can inflict harm, can be a form of oppression, imprisoning someone in a false, distorted, and reduced mode of being."[13] Due and proper recognition, Taylor concludes, is not simply a matter of courtesy and respect, but a vital human need. Hegel's allegory of the master-slave relationship also implies a normative principle that has political consequences. For Hegel, according to Taylor, "the struggle for recognition can find only one satisfactory solution, and that is a regime of reciprocal recognition among equals."[14] Taylor applies this Hegelian notion to the contemporary world to argue that if modern societies are to satisfy the principle of recognition, they must grant public recognition in one form or another to all citizens because everyone is the bearer of a particular cultural identity. Taylor refers to a range of social and political issues – feminism, aboriginal land claims, the status of once-colonised peoples, and Quebec as a distinct society – that he regards as reflecting a theoretical background that requires the distinctive characteristics of a particular group be recognised. In terms of the "problem of Canada," for example, he says that the "root cause of [Canada's] impending fracture can be put in one word: 'recognition.'"[15]

The problem, says Taylor, is that the demand for recognition often conflicts with older traditions of difference-blind liberalism, and his fundamental purpose as a political philosopher is to reconstruct a substantive liberalism that can, in his view, more adequately respond to this demand. For example, Taylor refers to feminist claims that a traditional patriarchal society imposes a negative self-understanding on women. Even when the removal of social and legal barriers has emancipated women, the lingering influences of a male-dominated society impose themselves on a woman's sense of self. And this internalised misrecognition continues to impede a woman's freedom to achieve authentic selfhood. Taylor sees similar examples of misrecognition in relations between whites and blacks. White society, he suggests, projects a demeaning image onto blacks that blacks have difficulty overcoming. Likewise, the failure of European society to properly recognise aboriginals ensures that some aboriginals even accept a degrading view of themselves as savages.[16] Thus, says Taylor, the failure to adequately recognise the "other" is not merely bad manners or a lack of respect, rather "[i]t can inflict a grievous wound, saddling its victims with crippling self-hatred."[17]

Taylor's argument raises the question of exactly what is meant by the term *recognition,* particularly in the context of debates about cultural or social identity. Patchen Markell suggests that *recognition* refers to a certain kind of public acknowledgment of the particular social or cultural identities of a person or group. Because these identities are connected to the concept of recognition, the idea of recognition itself is to be regarded as a thicker or more substantive good than more common notions of tolerance and respect. Toleration can be only reluctantly given and need not involve any real knowledge of the other. Respect can be granted despite animosity toward or dislike of another's cultural or social identity. Recognition, however, instantiates a deeper or thicker respect – that is, a respect rooted in awareness and knowledge of the identity of the other. Markell makes the further point that, at a deeper level, recognition involves an element of reflectiveness or self-consciousness. This emphasis on reflectiveness opens up the common understanding of the word *recognition* to suggest a dimension of re-cognition, or rethinking, and hence of the recovery of something once known but forgotten. Thus, as Markell puts it, recognition involves "respect grounded in the knowledge or understanding of someone's identity in all its particularity."[18] Anthony Appiah also captures this thick sense of recognition in arguing that the politics of recognition holds that people have a right not to be simply respected or tolerated on the basis of their common humanity, but "to be acknowledged publicly as what they already really are."[19]

Taylor's thought reflects this understanding of the concept of recognition. As such, his use of the concept is essentially Hegelian in that it reflects an attempt to reconcile the universalism of the Greek notion of the honour due equals with the homogeneous Christian notion of the equality of all people before God. This "thick" understanding of "recognition," with its emphasis on knowledge or reflection, is associated with a particular view of the character of identity. Taylor refers to this linkage of recognition and identity as authenticity. All individuals possess an authentic identity that distinguishes them from others and provides them with their own original and unique way of being. However, Taylor also extends this notion of authenticity, of being true to one's own originality, to groups and communities, making them the bearers of a collective or cultural identity. Whether individual or group, authenticity of identity is linked to recognition in that all are the objects of the acknowledgment of recognition. The politics of recognition requires that the unique identity of every individual and every group be acknowledged.

Taylor's view of authentic identity clearly implies that the identity of an individual or group is somehow independent of the judgments or attitudes of others. The idea of authenticity, as elucidated by Taylor, has its historical roots in the subjective turn of modernity – that is, in the idea that individuals possess an inner voice, or an inner moral sense, to which they must be true in order to be authentic. But does this not imply that only to the extent that our inwardness remains independent of the impositions of others can our subjective sense of identity serve as a standard for judging situations of misrecognition? And if so, does this way of understanding recognition and identity not make it difficult to justify the argument that misrecognition constitutes, as Taylor says, a "grievous wound"? Taylor insists that misrecognition is in itself harmful, constituting a kind of oppression in which an individual or a group is forced into "a false, distorted and reduced mode of being."[20] But if our sense of identity is so inward, why should the judgments of others affect us? Taylor's concept of recognition suggests that if an individual can be harmed by the misrecognition of others, then it must be because his identity is bound up in others, that his inwardness is not autonomous. This notion underscores Patchen Markell's previously noted description of recognition as a mode of public knowledge or self-conscious awareness of the particular social or cultural identity of another individual or group. Does this mean that authentic identities are social constructs? How does this fit with Taylor's claim that the authentic identity requires individuals to discover their inner self, an original way of being that cannot be derived socially but needs to be generated inwardly? How can this inner self be independent of others but at the same time require the recognition of others to be fully authenticated? Taylor seems to suggest that modern individuals cannot claim an identity that is entirely socially determined, but he also seems to say that neither can they seek a purely autonomous identity.[21]

Taylor responds to this apparent conundrum by asserting that there is no such thing as a monologically created inner self. Our sense of inwardness, the notion that we possess inner depths to which we must be true, is a dialogical product. To understand the close connection between identity and recognition, we need to understand that the crucial feature of human existence is its fundamentally dialogical character. As Taylor puts it, "[M]y discovering my own identity doesn't mean that I work it out in isolation, but that I negotiate it through dialogue, partly overt, partly internal, with others."[22] Individuals acquire self-agency and the capacity to comprehend each other through the acquisition of languages of expression, by which Taylor means not only words but also the languages of art, love, and what he calls "gesture." These languages are not something we acquire in isolation. We acquire the languages of expression through interactions with significant others. The languages acquired through these interactions are necessary not only for self-understanding, but also as the source of consciousness itself. This identity-generating dialogue, along with development in consciousness and self-understanding, continues throughout our lives. Indeed, our significant others include our parents, who are always with us, even if only in memory, our partners in relationships, our children, and others who provide the context of our social and political existence. In this regard, Taylor sounds very much like John Watson in his promotion of the symbiotic relationship of the individual and the community. Individual identity is not something that precedes recognition, but is the consequence of continuous relationships with others. We are always interacting with others; hence, the process of identity formation in and through others is not subject to some "monological ideal" in which we finally free ourselves from the influences of others, particularly our parents, and attain our true identities. "[T]he making and sustaining of our identity in the absence of a heroic effort to break out of ordinary existence remains dialogical throughout our lives."[23]

It is this symbiotic condition of human identity that makes the concept of recognition so crucial for Taylor, especially when it is attached to the idea of authenticity. Our individual identity greatly depends on the conduct of others. Who we are, our identity, is intimately tied to what others think of us. Taylor says that people understand this requirement of mutual recognition in the private or intimate sphere, especially in their dealings with their significant others. But this concern with recognition is also played out in the public sphere, in which the political culture is increasingly under pressure to practise a politics of equal recognition.[24] Indeed, Taylor's main political concern is with the rise of the modern demand for recognition in the public arena. This demand, he argues, is at the root of contemporary demands for the protection and elevation of minority groups and cultures in majoritarian societies. In his essay "The Politics of Recognition," Taylor argues that the mistreatment of others is often a matter of misrecognition. Failing to properly recognise individuals or minority groups as possessing a distinct and worthy identity is damaging to that person or group because negative perceptions from others affect our sense of self-worth.[25]

Taylor argues that the politics of equal recognition reflects two different, if interconnected, political trends in modern democratic societies. He calls these trends "the politics of equal dignity" and "the politics of difference." The politics of equal dignity is an outgrowth of our desire for equal recognition, and both are associated with the desirability of individual identity and the ideal of authenticity. The second trend, the politics of difference, comes out of the politics of dignity. In this trend, which is also universalist in its claims, we are expected to recognise the supposedly unique identities of individuals and groups that set them apart from other individuals or groups. This political trend adds a new dimension to the egalitarian principles of the Enlightenment. "The idea is that it is precisely this distinctness that has been ignored, glossed over, assimilated to a dominant or majority identity. And this assimilation is the cardinal sin against the ideal of authenticity."[26]

Taylor connects both trends – the politics of equal dignity and the politics of difference – to the collapse of pre-modern hierarchical societies with their concepts of honour. Despite the disappearance of such societies, the desire for honour that these societies once satisfied persists in the modern world, albeit in a different form. In pre-modern hierarchical societies, individuals could distinguish themselves from others and, when their conduct met some existing standard of excellence, be rewarded with greater social status than that given to others. The implications are obvious. Only a few could be so honoured, for if everyone was honoured in the same way, there would be no honour for anyone – the concept would lack any substantive meaning. Most people thus had to go unrecognised to a greater or lesser extent.[27] Thus, says Taylor, pre-modern honour is "intrinsically linked to inequalities. For some to have honour in this sense, it is essential that not everyone have it."[28] This is no longer acceptable in our democratic, non-hierarchical world. Since the time of the Enlightenment, the generally accepted notion of human nature presumes the inherent equality of individuals. This notion undermines not only traditional social and political hierarchies, but also the concept of honour itself. In modern egalitarian theory, all individuals should be equally honoured in their innate dignity as a human person. However, just because the traditional hierarchical notion of honour has faded does not mean that the individual desire for recognition has waned. The concept of honour has acquired its modern surrogate in the concept of human equality; in this latter concept, not only the equality of individuals is acknowledged but also the ostensible uniqueness of each individual. As Taylor states, "There is a certain way of being human that is my way. I am called upon to live my life in this way, and not in imitation of anyone else's life. But this notion gives a new importance to being true to myself. If I am not, I miss the point of my life; I miss what being human is for *me*."[29]

According to Taylor, the intermingling of these two ideas about human nature – one emphasising the abstract equality of everyone and the other the uniqueness of the individual – accounts for the deep longing that moderns bring to their personal and public relationships: "On the intimate level, we can see how much an original identity needs and is vulnerable to the recognition given or withheld by significant others. It is not surprising that in the culture of authenticity, relationships are seen as the key *loci* of self-discovery and self-affirmation. Love relationships are not just important because of the general emphasis in modern culture on the fulfilment of ordinary needs. They are also crucial because they are the crucibles of inwardly generated identity."[30]

This need to assert one's uniqueness, to maintain some modern version of honour, also plays out on the social plane. And it is on this plane that Taylor considers the distinctions and tensions between the politics of dignity and the politics of difference. On the surface, the two types of politics seem to point in opposite directions. The first posits a universalist understanding of equality that denies differences between individuals and makes everyone equal before the law, says Norman Barry. As individuals, all are equal in dignity, and thus all are entitled to be treated the same way as everyone else regardless of differences of sex, race, religion, and nationality. This egalitarian form of recognition does not preclude the retention of particular cultural characteristics that emerge organically from societal interaction, Barry notes, but it does exclude the kind of constitutional and legal arrangements that would privilege a particular group or culture.[31]

For Taylor, Barry argues, this universalist application of the principle of equality can threaten the survival of particular cultures. Taylor seeks an alternative doctrine, the politics of difference, in which people are identified by those cultural characteristics that differentiate groups and that would require the suspension of universalist principles if they would result in one group dominating others or even distorting their cultural integrity. "With the politics of equal dignity, what is established is meant to be universally the same, an identical basket of rights and immunities; with the politics of difference, what we are asked to recognise is the unique identity of this individual or group, their distinctness from everything else."[32]

Avoiding this sin is problematic. Although everyone might have an equal right to their cultural identity, minorities within a culture are often under pressure to conform to the majoritarian culture. However, Taylor argues that assimilationist pressures can be eased and members of these minorities enabled to attain the equality of the majority if the means can be found to recognise these minority identities. In effect, one acknowledges what is universally accepted – that everyone has an identity of equal value – by recognising what is distinctive about everyone. Thus, the politics of difference emerges out of the politics of universal dignity as the consequence of "a new understanding of the human social condition [that] imparts a radically new meaning to an old principle."[33]

In making this argument, Taylor underscores the challenge that the concept of recognition poses for the traditional understanding of liberal society. As he remarks, charges have been levelled against procedural liberalism and its purported "difference-blindness" – that is, its claim to provide a neutral ground that allows people of all cultures to coexist. But Taylor points out that Western liberalism is not the secular, post-religious culture that liberal elites like to claim, but rather a product of Christianity. The division of church and state, for example, reflects a view, dating from early Christianity, that sees a separation between the sacred and the profane. Liberalism, in this light, is not a meeting ground for all cultures because it is itself "the political expression of one range of cultures, and quite incompatible with other ranges."[34] Taylor's references to the cultural specificity of liberalism are intended to promote a different kind of liberalism, one that would acknowledge collective aspirations while, at the same time, safeguarding the fundamental rights of those who do not share those aspirations.

But there are difficulties with this more substantive liberalism. Taylor wants political society to provide two supports to individuals that on the face of it seem mutually contradictory. One support is grounded in what is perceived to be the fundamental Enlightenment liberal notion that the individual shares a common equality with all others. The other support is rooted in the idea that the individual or the cultural group possesses a supposedly unique particularity that sets him or them apart from all other individuals and groups. So what you have, on the one hand, is the politics of equal dignity that requires everyone to be treated in a difference-blind manner, and on the other, the politics-of-difference requirement that everyone's uniqueness be recognised and even fostered. To be sure, both those who promote equal dignity and those who push for the recognition of difference are concerned with equality. But as Andy Lamey puts it, those who promote equal dignity claim that the promoters of difference violate the principle of non-discrimination, while the promoters of difference say that the advocates of equal dignity push people into a homogeneous mould that denies their capacity for individual authenticity.[35]

This tension is evident in debates over multiculturalism. Advocates of multiculturalism argue that Western societies promote the ideal of difference-blind liberalism only because until recently their populations were largely homogeneous and, thus, they were able to regard many of their political practices and social policies – from who gets their portrait on the national currency to the language of instruction in schools – from a position of unquestioned universalist assumptions. But the emergence of more heterogeneous societies in the West as a result of globalisation and mass immigration exposes the extent to which liberal policy-making is not difference-blind, but reflects culturally influenced ends.[36]

Taylor highlights this argument against the claim of difference-blind liberalism. Supposedly, in a multicultural society, differences between people and cultures are accepted and need not be suppressed. In reality, however, the ostensible principles of multiculturalism conflict with other principles of liberal society, particularly those of majoritarian rule and popular sovereignty. Majoritarian groups, like minoritarian groups, tend to regard the "other" according to their own standards and values, and to find them wanting if they do not meet those values. Taylor sums up the multicultural perspective in his critique of neutral liberalism: "The claim is that the supposedly neutral set of difference-based principles of the politics of equal dignity is in fact a reflection of one hegemonic culture. As it turns out, then, only minority or suppressed cultures are being forced to take alien form. Consequently, the supposedly fair and difference-blind society is not only inhuman (because suppressing identities) but also, in a subtle and unconscious way, itself highly discriminatory."[37]

Taylor's project of reconciliation clearly promotes a form of liberalism that attempts to satisfy often-conflicting demands. The politics of equal dignity that is vouchsafed in a system of liberal rights is, he says, inhospitable to the politics of difference because it requires the uniform application of the rules defining those rights and is sceptical of collective goals. While he does not accuse liberalism of denying or trying to abolish cultural differences, he argues that "it can't accommodate what the members of distinct societies really aspire to, which is survival."[38] This aspiration, if it is to be satisfied, requires variations in the standard liberal rules of politics.

Taylor, it seems, wants moral standards that reflect universal rights regarding human dignity, including rights to life, freedom of expression and association, and the judicial protection of those rights. At the same time, he insists that these universal rights must not undermine collective identities. Hence, he promotes a form of liberalism that distinguishes fundamental rights from those rights that relate to the importance of cultural survival, and that, when necessary, favours cultural survival. Taylor argues that, given the way more and more societies are becoming multicultural, in the sense of including more than one cultural community that seeks its own survival, "the rigidities of procedural liberalism may rapidly become impractical in tomorrow's world."[39]

Can liberalism be altered in the way Taylor's urges? Is it a good idea even if it can be done? Before I can address these questions – and Taylor's own answers – it is necessary to consider his philosophical antecedents in order to understand how, as it were, Taylor reaches his conclusion about the impracticalities of liberalism.

18

A Philosophical History of Recognition

For Taylor, the most prominent feature of the modern identity is its inwardness. While inwardness was a feature in the thought of both Plato and Augustine, the identity articulated by modern thinkers such as René Descartes and John Locke is characterised by a radical turn inward for moral sources. No longer is morality grounded in a good or a god beyond us. Rather, we attempt as moderns to find our morality within ourselves. The modern idea of the individual, and, indeed, our whole notion of individualism, derives from the waning of those external horizons of meaning that provided pre-modern individuals with a sense of place within the larger whole and helped make their lives intelligible. Taylor attributes this loss to the erosion of the pre-modern cosmological and theological foundations by modern natural science. The collapse of these horizons undermined the legitimacy of traditional social hierarchies according to which individuals were recognised as existing within a natural or God-given chain of being. Under the pre-modern dispensation, everyone knew his or her place, and there was a place for everyone. The loss of traditional horizons of meaning has forced the individual to turn inward in order to find meaning and purpose.[40]

Taylor locates the loss of the pre-modern horizon in the split between ancient and medieval thought and modern thought. Between these two periods, our moral sources shift from a cosmic order that is external to the individual to one in which the sources of morality are found within the individual. But there is also a divide within the modern period that sees the idea of the individual as the source of morality increasingly radicalised until, with the Enlightenment, the idea of the autonomous, atomised self emerges. Then, with the Romantic reaction to the Enlightenment, the idea of the self was further radicalised by "the massive subjective turn of modern culture, a new form of inwardness, in which we come to think of ourselves as beings with inner depths."[41]

Taylor begins his philosophical history of this "new form of inwardness" with Plato.[42] It is with Plato that the concept of reason and reflection – "the ideal of rational contemplation," in Craig Calhoun's words – first gains ascendancy over the Homeric ethic of unreflective action and the desire for glory. Homeric Greece, according to Taylor, does not provide the idea of a unique and unitary self because it does not see the individual as the locus of identity and, therefore, cannot begin the process of internalisation that has become the hallmark of the modern self. With Plato, human consciousness becomes a unitary sensorium in which the order of the cosmos can be known through reason. Taylor is careful to point out that Plato's conception of reason is not that of the modern world. Plato does not conceive of reason as calculative, a means of deciding proper actions on the basis of the objective evidence. For Plato, rational contemplation is an attempt to attune human consciousness to the proper order of the cosmos and, in this attunement, to perceive the ethical truth intrinsic to that order. The best function of a man is to use his reason to attune himself to the external order of the cosmos. The knowledge of Plato's Forms includes the comprehension of both metaphysical and ethical truth. The Delphic injunction of "Know thyself" is not a promotion of narcissism but rather an admonishment to align oneself, intellectually and ethically, to the comprehended cosmic order. As Taylor puts it, Plato provides a substantive concept of reason in which "rationality is tied to the perception of order; and so to realise our capacity for reason is to see the order as it is."[43]

Taylor also attributes Plato's notion of "reason as attunement" to another development of modern inwardness, the idea that the individual, as a sensorium of the given cosmic order, is responsible for his own life and therefore must act with "rational self-mastery" to control the conflicting desires of the psyche and so harmonise himself with that order. In Taylor's view, Plato's call to self-mastery, to the control of one's appetites and desires, provides the first inward shift and hence the first move away from a morality grounded in external sources. With Plato, the gods no longer inform human consciousness as they do in the Homeric epics. After Plato, individuals are self-identical and therefore self-responsible.[44]

Augustine, however, is the pivotal transitional thinker who bridges the ancient and modern worlds. Augustine, says Taylor, moves away from a morality infused by external sources toward a morality sustained by the individual's inner resources. Following the teachings of Plotinus, Augustine takes Plato's dualities of spirit and matter, eternity and time, and recasts them in terms of inner and outer to produce a new Christian interiority. Augustine also identifies the Platonic forms with the idea of a god who creates the world *ex nihilo*. The created world receives its form through God, through its participation in the manifestations of His thought. Everything has being insofar as it participates in God. But the Augustinian synthesis is not simply the transference of the classical external cosmic order to an external Christian cosmos. Augustine's claim is that our knowledge of the divine comes not through some attunement to the external objects of the created order – although they are expressions of God's mind – but rather through our love of God. We have our being in our knowledge of God's created order, which implies that our relationship to the other, whether God or community, is a matter of knowing what it is that has created us. In this manner, Plato's notion of rational contemplation is recast in the language of inwardness.[45] Craig Calhoun explains the matter succinctly: "Augustine introduced a radical sort of reflexivity to the Western tradition, for his arguments involved not only taking care of oneself – making oneself the object of one's own attention – but also understanding the world through one's first-person experiential relationship to it. Radical reflexivity involves attempting to experience our experiencing."[46]

For Taylor, Augustine's notion of a personal god, whose love both created and redeemed the self, demonstrates an intimacy between self and other – soul and God – far deeper than anything Plato contemplates with his erotic union of the psyche and the Forms. Indeed, the relationship runs so deep that it suggests that our only knowledge of truth is through our inward access to the divine mind. This implies, however, that knowledge of the truth is related to loving that which is within ourselves. Taylor quotes Augustine's passage from *De Vera Religione* to this effect: "Do not go outward; return within yourself. In the inward man dwells truth." It is in knowing and loving ourselves – seeing the inner light, the light in the soul, as it were – that we may find God and thereby moral truth. But this also suggests that the truth of the self is ultimately tied to the first-person perspective, since God created that self. Taylor calls this "radical reflexivity," arguing that Augustine "bequeathed it to the Western tradition of thought" and, in doing so, "inaugurated a new line of development in our understanding of moral sources, one which has been formative for our entire Western culture."[47]

Taylor is careful to note that this radical reflexivity means more than the reified and solipsistic forms of modern subjectivism. Augustine's inward turn does not mean "taking care of yourself" – that is, making yourself the essential object of your attention. Rather, it means knowing the Truth of the world (which is God) through your first-person experiences of that Truth. In other words, radical reflexivity refers to a self-conscious awareness of the ground of reality, understanding the world not merely as an external collection of objects, but as something there for us to know and love. Nonetheless, Augustine's inward turn is the source of modern morality, according to Taylor. Augustine is also the source of Cartesian epistemology, the originator of the Cartesian *cogito*. And the Reformation in the sixteenth and seventeenth centuries can be regarded as the "immense flowering of Augustinian spirituality," a development that, as Taylor notes, carried on in its own fashion through to the Enlightenment.[48]

For Taylor, modernity begins with Descartes's recasting of Augustine. Descartes is "profoundly Augustinian,"[49] both in his reflexivity and in the emphasis he places on the *cogito*. What is different is Descartes's new mechanistic perspective on the world, as provided by modern natural science. This worldview undermines the older teleological view of the world, dissolving the Augustinian and Platonic linkage between the cosmos and human conduct and self-understanding. Yet, even if the natural world is no longer the source of morality, Descartes retains and even enhances the Augustinian self as the source of morality. Descartes radicalizes Augustine by centring the moral sources within man rather leaving them with the Augustinian god, who was the ultimate object of inward reflection. This marks a major shift in human self-understanding, says Taylor, especially in the relationship of man and God. With Descartes, the divine is no longer the basis of either our knowledge of the world or our morality: "God's existence is a theorem in *my* system of perfect science."[50]

Descartes's transmutation of Augustinian thought reflects his reliance on modern science's epistemology. Where Augustine (and Plato) understands "knowing" as the union of the mind to a cosmic order that makes the world intelligible, modern epistemology understands knowing as dependent on the mind's capacity to determine which of its representations most accurately correspond to the external objects of the world. Reason, according to this epistemological model, is no longer a matter of rational contemplation, attunement to the reality of the world, but a capacity to construct orders that meet certain conceptual standards or understandings. Or, as Gary Gutting puts it, with Descartes, "rationality could now be understood in a purely procedural way, that is, as the proper following of the rules of evidence and argument."[51] The problem with the Cartesian approach, at least from the perspective of the ancients, is that it creates a conceptual gap between reason and truth, a divide between the knowing mind and the object of the mind's knowing. The mind is now detached or disengaged from the world of experience. The world becomes an object for our subjective desires. Augustine understands reason as the means for obtaining clearer insight into our souls; to be fully rational is to have experiential knowledge of God's Truth. For Plato, to be rational is to be right-minded about the order of the cosmos.

With Descartes, however, reason becomes the instrument by which we construct claims regarding the reality or nature of objects external to ourselves. The mind is no longer a sensorium of direct engagement in and with the world, but is, as Taylor says, "'disenchanted', as mere mechanism ... devoid of any spiritual essence or expressive dimension."[52] Descartes might retain Augustine's and Plato's emphasis on rationality and inwardness, but he reorients the source of morality away from the pre-modern sources of the Good or God toward a subjective, self-certifying procedural rationalism. He reconstructs the first-person experience as the result of external forces impinging on internal capacities. Rationality becomes an internal element of subjective thought, rather than an attribute of reasoning related to a vision of reality. Augustine saw the divine at work in every aspect of an individual's life, and regarded the individual's failure to experience the divine source as a matter of sin. Descartes' epistemological shift opens up the possibility that the failure to find a source of morality is because there is no source to find. In other words, with Descartes, rational inquiry, coupled to modern natural science, opens the door to a rejection of religious faith.[53] As Taylor says, "this new conception of inwardness, an inwardness of self-sufficiency, of autonomous powers of ordering by reason, *also* prepared the ground for modern unbelief."[54]

Taylor devotes much of his philosophical project to tracking the consequences of the Cartesian shift. One path of inquiry leads to Locke and what Taylor refers to as the "radical Enlightenment" and its notion of the individual as an ahistorical atom. The other path leads to the Protestant affirmation of everyday life and the Romanticism of Rousseau and Herder and their idea of an expressive self with inner depths nourished by nature and membership in the community. Taylor opts for the Romantic view of modernity, arguing that seeing ourselves as autonomous individuals or atomised selves undermines moral existence. The main target in his critique of the atomised self is John Locke, who, he says, extends Descartes's disengaged self into a radically autonomous self. Descartes maintained the idea that humans have an innate inclination toward reason. Locke denied any form of innate ideas. Additionally, Locke rejected any teleological understanding of human nature, whether in terms of epistemology or morality. For Locke, humans have no particular natural inclinations, whether in the

ancient cosmological sense or in the more modern notion of innate rationality. The Lockean self, lacking innate ideas, is no longer even a bearer of
truth in any substantive fashion, and becomes itself an object of disengaged inquiry. These rejections form the basis of Locke's "punctual self."
The punctual self, says Calhoun, is even more self-contained and self-
sufficient than that of the Cartesian disengaged self. The punctual self is
merely a consciousness examining its sensory and cognitive experience. In
effect, reasoning begins by clearing the cognitive foundation of anything
that might hinder the acquisition of truth. While experience, sensation, and
thought remain basic functions, they are not the consequence of action but
the beginning of inquiry. Minds receive ideas; they do not create them.[55]
In Taylor's words, "Locke reifies the mind to an extraordinary degree," em-
bracing a mechanistic, atomised concept of it. "Our understanding of
things is constructed out of the building blocks of simple ideas ... The at-
oms themselves come into existence by a quasi-mechanical process."[56]

What sets Locke apart, says Taylor, is the extent of his detachment of the
self from any embeddedness in the world. Not only does Locke's rational
inquiry question all external authorities, but it also questions all internal
assumptions. But how does Locke avoid a self-destructive scepticism? Only,
according to Taylor, by insisting that the mind is passive and that what it
grasps is outside its own power. On this basis, reason asserts procedural
rules; that is, logical deduction and probable evidence allow the construc-
tion of the truth about the world. Taylor writes: "In effecting this double
movement of suspension and examination, we wrest the control of our
thinking and outlook away from passion or custom or authority and assume responsibility for it ourselves. Locke's theory also reflects an ideal of
independence and self-responsibility, a notion of reason as free from established custom and prevailing authority."[57] With Locke, then, Taylor sees
the philosophical beginning of the radically modern notion of the detached and autonomous self. This view of the self has political implications.
For one thing, it is anti-authoritarian in that it devalues knowledge of social
customs and traditions with the assertion that knowledge is rooted in personal experience and self-understanding, which is a more radical notion of
individual autonomy and self-responsibility. The Lockean individual can
examine himself as an object and can recast himself accordingly to suit his
own subjective desires.

This subjectivity is a radical transformation of Plato's idea of rational
self-control, says Taylor. Unlike the ancient notion of the citizen being
embedded in a community (or cosmos) and deriving his essential meaningfulness from his proper attunement to that community (or cosmos),

the modern individual finds his meaning and self-worth in his ability to re-make himself independently of that which is other to himself. "Radical dis-engagement," Taylor says, "opens the prospect of self-remaking."[58] Yet Taylor sees a paradox here. Locke links an ideal of individual independence with concepts of disengagement and procedural reason that foster the notion that the individual, too, can be an object who is the subject of detached rational inquiry. We become, in short, objects to ourselves. We experience our freedom in the first person but understand the entity that enjoys that freedom in the third person. In Taylor's words, "Radical objectivity is only intelligible and accessible through radical subjectivity."[59]

For Taylor, this is one of the great puzzles of modern philosophy. Modern epistemology calls for a radical disengagement from the engagements of ordinary experience. At the same time, the demands for self-responsible freedom and self-exploration, in awakening notions of dignity and authenticity, require a deeper engagement with our ordinary individual circumstances. On this point, Taylor recalls that for both Plato and Aristotle there was a distinction between "life" and the "good life," with the former a necessary if insufficient condition of the latter. You left the life of the household, the realm of economics, for the good of public life, the realm of politics and philosophy. With the advent of modernity, however, "ordinary life" – by which Taylor means family, marriage, work, and other similar matters – becomes a fundamental value. Work and family, production and reproduction, are no longer deemed lower than achievements of public honour or philosophic contemplation; indeed, they are even higher ideals. "[T]he fullness of Christian existence was to be found within the [ordinary] activities of this life, in one's calling and in marriage and the family."[60]

Taylor follows Hegel in tracing this affirmation of ordinary life to the Protestant Reformation. But he also points out how the emphasis on ordinary life is supported by modern science. While Baconian science may have originated in experimentation, it culminated in the technological impulse to improve the human condition. Science, rather than being an elite activity of rational contemplation, has become a pursuit dedicated to the betterment of ordinary life. Citing Bacon, Taylor writes that, for moderns, "science is not a higher activity which ordinary life should subserve; on the contrary, science shall benefit ordinary life."[61] In a similar fashion, the Protestant rejection of a priestly elite that has renounced profane life in order to mediate the presence of the divine reflects the notion that ordinary life gives everyone equal access to the sources of moral order. In this way, the Protestant denial of Catholic hierarchies leads to a rejection of distinctions between sacred and profane, between higher and lower. This not only fosters a heightened affirmation of ordinary life, but also undermines traditions of social hierarchy. At the same time, the Protestant emphasis on work encourages science in its efforts to improve the human condition. In an argument that recalls George Grant's acknowledgment of the spiritual sources of technology, Taylor says that this turn to science means that "the instrumental stance towards the world has been given a new and important spiritual meaning ... *Instrumentalizing* things is the spiritually essential step."[62] For moderns, control of the world is godliness.

But is there not a danger that this effort to master the world might lead to attempts to master ordinary life by means of technological intervention? In an argument that is again very close to Grant's, Taylor claims that this has in fact taken place because modern instrumental science denies its own spiritual sources and its original moral purposes. Taylor's purpose in attempting to recover the positive aspects of modernity – the ethic of benevolence, as he calls it – is to find those sources that have been subordinated to the dominance of "instrumental" rationality. For Taylor, those sources include the Romantics, such as Rousseau and Herder. It is with them and their expressivist notions of freedom and authenticity that we can recover a moral ground to address the tension between the individual and the community.

19

Expressivism and
the Ethic of Authenticity

Taylor regards the notion of authenticity, and the various modes of recognition it engenders, as the latest development in the history of the individual. He traces the origins of this development to nineteenth-century Romanticism, which sublated the previous forms of individualism articulated by Descartes and Locke – the "disengaged reasoner" and the "punctual self," respectively. The Cartesian and Lockean understanding of individualism reflected an instrumental attitude toward the world in which the individual, as a rational agent, is required to bring the external world under control in order to be free to decide upon his self-chosen purposes and realise them most efficiently. Much of Taylor's thought is a critique of this view of the individual. At the same time, though, Taylor recognises that the early moderns' concepts offer a moral ideal that valorises the freedom and dignity of the individual. The individualism of the early moderns, he writes, "signifies a rejection of the previously dominant notion of a hierarchy, according to which a human being can be a proper moral agent only when embedded in a larger social whole, whose very nature is to exhibit a hierarchical complementarity."[63] The Romantic "ethic of authenticity" is a response to the individualism of disengaged rationality and to the political ideas of contractarianism and procedural liberalism such an ontology produced.

Taylor's defence of authenticity is, in effect, an attempt to weave his way between those who applaud and those who disparage modernity. The boosters include those post-modern deconstructionists and neo-Nietzchean feminists, as well as the technologists and scientific administrators, who favour the concepts of individual authenticity and freedom precisely because there are no absolute horizons or moral standards for human conduct against which individuals must justify their own desires and claims to power. The knockers include those who regard notions of authenticity as little more than the promotion of a culture of narcissism, hedonism, and nihilism, a society devoid of moral ideals. According to Taylor, what both sides share despite their differences is a debased understanding of authenticity that reduces freedom to unconstrained, egocentric choice.[64] As he notes, even relativism is rooted in the moral claim that we all have the right to develop our own way of life based on our particular values. Taylor's aim is to recover authenticity as a valid moral ideal, since it is one that cannot be easily rejected by moderns.[65] We may object to the new-age narcissism and self-indulgence that have been the by-products of the ideal of authenticity, but the ideal itself resides at the core of our modern self-understanding. It is Taylor's task to show why both the boosters and the knockers are mistaken about authenticity, and why we should appreciate it. Indeed, Taylor suggests that a persuasive understanding of authenticity would provide the means for the reconciliation of the individual and the community. He writes: "What we ought to be doing is fighting over the meaning of authenticity ... we ought to be trying to persuade people that self-fulfilment, so far from excluding un-conditional relationships and moral demands beyond the self, actually re-quires these in some form. The struggle ought not to be *over* authenticity, for or against, but *about* it, defining its proper meaning. We ought to be trying to lift the culture back up, closer to its motivating ideal."[66]

Taylor's argument sounds very close to John Watson's regarding the symbiotic nature of the relationship between the individual and the community, in which each ideally serves the ends of the other. Taylor, too, believes that the authentic individual is the individual who is open to those things that transcend him and to unconditional moral relationships (communal belongingness, in other words) that are not merely the means for satisfying egocentric desires. Yet, such a claim raises the question: How can individual identities be authentic and unique and at the same time be dialogical and socially constructed? Perhaps the best way to approach this question is to examine Taylor's theory of expressivism[67] and the thinkers he draws on – Hegel, Herder, and Rousseau – to argue the ethic of authenticity. Taylor says that collectively these thinkers offer an expressivist understanding of the individual that both deepens and subverts the radical Enlightenment's mechanistic and instrumental understanding of the individual. As well, he contends that expressivism provides the theoretical means for the reconciliation of the individual and the community.[68]

Taylor's concept of authenticity is sustained by his view of human agency; that is, humans are self-interpreting animals. This expressivist interpretation of human beings provides Taylor with a corrective to the mechanistic understanding of human nature that came out of the scientific revolution and the Enlightenment. Taylor rejects the naturalist notion that values are projections of subjective desires and not aspects of reality. He holds that humans are endowed with a moral sensibility that runs deeper than an instrumental calculation of consequences. To be in touch with human passions and desires – the moral sentiments – is a requirement for realising our humanity. The individual is most himself when he feels that he is part of a community, part of a "we." And according to Taylor, this expressivist understanding of the symbiotic relationship between the individual and the community is embedded within modernity, or at least within the Romantic version of modernity, and hence is available for recovery.[69]

Taylor gives the credit for expressivism's origins to Rousseau, who, he says, further develops the inwardness already established in modernity by highlighting the autonomy of the individual. Rousseau does this not by accepting Locke's punctual self, but by arguing that individuals naturally possess an inner virtuousness that needs to be cultivated as an authentic identity. This, says Taylor, is the point of Rousseau's claim that "conscience, our inner guide, 'speaks to us in the language of nature,'"[70] although too few hear it. Our ability to hear this inner voice of nature is blocked by the passions and desires we have been taught to value through our dependence on others, which is to say, by society. Moral salvation requires reconnecting to our natural inner self. This inner virtue cannot be achieved from some ostensibly objective perspective as required by the natural sciences, but can only be accessed through personal experience. Rousseau, however, does not propose a return to some pre-social state of nature, which is impossible in any case. Taylor emphasises that Rousseau's recovery of our inner authentic nature is an attempt to realign reason and nature in harmonious unity. "Conscience is the voice of nature as it emerges in a being who has entered society and is endowed with language and hence with reason."[71] Individual authenticity – the capacity to articulate the inner voice – entails entering a dialogue with others. For Rousseau, "the good political community is bound together by a sentiment which is an extension of the joy that humans feel in each others' company even in the most ordinary and intimate contexts."[72] And that sentiment, as Taylor observes, is the "general will," understood not as the aggregate of all wills but as the right or rational will. By means of the general will, Rousseau aims to reconcile individual freedom and communal belongingness. The general will is manifested in a social unity whose source is to be discovered within each individual, a reconciliation grounded in freedom and the recognition of authentic identity through attention to nature's inner voice. Rousseau thus defines freedom and morality, the individual and the community, in symbiotic terms.[73]

Taylor argues that one of the consequences of Rousseau's thought was to further the collapse of the pre-modern social hierarchies that maintained a concept of honour in which recognition is granted only to a few. Rousseau promotes a system based on the value of equal dignity, in which everyone, in theory, is recognised. And it is this Rousseauean requirement for equal recognition that underpins the modern demand for authenticity (that is, the moral injunction to be true to each individual's uniqueness) not only in relation to the individual but in relation to the group. In approaching the issue of the demand for authenticity, Taylor compares Rousseau's discourse about honour and dignity to the pre-modern concept of honour. Rousseau argues that honour fosters pride and the striving after preferences. This, in turn, leads to social and political divisions, and hence to a dependence on others' opinions, which mute the inner voice of nature. In a society where individuals determine their own goals and purposes in isolation from others, the result is social hierarchies that engender oppressive self-definitions. In effect, those with power are able to impose their purposes on those with less power. The concept of equal dignity, however, reconstitutes the human need for self-esteem and turns it toward equality, reciprocity, and unity of purpose.[74]

This claim is reflected in Rousseau's concept of the general will. Behind the general will is the notion that personal autonomy should not be oppressed by social hierarchy. If each individual has this same unity of purpose in his deepest self, then it does not matter where that individual resides socially, since that person is free to fulfil his purposes. Since these purposes are ultimately identical to those of everyone else, then, with everyone participating willingly in a common purpose, the inner voice of all individuals is esteemed equally and, thus, all are recognised and all feel they are members of the community; the "I" becomes a "we." Rousseau, Taylor observes, tries to solve the puzzle of how individuals can be recognised without the invocation of cultural differences, and he does so by offering the ideal of civic republicanism, in which citizens who care about what others think of them accept living highly public or community-oriented lives.[75]

Rousseau is particularly concerned about the kind of vanity, or *amour propre*, produced by economic competition. He sees such competition as rooted in pride, which creates a form of subservience or dependence on others that can only be surmounted by an unqualified attachment to the community, in which everyone is an equal member. Vanity, of course, reflects the desire for recognition. But it is also a feature of human psychology that fosters the kind of differentiation Rousseau's general will seeks to overcome. The general will, then, amounts to an attempt to avoid the social alienation and conflict resulting from demands for recognition from everyone by having all individuals recognise their interdependence. Individuals can enjoy the mutual reciprocity of recognition by removing the elements of hierarchical or superior (including economic) judgment. As Taylor concludes, "Under the aegis of the general will, all virtuous citizens are to be equally honoured. The age of dignity is born."[76]

Taylor questions what he sees as the three inseparable elements of Rousseau's political philosophy – "freedom (non-domination), the absence of differentiated roles and a very tight common purpose"[77] – all of which he recognises as having totalitarian potential. The general will, while satisfying the communitarian concern for belonging, eliminates the kinds of cultural and psychological differences that give individuals and individual groups their sense of identity. Taylor accepts Rousseau's anti-individualism program (particularly in its economic consequences), as well as his egalitarian and democratic impulses. But he questions Rousseau's lack of concern for cultural differences, finding it unacceptable because it risks the creation of subjective will, which tends to assert itself in an unthinking manner and produce such phenomena as the Terror of the French Revolution.[78]

Taylor may regard Rousseau as the originator of the age of dignity, but his endorsement is problematic and, arguably, exposes the dilemmas in his own thought. Hegel questions the tilt toward subjectivism in Rousseau's thought, seeing in the general will the absence of any reference to concrete laws and institutions. Rousseau's general will fails to account adequately for the inner rationality of the social and political arrangements of the community, its laws and constitutional arrangements, and, as a consequence, leaves the community open to potentially destructive tendencies.[79] Taylor is certainly aware of this and follows Hegel in objecting to a system of equal esteem that "requires a tight unity of purpose that seems incompatible with any differentiation."[80] Given this, it is not unreasonable to question whether Taylor's doubts about such a central aspect of Rousseau's political philosophy might carry over to his own thought. Might the "politics of recognition" possess its own inherent tensions?

Taylor distinguishes between the politics of equal dignity and the politics of difference. But if the politics of dignity and the politics of difference are *de facto* substitutes for the pre-modern concept of honour, as Taylor argues, they would seem to veer in different directions in terms of providing equal recognition. The politics of dignity posits a universal understanding of equality that ostensibly extinguishes differences between people and makes them equal before the law. Everyone is equal in dignity by the fact of their personhood, and thus everyone is entitled to the same protection and opportunities for self-expression regardless of differences in sex, religion, race, or ethnicity. As Norman Barry notes, this does not exclude the development of characteristics that distinguish one group from another, but it does seem to preclude altering the existing systems of legal egalitarianism and liberal constitutionalism in ways that privilege one group over another. Differences between groups are allowed only if differences can be sustained in ways compatible with the neutral application of law.[81] Taylor, of course, recognises this formulation as the bedrock for difference-blind liberalism. Citing Ronald Dworkin, he defines a liberal society as one that neither holds nor adopts a particular substantive view about the ends or purposes of life. What unites liberal society is its procedural commitment to treat people with equal respect. Sustaining this society is the Kantian notion that individuals are autonomous and free because they possess a natural rationality that allows them to transcend their particular circumstances and engage principles that are transhistorical and universal. Such a view regards human dignity as bound up with autonomy; that is, each individual has the capacity to determine his own notion of the good life.[82]

Taylor's communitarianism emerges on this point, challenging the notion of individual autonomy as traditionally understood by procedural liberalism. Taylor argues that universalist legal egalitarianism threatens those cultural differences that provide the kind of deep-level authenticity now being demanded by individuals. For Taylor, the individual is situated in and thus constituted by a complex matrix of influences – tradition, culture, and relationships. Such a contrast prompts questions: Are we bounded selves who should create societies based on autonomy and individualism and on what distinguishes each of us from the other? If we are essentially connected selves, should we strive for societies that recognise our basic communality? Liberalism emphasises the autonomous society with its reliance on legal and constitutional procedures and institutional mechanisms to provide bridges between atomised individuals. Communitarians, on the other hand, focus on the communal good or purpose, claiming that the liberal reliance on procedures is in itself grounded in an underlying notion of the good life. Like most communitarians, Taylor criticises liberalism for its focus on procedural rights, arguing that an individual's sense of belongingness or community is contingent upon a relaxation of the universal application of atomistic liberalism. This is Taylor's politics of difference. This type of politics seeks the recognition of the unique identity of individuals and group, their distinctiveness from all others. But can the communitarian "connected" self and the liberal "bounded" self be reconciled? Why is the politics of difference dissatisfied with the politics of equal dignity? The answer, according to Taylor, is precisely because the politics of difference ignores what makes each person or group distinctive, assimilating them into a dominant or majoritarian identity. And, for Taylor, assimilation is contrary to the ideal of authenticity in that "the supposedly fair and difference-blind society is not only inhuman (because suppressing identities) but also, in a subtle and unconscious way, itself highly discriminatory."[83]

To be sure, Taylor is careful to hedge his critique of liberalism. He takes pains to situate himself within the liberal tradition, insisting that he is a firm supporter of traditional liberal civil liberties. His objection is to the ontological foundations of liberalism, its grounding in atomistic individualism at the expense of the individual's communal situatedness. With this qualification, Taylor attempts to go beyond traditional liberalism to argue that it must be open to a collective sensibility. He seeks not merely the maintenance of the neutral laws of procedural liberalism that protect individual liberties, but also the positive affirmation of the distinctive features of particular cultural groups that enhance the individual's sense of community. Can you have both?

Rousseau tries with the notion of the general will to find a way to achieve the recognition of the individual without invoking societal features that tend to differentiate individuals. Taylor rejects this aspect of Rousseau's thought. He accepts Rousseau's anti-individualism, but he cannot accept Rousseau's disregard for cultural differentiation. Taylor, it seems, wants a version of liberalism that can reconcile conflicting demands. It must embody a morality that reflects universal values of individual equality and freedom and the juridical capacity to uphold those values, but at the same time, it cannot override collective needs. What Taylor clearly wants is the reconciliation of Rousseau's substantive democracy and Kant's procedural liberalism. Indeed, he reveals this goal when he describes the problem of Canada as a concrete manifestation of conflict between two theories of autonomy, namely Rousseau's and Kant's.[84]

Taylor's appropriation of Rousseau is reflected in his arguments about Canadian multiculturalism, particularly in his distinction between what he calls "first-level diversity" and "deep diversity." Taylor argues that Canadian society, at the level of deep diversity, should accommodate various forms of government within itself to satisfy the recognition requirements of different groups. In defending deep diversity, Taylor attacks first-level diversity, which he sees as a weak acceptance of cultural diversity within a state in which all groups are treated equally. First-level diversity, he says, has the potential for harmful misrecognition because in its insistence on the uniform application of rules it is "inhospitable to difference"[85] and, consequently, does not really treat different cultures with equal dignity. The result is that certain groups remain alienated from Canadian society as a whole; that is to say, their inner voice, their sense of authenticity, finds no articulation in the greater community.

Taylor, of course, seeks reconciliation at both the theoretical and the political levels. He attempts this through his appropriation, first, of Herder, and then, of Hegel, who together substantiate his ethic of authenticity.

20

Herder and the "Measure" of Expressivism

Taylor credits Johann Gottfried Herder with offering a new way to express the modern identity, both for individuals and for groups. Herder, he writes, offers the idea that each person has "an original way of being human: each person has his or her own 'measure.'"[86] This individual measure is embedded in a cultural framework essential for the individual's development, but this does not imply conformity to a Rousseauean general will or an excess of unity. Instead, it points to the capacity of individuals to use reason to attain autonomy even in realising that they are rooted in a culture and its particular horizon of meaning. In appropriating Herder, Taylor attempts to reconcile Rousseau's concern to hear the inner voice with the Herderian presence of many other external voices. Taylor does this by grafting Rousseau's concept of authenticity onto Herder's concept of language, arguing that the discovery of one's authentic self is manifested within language rather than in the isolation of an autonomous conscience. "In language," says Vasanthi Srinivasan, "Taylor finds the mystery of a larger order that provides the basis for community."[87] That is to say, Taylor finds in Herder's concept of language the means to reconcile autonomy and heteronomy, self and other, the individual and the community. It is this reconciliation that Taylor claims for his notion of authenticity.

Taylor's understanding of authenticity implies that identity, whether that of an individual or a group, is somehow independent of the views of others. This understanding certainly justifies regarding the concept of authenticity as a development in the history of inwardness inaugurated by Augustine and culminating in Rousseau's inner voice of nature. But the concept of authenticity also implies autonomy from other-dependence. The authenticity of the individual identity remains authentic so long as it is somehow ultimately invulnerable to the impositions that come with being

enmeshed in a particular culture and its horizon of meaning. Furthermore, this way of conceiving authenticity seems to suggest that our sense of
identity is always under threat of misrecognition by the presence of others.
As Taylor says, "nonrecognition or misrecognition" can be "a form of oppression."[88] But how can misrecognition be oppressive if we possess an inner self that is independent of the views of others? Taylor answers this
question by asserting that our sense of authenticity is in fact vulnerable to
others because it is shaped in part by the recognition (or misrecognition)
coming to us from others. But how exactly can identity be authentic if it is
shaped by others?

One of the paradoxes of modernity is our confusion about the nature of
the self and its moral obligations, if any. The promise of modernity is the
idea of freedom, but freedom in the modern world seems to entail a high
degree of interdependence. Even in asserting our freedom, we are dependent on others. As Alan Wolfe says, there is "a sense that something in missing": "[People] are confused when it comes to recognising the social
obligation that makes their freedom possible in the first place. They are, in
a word, unclear about the moral codes by which they ought to live ... When
capitalism and liberal democracy combine, people are given the potential
to determine for themselves what their obligations to others ought to be,
but are then given few satisfactory guidelines on how to fulfil them."[89]
Taylor's ethic of authenticity aims to overcome this absence by articulating
what he believes is missing in the relationship between freedom and moral
obligation, between the individual and the community.

In the essay "The Politics of Recognition," Taylor identifies a contemporary form of inauthenticity in society's focus on selfhood, which, he says,
promotes inordinate self-absorption or self-centredness. Modern society
skews the ideal of individualism, flattening it such that individuals tend to
focus on their own narrow lives, ignoring the multiple concerns and interests that constitute a wider life. In focusing on the self, we lose sight of
others and our responsibility to recognise them. The modern notion of individualism is a degradation of the ideal that an authentic sense of self
brings with it a moral sensibility. Nevertheless, Taylor argues that the modern individual has the potential for authenticating himself in the reconciliation of freedom and morality, for achieving a "potentiality that is properly
[his] own."[90] This notion reflects the Rousseauean view that you have to be
in touch with your inner nature in order to be true to your self. However,
Taylor argues that this self-knowledge is discovered only through its articulation, which, he says, requires a language community.[91] The discovery of
the self, the attainment of authenticity, is a creative process. And it is in this

process of creation that we come to realise the basically dialogical character of the self through our relationships. We recognise our lives as relational and are thereby able to mitigate the isolation and atomism of hyper-individualism. Taylor describes the dialogical nature of the self in this way: "There is no way we could be inducted into personhood except by being brought initiated into a language. We first learn our languages of moral and spiritual discernment in our encounter with the ongoing conversation by those who bring us up."[92]

Taylor uses the word *language* in a broad sense, referring not only to words in speech but also to other modes of expression, including the languages of art, symbolic gesture, and love. We are inducted into these languages, he says, through our exchanges with others. We cannot on our own acquire the languages necessary for an authentic self. Language is not merely an instrument by which we have knowledge of our lives, but a medium that creates our lives. Through language we actualise our self-consciousness and reflectiveness. "The genesis of the human mind is in this sense not monological, not something each accomplishes on his or her own, but dialogical."[93] This dialogical reality makes recognition a crucial moral concern for Taylor, because our identities are formed in and through others, whether in agreement or conflict with their recognition or misrecognition. On this claim Taylor clearly echoes John Watson's understanding of the symbiotic nature of human relationships. But he also reflects the dynamics of Hegel's master-slave dialectic in recognising that we define ourselves not only through similarities and affirmations, but also through conflict and negation. Our identities are not some "reality" that precedes the act of recognition; they are the result of repeated interactions with others, positive and negative.

Taylor's promotion of an expressivist view of human conduct is, in part, related to his critique of the modern tendency to understand human life and behaviour in terms drawn from natural science.[94] According to Taylor, the natural sciences are informed by an attitude of detachment regarding their objects of inquiry. Natural scientists investigate the world not as it is *for us*, but as it is in and of itself.[95] Naturalism, Taylor argues, holds a certain understanding of human agency, in particular the idea of the individual's "ability to act on [his] own, without outside interference or subordination to authority," and it links this capacity to the modern "ideals of efficacy, power [and] unperturbability."[96] Hegel, says Taylor, recognises this modern epistemology and how it fosters the interpenetration of the scientific and the moral. In *The Phenomenology of Spirit*, Hegel speaks of a "'fear of error' that 'reveals itself rather as fear of truth.'" Hegel shows "how this stance is bound up with a certain aspiration to individuality and separateness, refusing what he sees as the 'truth' of the subject-object identity."[97] The naturalist view offers knowledge that can promote individual freedom as a kind of escape from existence, a lust to control the world rather than participate in it. This naturalist detachment promotes the application of conceptual postures such as the Cartesian mind-body dualism, utilitarianism, behaviourist ideas about human psychology, and the application of engineering models to matters of social policy and human affairs.[98]

The naturalist stance also promotes a certain kind of politics, what Taylor labels as liberal "neutralism" and "proceduralism." Both, he says, are grounded in naturalist assumptions of a disengaged identity and the attendant notion of freedom that "generates an understanding of the individual as metaphysically independent of society."[99] Like John Watson, Taylor refers to this metaphysically independent individual as atomistic. And, again like Watson, he regards atomism as the basis for many features of modern liberalism, including contractarianism, the idea of the state as neutral on conceptions of the good, the insistence on the priority of the right to the good, and a reliance on procedural legal systems.[100] In opposition to atomistic politics, Taylor, again like Watson, wants to establish the holistic idea that individuals are constituted by a language and culture that can only be maintained in communities with which the individual feels a sense of identity.

Taylor attempts this anti-atomist recasting by setting Herder's expressivist theory of language against the naturalist-inspired designative theory of language and meaning. These contrasting theories reflect the tension between the Enlightenment's atomised understanding of the autonomous individual and Romanticism's more holistic view of the interrelations of self with society and nature. Designative language, Taylor argues, follows Enlightenment epistemology and modern scientific thought. In the same manner that science aims to free individuals from religious thought by claiming that knowledge obtained by means of empirical observation is truer knowledge, so, too, do early modern linguistic theories seek to free language from its theological framework and give it over to instrumental reason. Enlightenment thinkers such as Hobbes, Locke, and Condillac try to break language down into its constituent elements and give it an objective order separate from its communal experience. As scientists of language, they assert that since our knowledge of the world is informed by language, then language must be mastered by reason if we are to know the world as it is in itself.[101]

Under the designative theory of language, words obtain meaning by being used to designate objects. We know the meaning of an object, or more precisely we give it the meaning of a sign or a word, by pointing to or referring to those objects or relations that "belong" to the word or sign being used. While designation is a useful aspect of word function, Taylor argues that it also makes the correlation between a word and an object the most essential aspect of language and, thus, the source of meaning. But such a close correspondence between the word and the object it describes is predicated on an observed external relationship that is indifferent to the subjective perspective of the language user. This mode of language usage reduces meaningfulness and comprehension to the efficacy of the speaker's and listener's production of and response to language signals. Thus, as Patchen Markell concludes, language becomes a symbol of things, detached from a sense of connection between the observer and what is being observed. This linguistic separation of self and world is reinforced by the idea that language is an individual creation, a discovery independent of others.[102] And this, in turn, buttresses the modern view of the individual as a free and independent agent capable of mastering the world. Citing Thomas Hobbes, Taylor points out that early modern thinkers regarded language as "an assemblage of separable words, instruments of thought that lie, as it were, transparently to hand and can be used to marshal ideas ... Ideally we should aspire fully to control and oversee its use, taking care of our definitions, and not losing them from sight in inconsiderate speech, whereby we become 'entangled in words, as a bird in lime twigs.'"[103]

Language, then, as far as the Enlightenment *philosophes* are concerned, is intended to control the world. Without control of language, one's freedom is threatened because it is possible "to slip into a kind of slavery; where it is no longer I who make my lexicon, by definitional fiat, but rather it takes shape independently and in doing this shapes my thought. It is an alienation of my freedom as well as the great source of illusion."[104] Taylor, of course, argues against regarding language as an instrument of control, insisting that it can never achieve the desired level of security. This is because, as users of language, individuals are always embedded in a matrix of language that they did not create because it preceded them. Thus, language is ultimately beyond any individual's control. Language "is rather something in the nature of a web," and "to speak is to touch part of the web, and this makes the whole resonate."[105] And because the words we employ are sensible only in and through their place in the web, we can never claim an overarching comprehension of the consequences of what we say at any given moment, since we cannot know every strand of the web. Language extends behind and beyond us and, as such, is always being recreated and extended. It is an endless activity and therefore ultimately uncontrollable.

Taylor sets the idea of expressive language against designative language. He argues that human language is distinct from mere signalling because of its sense of rightness. This sensibility is to be understood not in terms of its task-oriented efficacy, but in terms of its subjective meaningfulness to its user. We do not merely match signs and objects, but respond to signs in light of their sense of truthfulness, descriptive rightness, or power to evoke or express moods and emotions. Language reveals that our acts of thinking, speaking, and understanding are manifested in terms of subjective understanding. We do not think and then speak, but rather our expressiveness constitutes our thinking and feeling and hence the understanding that informs our identity. As Taylor puts it, "To be a linguistic creature is to be sensitive to irreducible issues of rightness … We just talk and understand."[106] Taylor cites Christian symbolism as an example of expressive language. For Christians, language constitutes a vast symbol system that represents divine speech. This language, or symbol system, developed through a dialectical process involving the whole of the Christian community. Language for the Christian community expresses the cosmic order and reflects the individual speaker's perception of that order, giving him a sense of the meaning of the cosmos and his place in it. Thus, for Taylor, as Richard Nutbrown succinctly states, "[h]uman communication [is] held to embody what we are essentially, the expression of which is the making manifest of these embodiments."[107] Or, in Taylor's words, language is "a pattern of activity by which we express/realise a certain way of being in the world."[108] There first appears the subject, the agent of perception, who has a thought about or an emotional response to an object. The agent's reflective response and the meaningfulness of the experience are manifested in some form of language, such as words, painting, music, or even bodily action. Taylor sums up Herder's expressivist concept of language this way: "Language is no longer an assemblage of words, but the capacity to speak (express/realise) the reflective awareness implicit in using words to say something. Learning to use any single word presupposes this general capacity as background. But to have the general capacity is to possess a language. So that it seems that we need the whole of language as the background for the introduction of any of its parts, that is, individual words."[109]

According to Taylor, then, language, broadly understood, informs our understanding of the world, which, in turn, is manifested by our reflective expression of what it is that we comprehend. By this means, we are able to influence our social world but are never completely in control of it, at least to the degree the theorists of designative language would like. Given this, Taylor argues that greater significance must be given to how our identities are informed by the language community in which we exist. "The language I speak, the web which I can never fully dominate and oversee, can never be just *my* language, it is always largely *our* language."[110] Taylor's communal notion of language highlights the wider social and political implications he sees in Herder's language theory. If language is essential to thought, as Taylor argues in his explication of Herder, and if the activity of thinking can only be expressed in and through language, it follows that different languages express the particular way in which a group of people realises the human essence.[111] This view, in turn, suggests that the development of an authentic identity is linked to our identification with and articulation of the culture in which we find ourselves embedded. This dialogical notion of the community as an individual's horizon of meaning contrasts with the atomistic idea of the individual achieving freedom through his capacity to transcend the community.

To be sure, Taylor insists that this does not mean that individuals are subordinate to the community. Like John Watson, he sees the community and its horizon of meaning as providing the means for achieving a more authentic freedom than that offered by atomistic theories. Where in the Enlightenment view of freedom the individual is a self-defining subject able to act and think independently of external control, freedom according to expressivist theory consists of authentic self-expression. The community's ethics provide individuals with a context in which they are able to attain the self-awareness by which they can achieve genuine freedom. We define ourselves against the backdrop of culture, history, society, and the natural world – what Taylor refers to as "social imaginaries." To bracket out social imaginaries is to eliminate all context of meaning and, therefore, all possibility of individuality. Only to the degree that we live in a society that coordinates as best it can history, the necessities of nature, and relations with others are we able to achieve an identity that is more than the mere slaking of random appetite and incoherent desire. For Taylor, authenticity is not an escape from external requirements; authenticity presupposes such requirements.[112]

Taylor's expressivist reconciliation of the individual and the community resides at the core of his communitarian politics. Such a position stands in sharp contrast to notions about the unencumbered self, the punctual self, or the disengaged self.[113] Indeed, Vasanthi Srinivasan argues that Taylor's expressivist claim makes language the basis for national communities. Since modern nation-states are the overarching community in the modern era, their constitutional orders, if they are to be authentic, have "to be expressive of distinct identities without jeopardising some fundamental rights."[114] In this claim, Taylor is again appropriating Herder, who believes that each people has its own particular guiding theme or manner of expression that should never be suppressed and that can never simply be replaced by attempts to duplicate the cultural expressions of others.[115] Taylor acknowledges that this identity of language and nation, when combined with chauvinistic appeals to national characteristics and claims to power, can produce the darker side of nationalism.[116] Nevertheless, he maintains that Herder's nationalism reflects the belief that only by identifying with their language are individuals able to achieve the authenticity in which their freedom and their need to belong are reconciled. A communal language allows the individual to authenticate himself, and at the same time enables him to negotiate the expression of that authenticity into a form acceptable to the community. Under the Herderian concept of *volk*, language – understood in its widest sense – is the basis of authentic individuality *and* authentic community, the means by which both can be true to themselves.[117]

Language must be the foundation of nationhood because it provides the means by which people are able to achieve an identity that carries them beyond being merely an agglomeration of atomistic individuals or an invented contractual arrangement between competing interests. For Taylor, a nation expresses "something constitutive of the people's autonomous humanity, something essential to being human."[118] And since language, whether in the form of art, music, architecture, or history, reflects and embodies a particular understanding of, and a way of being in, the world, it is the basis of nationhood. Language articulates the unique character of a specific people. It is worth quoting Taylor at length on this point:

> Language is the obvious basis for a theory of nationalism founded on the expressivist notion of the special character of each people, language conceived in Herderian fashion, that is, in terms of an "expressive" theory. It is a concept which roots the plurality of states in the nature of things, but not in a natural order conceived in the old hierarchical mode. It claims to find the principle of a people's identity – what makes it more than an aggregation – as something already given, not arbitrarily determined, but rooted in its being and past; while at the same time this principle is no external allegiance but something constitutive of the people's autonomous humanity, something essential to being human. Language is obviously a prime candidate for this constitutive, essence-defining role, especially in a Herderian perspective.[119]

Taylor makes this point repeatedly in regard to his defence of Quebec nationalism. He even refers to Quebec as a "language-nation." I shall discuss the implications of this claim momentarily, but before I do, it is
necessary to consider how Taylor's Herder-inspired communitarianism
fits in with his appropriation of Hegel's concept of recognition. Or,
rather, if it does.

21

Freedom, Community, State:
Hegel contra Taylor

Taylor places Hegel in the civic humanist tradition even though he thinks there is something "complicated, ambivalent, and double-sided," and even "potentially dangerous," in his contribution to modern liberalism.[120] Hegel can be described as a civic humanist because even though he accepts the liberal assumption that an "invisible-hand mechanism" operates at a certain level of society, he does not think that this is adequate for reconciling individual freedom and the good of the community. A humanist society, according to Taylor, is one founded on a common understanding among its individual members about the good and their shared communal enterprise. Such a society differs from a liberal society, which sets the rights of the individual ahead of the good. Hegel's political theory attempts to hold the good and the right together with its concepts of *Sittlichkeit* and *Moralität*.[121] Or, put differently, Hegel seeks an intersection of two sets of distinct concepts: the first set consisting of those goods sought solely by individuals and those collectively desired by the community, and the other of a morality of abstract universal principles and a morality based on community obligations. These are the two ways in which a free society based on civic humanist principles differs from one based on a liberal tradition of giving priority to rights, Taylor argues, and what makes Hegel "interesting" is his effort to weave these distinctions together by formulating "the main-line humanist argument that a free society cannot remain a free society without these elements of bonding."[122] For this reason Taylor believes that there is much in Hegel's thought to demonstrate the inadequacy of a liberal society based on atomised, self-seeking individualism.[123]

Taylor, like John Watson and George Grant, locates the source of Hegel's portrait of the relationship between individual freedom and communal bondedness in his master-slave dialectic, in which he establishes the connections between self-consciousness and recognition. Taylor extracts a particular lesson from the dynamics of this dialectic: to count as an individual requires having a sense of worth as an individual, and this worthiness is intimately linked to and dependent upon the community. "Persons exist only in a certain space of evaluation," and this space "is intrinsically and inseparably a public space."[124] What links the space of evaluation and the public space is language. There can be no evaluation of an individual, and no place for that evaluation to occur, without a language to articulate that evaluation. Language, however, presupposes a community of some sort that precedes the individual in the sense that it existed before the existence of the individual; there is a "we" before there is an "I." I become individual only by entering the "space of value" that is a community, and that value is elaborated through a shared language. My sense of worth as an individual, my sense of authenticity, is lessened if this "space of value is so laid out as to negate or denigrate me."[125]

Nevertheless, while this dynamic of recognition might be the locus of Hegel's master-slave dialectic, Taylor finds this aspect of Hegelian thought troublesome. As he explains, to be an individual, I seek recognition and am ready to fight for it. But fighting over recognition is a contradictory act because both the admission that I need recognition and the language that sustains the community where this recognition can take place must already be "constituted by conversation" between myself and others. "What powers the master-slave dialectic, and drives it on, is that the very struggle to gain recognition is fated to self-frustration because it can never be properly achieved until we reach the kind of community described in the passage which ends this section of the *Phenomenology*: a society where the I is a we and the we is an I."[126] In effect, Taylor concludes, Hegel grounds his civic humanism, and its insistence on the mutual recognition of self and other, in a philosophical perspective that links individual recognition to the nature of language itself. This leads Taylor to suggest that language is the necessary condition for recognition and, hence, for the possibility of a reconciliation of the individual and the community. Therefore, there has to be a conversation – a community of shared language – that precedes the struggle for recognition. In other words, some condition of *pre-recognition* must precede dialectical recognition. We must have a sense of community before we engage in dialectic acts that constitute or negate individual identity.

Hegel's civic humanist model is flawed, Taylor argues, because it does not go back far enough to this pre-recognition stage of the dialectic. Hegel's concept of recognition rests on a philosophical anthropology rooted in a fundamental subject-object dualism. As a result, his social philosophy provides a problematic legacy. To be sure, Hegel reveals the nature of a free society and demonstrates how such a society cannot be entirely structured around the classical liberal notions of invisible-hand mechanisms. He pictures a society that defines individual freedom in terms of a citizen's capacity to identify with and participate in his society – "a vision of embodied subjectivity."[127] Yet Hegel's thought is flawed by "great inadequacy" in that his social theory is informed by a metaphysical "conception of subject/object identity" taken from Johann Fichte. And this, Taylor concludes, makes Hegel "in the end a very bad model for a political society." The Hegelian model for reconciling the individual and the community "is a model for a kind of unity of society which, in the end, gives no place to the *agon*, to competition, to unresolvable differences." Hegel "had this completely unrealistic view about how representative institutions could work simply in a one-way direction to bring people in and create a consensus, rather than to be the arena in which deep dissensions can be worked out in a way that nevertheless helps to bond to a common allegiance." And this means, says Taylor, that "the whole Hegelian model is flawed."[128]

Taylor's criticism of Hegel – Hegel wants too much unity – clearly echoes Aristotle's criticism of Plato. It even shares similarities with the criticism levelled against Hegel by the British theorists of John Watson's day. The question is whether Taylor, with his Herderian perspective, reads Hegel right. In his essay "The Politics of Recognition," Taylor observes that in pre-modern Europe the question of identity and individual authenticity was not an issue. "In pre-modern times people did not speak of 'identity' and 'recognition' – not because people didn't have (what we call) identities, or because these didn't depend on recognition, but rather because these were then too unproblematic to be thematized as such."[129] Only in the modern age, in which traditional hierarchies of social order have been undermined, has the inwardly generated ideal of authenticity arisen and become problematic. With modernity has come the potential for conflict between the individual's sense of selfhood and various forms of socially imposed roles and categories of conduct. "What has come about with the modern age is not the need for recognition but the condition in which the attempt to be recognised can fail."[130] The question of identity and the recognition involved in that identity has become a matter of the quality and degree of interaction between the individual's inner voice and the external impositions of a collective identity.

Taylor's account of this tension between self and other is, of course, at the core of his politics of recognition. Like Hegel, he seeks a reconciliation of the diremptions generated by modernity's destruction of the pre-modern hierarchical social order. He also acknowledges that there can be no return to these older orders. Echoing Hegel's concept of *Aufhebung*, or sublation, he recognises that the modern sensibility can only be incorporated into a more complex, reflexive totality. But how specifically is this reconciliation of self and other to be achieved? Essentially, as I have argued, Taylor invokes Hegel's concept of *Sittlichkeit*, or ethical life, as the means by which the individual's desire for authentic identity and freedom and the concomitant longing for community can be brought together. However, Taylor recasts *Sittlichkeit* in terms of satisfying the desire for identity. Yet, as Srinivasan observes, Taylor also seeks "to restore Herder's idea of *Volk* not as a primordial essence but as an ongoing exploration of a horizon of meanings embedded in language and culture."[131] But this, she notes, is to apply Hegel's concept so broadly that everything from constitutions and law to cultural practices and customs becomes relevant for politics.

The implications of the effort to unite *Sittlichkeit* and an expressivist vision are readily apparent. The institutions of modern liberal society can be reworked to reflect not so much the liberal principles of abstract freedom and rights, but the desire of individuals to belong to a specific community. But would this not give primacy to community over individual freedom? Is there not a danger that the desire for community could undermine the principle of freedom? Nationalist sentiment is often used to justify repression and enforce social conformity. Nationalism is also vulnerable to the abuse of power, such as when governments suppress dissent or one group justifies its oppression of another in the name of the national interest. Taylor is aware of these dangers, but does his assertion of the priority of community not open the door to totalitarian impulses? Taylor may argue that communal identities are dialogically negotiated through politics and history and that the struggle for recognition need not descend into bloody conflict, but what happens to the principle of freedom when, for whatever reason, a society deems some aspects of its communal identity too important for negotiation? What if a particular community – the Taliban in Afghanistan, for example – prefers a hierarchical and authoritarian political order to one that emphasises universal equality and individual rights?[132]

There is considerable similarity between Hegel's understanding that freedom has a moral dimension beyond abstract rights and Taylor's expressivist view that individuals enjoy their freedom only in a community with which they can identify. However, Hegel's reconciliation of the individual and the community differs from that of Taylor's. Hegel's project of reconciliation, his ground for community, is rooted in the individual's inherent reason and the desire for freedom to which reason leads. Taylor, on the other hand, promotes community on the basis of a people's sense of identity, of some authentic way of being. Where Hegel responds to the question of recognising particular nations and cultures in terms of their self-conscious awareness of freedom, Taylor asserts that a people's attainment of modern ethical life is related to their ability to maintain an authentic identity. Freedom, it seems, is secondary. To recall, Hegel defines freedom in terms of self-direction, holding that the two main ingredients of freedom are achieving one's ends and acting on the basis of self-volition. This positive definition of freedom contrasts with Taylor's expressivist linkage of freedom and authenticity through communal attachment.

On this point, Taylor's desire to salvage the community from the ostensible excesses of atomistic liberalism becomes salient, and a direct comparison of his thought to that of Hegel's becomes necessary. Hegel's metaphysic of freedom is, of course, influenced by the Kantian idea of autonomy. But as I discussed in Part 1, it is also influenced by Fichte's notion of absolute self-sufficiency. Taylor argues that Hegel's social philosophy is flawed because it rests on Fichte's assumption of subject/object identity and thus would result in a reconciliation of the individual and the community that requires excessive unity.[133] Taylor misconstrues this influence, however, as Hegel is critical of both Kant's and Fichte's notions of freedom. This is evident in Hegel's concept of *Sittlichkeit*, or ethical life, in which the "ought" has been sublated according to his concept of *Aufhebung* and thus freedom is identified with duty. While Hegel draws on Kant's notion of autonomy and Fichte's conception of self-sufficiency to promote his concept of freedom, he argues against their view of the relationship between the self and the other. Taylor interprets Hegel's ethical life as promoting an excessive reduction of the other to the same, and it is this critique that makes him ambivalent about Hegel's legacy for liberalism. Taylor worries that Hegel's identification of Spirit (or freedom) and ethical life makes no allowances for differences that cannot be resolved.

Hegel's concept of *Sittlichkeit* is subtler than Taylor allows. For Hegel, the lesson of the master-slave dialectic is that freedom *is* ethical life in that freedom consists in being with oneself *in* another. The other does not restrict one's freedom but makes that freedom possible. Self-consciousness – and therefore freedom – is attained through those opportunities for recognition provided by the various forms of *Sittlichkeit* – the family, civil society, and, finally, the rational state – in which self-consciousness and freedom achieve actualisation. Hence, Hegel posits community *within* freedom.

Sittlichkeit, says Srinivasan, shows us that freedom is not solely a matter of abstract rights or an absence of restraint; it is about "belonging" to the community by means of those mediations and institutions that we choose for ourselves because they reflect our deepest (or best) will.[134] This is the interpretation of Hegel presented in Watson's political philosophy.

By contrast, Taylor's interpretation of ethical life reflects his concern with maintaining cultural identity and the individual's sense of communal belongingness. This is apparent in Taylor's reading of Hegel's master-slave dialectic. He argues that Hegel's interpretation of this relationship remains rooted in a pre-modern hierarchical notion of honour and, as such, is "crucially flawed" because it does not answer the question of why people seek recognition at all. In the master-slave dialectic, the self-consciousness that fails to win honour remains unrecognised, but even the self-consciousness that does win honour is, in a sense, frustrated because it attains recognition from an inferior. Such recognition is simply not satisfying, since it comes from an unequal and unfree being. "The struggle for recognition can find only one satisfactory solution, and that is a regime of reciprocal recognition among equals."[135] Such a reading of the master-slave dialectic implies that the moment of recognition must be a balanced exchange in which both self-consciousnesses recognise and respect each other's dignity and worth. From this perspective, Hegel's set piece suggests a breakdown in the dialectical relationship, a psychological slippage in which one self-consciousness fails to honour the other. As Taylor puts it, the "slave is forced to recognise the master, but not vice versa."[136] Hegel's master-slave dialectic amounts to the claim that our inability to get along with one another stems from our failure to properly respect each other's dignity. And that, in turn, implies that if we are all to be fully authenticated, we need each other. Authenticity is *dependent* on community, and our failure to achieve it is the consequence of our having inadequate means for giving and receiving the recognition that can create community. Thus, while Taylor may accept Hegel's understanding of freedom as self-consciousness, he maintains that the actualisation of freedom necessitates a community in which individuals see themselves and their deepest desires objectified in the community's institutional order. Hegel's political philosophy, he contends, "can be seen as an attempt to realise a synthesis that the Romantic generation was grasping towards: to combine the rational, self-legislating freedom of the Kantian subject with the expressive unity within man and with nature for which the age longed."[137] But Taylor argues that as a consequence of its emphasis on the individual, contemporary society has failed to achieve this Hegelian reconciliation. The struggle for recognition continues because the myriad self-consciousnesses that make up society continue to try "to wrest recognition from one another without reciprocating."[138]

By Taylor's account, then, the struggle for recognition is fundamentally social and political, as distinct from Hegel's ontologically oriented account. Hegel conceives of social and political institutions as the means by which the individual and the community can find common ground and establish institutions through which each individual gives and receives recognition. It is this dimension of Hegel's thought from which Taylor draws his communitarian discourse of recognition. For Taylor and other communitarians, recognition comes from groups of people within a particular state, and the state provides the means for satisfying claims for recognition that would otherwise go unsatisfied. But, as David Duquette observes, the institutions of the state also serve a more metaphysical purpose in Hegel's thought. For Hegel, "it is the ethical life of the modern state which purportedly provides a solution to human conflict arising from the struggle for recognition."[139] The state and its institutions, in serving as mediating conduits for exchanges between self-consciousnesses, become the highest expression of Objective Spirit and the *final* reconciliation between self and other. As Duquette states, "What distinguishes the mediation of self and otherness provided in the state is the ultimate harmonization of social life in which the struggle for recognition is finally overcome."[140]

Taylor misconstrues this point in criticising the Hegelian resolution of the struggle for recognition as a bad model for political society in that it demands too much unity. Admittedly, Hegel's reliance on the universality of modern institutions is problematic, particularly in the contemporary world where institutions can be oppressive. But Hegel is more careful than Taylor acknowledges in delineating the interdependence – or, a better word, symbiosis – of freedom and belongingness. In *Philosophy of Right*, for instance, Hegel is clear that the individual and the state (or community) are reconciled only insofar as each manifests the freedom and rational development of the other.[141] With his focus on authentic identity and its communal grounding, Taylor seems to insist that the actualisation of the individual is only available through the expressive community. Does this imply giving priority to the community over the individual? If so, it might be argued that in employing his theory of the expressive self to defend the community against excessive individualism, Taylor opens the door to elements that have the potential for totalitarian expression. To give priority to the community over the individuals who compose it effectively dismantles a reciprocal dialectical relationship between citizens and their community. In seeking to safeguard the community from the apparent corrosion of atomistic individualism with his conception of the expressive self, Taylor arguably skews Hegel's delicately balanced *Sittlichkeit*. I shall try to demonstrate this in considering Taylor's response to the endless "crisis of Canada" – that is, to the question of Quebec.

22

Quebec, Trudeau, and
the Crisis of Canada

The case of recognition with which Taylor is most concerned is, of course, Quebec. Taylor regards francophone Quebecers' concerns for cultural survival and the threat that such concerns pose for the unity of Canada as a manifestation of the Hegelian struggle for recognition. As he says, "The root cause of our impending fracture can be put in one word: recognition."[142] From a theoretical perspective, the problem of Quebec nationalism – the crisis of Canada – reflects an ongoing struggle between Enlightenment rationality, with the atomistic individualism it promotes, and the longed-for expressive unity of the Romantics that finds its contemporary expression in communitarianism.[143] More concretely, Taylor holds that in cases like that of francophone Quebec, where a minority culture is threatened by absorption into a larger culture, there is a need for special rights and privileges that acknowledge the culture's distinct history and group identity. Substantive equality can require subordinating basic assumptions of procedural liberalism. Taylor's formula for Quebec's recognition and the reconciliation of the two solitudes is to argue for a form of substantive liberalism that he believes to be more supportive of cultural rights. In this regard, Taylor's consideration of the problem of Quebec amounts to a *de facto* illustration of the alternative liberalism that can, in Taylor's view, provide Quebec the recognition it seeks while protecting the fundamental rights dear to English-speaking Canadians. Or, put differently, Taylor sees in the crisis of Canada a challenge to resolve the Hegelian dilemma of reconciling expressive unity with radical autonomy through a form of liberalism that takes into account Rousseau's substantive democracy and the Kantian claim of the radical freedom that underlies procedural liberalism.[144]

Taylor is not the first to promote group rights in apparent contradiction to liberal theories about individual autonomy and the state's neutrality regarding communal goods.[145] But it needs to be remembered that Taylor's objection to liberalism focuses on its assumptions of atomistic individualism, not on its concrete prescriptions regarding, say, freedom of speech or *habeas corpus*. Taylor objects to the traditional liberal notion of a self that can be abstracted from a pre-existing social context. His concern is that the autonomy and freedom prized by liberal theory is possible only within a community and sustainable only on the basis of that community's cultural resources. The historical developments that produced modern individuality have fostered significant scepticism toward the notion of community or belongingness among those who assert the primacy of their freedom.[146] But Taylor's individual is holistic – that is, a self defined by its attachment to communal goods and its resistance to the liberal idea of autonomous individuality. Taylor prefers the notion of individuals as "strong evaluators," individuals who make decisions within a "language" that has pre-shaped their moral understandings and, hence, their life choices. From this position, Taylor argues that procedural liberalism, with its formal claim to treat everyone equally, is insufficient for protecting the language of a particular cultural community that would satisfy the need of individuals to belong to a community where they would feel authentic. In the modern world, individuals need some way to affirm their sense of self. According to Taylor, this can best be achieved through a group identity that cannot be reduced to individualistic, monological liberalism. "In the search for a conception of situated freedom, reductive, mechanistic theories of human thought and behaviour are of no avail."[147] The issue for Taylor, then, as Nicholas Smith argues, "is whether a theory that excludes a socially endorsed conception of the good has the categories available for making sense of a viable modern democracy."[148]

Following from his critique of procedural liberalism – and in support of Quebec's aspirations – Taylor applies his concept of deep diversity and its claim that different cultures can be accommodated within a single Canadian state in such a way as to satisfy a "plurality of ways of belonging."[149] Canada, along with much of the rest of the world, needs models other than that of the identity-neutral liberal state if other less-constraining modes of political existence are to be possible, Taylor argues. The point of deep diversity, it will be recalled, is to recognise the worth of different cultures regardless of their history and traditions and to avoid imposing a single overarching cultural system on them. With first-level diversity, on the other hand, cultural differences may be accepted or tolerated, but they are not treated differently or given special recognition that is not accorded to any other group. According to Taylor, this kind of cultural equality actually results in the unequal treatment of different cultures. Such is the case for both Quebecers and aboriginal peoples within Canada, he argues. Canada is dominated by an English-speaking majority that generally subscribes to the traditional liberal political model of a value-neutral, procedurally oriented state. This contrasts with the situation of Quebecers whose "way of being Canadian" is to belong to *la nation québécoise*. The same holds for aboriginal peoples and their sense of communal identity. Neither group's way of being Canadian can be easily recognised by the first-level diversity offered by the traditional value-neutral liberal state. Only by allowing for second-level, or deep, diversity can these and other ways of being Canadian be accommodated.[150]

Taylor is vague on exactly how this deep diversity is to be accomplished, except to say that it means an individual's sense of belonging to Canada would "pass through" some other community before attaching itself to the Canadian nation-state. He insists that while this means accepting "more than one formula for citizenship," it does not mean the fragmentation of the country. He also rejects the idea that individuals adopting different ways of being citizens would threaten Canadian unity or undermine the principles of equal rights for all citizens. Indeed, he maintains that only to the degree that other cultures are fully recognised and able to develop substantive societal structures and identities will Canada remain politically united. According to Taylor, the stumbling block in Canadian history has always been the failure of French-speaking and English-speaking Canadians to understand and respect one another's motives. Because of this failure, each group attempts to impose its views on the other. "Each side would require the other to be something it is not in order to fit the formula within which it can itself be comfortable."[151] What sets Quebec apart from the rest of Canada is its concern with preserving its language and culture. Francophone Quebecers, unlike English-speaking Canadians, recognise the intrinsic importance of language as the bedrock of cultural preservation. For francophones, language defines their community, a point Taylor emphasises in a 1992 essay: "The real point here is that [a country] makes the survival and flourishing of [its] nation/language one of the prime goals of political society."[152]

Taylor seeks to articulate Quebec's search for recognition in a way that is acceptable to non-Quebecers and at the same time offer Quebecers a form of liberalism that would not be alien to them. He wants Quebec's efforts to protect its culture and ensure its survival to be understood by the rest of Canada as a form of liberalism that continues to protect fundamental rights even when it abandons the notion of neutrality about the good and asserts the central need of group recognition. English-speaking Canadians should bracket their cultural standards in order to more readily identify with Quebec's aspirations. In this way, Canadians could achieve a "fusion of horizons" that would provide them with a more open intercultural perspective. Is this possible? Should it be? Arthur Ripstein argues that a group possessing majority status within a political order does not – or should not – be granted the right to "use the coercive apparatus of the state to enforce their hopes."[153] One way to address these questions is to compare Taylor's views on the Meech Lake Accord with those of critics of the would-be constitutional deal. According to some critics, the failure of the Meech Lake Accord in 1990 and the Charlottetown Agreement in 1992 demonstrated irrevocably that the two-nations idea on which Quebec based its desire to be recognised as a state *equal* to the Canadian state was untenable. English-speaking Canada's refusal to give constitutional recognition to Quebec as a distinct society showed that Quebec's ultimate political aspirations can never be accommodated as long as Quebec is a province of Canada.[154]

Whether the Meech Lake Accord or the Charlottetown Agreement would have solved the crisis of Canada is, obviously, debatable. But there is no doubt that if either of them had come into effect, they would have radically altered Canada's political structure. For example, the Meech Lake Accord's main provision was the constitutional recognition of Quebec as a distinct society and the Quebec government as alone having the authority to "promote and preserve" this distinctiveness. This certainly would fit Taylor's prescription for the Quebec government: "It is axiomatic for Quebec governments that the survival and flourishing of French culture in Quebec is a good ... Political society ... involves making sure there is a community of people here in the future that will want to avail itself of the opportunity to use the French language."[155] One major consequence of this provision would have been the requirement that the courts interpret the Charter of Rights and Freedoms in such a way as to recognise the overriding principle of Quebec's existence as a distinct society. Critics, however, charged that the accord would have led to a highly decentralised Canada, the enfeeblement of the federal government in terms of formulating national policies, and the erosion of the rights of individuals and minorities. The authority given to Quebec to preserve and promote its distinctiveness would have allowed the Quebec government to extend its legislative powers into areas not available to other provinces. Legally speaking, Canadians would be divided into two groups, those who lived in Quebec and those who lived elsewhere. Moreover, constitutional recognition of Quebec as a distinct society would allow the Quebec government to use special restrictions on individual rights and freedoms for the sake of the overriding good of protecting the cultural identity of francophone Quebecers. This, critics said, was a violation of the Charter of Rights and Freedoms in that it effectively set the notion of distinct society status – or francophone Quebec's collective rights – against the principle of individual rights and the equality of all citizens that prevailed in the rest of Canada. As Barry Cooper and David Bercuson put it, "The Meech Lake Accord would have been the penultimate blow to Canada as a nation."[156]

The Meech Lake Accord's fiercest critic was, of course, former prime minister Pierre Trudeau. Trudeau always maintained that his political actions were based on his political philosophy, and so given the results of his intervention in the Meech debate, it is necessary to provide a brief consideration of that philosophy. I shall restrict my commentary to those aspects of Trudeau's political thought that readily apply to his intervention. Presumably, a consideration of Trudeau's thought on the question of Quebec will cast Taylor's philosophic position into higher relief. Trudeau and Taylor can be profitably compared on their different views on multiculturalism and nationalism or their contrasting positions on federalism – Trudeau as a centralist and Taylor as a decentralist, for example.[157] Another approach would be to compare Trudeau's civic view of Canada with Taylor's dualist vision.[158] For my purposes, though, the best method of comparison is to consider their contrasting positions within the liberal-communitarian debate. Trudeau clearly waves the flag of the liberal camp, while Taylor flies the communitarian banner. This is too simplistic, of course, since there are communitarian elements in Trudeau's liberalism – after all, the charter makes provisions for the collective rights of francophones and aboriginals – just as there is an abiding regard for certain forms of liberalism in Taylor's communitarianism.[159] Taylor, in fact, insists that "a society with strong collective goals can be liberal."[160] Nevertheless, it is reasonable to approach Trudeau and Taylor from within the liberal-communitarian debate because their different views on individual rights and collective purposes were so strikingly evident in the Meech Lake debate. Trudeau's liberalism was front and centre in his warnings that ratifying Meech would undermine the Charter of Rights and Freedoms, while Taylor's support for Quebec's distinct society and the Meech Lake Accord demonstrated his communitarian concerns.

For Trudeau, the charter was intended to serve two fundamental purposes that he thought, rightly or wrongly, would foster Canadian unity. Trudeau believed that the charter would foster a Canadian identity based on the possession of rights – a dash of communitarian spice in the liberal pottage, if you will – and establish once and for all the sovereignty of Canadian citizens.[161] Trudeau wanted to resolve the historical tension in Canadian political existence, wanted an end to the never-resolved quarrels over power and jurisdiction between Quebec and the federal government. Resolution of this tension was the ostensible purpose behind federal multiculturalism policy, as well as the fundamental purpose of the charter. Trudeau, in effect, wanted to create a nation-binding faith, a national myth that would appeal to all Canadians, French and English. The charter and his policy of multiculturalism were his chief institutional means for establishing this new order. "With the Charter in place," Trudeau wrote in his 1993 memoirs, recalling the constitutional conferences of the early 1980s, "we can now say that Canada is a society where all people are equal and where they share some fundamental values based upon freedom. The search for [a] Canadian identity, as much as my philosophical beliefs, had led me to insist on the Charter."[162] For Trudeau, then, the essential political purpose of the charter, beyond its unifying or nation-building element, was to counterbalance the decentralising leanings of the provincial governments, particularly Quebec's, by giving all citizens a symbolic and practical expression of national identity independent of their regional loyalties.[163] As Trudeau put it, sounding distinctly Hegelian or, via T.H. Green, vaguely Idealist: "I saw the Charter as an expression of my long-held view that the subject of law must be the individual human being; the law must permit the individual to fulfil himself or herself to the utmost."[164]

The problem, according to critics, is that the charter is rooted in differing moral and political principles, assumes different conceptions of unity, and diverges widely in its implications for the Canadian federal system. Much of the analysis of Trudeau's legacy since his death in 2000 has focused on the failure of the charter to achieve its nation-binding purpose. Two decades after its adoption, some scholars have concluded that rather than unifying the country, as Trudeau hoped, the charter is contributing to disunion.[165] "A strategy designed to transform the way in which Quebecers see Canada has little effect in Quebec, but it transforms English Canada," says Kenneth McRoberts. "Rather than undermining the forces of Quebec separatism, the strategy strengthens them, bringing Canada to the brink of collapse ... In light of the Trudeau strategy's original purpose of securing national unity, there can be no doubt that it has failed."[166] Such views may seem harsh, but considering that Trudeau entered politics to solve the Quebec question, it is not unreasonable to judge him on the consequences of that effort. McRoberts argues that Trudeau's efforts to achieve national unity through multiculturalism, bilingualism, and the charter's guarantee of civil rights have not worked because these policies, rather than accommodating enduring historical forces of regionalism within Canada, have sought to smother them. And that, McRoberts concludes, cannot be done, at least in a democratic system. Trudeau's strategy not only failed to alter how Quebec francophones regard Canada, he says, but has in fact strengthened their identity as Quebecers. At the same time, the Charter of Rights, multiculturalism, and equality of the provinces "have become central to English Canadians' view of Canada, so they have destroyed any willingness to recognize Quebec as a distinct society."[167]

Taylor would probably agree with such criticism. He, too, regards Trudeau's vision as a turning away from the two-nations, or dualist, historical understanding that, in his view, framed relations between Quebec and the rest of Canada and, arguably, allowed the country to remain united. But even more than this is the fact that the charter, in its essential principles, is an American document, philosophically, historically, and culturally. It places individual freedom as the central value of political order, effectively displacing the traditional – and more communitarian – ideal of "peace, order, and good government." English-speaking Canadians may have embraced the charter with enthusiasm, but that, as Robert Martin observes, only shows the degree to which they have been Americanized. The charter, says Martin, "symbolizes our loss of any uniquely Canadian sense of ourselves. To the extent that the Charter does provide a unifying national idea, it is an idea that trumpets the abandonment of our autonomy and our uniqueness."[168] Louis Balthazar shares this view, arguing that francophones have traditionally been faithful to the confederation arrangement of a decentralized federal state because it allows them to maintain a distinct society within Canada. But in the wake of the 1982 Constitution and its accompanying charter, it was clear that the Trudeau government was intent on pursuing "a quasi-American concept of Canadian union" that would not be acceptable to most Quebecers. As a result, says Balthazar, Quebecers "may break from the Canadian federation precisely because recent developments have made it alien from its original intent and more similar to the American concept of national union." Trudeau may have believed that multiculturalism and the charter would create "a new Canadianism," but as far as Quebecers were concerned, the federal principles on which the confederation arrangement was based have been diluted.[169]

On this argument, it is worth recalling that the basic philosophy on which Trudeau based his vision of the charter was rooted in his appropriation of the thought of T.H. Green. The British Hegelian, Trudeau once said, taught him that in politics "the focal point was not the state but the individual – the individual seen as a person integrated into society, which is to say endowed with fundamental rights and essential liberties, but also with responsibilities."[170] That certainly sounds Hegelian, which, of course, suggests that the Charter of Rights possesses a Hegelian pedigree. Should the charter be seen as a manifestation of Hegel's Objective Spirit? Such a question may seem fanciful, but there is nothing in Trudeau's statement with which Hegel or, for that matter, John Watson would quarrel. Trudeau even seems to share Watson's main political concern about how to establish the proper relationship between the individual and the state (or public authority). In a 1958 article, "Approaches to Politics," Trudeau examines what he describes as the "only question" in political philosophy: "How does it happen that one man has authority over his fellows?"[171] Change the words "one man" to "the state" or "the community" and you have Watson's question. Given the sources of Trudeau's philosophical thought, and the way that thought was translated into political action, it is not unreasonable to suggest a certain Hegelian influence on Canada's new "founding" document. An equally pertinent observation is how the philosophical differences between Trudeau and Taylor reflect differing appropriations of Hegel.

Given Trudeau's emphasis on the rights of the individual, there is little question that the Constitution of 1982 and its charter were grounded in the kind of liberalism in which principles of equality and individual autonomy are primary. Generally speaking, individual rights and non-discrimination among citizens take precedence over the collective goals that members of a society might assign themselves. This notion of liberalism, strictly applied, restricts the state from promoting and even protecting a public concept of the common good. According to Taylor, though, such a view of liberalism ill serves Quebec, which stresses the importance of collective goals (without neglecting individual rights) and sees the survival of its distinct society as imperative. In an argument that has parallels to George Grant's criticism of the Americanising consequences of Trudeau's rationalist politics, Taylor says that despite Trudeau's hopes that the charter would foster Canadian unity, it actually "makes us more like the United States" and reflects "the growing force of procedural liberalism" in North America. Likewise, the defeat of the Meech Lake Accord only reiterated the post-charter spread of this form of liberalism in English Canada, a form of liberalism, Taylor asserts, that is alien to francophones and something Quebec could never accommodate without surrendering its collective identity.[172]

Is Taylor right in judging Trudeau as having no regard for a common good in his opposition to Quebec's claims of cultural distinctiveness? Does Trudeau ignore the need of people for a communal identity? It is true that

Trudeau places the locus of the state on individual rights and the need to protect the individual from collective impositions? He certainly regarded the charter as "in keeping with the purest form of liberalism," according to which individuals "enjoy certain fundamental, inalienable rights and cannot be deprived of them by any collectivity."[173] And his opposition to Meech Lake's dualist vision of Canada accords with his liberal principles. Given this, there is little reason to expect that Trudeau would accept Taylor's argument that Quebec society is, or should be, based on another, more collectivist-oriented form of liberalism. Nevertheless, it is not quite accurate to say that Trudeau had no notion of the common good. Trudeau's notion of a just society requires not only individual freedom, but the opportunity to enjoy that freedom. As Trudeau writes, "The common good (in a parliamentary democracy) may be more or less inclusive, and may be defined in different ways by different men. Yet it must in some way include equality of opportunity for everyone in all important fields of endeavour."[174] Max Nemni points out that Trudeau's economic and social policies, whatever their practical failings, were based on the idea that individual freedom includes freedom from want and fear. Trudeau, he says, "considers that economics must contribute to the common good, as must every important social field of endeavour."[175] Thus, it cannot be said that Trudeau has no conception of the common good. Certainly, he does not define it in the proceduralist manner that Taylor suggests by asserting only the formal equality of citizens before the law.

That is, it is evident that Trudeau's notion of the common good always redounds to the individual. As he writes in a 1990 essay, "The Values of a Just Society," "only the individual is a possessor of rights. A collectivity can exercise only those rights it has received by delegation from its members."[176] The operative word here, I suggest, is *delegation*. Trudeau's common good, with its focus on the freedom of the individual, reflects Hegelian concepts. Trudeau, like Hegel, sees a society's good emerging through the mediation of institutions in which men are free to participate. In this regard, Trudeau's notion of the relationship between the common good and individual freedom is of a piece with Hegel's concept of *Sittlichkeit*. This can also be seen in Trudeau's opposition to the Meech Lake Accord. In his view, the accord, and its notion of Quebec as a distinct society, violated his notion of institutionally mediated freedom: "Now the consequences of 'distinct society' become clear. The Charter, whose essential purpose was to recognise the fundamental and inalienable rights of all Canadians equally, would recognise thenceforth that in the province of Quebec these rights could be overridden or modified by provincial laws whose purpose would be to promote a distinct society and more specifically to favour the 'French-speaking majority' that has a 'unique culture' and a 'civil law tradition.'"[177] What might this mean, Trudeau asks, for those Quebecers of Irish, Jewish, or Vietnamese origin? Would these minorities have trouble belonging to this distinct society if they attempted to protect their charter rights against discriminatory laws imposed by the francophone majority in its assertion of collective rights?

Trudeau's concerns are shared by other critics of Taylor. Russell Hardin argues that in supporting Quebec's language laws Taylor effectively imposes the self-interested claims of one particular generation on future generations: "The forcible institutionalization of minor languages as required for official and business transactions, and other such communally motivated policies, often have as their sad consequence the fettering of the lives of future generations, who, in a sense, are used by the present generations merely to make life a bit more comfortable for themselves."[178] Jürgen Habermas likewise warns that Taylor's efforts to ensure francophone cultural survival might well lead to its ossification. The pace of change in the modern world "explodes all stationary forms of life," he argues, and cultures can only flourish if they have "the strength to transform themselves through criticism and secession."[179] Mark Redhead picks up on this theme in arguing that by not recognising how procedural liberalism helps cultures retain their dynamism, Taylor "runs the risk of promoting a deeply diverse Canadian federation that perpetuates cultures unable to cope with the changing world around them." He points out that it was this kind of fly-in-amber culture that Trudeau found in Duplessis's Quebec and that he feared would return under the mantle of Quebec nationalism. Taylor might share these concerns, says Redhead, but "the manner in which he seeks recognition and accommodation of Quebec in his deeply diverse Canada contains no means of preventing these fears from being realized."[180]

From another perspective, Andy Lamey detects a paradox, if not incoherence, in Taylor's position. On the one hand, Taylor opposes assimilationist policies that would see minorities homogenised into majorities because he fears that this would lead to the grievous wounds of misrecognition. Yet, as Lamey points out, Taylor supports Quebec's language laws that "'actively seek to *create* members of the community.'" Lamey continues: "In other words, were Quebec's francophones to be subsumed into Canada's English majority, the result would be a serious injustice. But the French goal of culturally assimilating other minorities is perfectly laudable. Strangely, Taylor's concern over unwanted assimilation leads him to endorse government measures the explicit aim of which is … unwanted assimilation." Such a position, Lamey says, creates the conditions for the kind of misrecognition that Taylor ostensibly wants to avoid. Taylor, he concludes, is reduced to making a claim of power, not principle – "the only difference in the Quebec case being that the burden of having an external culture inflicted upon them is shifted to cultures with less power than the French: the immigrants."[181]

Such commentary suggests that Taylor's communitarianism might not be all that amenable to liberalism. Steven Rockefeller touches on this possibility when he says that Taylor gives too little consideration to the possibility that the imposition of laws to guarantee the cultural survival of francophone Quebec may well lead to "an erosion over time of fundamental human rights growing out of a separatist mentality that elevates ethnic identity over universal human identity." Rockefeller suggests that there is an "uneasy tension" between Taylor's promotion of the principle of cultural survival and his simultaneous endorsement of the need to be open-minded toward other cultures. It is naïve, says Rockefeller, to believe that francophone Quebec will be open to what Taylor refers to as a "fusion of horizons" when it is "preoccupied with the protection of one particular culture to the extent of allowing the government to maintain that culture at the expense of individual freedom."[182] This was Trudeau's concern, too. He argued that the Meech Lake Accord would undermine Canada as a bilingual and multicultural nation. As he wrote in a now famous 1987 newspaper article, Meech Lake would destroy the dreams of Canadians who saw the charter "as a new beginning for Canada, where everyone would be on an equal footing and where citizenship would finally be founded on a set of commonly shared values."[183]

Trudeau's attack on the Meech Lake Accord is credited with galvanising opposition to it.[184] Newly elected premiers in New Brunswick and Manitoba failed to go through with their predecessors' commitments to ratify the agreement in their legislatures. The Newfoundland premier even repealed his province's previous ratification. And in June of 1990 the accord died. A similar fate awaited the Charlottetown Agreement two years later. This agreement closely resembled Meech Lake in that Quebec was to be recognised as a distinct society, requiring the courts to interpret the charter in a manner consistent with Quebec's desire to preserve its distinctness. But there was also the "Canada Clause," which told Canadians who they were supposed to be as a people, entrenched the right to aboriginal self-government, provided for an elected Senate, and guaranteed that Quebec would always have 25 per cent of the seats in the House of Commons. Once again, though, the main question was whether the agreement had given too much or too little to Quebec. English-speaking Canada believed the former; most Quebecers believed the latter. Locked into their respective visions of the country, both French-speaking and English-speaking Canadians overwhelmingly rejected the Charlottetown Agreement in a referendum in October 1992, albeit for opposing reasons.

If the failures of the Meech Lake and Charlottetown accords reveal anything, it is the deep dissonance between Quebec's desire for recognition as a distinct society and the rest of the country's adherence, reflective or not, to the rights-based society of traditional liberalism. While the rights-model society promoted by the Charter of Rights and Freedoms may have the support of a majority of English-speaking Canadians, it causes francophone Quebecers to question whether their collective interests, their desire for cultural survival, are compatible with those of the rest of the country. English-speaking Canadians generally see the individual as the ground of sovereignty and majority rule as the basis of the federal government's legitimacy. Francophone Quebecers, however, do not necessarily regard the individual as the bedrock of sovereignty. They look, instead, to their community to provide the basis for sovereignty. The francophone perspective comes through most clearly in the 1991 report of the Commission on the Political and Constitutional Future of Quebec, better known as the Bélanger-Campeau Commission. The commission, to which Taylor made a significant contribution,[185] was set up by the Quebec government following the defeat of the Meech Lake Accord. It promoted the two-nations vision of Canada, claiming that the country was a pact between two peoples. It concluded that, after the imposition of the charter in 1982, Canada's constitutional order reflected a political ideology that denied Canada's dualist nature and, hence, was at odds with Quebec's concerns for its cultural survival. The commission focused in particular on the Constitution's enshrinement of multiculturalism, with its assumption of the equality of all cultures and cultural origins. According to the commission, not only was this was tantamount to denying French-speaking Canadians' historical claim to be one of Canada's two equal founding groups, but also, in the commission's view, it failed to provide constitutional recognition to people with a particular culture they wished to preserve.

This is also Taylor's argument in many ways. In his essay "The Politics of Recognition," he argues that the debate over Meech Lake reflects a clash between two different forms of liberal society. For English-speaking Canadians, the distinct society clause gave collective goals precedence over individual rights. Such a notion runs counter to the charter-inspired support in English-speaking Canada for the kind of procedural liberalism that insists

that the state remain neutral about the good life and proclaims the universalising principle of the equality of all citizens before the law.[186] Quebecers, on the other hand, because of their historical experience, hold to a
model of society organised around the definition of a collective goal,
which the Quebec government uses its powers to promote. For a majority
of Quebecers, the fundamental good is the survival of their culture. Francophones saw English-speaking Canada's opposition to Meech Lake as reflecting a charter-inspired view of society that sets individual rights above
collective or group rights. Such a society, Taylor says, is alien to Quebec,
one to which Quebecers can never accommodate themselves without
losing their identity.

According to Taylor, a resolution to the crisis of Canada depends on
whether two types of liberal society can coexist. He refers to these two types
as procedural liberalism and substantive liberalism.[187] Procedural liberalism, which has prevailed in English-speaking Canada as well as in the rest
of the Anglo-American world, recognises the individual as the locus of political value; the individual possesses inherent and equal dignity independent of group differences such as class, race, religion, or sex. Such notions
reflect particular philosophical assumptions, largely drawn from Kant's
thought, Taylor argues. This view regards individual autonomy – "the ability of each person to determine for him or herself a view of the good
life,"[188] as Taylor puts it – as the fundamental political value. Because this
value is pre-eminent, a liberal society must remain neutral in regard to notions of what constitutes the good life and restrict itself to ensuring that citizens with differing views of the good treat each other fairly and that the
state itself treat everyone equally. And because a society that follows this
model of liberalism cannot publicly promote ideas of the good life, it relies
on the procedures of judicial review to ensure the constitutional equality
of its citizens – hence the label procedural liberalism.[189]

With Quebec, it seems, we have to consider a different form of liberal society. Taylor readily acknowledges that a society with collective goals like
those of Quebec "violates" the procedural model of liberalism.[190] But he
argues that there is another conception of liberalism – substantive liberalism – that is equally valid in protecting individual rights, but also safe-
guards the community whose survival is crucial to the identity of the
individuals who are its members. Taylor maintains that recognising Quebec's right to maintain its francophone culture – a right that constitutes
the basis for its constitutional claim of equality and its bid for distinct society status – need not infringe on traditional liberal principles such as freedom of speech, association, and religion, so long as collective rights such as

language protection are acknowledged and permitted to override other rights when legitimate collective aspirations require it. What English-speaking Canada fails to understand, he says, is that the supposed recognition of equal individual rights provided by strict adherence to the charter would undermine Quebec's cultural identity and lead ultimately to the disappearance of the French culture in North America, something that francophones are not going to accept. Substantive liberalism is a form of liberalism under which a society will sacrifice *non-fundamental* rights for the sake of a collectively determined concept of the good life. In Taylor's view, applying the model of substantive liberalism to Quebec to safeguard that province's collective aspirations is an attempt to find a middle way between procedural liberalism and anti-liberal communitarianism.[191]

Taylor's prescription for ending the crisis of Canada thus amounts to permitting in Quebec a society that ostensibly surmounts the atomism and inequities of liberalism while, at the same time, maintaining the fundamental principles of liberal democracy. Since Quebec qualifies as a "differently" liberal society, the way to resolve the crisis is to recognise Quebec's version of liberalism as being as valid as the procedural mode that prevails in the rest of Canada. Canadians as a whole need to reconcile the liberal tradition of individual rights with the communitarian emphasis on collective rights, Taylor concludes. Canadians, in other words, must become deeply diverse.[192]

Taylor's argument has certainly been challenged, particularly his attempt to formulate an alternative model of liberalism that would satisfy Quebec's collective aspirations without violating fundamental tenets of liberalism. Michael Lusztig, for example, points to the examples of Meech Lake and Charlottetown, along with the experience of three decades of would-be constitution making in Canada, to suggest that Taylor's middle way of "command liberalism"[193] has produced considerable conflict and animosity among English- and French-speaking Canadians, even to the point of bringing the country near to breakup in the 1995 Quebec referendum when a tiny majority of Quebecers voted against separation. Others, like Cooper and Bercuson, go so far as to argue that the principles on which English- and French-speaking Canadians base their constitutional claims cannot be reconciled within Canada's existing political order. The Meech Lake Accord, they point out, contained Quebec's *minimum* demands, the least it was prepared to accept. But the accord still proved unacceptable to Canadians as a whole. And it was unacceptable because it effectively undermined the universal principle of equal rights and thus "posed a fundamental threat to the foundations of liberal democracy in this country by creating two classes of citizens and two classes of governments – those in Quebec and those outside of it. Whatever the implications for Canadian federalism, it [the accord] served to undermine completely one of the fundamental pillars of liberal democracy: equality of citizens before the law."[194] Cooper and Bercuson conclude that "irreconcilable differences" exist between Quebec and Canada and a divorce is necessary. In other words, regardless of the validity of their claims about the future of Canada, Cooper and Bercuson's argument suggests that Taylor's appropriation of Hegelian concepts in an effort to satisfy Quebec's desire for recognition within the current Canadian political order is not coherent.

Such comments raise the question of whether Taylor's appropriation of Hegel's concept of recognition and its application to the problem of Canada is flawed.

23

Illiberal Strands in Taylor's Thought

Taylor's arguments on behalf of Quebec's quest for recognition are instructive because they offer a concrete test case for his notion of authenticity. But does he coherently meld features of liberalism, as he understands them, with the politics of recognition? Or, to put the question another way, does the kind of society envisaged in Taylor's appropriation of Hegelian thought in his quest for community satisfy the individual's desire for belonging while, at the same time, avoiding the potential for authoritarian politics raised by critics?

Liberalism unquestionably contains elements – individualism and egalitarianism, for example – that conflict, at least potentially, with collective aspirations. The problem of Quebec is a clear demonstration of this tension within the Canadian state. Successive efforts at constitutional politics have shown that a majority of Canadians are not willing to grant Quebec special or distinct society status. By the same token, it is doubtful that a majority of francophone Quebecers are willing to recognise the autonomy of cultural minorities within Quebec in the same way that they expect English-speaking Canadians to recognise their claims. Observers such as Jürgen Habermas have pointed out that granting Quebec a *de facto* veto on constitutional amendments would affect the rights of Canadians both inside and outside Quebec. Taylor might argue that English-speaking Canadians will just have to bend their procedural liberalism to accommodate their francophone countrymen and acknowledge their wish to live by a different model of liberalism. But does this mean that the politics of recognition requires that a group's sense of dignity and cultural identity be respected and sustained even if that results in using state power to enforce ends that perhaps offend liberal notions of individual rights?

Habermas addresses that question in commenting on Taylor's notion of deep diversity, arguing that recognising Quebec as a distinct society or granting Quebec a constitutional veto would be wrong if such actions would contravene long-established principles of individual rights and were not debated and decided on in an open and democratic fashion. He points out that Canadians have found "a federalist solution" that accommodates Quebec's desire for cultural autonomy by decentralising certain powers to Quebec. This demonstrates, he says, that procedural liberalism's theory of rights "in no way forbids the citizens of a democratic constitutional state to assert a conception of the good in their general legal order, a conception they either already share or have come to agree on through political discussion." What the theory of rights does forbid, however, is "to privilege one form of life at the expense of others within the nation."[195] The crisis of Canada, Habermas concludes, is not so much about the principle of equal rights but about the nature and extent of powers available to Quebec within the Canadian federation. In other words, Habermas challenges Taylor's reading of liberalism's ability to accommodate collective aspirations. Taylor may believe there is a conflict between protecting community identities and protecting individual rights, but such a reading of liberal principles "attacks the principles themselves and calls into question the individualistic core of the modern conception of freedom."[196]

Habermas goes on to question Taylor's assumptions about rights. Individual rights are not, he says, a product of atomised individualism. Rights are intersubjective in character because they are "based on the reciprocal recognition of co-operating legal persons." Taylor's emphasis on group-based rights inadequately acknowledges the substantial level of community already embedded in a liberal system of rights. Habermas writes: "[P]rivate legal persons cannot even attain the enjoyment of equal individual liberties unless they themselves, by jointly exercising their autonomy as citizens, arrive at a clear understanding about what interests and criteria are justified." To insist on the primacy of a system of individual rights need not prevent recognising group difference. Liberalism's theory of rights may aspire to universality, but that does not make it blind to unequal social conditions or cultural differences once "we ascribe to the bearers of individual rights an identity that is conceived intersubjectively." Indeed, "a correctly understood theory of rights requires a politics of recognition that protects the integrity of individuals in the life contexts in which his or her identity is formed."[197]

Taylor may seek a compromise between the demands of liberalism that are grounded in the primacy of the individual and the claims of recognition that give priority to the community, but is such a compromise coherent, or does it open the door to illiberal possibilities? As Janet Ajzenstat observes, Taylor wants to see Quebecers build a way of life that distinguishes them from other North American populations, but he also hopes that Quebec's political and social order "will *not* differ from other jurisdictions in its adherence to broad principles of liberal-democratic justice." She concludes that Taylor is, in the end, an uncertain friend of liberal democracy: "He cannot believe liberal democracy is *sufficient* for human flourishing, and yet he continues to admire it." Thus, she regards his communitarianism as dangerous romanticism.[198] Similarly, Barry Cooper questions the coherence of Taylor's politics of recognition. Taylor, he says, claims that equal respect is owed to all cultures but that some cultures are more deserving or "thicker" than others. How, Cooper asks, do you tell them apart? Who decides? And on what basis? Taylor might presume that all cultures that have lasted for any length of time offer something of worth to the world, but what is the basis for this presumption? "Who determines what is important in the voice of a culture? Why should one respect only important cultures?" Such questions are not asked by procedural liberals, Cooper contends, because they regard culture as a private, non-political activity toward which the state remains neutral. Such questions are only asked when efforts are made to politicise culture, "when culture is conceived as being worthy or even capable of 'recognition.'"[199]

Such commentaries raise numerous issues. Why does Taylor's project of recognition require constitutional validation? Is the misrecognition of Quebec by the rest of Canada so egregious that it warrants the breakup of the country as a whole if proper recognition is not forthcoming? And what if the rest of Canada simply cannot offer that recognition without violating its own deepest principles? Do Quebecers not have some obligation to properly recognise the aspirations of English-speaking Canada, assuming, of course, that you can define (or find) English-speaking Canada? And if Quebecers cannot recognise those aspirations, should Quebec be "deconfederated" to preserve the liberal order in the rest of the country? To consider these questions I need to briefly recapitulate Taylor's communitarian politics.

Taylor seeks to demonstrate the importance of collective concerns in the establishment of individual identity. He criticises the social contract theories of traditional liberalism, arguing that they are inadequate for satisfying the individual's desire to belong. Against this liberal ontology, Taylor sets his communitarian perspective, affirming the collective aspects of life that make society possible and, indeed, engender the possibility of individuality. He insists that there are "irreducibly social goods" and that we need to drop the notion that "all social goods are decomposable" into individual goods. Accordingly, he attacks what he describes as an atomist view of politics that regards the common good as "constituted out of individual goods, without remainder."[200] For Taylor, community is the precondition for individuals to possess and exercise their individual rights. Even the concept of individualism is possible only within a particular culture, and culture is not a matter of individual choice but a collective enterprise. There is no way that a person could conceive of himself as an autonomous or free being or as a bearer of rights unless these goods are part of a pre-existing cultural context. Taylor draws on Rousseau to argue that it is also wrong to assume that individuals could even exist outside of the community, since the prerequisite of any social contract is the capacity for reason and language, both of which are attainable only in a social context.[201] The promotion of individual freedom points to the prior existence of social and cultural conditions that make such a good possible. In short, for an "I" to be, there has to be a "we." On this claim of the socially created individual, Taylor concludes that the individual who identifies himself as a free being has a moral obligation to the community that makes his identity possible. This implies that the primacy of the individual espoused by liberalism (in Taylor's interpretation) must give way to the primacy of the community.[202] Such an argument – the affirmation of individual good entails the affirmation of the community that makes such a good possible – harkens to Hegel's concept of *Sittlichkeit*. Indeed, Taylor argues that Hegel's concept refers to the obligations that individuals have to society: "What Hegel calls *Sittlichkeit* ... refers to the moral obligations I have to an ongoing community of which I am a part."[203]

I do not quarrel with Taylor's interpretation, so far as it goes, but I suggest that it does not go far enough. For Hegel, as I have previously argued, what makes a society and its institutions worthy of affirmation and obligation is its approximation to the Idea of freedom and its necessary embodiment in history. Taylor, as I have also noted, rejects Hegel's ontology – reason manifesting itself in greater human freedom through the historical process – as unacceptable nowadays. Nevertheless, he follows the Hegelian dialectic in arguing that the crucial characteristic of ethical life is how "it enjoins us to bring about what already is" – that is, to recognise that the pre-existing community life is the basis for one's obligation. "It is in virtue of its being an ongoing affair that I have these obligations; and my fulfilment of these obligations is what sustains it and keeps it being."[204] Taylor is not implying anything as simplistic as "my country right or wrong." Nor is he claiming that individuals are obliged to support their community regardless of its moral or ethical condition. And neither is he suggesting that individuals must remain loyal to corrupt regimes.[205] Nonetheless, his argument misses a salient aspect of Hegel's concept of *Sittlichkeit* – the community's obligation to the individual.

For Hegel, community is not primarily about individual *identity*, but about individual *freedom*. Hegel would probably agree with Taylor about the problems of atomistic individualism and the need for a sense of communal belonging, but his abiding concern is with promoting a politics of rights that enhance individual self-determination. Where Taylor focuses on the need for common conceptions of the good, Hegel seeks to strengthen those institutions and mediating associations that allow freedom. Rights for Hegel are situated within institutions that embody freedom. As Vasanthi Srinivasan observes, "The unencumbered self is countered not by replacing a politics of rights with a politics of the common good but by restoring the immanent reason within the institutions that secure rights."[206] Which is to say, our desire to belong, to identify with a community, has to be satisfied in and through freely chosen institutional arrangements (including constitutions) and not by recognising cultures that do not necessarily reflect the fundamental metaphysical ground of modernity – free will. As Hegel's *Philosophy of Right* makes clear, freedom is embodied in legal rights and political institutions. As rights-bearers, individuals live within a set of institutions – the family, the markets, civil society, a constitutional order, the state – that are rational to the degree that they live up to the modern principle of self-determination. Political community is important to Hegel because only through a community and its institutions can individuals claim their freedom. Language and culture do not necessarily enhance freedom. Hence, for Hegel, moderns must belong institutionally rather than culturally because what is ultimately at stake in the relationship between the individual and the community is freedom, not identity.[207]

The obvious question that arises from all this is whether Taylor's grounding of the reconciliation of the individual and the community in culture and language exposes an illiberal strand in his communitarian politics.[208] Given his concern with maintaining cultural identities, it is clear that Taylor does not base his concerns for the centrality of community on the primacy of individual freedom. To the contrary, he is adamant in claiming the independent nature of the community. Hegel describes the reciprocity of freedom and obligation that makes the relationship between the individual and the community symbiotic in that each requires the other achieve their respective rational moments. But Taylor, in making the fulfilment of the individual contingent on the existence of the community, opens up the possibility of communities taking precedence over the individual. And that, as Hegel knew from the Terror, is something to avoid. Hegel's position, with its emphasis on the reciprocal nature of the relationship between the individual and the community (or between freedom *and* belonging), is reflected in Hegel's Socratic model, which I discussed in Part 1. In considering Taylor's "illiberal strand," it is worth recalling that discussion. Hegel sees in Socrates' defiance of the laws of Athens an example of an individual's subjective will justifiably taking precedence over that of the community. The individual assumes primacy when he knows inwardly that he is right and the community is wrong.

> This subjectivity, *qua* abstract self-determination and pure certainty of oneself alone, as readily evaporates into itself the whole determinate character of right, duty, and existence, as it remains both the power to judge, to determine from within itself alone, what is good in respect of any content, and also the power to which the good, at first only an ideal and an ought-to-be, owes its actuality ... Once self-consciousness has reduced all otherwise valid duties to emptiness and itself to the sheer inwardness of the will, it has become the potentiality of either making the absolutely universal its principle, or equally well of elevating above the universal the self will of private particularity, taking that as its principle and realizing it through its actions.[209]

Given Hegel's argument, I would suggest that Taylor, in asserting an independent function for the community, also implies a dependent relationship between the individual, in terms of his capacity for achieving his purposes, and the community in which he exists. In doing so, Taylor denies the implications of Hegel's interpretation of Socrates' trial and execution: that individuals can be, and sometimes need to be, independent of the community, that they can have values outside the social context that provide meaning to their lives and a framework for self-understanding. Taylor, in short, wants too much unity.

Others also question Taylor's critique of liberalism along these lines. Will Kymlicka, for example, questions what he regards as Taylor's willingness to subsume the individual in the community. In making the individual's identity so dependent on the community, Taylor ignores the liberal claim that "we have an ability to detach ourselves from any particular communal practice." No community can morally justify requiring an individual to identify with it if such identification is not subject to individual judgment and the possibility of rejection.[210] Individuals in liberal societies are free to stand back and decide for themselves whether they want to belong to a particular community. Brian Barry makes a similar argument regarding Taylor's claim that the egalitarian principles of procedural liberalism are inhospitable to cultural differences. "It is 'difference-blind' liberalism that gets the right answers and the 'politics of difference' that should be rejected," Barry says, arguing that liberalism is able to accommodate precisely what Taylor says is inadequate: "'having the French language available (in Quebec) for those who might choose it.'"[211] In an analysis of Taylor's 1992 essay "The Politics of Recognition," Barry comments that social policies that require francophone parents to send their children only to French-language public schools lend the coercive powers of the state to those "'who value remaining true to the culture of our ancestors,'" but interfere with the freedom of "'those who might want to cut loose in the name of some individual goal of self-development'" to pursue their goals. Such policies offend fundamental principles of liberalism. "The notion that birth is fate – that simply in virtue of being born into a certain ethnic group one acquires the (potentially enforceable) duty to maintain its 'ancestral culture' – is continuous with the kind of ethnic nationalism that is profoundly at odds with liberalism."[212]

The illiberal potential of Taylor's communitarianism is demonstrated in an article Taylor published in 1989 about the Iranian *fatwa* against Salman Rushdie, author of *The Satanic Verses*.[213] Taylor acknowledges that writers cannot be expected to avoid dealing with sensitive religious symbols without betraying their own understanding of the world. Nevertheless, he maintains that in adopting the anti-religious and secular perspective of Western liberal society, Rushdie ignores the fact that religious symbols and dogmas mean a great deal to those who espouse them and that to mock those symbols is to mock those existential supports that provide people with the meaning in their lives. "Rushdie's book is comforting to the western liberal mind," Taylor says, "[because it confirms] the belief that there is nothing outside their worldview that needs deeper understanding."[214] In other words, Rushdie engages in a deliberate act of misrecognition, and, according to Taylor, to misrecognise someone, whether an individual or a group, is to do damage to that individual or group. Even fundamental principles of liberalism such as freedom of expression have to bend to accommodate the feelings and sensibility of others. "Any regime of free expression has limits which are justified by the possibility of harm on others,"[215] Taylor says, noting the existence of libel laws and the taboo on shouting "Fire" in a crowded theatre. In a world in which international migration is making societies less culturally homogeneous, he concludes that "the liberal mind will have to learn to reach out more."[216]

Using the analogy of libel laws as a way to challenge liberalism is a dubious intellectual stretch. Canadian libel laws offer redress to individuals – not groups – who think their reputations have been harmed. What individual Muslim did Rushdie libel? Can Taylor name an individual Muslim whose reputation Rushdie besmirched? In any case, how do you libel an entire religion? Taylor's standard, if taken to its logical conclusion, would disallow any criticism of religion because it is inevitable that some believer somewhere will be offended. As for the crowded-theatre standard, surely that is a matter of saving lives, not a matter of principle.[217]

Taylor argues that in a multicultural society it is insufficient to defend Rushdie's book by asserting the principle of free expression and the claim that this is the way we do things in the liberal West, because Western societies are becoming increasingly multicultural and there are "substantial numbers of people who are citizens and also belong to the culture that calls into question our philosophical boundaries."[218] Given that reality, Taylor argues, it is simply not tenable to say, "This is how we do things here," when the norms of one group conflict with those of another. However, Brian Barry points out that Taylor's argument implies that problems like Rushdie's *fatwa* would not happen if different ethnic or religious groups did not share the same geographical space and thereby impose conflicting demands on the presiding political order. In other words, conflicts like those stirred up by the Rushdie affair are the result of the West's immigration policies and its increasing heterogeneity. Does this mean that, in a more homogeneous culture, resorting to "This is how we do things here" is more acceptable? If that is the case, then there is nothing wrong with defending Rushdie's freedom of speech if that is how we do things in a liberal society. And that, of course, raises the awkward question of whether liberal societies are supposed to become less liberal to accommodate minorities that are not willing to live by liberal principles and premises.[219]

Taylor's communitarianism promotes the notion that individuals have to accommodate themselves to the pre-existing community for the sake of that community's survival. Does this standard apply to immigrant groups, too? Why did they come to the West if they were not willing to accommodate the pre-existing community they would find on arrival? Taylor's response to such questions – and to cultural conflict in general – may well be to urge compromise. But what do you do when you are confronted with a culture that does not value compromise? Moreover, can liberalism compromise on its most fundamental principles without becoming illiberal. As Brian Barry cogently remarks, "[A] liberal cannot coherently believe that liberal principles should themselves be compromised to accommodate the demands of anti-liberals."[220]

In "The Politics of Recognition," Taylor acknowledges that as far as a "mainstream Islam" is concerned, "there is no question of separating politics and religion the way we have come to expect in Western liberal society." What this means, he says, is that liberalism cannot be regarded as a difference-blind or neutral meeting ground for the world's cultures. The Rushdie case, in particular, demonstrates that liberalism is merely "the political expression of one range of cultures, and quite incompatible with other ranges." Taylor finds this disturbing because it points up the problems facing the liberal societies of the West as they become increasingly multicultural. He finds it awkward, however, having to tell immigrants from non-Western cultures, such as Muslims, that they have no basis for objecting to Rushdie's book because "this is how we do things here."[221]

This is the most troublesome aspect of Taylor's position in the Rushdie controversy. Taylor suggests, implicitly or otherwise, that the liberal mind must violate its civilisational foundations to accommodate a cultural mindset that denies those very principles. Why is Taylor's insistence on tolerance and proper recognition so one-sided? Why is Rushdie supposed to understand and tolerate the worldview of some Muslims when they are not obliged to understand or tolerate his worldview? Taylor is correct in saying that there is no universally accepted standard of freedom of speech because there is no single world culture. But why does he require the liberal West to retract its principles when confronted by those who not only misrecognise those principles, but would, if possible, destroy the civilisation based on those principles? Maybe "how we do things here" is the right way to do things and those who object should not come "here" if they cannot abide by that worldview.

To be sure, Taylor argues that the defence of "This is how we do things here" covers fundamental principles such as the right to life and freedom of speech, neither of which he wants to sacrifice. Taylor defends Rushdie on the ground that liberalism is not difference-blind. In fact, he refers to liberalism as a "fighting creed" that must be defended against those who would undermine its fundamental principles, such as rights to liberty, free speech, and freedom of religion. None of these fundamental rights, he says, can be compromised for the sake of preserving a culture: "One has to distinguish the fundamental liberties, those that should never be infringed and therefore ought to be unassailably entrenched, on one hand, from privileges and immunities that are important, but that can be revoked or restricted for reasons of public policy – although one would need a strong reason to do this – on the other."[222] With this statement Taylor tries to find theoretical space that would reconcile atomistic liberalism with its denial of the validity of cultural differences and the demands of minorities whose cultural traditions or religious beliefs would, if allowed, undermine the fundamental principles of liberalism.

Is this possible, or does Taylor merely want it both ways? Daniel O'Neill argues that Taylor's defence of Rushdie's right to free expression in "The Politics of Recognition" fits uneasily with previous statements in his 1989 essay "The Rushdie Controversy."[223] In the 1989 essay, while defending Rushdie's freedom to publish, Taylor seems to be saying that such freedom is limited to the liberal West. As he puts it, Rushdie's right to publish per-haps "applies to us. But does it necessarily apply across the board? Can we say that the ground rules which apply here ought to apply everywhere?"[224] Taylor, O'Neill observes, believes for both practical and theoretical reasons that such a question cannot be answered in purely general terms that would be applicable everywhere regardless of circumstances. At the practi-cal level, any society that endorses freedom of expression is already sus-tained by a broad consensus on what that freedom entails. And at the theoretical level, even in liberal regimes, limits on free expression are justi-fied by the potential harm some of its forms might inflict on others – hence the existence of libel laws. Taylor argues in the 1989 essay that there is no doubt that some Muslims were offended by *The Satanic Verses*, believing that the book ridiculed them and their religion. Thus, he says, it is "misguided to claim to identify culture-independent criteria of harm. What people are really doing who propose such criteria is endorsing the superiority of some culture over others. In this case, of course, the superiority of the West."[225] For Muslims, Rushdie's novel was blasphemous, and thus, in supporting the *fatwa* or demanding that the book be banned, Muslims were defending their faith; any denunciation from the West of their views amounted to an attempt on the part of Westerners to impose their cultural beliefs. As Taylor says, "I wouldn't be surprised if a Muslim saw an attempt on my part to convince him/her that our definitions [of freedom of speech] are universally correct as another way of imposing the standards of Christendom, i.e., as an effort at conversion, rather than that defining of an impartial principle."[226]

All this leads Taylor to conclude that there cannot be a universal defini-tion of freedom of expression without a single world culture. This, in turn, means that solutions to problems that work in one part of the world do not necessarily apply elsewhere. Besides, given the increasing levels of immigra-tion to the West from non-Western countries, "we are going to have to live with this pluralism for some time." Perhaps so, but why does Taylor assume that Western societies, with their hard-fought and long-established tradi-tions of secular liberalism, must be the ones that accommodate the claims of newcomers? Why, in other words, does Taylor require of liberalism a form of cultural conduct that is contrary to maintaining liberal society?

Taylor's solution to the problems raised by the Rushdie controversy is to argue that when it is not a matter of cultural survival, there is still a need to "recognize the equal value of different cultures; that we not only let them survive, but acknowledge their *worth*."[227] Why? If you accept Taylor's argument that liberal principles might not necessarily apply in non-Western countries, then the rejection of Muslim demands to ban Rushdie's novel is, by Taylor's own standards, merely the imposition of majoritarian will on a minority, the countenance of a liberal assault on the cultural values of an immigrant community. But as O'Neill points out, this was exactly the argument used by Western Muslims, who, even if they did not support the *fatwa* against Rushdie, denounced the publication of his book in the name of freedom as the imposition of secular liberal values on their equally worthy traditions. "Thus, Taylor's entire multicultural liberal project of distinguishing fundamental rights from privileges and immunities occurs within a specific cultural context that, based on his own argument, would seem to have no legitimate theoretical basis for trumping non-Western notions of justice in the international arena."[228]

This leads to the conclusion that Taylor, in promoting multicultural liberalism, is unable to offer a solid theoretical defence of the principles of liberalism on which he bases his politics of recognition. In both "The Politics of Recognition" and "The Rushdie Controversy," Taylor effectively says that the only real defence that Western liberals can offer in supporting Rushdie's freedom of speech is pragmatic and geographically bounded – that is, this is how we do things in the West. But O'Neill says that if this is liberalism's best defence, "it neither provides philosophical support for Taylor's multicultural liberal framework nor its substantive implications and will do little ... to convince Muslims of the theoretical desirability of the liberal position."[229] When push comes to shove, Taylor is unable to defend liberalism. He might seek a form of liberalism that ensures cultural survival as it maintains individual rights, but in the end, he finds no fundamental theoretical grounds on which to base a defence of liberalism and its principles as a universal fighting creed, even though those principles are essential to his communitarian creed. The Rushdie affair, O'Neill concludes, exposes "a potentially unresolvable tension at the heart" of Taylor's multicultural liberalism.[230]

The Rushdie controversy is not the only example where Taylor's theoretical claims fall short when applied at the concrete level. Taylor also criticises the American novelist Saul Bellow for purportedly saying, "When the Zulus produce a Tolstoy we will read him." Taylor regards this remark "as a quintessential statement of European arrogance, not just because Bellow is allegedly being *de facto* insensitive to the value of Zulu culture, but frequently also because it is seen to reflect a denial in principle of human equality."[231] But as Andy Lamey observes, Taylor's suggestion that Bellow is ignorant of Zulu culture and therefore unqualified to make his (alleged) judgment merely demonstrates Taylor's own ill-informed judgment. Bellow, it seems, was once a student of African anthropology, and he was "'speaking of the distinction between literate and pre-literate societies.'" Lamey also cites other experts, including Africans, who support Bellow's argument that Zulu literature has yet to achieve the level of quality or the universal appeal of the Russian novel. Which suggests that it is Taylor himself who is being condescending: "Zulu culture is not something Taylor feels he needs to acquaint himself with – engage in dialogue with – before lecturing on its essential 'equality' with our own culture." Such an attitude is not only condescending but, arguably, culturally destructive. As Lamey observes, the Zulu novels that do exist are a fusion of various cultural horizons, bringing together an African oral language and tradition and a European language and cultural form that is biblical in its roots. "For Taylor, however, it seems a matter of faith that what the Zulus have so far produced could not be anything other than utterly alien." Only Westerners, it seems, are capable of transcending their cultural horizons. And that leads to the conclusion that in promoting equality of cultures, Taylor effectively lowers the standards of quality. As Lamey concludes, Taylor's denunciation of Bellow "reveals the hollowness of Taylor's talk of fused cultural horizons and dialogical identity."[232]

Brian Barry extends this argument in pointing out that there is a difference between the claim that all *human beings* as individuals are entitled to equal respect and the claim that a similar respect should be given to every culture. Citing Taylor's essay "The Politics of Recognition," Barry questions the veracity of Taylor's claim that even to entertain the possibility that some cultures are less valuable than others is to deny human equality or even the presumption of equal value. In the case of Bellow's ostensible remarks, Barry says it is remarkably naive – he uses the word *feeble* – of Taylor to doubt that some cultures have produced works of art that are qualitatively and objectively better than that of others. No one would claim that there is no difference in quality between individual painters or writers, so why suggest there is no difference between cultures. Barry writes: "It is clear that some societies have created more valuable ideas and artefacts than others. In the same way, we are bound to judge that some cultures (in the anthropological sense of 'culture') are better than others: more just, more free, more enlightened, and generally better adapted to human flourishing."[233]

Where do such commentaries leave us? Recall John Dunn's observation that I quoted at the beginning of my consideration of Taylor's thought – "[I]n the face of distressing choices he [Taylor] is apt to cling tenaciously to both horns of the dilemma, refusing, for what are often humanly excellent motives, to let either of them go."[234]

For Dunn, though, this is a perilous position. It is worth quoting Dunn at length on this point because he succinctly encapsulates the conundrum in Taylor's thought:

> Since [Taylor] is a Catholic he could scarcely fail to see some force to demands that come from beyond our own desires or aspirations, be they from history, tradition, society, nature, or God. But, as well as being a Catholic, he is also very much a Romantic, [and therefore] he is strongly and personally committed to taking what comes from our own desires and aspirations at least equally seriously.
>
> The resulting amalgam can readily offend most readers. His liberal critics among American philosophers do not care for the Catholicism, and believe that it leads him to espouse a potentially (or actually) oppressive relation between a society and its individual members. No doubt his Catholic critics are less enthusiastic about the Romantic elements, seeing these as licensing a *louche* and excessively aesthetic approach to the art of life, and a correspondingly enfeebled grasp of the requirements of God's Law. Either may well be partly right.[235]

What does this theoretical tension suggest about Taylor's appropriation of Hegel's thought? Taylor, like Hegel, is engaged in an attempt to make whole what is fragmented. He seeks to bring to our attention the deeper existential commitments that are inherent to the modern project, attachments that if properly understood offer, in his view, a kind of salvation. What we get in Taylor's thought is both a critique of modernity and a defence of modernity. Taylor shares the communitarian concern regarding the perceived excesses of liberal individualism: a centring on the self and a concomitant unawareness of the greater concerns – religious, political, historical – that transcend the self. However, he insists that he is not completely opposed to modern liberalism or, for that matter, to modernity. While he generally accepts the communitarian critique of modernity, he argues that there are forms of self-interpretation and understanding within modernity that can mitigate its excesses. At the centre of Taylor's project, then, is the idea that modernity provides moral grounds, or sources, for overcoming the reification of individualism and its attendant self-absorbed subjectivism. He holds that if we try hard enough to understand why modernity has come to be what it is – why, for instance, the modern self is so needful of an authentic identity – we will discover the modern aspirations to be both reasonable and worthwhile.

This makes Taylor's enterprise akin to Hegel's in the sense that it regards the modern identity as having "unfolded as an intelligible story."[236] What Taylor provides, Ronald Beiner observes, is a narrative of the self-development of the modern identity such that, at the deepest level, the essential moral purposes of modernity can be seen as intelligible, coherent, and worthy of aspiration. The problem, though, is that without Hegel's metaphysical foundation, Taylor has difficulty maintaining confidence in the immanent narrative structure of the modern project. The result is an abiding tension in Taylor's thought. To appropriate Beiner's view, Taylor's purpose "is to try to do the utmost interpretative justice to the aspirations of people in modern society to both express their individuality *and* to satisfy their longings for community. (In this sense he is a communitarian *and* a liberal.)"[237]

Can you be both a communitarian and a liberal without contradiction? Or, put differently, has Taylor's Hegelian appropriation allowed him to reconcile the individual and the community in a coherent fashion that supports the modern demand for individual freedom and self-rule? I leave my response to these questions for my concluding remarks in the next section. It is sufficient here to note that at least in the cases of Rushdie and Bellow, Taylor urges a generosity toward religious and cultural communities that he does not accord those who would defend Western cultural standards and philosophic principles. Similarly, while he insists on a sympathetic understanding of Quebec's aspirations, he does not require a reciprocal understanding of the concerns of the rest of Canada. For all his talk of cultural equality, Taylor wants to recognise "the superior position of the francophone ethnic group,"[238] at least within Quebec. But this is to promote the imposition of a collective goal on other Quebecers who reject that goal – a strategy that Taylor denies English-speaking Canada having any right to pursue in its relations with Quebec. Moreover, Taylor himself acknowledges the dangers of promoting Quebec's distinctiveness:

> I recognise the principle commitment of the *indépendentiste* leadership in Quebec is to building an open, tolerant, pluralistic society, with a place for minority cultures. But I sense in the dynamic of the independence movement itself, in the passions it feels required to mobilise, the harbingers of a rather narrower and more exclusionist society. And very much

the same can be said, *mutatis mutandi*, for the movements in English Canada which would be glad to see Quebec go. Separation would not only mean the failure of the Canadian experiment in deep diversity but also the birth of two new states in some ways even less amenable to diversity than our present condition.[239]

Such uncertainties on Taylor's part open the door to numerous concerns: What matters when it comes to cultural survival? If liberalism is a "fighting creed," why such hesitation in fighting for its survival? Are only minorities and other cultures allowed to claim the right of survival? Can a majority preserve itself or its self-understanding? If Quebec were to separate or be removed from the Canadian state, would it have to sacrifice its majoritarian culture for the sake of its minorities in the same way that English-speaking Canada is supposed to sacrifice its English-speaking culture in order to accommodate Quebec? And if the francophone majority is unwilling to do this, would they not violate the liberal principles Taylor says he wants to preserve?[240]

Such questions raise the issue of whether Taylor's communitarian elevation of communal identity over and against the liberal principles that give priority to the individual as a bearer of universal rights would "weaken the foundations of liberalism and open the door to intolerance."[241] For example, Steven Rockefeller, in a commentary on Taylor's essay, "The Politics of Recognition," is sceptical of Taylor's "Quebec brand of liberalism." Says Rockefeller: "I am uneasy about the danger of an erosion over time of fundamental human rights growing out of a separatist mentality that elevates ethnic identity over universal human identity."[242] Even a sympathetic critic like Mark Redhead acknowledges the veracity of some critics' judgments that Taylor is "guilty of potentially promoting a limiting schema for belonging to a state like Canada that stands in tension with the openness to diverse identities that he espouses."[243] In other words, rather than carry forward Hegel's project of reconciliation, Taylor's project of deep diversity might do more harm than good to Canada's federal system.

PART FIVE

Northern Spirits –
An Iterative Conclusion

24

Taylor's Tale of Multiculturalism

INTRODUCTION

I argued at the beginning of this essay that Canada exists in tension between those factors that promote disunity and those that foster unity. The
underlying narrative of Canadian political and social history has been the
effort to reconcile this tension. Intrinsic to this project of reconciliation is
"a passion for identity," as David Taras puts it: "The desire to come to
terms with oneself in place and time and in relation to others is itself a national instinct."[1] Which is to say, the desire for reconciliation runs deep in
the Canadian psyche. It is this desire for reconciliation that has attracted so
many Canadian intellectuals to Hegel. This essay has explored some ways
in which Hegel's thought has been appropriated in response to the tensions, conflicts, and concerns with respect to Canada's political existence.
The fundamental question to which this essay is a response is, in metaphor-
ical terms, How has Spirit manifested itself in the Canadian mind? I would
like to think I have provided some reasonable – and reasoned – answers.
My argument, in a nutshell, has been this one: Watson finds in Hegel
support for urging Canadians into imperial citizenship; Grant, conversely, regards Hegelian rationalism as a formula for subsuming the "idea" of Canada
into a continental empire; and Taylor finds in Hegel a source that may
help Canada maintain a pluralistic society within a single unified state.

It is not that simple, of course. The thought of all three political philosophers is complex and sometimes contradictory. Drawing on Hegel's
thought, both Watson and Grant oppose the idea of a world-state. But
where Watson employs Hegelian principles to justify empire and, by implication at least, to urge Canada into a greater imperial role, Grant sees
those same principles leading to Canada's disappearance. Where Watson

looks forward to Canada's future Spirit, as it were, Grant looks back and laments the passing of a particular Spirit. Taylor, on the other hand, sees a Spirit that expresses a worldwide phenomenon of multicultural societies in formation. All three share communitarian concerns, but Watson leans more toward the individual, while Grant and Taylor incline toward the primacy of community. Where Grant sees multiculturalism as a homogenising force, and hence possibly leading to tyranny, Taylor regards multiculturalism as a necessity to which Canada must accommodate itself in order to preserve Canadian unity. All three, again drawing on Hegelian concepts, agree that extreme individualism undermines community and authentic human freedom. They share a similar critique of the atomising features of modern liberalism, including its contractarian politics and the idea of the neutral state. They also share concerns about the consequence of modernity's reduction of classical reason – that is, philosophy – to modern instrumental rationality, and they fear a modern scientific project that regards humans as objects to be analysed and manipulated in the same way as nature is to be conquered.

Such examples point up the numerous areas where my three Hegelians converge and others where they diverge – even as they draw on the same Hegelian concepts. This makes it difficult to claim some definitive commonality regarding their appropriations of Hegelian thought. Nevertheless, I think I have shown that if there is one issue with which all three are concerned it is the question of the proper relationship between the individual and the community or, more abstractly, between the self and the other. The responses of Watson, Grant, and Taylor to this question, different as they may be, are very much tied to their respective readings of Hegel, particularly the master-slave dialectic and its struggle-for-recognition theme. Watson finds in the master-slave dialectic a theory for a federalist empire, while Grant sees the dark formula for a tyrannical world order and Taylor finds the metaphor for expressivist politics. That there should be such different responses to the same thought should not be surprising: what a philosopher meant is not necessarily what he comes to mean. Still, it is surprising that Hegel's central philosophic trope could produce such contradictory "meanings."

It is with this abiding conundrum in mind that I want to return to and expand on some of the meanings that have emerged from my essay. My remarks are intended as an iterative summation, an attempt to situate the movement of Spirit in Canada, highlighting some of the more distinctive themes that have emerged in my study of these three Canadian Hegelians.

I also hope that my remarks point toward further inquiries into Spirit's sojourns in Canada, particularly in terms of the nation's future, whatever it may be. I begin with Taylor.

* * *

As moderns, according to Taylor, we are plagued by the sense that things are falling apart, that the centre no longer holds and the world is descending into anarchy. We might not fret about the decay of civilisation on a daily basis; we generally go about our everyday lives reasonably confident that whatever the future may conjure, things will not be too bad. Yet few would doubt that our confidence is being tested. Portents of uncertainty and disorder are everywhere, from the barbarous to the bathetic. On the international scene, we confront terrorist attacks on civilian populations, threats of war and failing states, while closer to home we perceive the weakening of traditional social and family structures, the atrophy of civic life, pervasive cynicism toward political elites, and growing mistrust between groups within society. Of course, every age has its fears, but it seems that the anxieties of our time tend toward the extreme and even the paradoxical. At least this is Taylor's conclusion: "What is special about our case is that we see the breakdown coming about in a particular way. We see it coming through hypertrophy, through our becoming too much what we have been. This kind of fear is perhaps definitive of the modern age, the fear that the very things that define our break with earlier traditional societies – our affirmation of freedom, equality, radical new beginnings, control over nature, democratic self-rule – will somehow be carried beyond feasible limits and will undo us."[2]

What Taylor is getting at is the perception that the crisis of Western liberal democracy, including Canada's version, is a crisis of excess, the consequence of too much of a good thing. At the core of this crisis is the concept of individualism pushed to its extreme. We have come to believe that people are (or should be) utterly autonomous and therefore able to create their own values irrespective of historic or cultural circumstances. This attitude has eroded the loyalties, customs, and attachments to what is beyond the self, including the family and the wider community. The result, says Taylor, is a crisis of legitimation.

In Part 4, I presented my understanding of Taylor's response to this crisis, particularly as it applies to the problem of Canada. In essence, he seeks to reconcile expressive unity and radical autonomy, appropriating

elements of Hegel's philosophy to do so. For Taylor, Hegel's contemporary relevance is due to his thought having played "an important part in
the intensification of the conflict around the modern notion of freedom."[3]
Taylor's own philosophic narrative seeks to rescue modern freedom from
the distortions of excessive individualism. Deploying Hegel's concept of
recognition, Herderian language theory, and Rousseau's notion of authenticity, Taylor promotes an idea of freedom that, he says, allows people to
maintain an individual identity that satisfies their need to belong. Hence,
he concludes that the proper response to hypertrophy and social fragmentation is to recognise community identities. The preservation of liberalism requires recognising and maintaining cultural differences – that is to
say, multiculturalism.

Before I pursue this line of thought, it is worth noting that Taylor's attacks on extreme individualism follow Hegel's distinction between *Verstand*
and *Vernunft* – that is, between a calculative "understanding" that isolates
objects in analysing them and a more holistic "reason" that comprehends
things in their totality and context. For Taylor, as well as for Watson and
Grant, the atomising manifestations of modernity reflect the practices of
Verstand, or instrumental reason. One of Taylor's main purposes is to undercut the idea that human life can be comprehended by means of the
particular understanding of the natural sciences, with their stance of disengagement toward the objects under observation. Such a naturalist perspective wrongfully presumes humans can be interpreted as objects that can be
known for what they are when detached from the social and natural worlds
in which they live. As well, this epistemological position fosters the notion
of the autonomous, self-responsible individual as the locus of value. This
leads, in turn, to the political idea that the individual takes precedence
over the needs of the community and that the state's function is largely
one of keeping order among self-seeking individuals. Against this view,
Taylor posits his expressivist theory and its claim that humans are not
things, but rather self-interpreting agents whose conduct is informed by
self-given meanings and purposes derived from belonging to a community.

Taylor by no means rejects all aspects of the Enlightenment project – the
increased respect for individual worth and the curtailment of authoritarian
politics, for example. But he argues that traditional liberalism's promotion
of the atomistic individual has created a society in which people are alienated from the communities in which they live. Traditional liberalism, he
says, downplays the reality that people gain meaning and purpose through
their relationships and attachments to others. People are not self-created;
rather, they are formed in and by communities. They are free and authentic

as individuals only when they know themselves as belonging to communities. And it is this "freedom in belonging" that necessitates a politics of recognition.

Taylor regards the crisis of Canada as a paradigmatic example of the politics of recognition. In the separatist aspirations of francophone Quebecers, we have a conflict between the principles of the radical Enlightenment and Romantic expressivism. Taylor seeks to ameliorate this conflict by promoting a politics of deep diversity that accepts "a plurality of ways of belonging"[4] and does not require individuals or groups to pass through some other more dominant community. The Canadian state should accommodate multiple cultures within a single political order. Taylor distinguishes this idea from the first-level diversity of traditional liberal societies, in which the diversity of cultural groups is acknowledged but all are treated equally by the state – "the politics of equal dignity," as he calls it. Taylor argues that such comprehensive equality cannot produce genuine recognition because it does not in fact provide equal dignity to different cultures. In particular, francophone Quebecers (along with aboriginals) are under pressure from English-speaking Canada to adopt forms of governance that conflict with their culture. But they fear that the Kantian liberalism of English-speaking Canada will have homogenising consequences and undermine the culture that gives them identity and meaning to their lives. Hence, Taylor concludes that imposing a blanket procedural liberalism on Quebecers constitutes a form of oppression: "The claim is that the supposedly neutral set of difference-blind principles of equal dignity is in fact a reflection of one hegemonic culture. As it turns out, then, only the minority or suppressed cultures are being forced to take alien form. Consequently, the supposedly fair and difference-blind society is not only inhuman (because suppressing identities) but also, in a subtle and unconscious way, itself highly discriminatory."[5] To end this oppression requires the rest of Canada to acknowledge that measures to maintain Quebec's francophone culture need not infringe on traditional liberal principles such as freedom of speech, association, and religion. There is room to allow collective rights such as language protection to take precedence over other rights when legitimate collective aspirations require it. English-speaking Canada should understand that the supposed recognition of equal individual rights provided by strict adherence to the charter would undermine Quebec's cultural identity and lead ultimately to the disappearance of the French culture in North America, which, of course, is something francophones cannot accept.

Taylor insists that what he is promoting will not lead to the fragmentation or balkanisation of Canada. Indeed, he warns that without such pluralistic recognition Canada will undoubtedly break apart. "Deep diversity is the only formula on which a united federal Canada can be rebuilt."[6] There must be more than one formula for citizenship, other models of liberal society that not only maintain the goods of procedural liberalism such as *habeas corpus* and other fundamental rights, but also recognise communal "goods." Canadians must reconcile the liberal tradition of individual rights with the communitarian emphasis on collective rights.

I have already detailed some of the criticism levelled against Taylor for his reliance on cultural identity in the establishment of communal goods. It is true that Hegel lends support to the communitarian position in regard to the importance of community and the value of family membership and citizenship. For Hegel, the purpose of citizenship cannot be reduced to the satisfaction of utilitarian desires or the protection of individual rights. However, Hegel praises community membership (and the institutions that sustain it) for its capacity to extend individual freedom. Where Taylor's Romantic approach highlights belongingness and cultural identity, Hegel makes the protection of individual freedom the primary purpose of the community. Taylor may argue that the community is a substantive good because it is only as members of a community that we find significant meaning in our lives, but Hegel makes the more nuanced point that a community can only constitute itself as good (or rational) to the degree that it maximises the freedom of its individual members. Hegel, in effect, seeks the reconciliation of the individual and the community through recognition of the interdependence of right and good, duty and freedom.

This is the function of *Sittlichkeit*, or ethical life, which is both the product and producer of freedom. While Hegel also seeks some form of shared identity between the individual and the community (the "Spirit of the people," as he puts it), he is careful not to base such an identity on a substantive account of the good. Furthermore, where Hegel emphasises individual self-determination as the essential purpose of *Sittlichkeit*, Taylor tends to foreground communal identity by subsuming the mediations between the individual and the community under expressivism. To be sure, Hegel would agree with Taylor about the dangers of individualism taken to excess, but he would also insist that the way to recast the politics of rights is by means of a more Ideal understanding of freedom. Instead of appealing to notions of authentic identity to respond to hypertrophy or to foster a sense of belonging, Hegel "appeals to the inner reason underlying modern freedom to argue for solidarity. Civic virtue is conceived in terms of trust, civility and rectitude rather than thick attachments."[7] Hegel is always aware that civil society has the potential to undermine freedom, and therefore, he mediates the relationship of the individual and the community through institutions and other concrete forms of subjective freedom. From Hegel's perspective, Aristotle's criticism of Plato probably applies to Taylor: he wants too much unity. Hegel does not seek Taylor's expressivist community, but rather promotes a cautious symbiosis of the individual and the community. In this regard, it is not unreasonable to question whether Taylor's promotion of multiculturalism and his prescription for resolving the crisis of Canada contain illiberal strands.

Taylor promotes multiculturalism in terms of demands for recognition of the other because "misrecognition has now graduated to the rank of a harm."[8] He argues that what is at stake in debates about multiculturalism is the recognition of the equal value of different cultures. In other words, not only is there the demand for recognition, but there is also the demand that what is sought is not merely acknowledgment of the other's cultural identity but an acknowledgment of the worth of the other's culture. We are obliged to grant equal worth to all cultures. To be sure, while he argues for the recognition of the values of different cultures, Taylor does not say that these values must be accepted as a good simply because they are attached to a particular culture. Society as a whole needs to deliberate on which cultural values and practices it can accept that do not undermine other overarching values.

Taylor's conclusions are, of course, open to question. Is it realistic to think that debates about cultural values can take place and not become struggles for power? Can a claim for special rights in the name of cultural survival undermine the rights, including the right of survival, of others? Does the group enjoying a majority in a particular jurisdiction have the privilege of using the state's powers to impose its will? Indeed, does a majority have the moral right to protect its own culture against the perceived threat of minorities asserting their special rights? For example, if Quebec separates, would the francophone majority still have the right to protect its language and culture or would anglophones gain that right against the majority francophone population? Similarly, if the rest of Canada wishes to detach itself from Quebec, would it have to retain constitutional provisions for bilingualism and French-language rights? Such questions suggest that Taylor's promotion of multiculturalism, tied as it is to a language-oriented or culture-based notion of community, is not unproblematic, particularly in its implications for individual freedom. It also has disturbing implications for the Canadian state. Can a highly multicultural society possess a meaningful national identity? As Todd Gitlin states, "if multiculturalism is not tempered by a stake in the commons, then centrifugal energy overwhelms my commitment to a common good."[9] Perhaps, though, Elizabeth Trott captures the conundrum of multiculturalism best:

> Multiculturalism as a policy requires that all cultures embrace it and hold it as a Canadian value to be celebrated. Yet it doesn't follow that each ethnic group or cultural community will automatically do so. After all, they are encouraged to celebrate their distinctiveness. Suppose a single culture begins to dominate that does not hold multicultural policies (and their incumbent duties) in high regard. Can we be assured that a dominant group will want to continue multicultural programs as exemplary of Canadian values if its members don't see themselves first and foremost as Canadians and not some hyphenated ethnic tribe?[10]

Taylor's notion of multicultural recognition presents a problem because its possible consequences lead to the opposite of what it purports to promote. Given the right (or, more appropriately, the wrong) circumstances, Taylor's culture-centred liberal order could, if taken to its logical extreme, produce anti-liberal communitarianism. If, as Taylor argues, a national culture is the deepest level of diversity, then, presumably, almost any political action could be justified to preserve it, including the oppression of those individuals or groups who are believed to pose a threat to the national culture. Similarly, there is a danger in according special protection to internal minorities in the name of group rights and communal identity. Does the privileging of francophone rights in Quebec open the door for the suppression of other cultures within Quebec? What about minorities within minorities? Does protecting the rights of a Muslim culture against the impositions of an Anglo-Celtic majority leave individual Muslim women vulnerable to group oppression? If Canadians value multiculturalism, asks Elizabeth Trott, why would they value cultures that do not value multiculturalism and that may only use the benefits of multicultural policies to avoid having to become genuinely multicultural themselves?[11] Obviously, this kind of speculation can regress to the point of absurdity. But that is the point. As Michael Lusztig observes, "[U]ltimately the only politically irreducible core is the individual. And once we begin to think of special rights for the individual, 'special' rights become a meaningless concept. We are back to liberal individualism. Not only are the 'special' rights of the individual specious, but the logic for privileging the group disappears as well."[12]

A number of critics have suggested that there is a potential for authoritarianism embedded in Taylor's attempt to make the survival of a particular culture an irreducible social and political good. Iris Marion Young, for example, suggests that a deliberate attempt to create future members of a particular community may well throw up barriers between groups and lead to the establishment of them–us distinctions, thus dividing society into distinctive and perhaps mutually hostile groups. Furthermore, the effort to ensure the cultural survival of a particular group can impose unwanted life-scripts on individuals within that group and thus leave little room for individuals to safely assert their distinctiveness from that of other members of the group.[13] Norman Barry says that Taylor's efforts to reconcile liberalism, with its emphasis on universal equality, and communitarianism, which insists on legal and social recognition of group distinctiveness, threaten the political instruments that can prevent conflict between groups: "Taylor's deliberate downgrading of personal choice in the liberal credo succeeds only in eliminating all those mechanisms that a properly articulated set of liberal institutions had developed for dealing with the problems of potential communal tensions."[14] Jürgen Habermas shares this concern. Arguing against Taylor's critique of value-neutral liberalism, Habermas maintains that liberal institutions in democratic countries are constantly subjected to ethical debate and reformulation. He defends the Hegelian discourse-based model of democracy, saying it does not need the imposition of collectivist-oriented language. While the state might foster conditions that enable cultural survival, it cannot guarantee that survival. To do so strips individuals of "the very freedom to say yes or no that is necessary if they are to appropriate and preserve their cultural heritage."[15]

Andrew Schaap extends this argument, warning that trying to ensure the survival of particular cultures may force individuals within that culture into social roles with which they do not identity or they find inauthentic to themselves as individuals. Which is to say, cultural survival through state coercion may well foster the kind of misrecognition that Taylor otherwise denounces. Schaap writes: "By scripting an identity too tightly, a policy of cultural survival may replace one form of tyranny with another."[16] A politics of recognition that seeks to achieve a common identity among individuals leads to a kind of anti-political stance that effectively closes off the potential of the "other" to achieve genuine recognition. Taylor may promote the possibility of reconciliation of groups or individuals by means of a dialogue that aims at some fusion of horizons, but as Schaap argues, there is a "violent appropriation inherent in the logic of recognition that curtails the possibility of reconciliation." Hence, "Taylor's optimism about the possibility of reconciliation through a struggle for recognition is unwarranted."[17]

The problem with Taylor's politics of recognition, says Schaap, is that it too readily assumes that all conflicts over identity are open to solution through communicative exchange – that is, adequate recognition achieved through communicative exchange leads to reconciliation. But this assumes that the search for identity is the source of political conflict as well as its end, that the end of dialogue is in community. In other words, Taylor's project of reconciliation *assumes* that there is a "we" to be found. But Schaap argues that such assumptions are not necessarily warranted. Drawing on the thought of Emmanuel Levinas, Jean-Paul Sartre, Franz Fanon, and Majid Yar, Schaap points out that the act of recognition can be a kind of violence in that "the knowing look of recognition over-determines the other and so constitutes the death of his or her possibilities. To render the other 'known, understood, interpretable, is to rob her of her alterity or difference, to appropriate and assimilate her into a sameness with my own subjectivity.'"[18] Colonial politics, in particular, demonstrate the "violent appropriation" involved in recognition. The colonised subject may believe that liberation is possible if he demonstrates his equality to the coloniser. But this effort to gain recognition requires adopting the values of the colonising culture. And that, says Schaap, shows how "assimilation entails self-negation." By accepting the coloniser's values, self-consciously or otherwise, the colonised man denies his original identity. Since this is psychologically untenable in terms of actualising an original identity, the colonised individual tries to reverse the colonialist's misrecognition by inflating the worth of his denigrated culture through the recovery of indigenous values and traditions. This revaluation is problematic because the colonised man still has to acknowledge what it is that makes him different from the coloniser. He continues to "'think, feel and live against and, therefore, in relation to the coloniser.'"[19] Real liberation, and hence genuine authenticity and identity, requires not mutual recognition between colonialist and colonised, but the destruction of the terms and conditions of colonialism itself, since it is those terms and conditions that shape the identities of both the colonised and the colonialist.

But this, too, is complicated, says Schaap, referring to Fanon's insight regarding the contradictions involved in Africans trying to recover an original identity in the post-colonial era. The recognition supposedly offered by the former colonial master remains tangled in relations of power regardless of the colonialist's good intentions. Even though the former coloniser and the one-time colonial each desire the recognition of the other, such recognition cannot help but limit the previously colonised man's possibilities for self-creation. Fanon doubts not only the possibility that the colonised can recover an original identity in the post-colonial world, but also the possibility that the struggle for recognition can produce shared horizons. Just as Hegel's master initially requires no need for the slave's recognition, so, too, does the coloniser evince no particular interest in wanting recognition from the colonised, and he may, in fact, regard the colonised with indifference. "The zones of settler and native, though opposed, are 'not in the service of some higher unity.' Mutual recognition is impossible because the native is not complementary but superfluous to the settler. As such, there is no intersubjective struggle"[20] that could result in recognition and reconciliation.

In any case, recognition brings with it its own problems. While individuals may depend on others for recognition to attain self-consciousness, to be the object of another's "look" is a kind of violation of the self because recognition also imposes boundaries on the self. You cannot be both subject and object at the same time; you are either the subject that sees the other or the object that is seen by the other. The only way to surmount this objectification by the subject who sees, is to reverse the gaze, to turn the subject into the object and the object into the subject. But this, says Schaap, means that *real* recognition entails conflict: "Intersubjective life is characterized by a perpetual, antagonistic struggle of mutual objectification."[21] In other words, recognition involves relations of power. And power, its use and abuse, is what politics is all about.

By this argument, Taylor's assumption of an implicit "we" in the politics of reconciliation is highly questionable given the apparent impossibility of achieving a condition of reconciliation that truly surmounts the inherent antagonism of intersubjective life. According to Schaap, positing a shared horizon in which two othernesses can achieve reciprocal recognition leads to an "anti-political moment" that tends to undermine the possibility of reconciliation by overdetermining the terms of identity in which a politics of recognition can even be attempted. In effect, Taylor's theory of recognition would eliminate the risk of politics but makes no provision for the possibility that failures of recognition can lead to conflict. But the desire to avoid conflict at all costs is tantamount to a denial of freedom in that it reduces the other to *a priori* terms of identity that are not of the other's choosing. Thus, says Schaap, "Taylor's optimistic account of the struggle for recognition is unwarranted ... [T]here is a certain anti-political moment inherent in the logic of recognition that leads to reduction and violent appropriation of the other."[22] This anti-political moment of recognition – and the potential for the "violent appropriation of the other" – emerges most clearly when recognition is institutionalised to ensure cultural survival. Taylor's optimism about setting up regimes of reciprocal recognition to ensure the cultural survival of particular communities makes him "insensitive to the anti-political moment of recognition" and the possibility of "repressive authenticity."[23] In response to Taylor's anti-political moment, Schaap advocates "agonistic reconciliation," which is a form of political reconciliation that understands how "a relation of antagonism might turn out to be ethical and integrative." Rather than think of reconciliation in terms of a struggle for recognition as the necessary precondition for achieving community and ending conflict, one should conceive "an agonistic reconciliation [that] would be predicated on an awareness that community is always not yet." The point is not to achieve a common identity, but rather "to make available a space for politics within which citizens divided by the memories of past wrongs could debate and contest the terms of their political association."[24]

Schaap's idea sounds very much like an endorsement of the kind of Hegelian liberalism in which institutions and laws exist to mediate relationships and conflicts between individuals, as well as those between communities within the state. In this regard, Taylor's multicultural solution to the crisis of Canada can be challenged, both theoretically and pragmatically, for its coherence. If the cultural differences between Quebec and the rest of Canada are disappearing, and if both adhere to liberal values of "'equality, non-discrimination, the rule of law, [and] the mores of representative democracy,' then why are the two political societies so far apart on constitutional issues?"[25] Taylor's politics of recognition presumes the possibility of mutual agreement, the anti-political moment. Is it not possible that recognition on terms satisfactory to both communities is simply not possible and that the best that can be achieved is along the lines of Schaap's agonistic reconciliation? To put the matter in more colloquial terms: "We recognise that conflict would be ruinous to both sides, so we agree to disagree and hope for the best." Schaap's agonistic reconciliation might well serve as a derivation of the kind of creative thinking Leslie Armour urges in his notion of "rationalist pluralism," which I touched on in Part 1. For reasons of history, geography, and culture, Canadians "have never really been able to conceptualize Canada as a simply cultural unity and have had to think in terms of plurality, but, more importantly, that the tensions in this plurality have always been endemic to it."[26] In other words, sometimes mutual recognition is impossible and the best you can hope for is to act reasonably and avoid the appropriation of violence – in other words, agonistic reconciliation. It is questionable whether even a federal state like Canada can accommodate both first-level and deep diversity. Decades of constitutional quarrels have undermined Canadians' confidence in their political institutions and in constitutional formalities. The difficulty facing Canadians, one that makes Taylor's appeals to substantive liberalism doubtful, is that there is no ready substitute for the mechanisms and institutions of procedural constitutionalism. As the failures of the Meech Lake and Charlottetown accords demonstrate, turning away from procedural constitutionalism provokes immoderate opposition to Quebec's aspirations, and this in turn fosters Quebecers' notions that the rest of Canada is against them and secession is the only solution. In Janet Ajzenstat's words, "What we are seeing is not a battle between two forms of liberalism – substantive and procedural – but the breakdown of the procedural constitution."[27]

Taylor claims that the community provides the individual with his moral capacity and thus the conditions necessary for identity and freedom. In effect, even though Taylor denies the metaphysical foundations of Hegel's thought, he promotes a secular metaphysic that makes the individual's attainment of selfhood dependent on the community.[28] He then advocates policies of multiculturalism to ensure the community's survival on the ground that multiculturalism is necessary for the individuals in that community if they are going to be able to enjoy their identity and freedom. But this amounts to a potentially dangerous reification of culture, calling into question how Taylor's support for economic and social liberalism can be squared with his philosophical critique of liberal individualism.

Taylor's extension of his secular metaphysic into the crisis of Canada is a case in point. Language allows francophone Quebecers to discover a common moral ground that encourages political and social bonds. But this links the moral and political spheres of an individual's life with his participation in community, effectively making that person's authenticity dependent upon his sense of identity with that community.[29] The result is that in trying to protect the community from the hypertrophy of atomistic liberalism, Taylor is impelled "to include elements in his vision of society that could easily be brought into the service of a totalitarian community."[30] Thus, Taylor's concern for community creates the potential for a return to unreasoned community, a restoration of irrational Romanticism in politics that would see the individual engulfed by the collective. Such a potential suggests that Taylor's communitarianism may be self-defeating in its effort to preserve pluralism. The hesitation of the French-speaking majority in Quebec to recognise the autonomy of cultural minorities within the province is sufficient to raise this problematic aspect of Taylor's communitarian aspirations. As Norman Barry remarks, "One suspects that Quebec is similar to most of the conventional candidates for secession throughout the world. They themselves are not normally good examples of cultural homegeneity."[31] To recognise Quebec along the lines Taylor argues might well lead to the imposition on Quebec's minorities of values that Taylor would find offensive if applied to francophones by Canada's English-speaking majority. "The deliberate propagation of Frenchness by coercive law is logically no different from the imposition of Englishness through an allegedly universal set of liberal constitutional principles."[32] This suggests that Taylor's aims are ultimately collectivist when taken to their logical end and that they therefore undermine the liberal principle of individual freedom.

Taylor, it seems, does want it both ways.[33] He has difficulty accepting the idea that liberalism is sufficient for human social and moral fulfilment, yet he acknowledges that liberalism is worthy of admiration. In the same vein, he supports the desire of Quebecers to live distinctly from other Canadians (and North Americans), but he hopes that even in their distinctiveness they will continue to abide by the principles of liberal democracy practised in rest of the continent. On the issue of multiculturalism, Taylor argues that Westerners need to be more open to non-Western cultures, but he does not require non-Western immigrants to extend the same courtesy to their hosts. As recent events attest, some non-Western immigrants to Western countries have shown little interest in partaking of Western culture. Some are even hostile toward their hosts. But then multiculturalism is a Western ideal, just as notions of rights and recognition are Western concepts. This means that multiculturalism and the politics of recognition are really "a politics of integration, which does not increase but decreases diversity or pluralism."[34] Which is to say, the Spirit of recognition that Taylor appropriates from Hegel might well foster the kind of integrative, centralised, and even potentially authoritarian politics he says he abhors. George Grant, who shares many of Taylor's communitarian concerns, certainly thought so.

25

Grant and the Conundrum of Canada

In their survey of Canadian philosophy, *The Faces of Reason*, Leslie Armour and Elisabeth Trott observe that while philosophies are not necessarily "mirrors of a national mind," they often emerge in response to "some felt need," "to what one thinks the world needs rather than reflections of the way in which it is."[35] If we apply this view to Grant, what might we conclude about his "felt need" in the context of his appropriation of Hegelian thought? In a 1957 letter to his wife, Sheila, Grant acknowledges that Hegel possessed a "truer recognition of evil than other moderns."[36] Yet, at the same time, Hegel seems to accept the necessity of evil as something that serves the ultimate good of freedom. While Christianity accepts suffering as part of the soul's journey to God, Grant thinks Hegel too quick to accept evil in history as the price of progress. Hegel may identify his philosophy of history with the actions of divine providence in the world, but this, in Grant's mind, is to call good evil and evil good. But it also implies, insofar as the Hegelian project is embodied in modern liberalism and its fundamental belief in freedom,[37] that liberal humanism, and the modern project as a whole, has too easily reconciled itself to evil and, as such, amounts to a theology of glory.[38] Such an argument implies that Grant sees modern philosophy as complicit in evil. Is that the case? The question requires another look at the intellectual relationship between Grant and Strauss.

Leo Strauss sees the possibility of recovering a philosophic comprehension of the world in turning the historicist truth claim on itself. He argues that the application of historicist premises to historicism itself results, ultimately, in a non-historicist recognition that the fundamental problems that require man's theoretical attention have remained unchanged throughout history.[39] Rather than legitimising historicism, history demonstrates that all human thought is concerned with much the same fundamental themes

and problems, regardless of time or place. For Strauss, this suggests the existence of an unchanging framework of theoretical concerns that persists despite changing historical conditions and epistemologies.[40] Furthermore, if
one applies historicist standards to historicism, then historicism must be regarded as merely another form among many of man's reasoning about the
world. Consequently, historicism must also reject the view of history as progressive, rational, or even evolutionary because every understanding, however theoretical, implies specific evaluations that are intrinsically value-laden.
In the first place, historicism subordinates the world of nature to the world of
human action, thus ignoring a universal *a priori* of human existence in nature. But the natural ground, says Strauss, is the source of any effort to understand human existence, and thus it is the source of all thinking regarding
morality. This means that historicism, lacking a teleological philosophy of
nature, can posit no knowable order, including history.[41] "Historicism asserts
that all human thoughts or beliefs are historical; and hence deservedly destined to perish; but historicism itself is a human thought; hence historicism
can be of only temporary validity, or it cannot be simply true. To assert the
historicist thesis means to doubt it and thus to transcend it ... Historicism
thrives on the fact that it inconsistently exempts itself from its own verdict
about all human thought."[42] For Strauss, then, historicism, the historical
consciousness, is an arbitrary and abstract interpretation imposed on reality.

Grant accepts Straus's view in arguing that historicism assumes all thought
to be historically bounded and therefore unable to grasp anything
eternal.[43] He, too, finds in the persistence of fundamental concerns the
possibility for a renewed philosophy of nature that might serve as an adequate response to historicism.[44] But it is not to Strauss that Grant looks
for this possibility. In the last section of his essay "Tyranny and Wisdom,"
Grant criticises Strauss for not giving due consideration to Jerusalem, or
to biblical revelation. While he sides with Strauss in rejecting the historicist ontology of "Kojève-Hegel," he also observes Strauss's "remarkable
reticence" in tackling the central issue of the debate between the ancients and the moderns, namely "whether Machiavellian and Hobbesian
politics are at least in part a result of the Biblical orientation of western
society."[45] Similarly, while he shares Strauss's concern that modern liberal society is largely determined by the technological imperatives of efficiency, Grant questions whether Strauss has shown due regard for the
concepts of universal justice and equality embedded in the liberal ideal.
To deny the validity of this essentially Christian ideal, to reject the idea of
technological change and development, one must consider the consequences for those less fortunate than oneself. The "poor, the diseased,

the hungry and the tired can hardly be expected to contemplate any such limitation with the equanimity of the philosopher."[46]

But Grant issues his strongest challenge to Strauss when he questions why, despite Strauss's distinction between esoteric and exoteric writing, he does not more adequately account for revelation – and hence the virtue of charity. How, Grant asks, is the Christian virtue of charity related to the Greek idea of contemplation? Which one takes primacy, charity or thought? Or is it possible that they are interrelated and interdependent? Strauss shows Grant how modern philosophy has lowered the standards of human excellence to the desire for self-preservation, recognition, and the liberation of the passions, effectively rejecting the self-restraint and discipline required by both Christianity and classical philosophy. But Grant is puzzled as to why Strauss leaves unanswered the question of the relationship between Christianity and philosophy, as well as the connection between Christianity, technology, and the coming-to-be of the universal and homogeneous state.[47] For Grant, Christ's Incarnation demonstrates the primacy of charity – the theology of the Cross – and the underlining notion of the essential equality of all humans. And he holds that regardless of how secularised this concept has become, it still informs the ideals of liberal egalitarian politics and justice. Thought that does not reflect charity is tantamount to a theology of glory and is as deficient as theology that does not respect man's capacity for reason. Grant rejects the Hegelian account of the relationship between philosophy and biblical religion as inadequate in part because he agrees with Strauss that Hegel's philosophy of nature is essentially Hobbesian and therefore cannot be reconciled to Plato's understanding of a beneficent nature and the pursuit of transcendent good. Yet Grant questions why Strauss does not speak of the relationship between Hobbesian, or modern, political philosophy and biblical religion. "I find it impossible to know whether he [Strauss] thinks there is in the Bible an authority of revelation which has a claim over philosophers as much as other men."[48] Grant assumes that this reticence implies a particular position regarding Christian revelation.

What might that position be? And if that position can be discerned, what might Grant's response be? Is there a connection between Grant's questions about Strauss and his own concerns regarding the "disappearance" of Canada? As Yusuf Umar comments, Grant's interpretation of the debate between Strauss and Kojève constitutes "the intellectual or philosophical context within which his reflections on Canada and on its fate may best be understood."[49] At least one point can be made without hesitation: Strauss freed Grant from his admiration for Hegel, but he does not in Grant's view adequately account for the way in which modern ideals – justice and equality for all and the alleviation of want and hardship by means of technology – were derived from biblical theology and its emphasis on charity. In the words of H.D. Forbes, "This essentially religious idea of human unity on the basis of human equality has become in recent centuries the core of a practical political program."[50]

Strauss, like Grant, recognises that the modern demand for freedom from necessity leaves man without any standard beyond himself to limit his attempts to satisfy his desires, and sees that this can lead to great evil. Both classical philosophy and Christianity maintain transcendent standards – the good and God – to restrain these desires, and within both it is understood that freedom detached from obedience to a transcendent standard can be destructive. Thus, both Grant and Strauss accept the necessity of limits as good for human beings. Where they part is on the ultimate source of that limit. While Strauss may be reticent in criticising biblical theology in *On Tyranny*, as Grant observes, he shows no such reticence elsewhere in asserting the primacy of philosophy over religion. Like Simone Weil, Strauss accepts the necessity of limit, but unlike Weil, he does not say where he thinks the source of that limit is embodied – in classical natural law or the positive law of the Bible. "The Bible," Strauss once said in a lecture, "confronts us more clearly than any other book with this fundamental alternative: life in obedience to revelation, life in obedience to human freedom, the latter being represented by the Greek philosophers."[51] Strauss clearly opts for the life of philosophy. Unassisted reason is sufficient for humans to have knowledge of the whole.[52] In fact, Strauss argues that Christianity, in trying to reconcile reason and revelation, deprived philosophy of the "inner freedom from supervision" it had enjoyed under Judaism and Islam.[53]

Grant, of course, accepts the authority of Christian revelation. His hope is – as his initial admiration for Hegel implies – to bring reason and revelation together. He holds that "rational theology must never detach itself from Biblical tradition."[54] The fundamental difference between Grant and Strauss thus comes down to their differences on the relationship between philosophy and biblical revelation. This difference, says H.D. Forbes, can be seen in their contrasting interpretations of Plato's account of the good in the *Republic*. Grant sees Plato referring to a good that is "beyond being," or to God. Strauss holds that there is nothing beyond being and that the idea of the good is simply the idea of the whole.[55] This difference between Grant and Strauss on the relationship of reason and revelation helps to account for why Grant questions the comprehensiveness of Strauss's understanding of the linkage between modernity and Christianity. This is particularly important in light of Grant's insistence on a form of knowing distinct from that of modernity's instrumental reasoning. Christianity, he says, stands or falls with the assertion that there is knowledge beyond that available to human reason. He refers to this knowledge as faith, understood as the union of love and knowledge, or, put differently, as the union of charity and reason. "Faith is the experience that the intellect is illuminated by love," he says, borrowing from Simone Weil.[56] Such thought on Grant's part suggests that while Strauss denies the possibility of a Hegelian synthesis of philosophy and religion, of reason and revelation, Grant still holds out hope for some kind of reconciliation. In this sense, Grant retains the Hegelian imprimatur long after his turn from Hegel (describing him as a reluctant anti-Hegelian would be an accurate, if awkward, way to put it). Indeed, in arguing that we can only fully comprehend modernity by thinking reason and revelation, Plato and Christ, together, Grant still asserts the overarching motive of the Hegelian project. That Grant came to see such a reconciliation to be impossible does not take away from the fact that it reflects his deepest spiritual and intellectual longing.

It was Simone Weil who taught Grant "what it is to hold Christ and Plato together."[57] Weil provided Grant with the means to respond to the perceived inadequacies of Strauss's account of the modern project. From Grant's perspective, Strauss's assertion of the self-sufficiency of human reason resembles a continuation of the theology-of-glory tradition that sets human reason above other ways of knowing and, in effect, idolises the intellect. Weil is Grant's counterfoil to Strauss. Yet – and this is one of the abiding conundrums in Grant's thought – even though his commitment to Christian charity left him sympathetic to the ideas of Kojève-Hegel, Grant accepts Strauss's judgment regarding the tyrannical tendency of modern philosophy. Grant recognises that man might be the creator of the modern project, but Grant does not believe it to be a project that serves humanity's greatest good. We dwell in a dark time in which we have diagnosed the discontents of modernity and are aware of its deprivals, but are unable to articulate a coherent alternative. We are trapped in Hegel's magic circle. As Grant writes in the essay "A Platitude," "The drive to the planetary technical future is in any case inevitable; but those who try to divert, to limit, or even simply stand in fear before some of its applications find themselves defenceless, because of the disappearance of any speech by which the continual changes involved in that drive could ever be thought of as deprivals."[58] Of course, Grant insists that there is another discourse, another way of thinking, available to moderns. There is Christian faith, and "ancient philosophy gives alternative answers to modern man."[59] But Grant is also aware that such an assertion no longer attracts most moderns. His alternative points to an eternal order that is no longer widely accepted because of the historicism that resides at the core of the modern project, the result of which has been the transfer of God's attributes to humans. Grant accepts that Kojève's Hegel reflects the modern consciousness.

Taylor, it will be recalled, believes that we can still find sources within modernity that will enable us to overcome the conflicts of modernity, but Grant is clearly more doubtful. The difference between them is highlighted by their views on multiculturalism. Taylor sees multiculturalism as a means for reconciling the fragmentary tendencies of Canadian political life. Grant, however, sees multiculturalism in a more problematic light, evidenced in his insistence that "a society only articulates itself as a nation through some common intention among its people."[60] On this point, Grant follows Hegel, who holds the view that nations are to be understood by reference to their self-understanding. Grant's political thought is thus grounded in the notion that a nation or a community is a partnership that can be understood primarily through the articulation of the purposes of the partners in establishing their union. In Grant's view, the fundamental purpose of Canada is the maintenance of its French- and English-speaking partnership. The accommodation achieved in 1867 between the French- and English-speaking colonies of Canada is, for Grant, the unique and central feature of the Canadian nation-state. If Canada is to survive, it has to be anchored in the reconciliation of these two national communities. Without that ongoing arrangement, the idea of Canada will die, and with it Canada's political existence.

Grant faults John Diefenbaker for his ignorance of this bedrock of Canadian unity. Diefenbaker, he writes in *Lament for a Nation*, inadvertently promoted a multicultural version of Canada in his appeal to "one united Canada, in which individuals would have equal rights irrespective of race and religion: there would be no first- and second-class citizens." While Grant does not quarrel with this idea as far as it applies to the civil rights of individuals, he argues that "the rights of individuals do not encompass the rights of nations, liberal doctrine to the contrary." For Grant, Diefenbaker's multicultural vision is too close to the homogenising universalism of the United States. What distinguishes Canada from the United States is the common purpose of two nations – the French and the English – to unite into a single state to avoid becoming American. Diefenbaker's notion of "the unity of all Canadians" was an Americanised interpretation of the Confederation partnership. In Grant's view, this multicultural unity did not have the strength of purpose of the old two-nations partnership: "It could not encompass those who were concerned with being a nation, only those who wanted to preserve charming residual customs."[61]

Therefore, even though Grant shares many of Taylor's communitarian concerns, including a concern with the survival of francophone Quebec, his idea of Canada precludes Taylor's multicultural prescription. For Grant, multiculturalism is tantamount to a denial of cultural identity, not a protector of that identity. Where Taylor sees multiculturalism as a means to help disparate groups find their identity within the whole, Grant sees multiculturalism as an expression of modernity's universalising and homogenising consequences. Multiculturalism is another means by which liberalism subsumes different cultures into the technological mixing bowl where once-authentic ways of life are reduced to cultural kitsch. Grant had Trudeau's multicultural policies in mind on this claim, for he regarded those policies as having eroded authentic Canadian political identity. Thus, Grant sees multiculturalism as yet another manifestation of instrumental rationalism, one that leads toward Canada's disappearance.

Grant, as I have discussed previously, detects this rationalist mindset in other aspects of Canadian politics. While liberalism wants equality, moral progress, and happiness for all, it has at its core an ascription to the instrumental rationality of science and technology, both of which have made plain, in Grant's view, that reason regarded as an instrument cannot teach us how best to live. Modern liberalism, penetrated by the instrumental rationality of science and technology, reduces freedom to the satisfaction of desires. And this, according to Grant, has resulted in politics being "increasingly replaced by administration," as exemplified by the Trudeau government.[62] Grant's criticism of modern bureaucracy has to be considered with this broader philosophic argument in mind. Contrary to Hegel's view that the universal class is necessary to sustaining the state, Grant sees Canada's bureaucrats and its corporate leaders furthering the Hegelian universal and homogeneous state. In particular, Trudeau's linkage of national interests and universalist values and his emphasis on techniques of cybernetic politics and rational administration amount to a denial of the worth of any local or particular culture, especially one living in such close proximity to the heartland of the technological world order. In other words, Canada's fate, its impossibility, is part of the wider sweep of technological modernity.

Against this disappearance, Grant's love of his own is rooted in his affection for the particular, as he experienced it.[63] But Grant also recognises that the imperatives of the modern project erode all particulars. Given this, it would be a mistake to think that Grant's turn from Hegel means that he is able to excise Hegel's influence, that he can step outside the magic circle of modernity. Grant is simply unable to reject Hegel in any absolute sense because he retains throughout his work the truth of the Hegelian account of modernity vouchsafed him through Kojève's interpretation of Hegel. Even Grant's post-Hegel thinking continues to reflect Hegel's abiding influence. As Michael Allen Gillespie writes, Grant's "more mature thought was characterized by a deepening reassessment of Hegel in light of what he saw as the failure of North American society to produce the human excellence that Hegel had predicted."[64]

I have tried to show that, for Grant, the character of modernity means the end of a truly sovereign and independent Canada and that this removal of what makes Canada "other" to the United States is but one example of the erasure of alternatives resulting from the fulfilment of the Hegelian project. This is not anti-Americanism on Grant's part by any means. He simply recognises that because of certain geopolitical and economic realities Americanisation is the way that modernisation is unfolding. Americans were the first members of the planet to be modernised. Canadians were second. The rest of the world has been following, however bloodily and reluctantly. By Grant's argument, we now dwell in a post-Canadian order, the world's first post-modern state. Grant certainly recognised this reality, however much he lamented it. In a 1964 letter to friends, he referred to his book *Lament for a Nation*, describing it as being "about Canada becoming part of the universal and homogeneous state." The letter expresses the puzzling sense that while everything has changed, nothing is different, at least on the surface. "It is finally true that one's home must lie in the transcendent, but what a business it is putting off one's finite hopes. Otherwise life goes on for us quite pleasantly day by day."[65] Donald Creighton said the same thing in describing Canada as merely "a good place to live."[66] More recently, the novelist Yann Martel echoed Grant and Creighton when he referred to Canada as "the greatest hotel on Earth."[67] While the formal trappings of nationhood linger – a flag, a border, Parliament, Canada Day (which used to be Dominion Day) – little of national substance remains.[68]

Lamentably, there is little serious prospect of recovering a substantively distinct Canada. As Grant learned from Nietzsche, horizons are "man-made perspectives by which the charismatic impose their will to power," expressions of "the values which our tortured instincts will to create."[69] Our historicist mindset tells us that nationalism is a fiction. Once we assume that horizons are relative and man-made, "their power to sustain us is blighted. Once we know them to be relative, they no longer horizon us. We cannot live in a horizon when we know it to be one. When the historical sense teaches us that our values are not sustained in the nature of things, impotence descends."[70] How can we sustain any genuine patriotism when we are self-consciously aware that our nation is an invention that exists at the sufferance (or indifference) of the modern project as embodied in the American empire?

Hegel's thought enables Grant to comprehend this reality, to see what the modern project ultimately means for Canada. For this reason Grant cannot "reject" Hegel even if he wanted to because his own thinking constitutes a response to Hegel. Grant's analysis of technology, his judgments on liberalism as a theology of glory, his lament for Canada – they all reflect variations in an ongoing philosophic dialogue with Hegel, who, as one critic puts it, is "the true voice of all that Grant opposes."[71] In this regard, Grant's reputation as a "father of Canadian nationalism" needs to be re-evaluated. And that reconsideration should be accompanied by a rejection of the notion that Grant's lament is nothing more than an indulgence in "longing for the past," an "Anglo-Saxon lament," or nostalgia for some pre-war myth of Canada's Britishness.[72] Certainly, Grant knows that his thought is informed by his being "brought up in a class which has almost disappeared."[73] But he also insists that only "simple people" would interpret *Lament* as mere nostalgia for "the passing of the British dream of Canada."[74]

Grant's use of the word *lament* provides the most conclusive evidence that, for him, Canada as a political alternative to the United States is truly finished. The word comes from the Latin *lamentum*, referring to a condition of wailing or grieving. To lament is to express grief for something that is lost but still remembered. There is no suggestion in the word that something can be saved or revived. The line from Vergil's *Aeneid* with which Grant ends his book – "Tendebantque manus ripae ulterioris amore" [They were holding their arms outstretched in love toward the further shore] – reinforces Grant's judgment. The phrase occurs in Book VI of the *Aeneid* where Aeneas follows the Sibyl of Cumae into Hell and encounters Charon, the ferryman of the Underworld who transports the shades of the dead across the river Styx. Charon refuses to carry those shades that remain unburied after death. They are left "a hapless host" that "may not pass the shore … until their bones have found a home and rest."[75] Grant's choice of this scene as the concluding statement in *Lament* implies that he sees post-Canadians as lost souls who will be unable to reconcile themselves to a new political order until they bury the bones – the flag, Parliament, Canada Day, etc. – of their former life.

If Grant's views on the relationship between philosophy and the political reality of Canada can be parsed to a single concluding statement, it might be this: if modernity constitutes the end of philosophy in favour of technology, then Canada is fated to disappear. This may seem an outlandish notion, but this is what Grant's diagnosis of modernity implies. If Hegel is right, if necessity and goodness are identical and the universal and homogeneous state is the political product of that identification, then Grant is correct to pronounce Canada's impossibility as a sovereign state.

26

Watson and the Return to Empire

Grant's concerns about the universal and homogeneous state are obviously similar to those of John Watson about world government.[76] Indeed, the arguments that Grant makes against the idea of the universal and homogeneous state being the best order closely resemble those put forward by Watson against the concept of a world-state. Where Grant speaks in defence of the love of one's own, Watson speaks of the need to maintain "ties of kindred and friendship, family and nation."[77] Watson also anticipates Grant's fear that a universal, homogeneous state would be a tyranny when he characterises a world-state that does not maintain differences between people and seek their highest good as "empty."

> We can only have a true World-State when we have developed to their utmost the possibilities of each Nation-State, just as we cannot have a true Nation-State without the institution of the family and of private property, with the various industrial and commercial relations which they imply, and without that free play of individuality which gives rise to decentralised forms of association. A World-State based upon the combination of variously differentiated Nation-States is a possible ideal; a World-State which abolishes all the differences of race and nationality and individuality is an empty ideal.[78]

Thus, while the logic of Watson's Idealism, like that of Hegel's, points to a universal state, Watson sees such a state as unworkable if it does not allow internal differentiation. For Watson, a world-state would be either too weak or too strong. If the latter, it would erase differences of nationality and individuality that provide people with the basis for their consciousness of themselves as belonging to a community. If the former, it would be

unable to provide individuals with the means for developing their awareness of themselves as spiritual beings – that is, their freedom.

The basic difference between Watson and Grant, then, is that Watson regards the world-state as an empty ideal. Any attempt to establish it will fail,
since people cannot possibly surrender those particulars that made them
different. Grant, following Strauss, sees the universal and homogeneous
state as all too possible because technology is gradually eliminating those internal differentiations, including the differences between philosophers and
non-philosophers. If Watson thinks that the world-state will be sabotaged because it is contrary to human nature, Grant believes that the world-state is all
too possible because technology is transforming human nature. Watson's
more positive view of world order is rooted in his acceptance of Hegel's notion of history as an intelligible realm of reality in which mankind is developing toward an end that reconciles the essential human aspiration to unite
the spiritual and the material, the universal and the particular. Like Hegel,
Watson sees human development logically progressing toward a universal
state. However, unlike Grant, Watson still holds out for the possibility of a
world order – although not a world-state – that would achieve the reconciliation of the universal and the particular. And, following Hegel, he applies
the concept of reconciliation to explain the symbiotic nature of the relationship between universal and particular interests.

Watson, it will be recalled, applies the Hegelian concept of reconciliation to the realm of politics and society, including international relations.
He applies this concept first to the fundamental political problem of reconciling individual freedom and public authority, and then to the relation of individual nation-states to the world-state. The state exists for the
establishment of those external conditions that enable the individual to
attain his highest ends, which are the identity of the individual and the
good of the community. This political theory reflects what Watson regards as the fundamental political problem: namely, the reconciliation of
freedom and authority.

In his Idealism, Watson appropriates Hegelian principles to underpin
his critiques of empiricism, utilitarianism, and American-style liberalism,
rejecting all three concepts on the ground that they fail to recognise moral
obligation. Thus, Hegel's thought provides Watson with a conceptual
model for reconciling the dualism of the common-sense school, the scepticism of the empiricists, the atomism of the utilitarians, and even the
materialism of the Darwinians. Hegelian thought shows Watson the interrelationship of all things: mind and matter, man and nature, philosophy
and science, and the individual and the community. Moreover, Watson,

again like Hegel, sees the individual as a product of social order, but, unlike Taylor, he is careful to avoid subsuming the being of the individual in the being of the community as a whole. This is the thematic point of Watson's use of Socrates' trial and death as the paradigmatic model to illustrate the problematic nature of the relationship between the individual and the community.

Watson's understanding of this relationship is worked out in his philosophic history and his discussion of various thinkers, from Plato and Aristotle through to Hegel and Nietzche, through whom he presents his own theories of individualism, freedom, and the state. Watson certainly resembles Taylor in attacking as incoherent the idea of the atomistic individual and the notion of social contract theory as the basis for political community. Watson, like Taylor, argues that individuality apart from the community is impossible. However, as his theory of relative sovereignty suggests, Watson wants to maintain a balanced reciprocity between communal goods and individual freedom. Where Taylor's politics of recognition arguably leads to illiberal results that can oppress the individual, Watson is careful to protect the fundamental reality of the individual. For Watson, while it is true that you cannot speak of the individual apart from the community, it is also true that Western society has undergone a long historical process that has seen increasing individual differentiation. Where some Idealists would dissolve the individual into the Absolute, Watson continually insists on the distinctive reality of the individual. In the same way that he does not follow Josiah Royce in substituting the Absolute with a community united by shared loyalties and sentiments, Watson would not follow Taylor in granting primacy to the community. Watson's theory of relative sovereignty requires that *both* the individual and the community, the particular and the universal, serve purposes that sustain and enhance the other.

Watson's theory of relative sovereignty demonstrates that he is less of a communitarian than either Taylor or Grant in that his support for community is focused on his concern for the development of the individual's highest nature. Watson understands Hegel to be promoting a symbiotic relationship between the individual and the community and to be arguing that freedom and belonging reflect and reinforce each other. Or, to put it differently, neither can be achieved unless the other can be as well. Watson maintains that the individual cannot exist apart from the community, but he also asserts that the development of the individual is the purpose or end of the community. Watson's Hegelianism stands exclusively neither in the communitarian nor the liberal camp. At the level of the individual-state relationship, Watson argues equally against both the liberal atomistic view that individuals take precedence over the state and the notion that the state takes precedence over the individual. His communitarianism more easily accommodates individualism than that of Taylor because Watson assumes that an individual, in seeking his own personal good, is in fact seeking the perfection of his nature; that is, he is seeking to achieve his "best mind." And, for Watson, this best mind is identical with the good of the rational community. Genuine individualism satisfies both freedom and belonging.

Conversely, the community fulfils its true purpose to the degree that it enables the individual to satisfy his personal good, which is his freedom. In a statement that recalls his paradigmatic model of the relationship of the individual and the community, namely that of Socrates and Athens, Watson writes: "The laws of the State may well be identical with his own real will; and if they are not, they are condemned as not realising their end. This at once explains the habit of obeying without question the ordinary laws of the State, and also the opposition to those laws, actual or opposed, which are not in harmony with man's ideal of himself."[79] The state provides the arena where individual freedom is possible. The individual experiences the freedom that is available to humans in and through his relationships with others. The state functions through its institutions to represent a community of interests that allows and fosters those relationships that provide the individual his substantive freedom. Thus, for Watson, the state exists to establish those external conditions by which the highest human life may be achieved, a life of freedom based on reason.

In *The State in War and Peace*, Watson extends the Hegelian principle of reconciliation into international politics, promoting a world order based on a type of multinational integration that constitutionally resembles the federalist model of the British North America Act. Nevertheless, Watson questions the idea of a homogeneous, all-encompassing world-state. On the one hand, he says that such a state, if it did not impose homogeneity on everyone, would be unable to provide the means for the greatest number of people to realise their potential as free and rational beings. On the other hand, he says that the ties of kindred and friendship, family and nation, would be lost if a world-state came to pass. This leads Watson to ask, as Grant does a generation later, whether such a state is the best political and social order in terms of fulfilling human aspirations. Watson answers no; such a state would not actualise the highest potential of people, since it does not recognise their differences. An individual must learn to set aside his individual desires and make himself an organ of the community in order to act morally; at the same time, he must be free to criticise the community if it fails to act in accordance with rational principles.

Watson also extends his Idealist reconciliation of the individual and the community to relations among nation-states. Individual states, like individual people, are differentiations of mankind's organic unity. The purpose of states is "to secure the best conditions of life for the citizens in harmony with and limited by the universal principles of morality." As a result, "the good of one State cannot be separated from the good of another."[80] Yet, in the same way that states must maintain differentiations among individuals and institutions if the good of the whole is to be achieved, so, too, in a world of sovereign states, must the differentiation of cultures and societies be maintained. As Watson asserts, "Each nation has its own special task, arising from differences in climate, economic, religious, artistic and scientific relations."[81] Which is to say, the independence of states is necessary for the good of mankind as a whole. On this point, as I noted in Part 2, Watson explicitly rejects an idea promoted in his time by Bertrand Russell, which was that people must surrender their patriotic attachments and establish an "International Authority" that would assume sovereign status over all national groups. In an argument that resembles Grant's view that love of the good is rooted in love of one's own, Watson expresses doubt that a federation of nation-states requires abandoning particular loyalties.

Despite his insistence on the political and cultural autonomy of nation-states, Watson defends imperialism. Civilised nations are duty bound to assume authority over those that are less civilised – if the purpose of that authority is the moral and material betterment of those people. Watson is careful on this claim, maintaining that the assumption of authority over a colonised people does not mean the suppression of their culture. The imperial power must not expect – or want – to maintain permanent authority over its colonial subjects. "There is no justification for the rule of a foreign government which does not seek to promote civilisation, liberty and progress in the subject people, and does not take the necessary steps to fit them for self-government."[82] If a civilised nation fails to live up to this principle, Watson argues, "its rule can only be regarded as an unjustifiable tyranny."[83] Watson believes that the British Empire came as close as practically possible to achieving this Ideal world-order. In his analysis of the post–First World War era, Watson promotes the British Empire as the most successful experiment in international governance. The empire, he writes, succeeded in "combining the freedom of the separate organs with the unity of the whole"[84] and provided the best means for lifting colonised people to higher levels of development, both moral and political. Grant, it will be recalled, shared this view early in his career when he saw the empire's mission as one of helping people in backward regions move toward greater political consciousness and the modern use of their resources. This is Watson's Ideal, too, and his appropriation of Hegel establishes a theoretical foundation for imperialism – or, what might be called the "Spirit of empire." Watson's Idealism provides him with a positive notion of imperialism in which empire becomes a means for the furtherance of mankind's moral potential and an enterprise devoted to military or economic ends.

Does Watson's Idealist view of empire have any relevance in our postcolonial era? A useful way to approach this question is to recall the question I asked of Taylor's multiculturalism. Taylor defends multiculturalism with the argument that in a world in which international migration is making all societies less culturally homogeneous, multiculturalism is the only way to go. "There are other cultures, and we have to live together more and more, both on a world scale and commingled in each individual society."[85] Economic globalisation, increasingly diverse nation-states, and even the creation of "diasporic identities" are a result of major shifts in the world's population, says Taylor. "We are living in multinational societies, and they will only become more multinational ... [W]e have to recognise that we cannot all share the same historical identity."[86] That may well be the case, but the question I asked was whether Taylor's ideal of multicultural recognition actually works to promote an acceptance of the deep diversity he desires. With its notion of the equality of all cultures, multiculturalism may very well undermine any substantive cultural identity and produce a substantially homogeneous world in which authentic cultural difference is diluted to lifestyle choice. As Michael Bliss observes, commenting on the consequences of Trudeau's multicultural policy, "a diverse people, celebrating their constitutional right to be different from one another, would obviously not have much of an identity. Canada was on its way to becoming almost as multi-ethnic, multicultural, and diverse a country as the United States, though without the glue of that intense sense of patriotism called 'Americanism.' We are not significantly British, not significantly northern, not significantly socialist, not significantly bicultural to be significantly different from the United States. At best, maybe, we're a little of all of those – small differences that do not add up to a distinction."[87]

Paradoxical as it may seem to contemporary sensibilities, it is this homogenisation of cultures that Watson's imperialism tries to avoid. Recall that for Watson the independence of each state is necessary for the good of humans as a whole because each state has its special mission. Moreover, Watson justifies empire on the basis that advancing a colonised people to a higher form of civilisation does not imply the destruction of a colonised people's culture or the imposition of an alien civilisation. Watson recognises that many cultures had made some "advance in civilisation," but were unable to maintain a civilised government after coming into contact with the West. Indeed, as he acknowledges, many of these first encounters saw atrocities perpetuated against the native race. But to Watson's mind such a situation makes it even more incumbent upon the more civilised power to assume the guardianship of the "lower" race. Given the similarities between Watson and Taylor in terms of the need to respect diverse cultures, there is considerable irony in the thought that Taylor's multiculturalism might be used to bolster a new kind of homogenising imperialism, or that Watson's imperialism may actually preserve the world's cultures.

Watson looks to India as an example of the overall beneficence of empire. He observes that in the mid-eighteenth century, when India was in a state of near anarchy, British statesmen reluctantly realised that Britain had to assume control of the country "in the interests of humanity and justice." Watson maintains that, whatever its numerous failings, British rule was an example of relatively enlightened imperialism. Whether these views are palatable today is neither here nor there. Watson's point is this: sometimes one state (or group of states) has to assume control of another when the latter is unable to maintain its sovereign status in a way that best serves the principles of justice and the greater good of mankind as a whole. Even though he would likely be dismissed nowadays as politically incorrect, Watson is careful to qualify his support for imperialism by arguing that even if one nation possesses all the highest qualities of civilisation – "a preposterous supposition," as he puts it – it would still not have the right to impose its culture on other nations by force.[88] In the same manner, Watson is also careful to delimit imperial rule:

> The rule of a foreign and subject people is a difficult and delicate task. The better elements in the older civilisation must be recognised and fostered. To destroy a people's faith in their traditional customs and laws can only lead to the overthrow of all moral rules and the introduction of moral anarchy. A whole foreign civilisation cannot be externally imposed upon a people. The foreign government must act so as to create a feeling of loyalty to itself in the minds of the subjects, while these must learn to look to it for security of person and property, for freedom of thought and speech, and for the defence of their special form of worship.[89]

In other words, for Watson, imperial rule can preserve cultural differences as well as foster the conditions that allow people to become self-governing and autonomous.

Watson's view of imperialism is worth considering because we may well be entering a new age of empire. Michael Hardt and Antonio Negri's much-praised and much-criticised book, *Empire*, has certainly given new currency to the concept of empire. They argue that while the age of nation-state imperialism may be over, a new imperial form of sovereignty is emerging.[90] But others, too, have come forward in recent years to argue that in an age of failing states and non-governmental terrorist organisations that threaten world order, the idea of empire needs to be recovered. Some even acknowledge that a new form of imperialism is a legitimate response to world disorder. Michael Ignatieff, for example, acknowledges that "America's entire war on terror is an exercise in imperialism."[91] But he defends the necessity of American imperialism by asking, "[H]ow can it be imperialist to help people throw off the shackles of tyranny?" While no one advocates a return to old-style imperialism, "no one in his right mind can want liberty to fail." If the Western world truly believes in freedom and democracy for everyone, and not just for itself, then an American empire is warranted. Ignatieff writes: "If the American project of encouraging freedom fails, there may be no one else available with the resourcefulness and energy, and even the self-deception, necessary for the task ... Big imperial allies are often necessary to the establishment of liberty."[92] And what about Canada in this new imperial order? According to Ignatieff, one of the crucial foreign policy challenges confronting Canada is "staying independent in an age of empire."[93]

Various terms have been offered to describe this new age of imperialism – *liberal imperialism, defensive imperialism, voluntary imperialism,* and even *empire lite.* Regardless of the label, as Hardt and Negri argue, in this new age of empire, sovereignty is being transferred from nation-states to a new global sovereignty that they call "empire" and define as "the sovereign power that governs the world." Such power does not adhere to any particular nation-state; rather, this new imperial sovereignty is manifested in a series of national and supranational organisms that are united "under a single logic of rule" – the logic of economic globalisation. Of course, the United States is the power at the pinnacle of this new imperial order. The United States and its collaborators have unleashed global market forces that are replacing the system of the old imperialistic nation-states with a new transpolitical global order in which economic considerations supersede all other concerns. This new empire establishes no territorial centre of power and does not rely on fixed boundaries. Hardt and Negri characterise it as a form of rule that lacks boundaries or barriers to its imposition: "It is a decentered and deterritorializing apparatus of rule that progressively incorporates the entire globe within its open, expanding frontiers."[94]

In true Hegelian fashion, then, Hardt and Negri recognise that ours is a time of birth. What is being born is a new concept of overarching authority. However, Hardt and Negri's *Empire* reflects a great deal of socialist nostalgia. Liberal democracies are described as "societies of control," enveloped in the "rhythm of productive practices and productive socialisation." The authors see revolutionary potential in a "counter-Empire" led by "the multitude" (a post-modern version of Marx's proletariat, presumably). The multitude includes all those who have been supposedly disenfranchised by globalisation – everyone from protestors and radical feminists to Third World revolutionaries and Islamic fundamentalists. Without ever defining how the multitude's "new forms of power" will be exercised, the authors predict that the politics of the new era will see the establishment of "global citizens" and an "absolute democracy" that will "take us through and beyond Empire."[95] They never actually provide a concrete description of what this abstract idea of "beyond Empire" means, which may be why their views have been dismissed as "thoroughly misguided."[96] Perhaps so, but that only reinforces the relevance of Watson's Idealist notion of empire. Hardt and Negri's empire looks like a tyrannical universal and homogeneous state, and the authors come across as theologians of glory, willing to make evil a good in arguing for the need of violence to establish this new empire. "The new barbarians" of the multitude must "destroy with an affirmative violence" that will "create and recreate" the human world in a "secular Pentecost." How this "affirmative violence" will manifest itself is, of course, never described, although the use of the word *Pentecost* provides a revelatory hint. The word refers to the Christian festival commemorating the descent of the Holy Ghost on the disciples after the Resurrection of Christ.[97] Hardt and Negri's *Empire* thus reflects a dangerous restoration of the totalitarian impulse that plagued the twentieth century.[98]

Words such as *empire* and *imperialism* still possess near-demonic associations for some. But as Deepak Lal observes, such views are not only naive, but historically unjustified: "Empires have unfairly gotten a bad name."[99] Indeed, according to Lewis Feuer, Western imperialism by and large brought improvements in social, economic, and political conditions to those it ruled – everything from better education and health to an end to slavery and tribal warfare.[100] No doubt, some will dismiss such claims as self-serving. And so they often are. But there is also considerable truth to them. For this reason, it is time to recover this more balanced view of empire. Feuer sounds very much like Watson in making a distinction between regressive and progressive imperialism.[101] The former, he argues, was devoted to pillaging their colonies, while the latter sought, at least to some

extent, to improve social and economic conditions. Feuer offers Mongo-
lian, Spanish, and Soviet imperialism as examples of regressive imperialism. The Alexandrian, Roman, French, Dutch, and British empires were
more progressive forms of imperialism in that, for all their errors and arrogance – the British Opium War with China in the 1840s, for example –
their rule was generally beneficial. In modern times, imperialism brought
improvements in social conditions and economic wealth to many regions
of Asia and Africa. As well, Britain's outlawing of slavery throughout the
empire largely put an end to the slave trade, except in the Arab world.[102]
Thus, Feuer concludes that

> [i]mperialism brought with it a tremendous rise in the populations of
> Africa and Asia. From West Africa to Java it put an end to the tribal wars
> that, periodically decimating populations, made genocide a recurring
> phenomenon. The death toll of epidemics was reduced by health
> measures. Although most of the colonial areas remained backward in
> technology, and pre-feudal, feudal or absolutist in their social systems,
> they received at the hands of the imperialist power a set of medical
> and political services that were the high achievements of the Western
> capitalist nations.[103]

With the terrorist attacks on New York and Washington in the fall of
2001 and the commitment of Islamist terrorists to attack the West in the
name of religion, it has become rather obvious that the world is undergoing some sort of political reordering. Empires, it seems, are good candidates.[104] As Tom Darby observes, "[W]hen you transform a civilisation into
a power unit you get an empire." Even the West may be fragmenting into
imperial power units, he says, and the European Union's efforts to set up
its own military arm outside NATO suggests that "the EU [is] becoming an
empire, and, in response, [the members of the] North American Free
Trade Agreement [are] becoming the same, and perhaps the 'rest' of the
non-West [is] forming imperial power units."[105]

Against such fragmentation, Robert Cooper argues that the West must
unite on the basis of "defensive imperialism." The existence of what he
calls pre-modern zones of chaos such as Afghanistan are too dangerous for
established states to tolerate, and as a result, "it is possible to imagine a defensive imperialism." If non-state actors, including crime or terrorist syndi-
cates start using failing states as bases from which to attack the West, "then
the organised states may eventually have to respond."[106] Western countries, perhaps acting under the mandate of the United Nations, might,

under extreme circumstances, need to take charge of these countries and provide good government, administrative competence, and institutional order until the locals can do it themselves – what Cooper calls the "imperialism of neighbours." That is to say, "[a] system in which the strong protect the weak, in which the efficient and well-governed export stability and liberty, in which the world is open for investment and growth – all of these seem eminently desirable. If empire has not often been like that, it has frequently been better than the chaos and barbarism it replaced."[107] To this end, Cooper calls for cooperative or voluntary imperialism as the only legitimate form of imperialism in a post-imperial era. Zones of potential chaos – Bosnia, East Timor, and Afghanistan, for example – could be placed under a form of trusteeship at the behest of the international community. While this kind of imperialism – "imperial liberalism," as Cooper calls it – lacks the clarity and decisiveness of traditional, nineteenth-century imperialism, in a post-modern era, international and voluntary imperialism can be legitimate. Besides, "in the end nothing else will work."[108]

Robert Conquest offers another form of empire. He observes that while the Western democracies, particularly the English-speaking nations, prevailed in the twentieth century's ideological wars, they are now losing the sense of purpose and common cause that once sustained them in their fight. And this, he says, is dangerous because the post–Cold War world is increasingly fragmented and fractious. He urges the establishment of an "association" of English-speaking nations and peoples, including Canada, the United States, Britain, Ireland, Australia, and New Zealand, as well as the peoples of the Caribbean and the Pacific Ocean. In a fragmented world, such a "political civilisation would be eminently prudent." Indeed, he argues that "closer integration of the English-speaking countries can create a centre of power attractive to the other countries with a democratic tradition and form the basis for a yet broader political unity in the long run. And this in turn could eventually be the foundation for a full unity of the democratized world."[109]

Deepak Lal seeks something similar in his defence of empire. He argues that with large regions of the world in disorder, a return to empire offers the most practicable means for quelling the potential chaos: "[T]he major argument in favour of empires" – for all their failings – "is that, through their *pax*, they provide the most basic of public goods – order – in an anarchical international society of states."[110] Given the disorder in the world, Lal insists that the United States – and the rest of the world – must recognise the necessity of "an American *pax* to provide both global peace and prosperity."[111] He dismisses notions of "ethical imperialism" and soft-power foreign policies as naive and likely to create even more disorder. It is only through "the beneficent exercise of power" that the United States and its allies will see their democratic values emulated elsewhere in the world. Certainly, parts of the planet will continue to fear and loathe the West, but as Lal observes, one of the key tasks of imperial statesmanship is to prevent this inevitable and unavoidable hatred from creating global disorder. "Wishing the empire would just go away or could be managed by global love and compassion is to bury one's head in the sand and promote global disorder."[112] Lal concludes that the United States has acquired an empire and needs to assume its imperial responsibilities in the same manner as Great Britain did in the nineteenth century. In the case of Africa, where Western development efforts have been an "abysmal failure," only "costly direct imperialism is likely to provide the good governance that is a prerequisite for the economic advancement of the continent." In the Middle East and Central Asia, the new imperialists need to see that the Muslim world embraces modernisation even if it rejects Westernisation. Sounding very much like Watson, Lal writes: "The most urgent task in the new imperium is to bring the world of Islam into the modern world, without seeking to alter its soul."[113] Lal's argument for the "beneficent exercise of power" clearly resembles Watson's endorsement of empire as a means to bring freedom and reason to the less civilised regions of the world. But Lal's rationale, along with Cooper's prescription for cooperative imperialism and Conquest's notion of an English-speaking association, also echoes Watson's Idealist claims for the British Empire – that the empire existed for a good beyond its own self-interest.

Words like *empire* and *imperialism* are much out of favour in our postmodern times, but some political leaders are resurrecting the ideals of nineteenth-century imperialism, at least rhetorically. In a speech in the fall of 2001, then British prime minister Tony Blair defended Britain's participation in the war against terrorism in Watsonian terms: "The starving, the wretched, the dispossessed, the ignorant, those living in want and squalor from the deserts of North Africa to the slums of Gaza to the mountain ranges of Afghanistan: they too are our cause."[114] And in the summer of 2006, Canadian prime minister Stephen Harper surprised an audience in England with a speech that praised the British Empire, saying that "'in the Canadian context, the actions of the British Empire were largely benign and occasionally brilliant.'" The prime minister pointed to imperial policies that helped ensure the survival of French culture, while Britain's policies toward Canada's First Nations peoples "'were some of the fairest and most generous of the period.'"[115] Except for the place names, the sentiment would not have been out of line with that of a nineteenth-century imperialist who, like Watson, regarded the British Empire as a civil-ising force in the world.

This kind of argument suggests that if a new form of imperialism is emerging, then Watson has something to say to Canadians even in our post-Idealist age, more so than even Taylor and Grant. Canada cannot be immune to imperial affairs, even though, as Ignatieff puts it, Canadians continue to indulge in the "naive narcissism" of believing themselves "im-mune from Islamist terrorism."[116] Given that both Taylor and Grant cast the crisis of Canada as a consequence of and a response to modernity, Watson's thought as it applies to the international arena may prove valu-able. Watson's version of empire – the imperial power that must act in such a way as to preserve diverse cultures and encourage responsible govern-ment – certainly fulfils Taylor's multicultural requirement for recognising different cultures. Watson's Idealist view of empire also offers a counter-part to Grant's vision of the tyranny of the universal and homogeneous world-state. A new age of empire might well allow the recovery of the Ideal-ist hopes for a larger, more dynamic role in the world for Canada, one akin to that promoted by Canada's nineteenth-century imperialists. Indeed, the ideas that Stephen Leacock, Andrew Macphail, and George Robert Parkin had for Canada as an imperial player parallel the kind of imperial role for Canada suggested in Robert Conquest's idea of an association of English-speaking nations. Conquest points out that countries such as Canada, Australia, and the United Kingdom lack the power to act autonomously with any but local effect. Yet their interests, like those of the United States, are deeply involved in the world scene. In acting together, they could make contributions far beyond their own areas that would help the whole world community. Within an association of like-minded liberal democracies, countries such as Canada, which have often felt themselves committed to actions or policies by the more or less unilateral decisions of the United States, would more fully share not only the responsibility of decision-making, but also that of military or other action. Conquest even suggests that Canada's membership in such an association might well mitigate sepa-ratist aspirations in Quebec, as well as mute secessionist inclinations in Western Canada: "On an Association basis, the former trend might be muted and the latter still largely satisfied." And if Quebec did secede, that would be even more reason for English-speaking Canadians to look upon the idea of association positively.[117]

Interestingly, Alexandre Kojève, in a 1945 essay, expressed ideas similar to those of Conquest, albeit on behalf of France. In his "Outline of a

Doctrine of French Policy," Kojève argued that if France was to have a significant role in the post-war world, it needed to promote and lead a Latin empire that would serve as a counterfoil to both the Slavo-Soviet empire and the Anglo-American empire. This sounds similar to what Grant was promoting at the end of the Second World War when he talked about the British Commonwealth (with Canada playing a leading role) providing a third way between the two superpowers. Behind Kojève's idea was his belief that the age of the nation-state had come to an end, that the nation-state system was "gradually giving way to political formations which transgress national borders and which could be designated with the term 'Empires.'"[118] According to Kojève, "the period of *national* political realities is over. This is the epoch of *Empires*, which is to say of transnational political unities, but formed by *affiliated* nations."[119]

Kojève drew a parallel between his would-be Latin empire and the British Commonwealth as it was in his time. But he argued that even the Commonwealth was still too national to maintain itself as an empire, given the realities of the post-war era. Only the Anglo-Saxon empire, which Kojève defined as the Anglo-American politico-economic bloc, was an effective and actual political reality. France, he argued, needed to emulate this Anglo-American empire with its own membership in (and leadership of) a Latin empire. If France insisted on remaining "an exclusive *Nation*, she will necessarily sooner or later have to stop existing as a State in the strict sense and as an autonomous political reality. She will end, fatally, by being politically absorbed by the Anglo-Saxon Empire."[120] Arguably, considering how the European Union has developed over the last fifty years, Kojève's seedling idea for a Latin empire has borne fruit.[121]

Kojève describes his Latin empire in terms, both moral and political, that Watson and the Canadian imperialists of the late nineteenth century, as well as Grant, would recognise. France, Kojève argues, no longer knows what it means to be a nation. France "does not have, or no longer has, a clear and conscious political idea." The contemporary Frenchman, regardless of where he stands on the ideological spectrum, "lives as a 'bourgeois' and not as a 'citizen.'" He no longer identifies with or feels himself subject to the demands of the "'universal' reality of the State and the means it uses to assert and preserve itself." Hence, "France is politically dead for once and for all *qua* nation-State."[122] At the same time, though, it can be reborn "through an international union of affiliated nations." Grant, it will be recalled, also argues that Canadians, like the people of Kojève's France, have lost the idea and purpose of Canada and given themselves over to a depoliticised consumer lifestyle. Grant describes how the death of Canadian nationalism and the loss of the British heritage means Canada's absorption into the American empire. Does this argument amount to a Canadian version of Kojève's argument that the death of France as a *nation*-state opens the door to a revival of French *nationalism* through their leadership of a new empire? Kojève also argues that France's membership in a Latin empire would provide the French with a renewed sense of transcendence. As he put it, a Latin empire would be "a manifestation of the French will to political autonomy and 'greatness.'"[123]

Kojève's arguments for empire echo those of the nineteenth-century Idealists like Watson, who argued that Canada's partnership in the British Empire provided it with a sense of purpose that would allow it to transcend the narrow psychology and small materialist aspirations of Little Canada. But the contemporary advocate of empire whose thinking most closely resembles that of Watson is Michael Ignatieff. While he eschews an Anglo-Celtic association, Ignatieff does favour a morally grounded form of imperialism as a response to Islamist terrorism and other forms of disorder. And, like Deepak Lal, Ignatieff also insists that the United States must stop denying that it possesses an empire. The failure of so many states in the post–Cold War era has reached such proportions that it has created "an ongoing crisis of order in a globalised world."[124] The exercise of imperial power is the only rational and coherent response to this disorder and the only way to help these states get back on their feet. And since power requires military capacity, the United States is the singular imperial power in the world and, thus, must accept the burdens of empire. But so, too, must Canada, says Ignatieff. Canadians cannot claim to believe in multilateralism and international legal institutions as the way to maintain order in the world if they are not prepared to defend those beliefs by force if necessary.[125] Ignatieff echoes Watson (and Hegel, for that matter) in arguing that stable institutions are the key to order and good governance. Democracy works best when it is supported by liberal institutions. Without these constitutional pillars, democracies can easily become populist tyrannies. And institutional order, domestically or internationally, ultimately depends, like it or not, on the threat of coercive force. Soft-power appeals to tolerance and diversity and notions that Canada can influence the world by being a "model citizen"[126] are dangerously incoherent when one is faced with opponents who do not subscribe to such values and, indeed, who reject the principles, political and ontological, underlying those values. When soft-power humanitarianism fails, when order is threatened by disorder, when dissent descends into civil war, "there [is] a case for temporary imperial rule, to provide the force and will necessary to bring order out of chaos."[127]

On this point, Ignatieff closely follows Watson in asserting a moral dimension to imperialism. Watson argues that imperialism is morally justified so long as its purpose is not to rule others for selfish purposes, but to serve an Idealist end. Similarly, Ignatieff says that the exercise of imperial power is not discreditable "provided that empire does more than reproduce itself, provided that it does eventuate in self-rule for nations and peoples."[128] Ignatieff is also enough of a realist to understand that the primary purpose of empire is to bring order to the "barbarian zones." Only when there is order are human rights, the rule law, and other institutions of democracy possible. Again, Ignatieff's imperial motives parallel those of Idealists like Watson, who regarded the British Empire's special mission to be one of bringing order and civility to the savages. "The only justification for the rule of a superior over an inferior people is that the former should regard as its special task the elevation of the latter to its own level,"[129] Watson says. This is not substantively different from Ignatieff saying "nation-building could be an exercise in solidarity between rich and poor, the possessors and the dispossessed."[130] To be sure, Ignatieff does not employ what some regard as politically incorrect language. Nevertheless, his justification for empire is no different from that of Watson: "Bringing order is the paradigmatic imperial task, but it is essential, both for reasons of economy and for reasons of principle, to do so without denying local people their rights to some degree of self-determination."[131] In fact, Ignatieff acknowledges that the key difference between the old imperialism of the Idealists and the new imperialism of the liberal humanitarians is the rapidity with which self-rule and self-determination are granted and the imperial power makes its exit.

What all this leads to is not an argument to promote empire or imperialism, but the recognition that if Canada, along with the rest of the world, is entering a new age of empire, then a nineteenth-century Canadian philosopher, John Watson, has a great deal to say Canadians (and other westerners, too). Philosophers, as Hegel taught, do not predict the future, but Watson's thought allows us to revisit the idea of imperialism without apology. That could prove valuable both in providing a theoretical warrant for a return to empire and in establishing an ethical code for defensive imperialism. If Western civilisation is threatened by failing states and non-governmental terrorist organisations, if the Westphalian system of nation-states is giving way to some reconfiguration of transnational order (or disorder, as the case may be), then Watson offers Canadians a way to think through their country's place in this new world order, a theoretical compass to lead them toward imperial citizenship. If a new form of imperialism is going to be the overarching form of twenty-first-century politics – *relative imperialism* would be a good term of description – then Watson's prescription for empire offers moral guidance even in our post-Idealist age.

SUMMARY

Grant argues that there is every possibility that a new age of empire would eliminate difference and diversity and tend toward tyranny. In this view, though, Grant is reacting to a version of Hegelianism in contemporary liberalism that bends Hegel's project of reconciliation toward the universal rather than the particular. Grant, while supportive of liberal rights, believes that the logic of the Hegelian system leads to the imposition of universal principles on all people – the universal and homogenous state – regardless of their preference for difference. Watson, however, argues, in effect, that a universal and homogeneous world-state would not succeed because it is impossible to impose homogeneity. Taylor seeks a form of accommodation – multiculturalism – that would reconcile the universal and the particular. Which thinker proves correct in the longer run remains to be seen, of course. Yet, if Spirit is ushering in the remaking of the world order, Watson, Grant, and Taylor offer intelligible ways of thinking about this new configuration of power, particularly as it relates to the future of Canada.

This movement of Spirit can perhaps be more readily imagined by resorting to an artistic image. In the National Gallery of Canada, there is a picture depicting a solitary tree trunk on a hill above a lake. The stump is split and twisted, its trunk smoothed of bark. In the background on the right, the sky bulks with dark-bellied clouds. On the left, the sky is clear, as though a storm has passed. Shafts of sunlight fall through a breech in the cloud cover, lighting one side of the trunk with a sharp luminous glow. The rest of the tree remains in shadow. Lawren Harris's 1926 painting *North Shore, Lake Superior* has long been recognised as an icon of Canadian art. The split trunk conveys the isolation of the individual amidst an overwhelming natural world, a figure divided between light and dark, longing to overcome the isolation and find meaning in that which is greater than itself. By this interpretation, Harris's painting is regarded as an aesthetic response to the problematic nature of living in a huge northern land, a symbolic exploration of the character, atmosphere, moods, and spirit of a particular geography of Canada.[132]

In one fashion or another, every generation of Canadians engages in an exploration of the country, seeking by various means – political, social, cultural, and philosophic – to articulate an understanding of what it means to occupy the top half of North America. Historically, we have a produced a number of self-definitions: once we were a British community, loyal to the empire and the inherited traditions of constitutional monarchy; we have also been a rugged northern people, consciously rejecting the corruptive lure of the United States; and more recently, we conceived of ourselves as a mosaic of diverse cultures whose ability to live together in peace would inspire the world. Nowadays, few are so bold as to declare without qualification what it means to be Canadian, to assert who we are as a nation or even to promote a national purpose or a national idea. One consequence of this reluctance is that we are dispossessed of an abiding sense of belonging. A popular columnist refers to Canada as the world's first post-modern state, a post-national state-nation.[133] A prominent historian asks, "[G]iven radical cultural pluralism is there anything other than language for an immigrant to assimilate ... Could we logically replace the existing population with an entirely new immigrant population and still have Canada?"[134] It appears we are not only unsure of who we are, but why we are; that is to say, we are unsure of why we remain together as a politically united state.[135]

Clearly, Canada's future is open to question, so much so that Grant's theoretical statement about the impossibility of Canada sometimes seems prescient even at the pragmatic level. A cursory reading of newspapers should be enough to convince anyone that Canada's claims to sovereign status are problematic. The American president refers to Canadian oil and gas as domestic supply. Canada, it is said, must become part of a continental defence system and better coordinate its immigration and customs systems with those of the United States. There is talk of harmonising policies in regard to a North American security perimeter. And, of course, there is the continentalising imperative of free trade. All of which leads some to conclude that Canada is little more than a suburb of the United States, and to proclaim that "a moment of national truth is approaching, a time when we have to face up to the implications of Canadian decline ... Eventually we may decide to negotiate some kind of union [with the United States] because nobody will remember the point of continuing to stay separate."[136]

Ignatieff reflects this *zeitgeist* with a remark that is distinctly Hegelian in its recognition of the dialectical nature of Canadian political psychology: "Canada just happens to be one of those countries that is committed, as a condition of its survival, to engage in a constant act of self-justification and self-invention." Sounding almost Grantian, Ignatieff says that to the degree that Canadians are weary of this endless dialogue, then they are weary of being Canadian. "Constitutional dialogue among regions and languages is

the very condition of our collective survival. To be tired of this is to be tired
of Canadian life." He warns that if our national institutions are no longer
able to hold Canadians together despite their differences, then "we might
find ourselves unwilling participants in an experiment unprecedented in
the annals of political history: not the break-up of a failed state, but the dissolution of a mighty, successful and admired G-8 country."[137]

Such views recall the context of this essay – the problematic nature of
Canada's political existence – and its purpose – to show how Hegel's
thought has been variously appropriated in responding to that problem. I
have offered a wide-ranging consideration of the responses of three Canadian political philosophers to the tensions they perceived in the Canadian
political community. I have demonstrated that the responses of Watson,
Grant, and Taylor to the crisis of Canada were informed, in part at least, by
their appropriations of Hegelian thought, particularly his project of reconciliation. Their respective readings of Hegel, either as elaborators or de-
tractors, are a testament to the continued presence of the Hegelian Spirit
on the northern half of the North American continent. So long as
Canada's political future remains uncertain, there is every reason to believe that Hegel will continue to have much to say to Canadians.

Notes

INTRODUCTION

1 Georg W.F. Hegel, *Lectures on the Philosophy of World History, Introduction*, trans. H.B. Nisbet (Cambridge, 1975), 162, 169–70.

2 John Burbidge, "Hegel in Canada," *Owl of Minerva* 25, no. 2 (1994): 218. Even a brief survey of the literature shows a long-held interest in Hegel on the part of Canadian thinkers. In the recent past, there are the studies by the dean of Canadian Hegelians, H.S. Harris, including his massive two-volume work, *Hegel's Development: Toward the Sunlight* and *Night Thoughts*, published in 1972 and 1983 respectively, which is widely recognised as the definitive intellectual biography of Hegel in the English language, and his subsequent masterwork, the two-volume *Hegel's Ladder*, which is a paragraph-by-paragraph commentary on Hegel's *Phenomenology of Spirit*, published in the late 1990s. There is also Emil Fackenheim's 1967 book, *The Religious Dimension in Hegel's Thought*; Charles Taylor's 1975 work, *Hegel*; Burbidge's 1981 *On Hegel's Logic: Fragments of a Commentary* and his 1992 study, *Hegel on Logic and Religion: The Reasonableness of Christianity*, all of which remain standards in the field of Hegelian scholarship. There are also numerous interpreters and interlocutors of Hegel, such as Tom Darby, Waller Newell, Peter Emberley, Barry Cooper, Leslie Armour, David McGregor, James Doull, John Conway, Philip Resnick, Ian Angus, Theodore Garaets, and George Giovanni, to name a few. Literary critics, historians, sociologists, and film critics – Northrop Frye, Harold Innis, Bruce Elder, Robin Mathews, Stanley Barrett – have all employed Hegelian dialectical approaches in their work. And, finally, there is Pierre Trudeau's acknowledgment of the influence of the British Hegelian T.H. Green on his political thought.

3 David MacGregor, "Canada's Hegel," *Literary Review of Canada*, February 1994, 18–29. Robert Fulford makes a similar point in "Keeping the Hegelian Spirit

Alive," *Globe and Mail,* 1 February 1995, A9. For example, Tom Darby's *The Feast: Meditations on Politics and Time* (1981; reprint, Toronto, 1990), was the first English-language study in Canada to undertake an interpretation of Hegel's end-of-history thesis. Barry Cooper's *The End of History: An Essay on Modern Hegelianism* (Toronto, 1984) also considers this theme.

4 Leslie Armour and Elizabeth Trott offer an overview of this phenomenon in *The Faces of Reason* (Waterloo, 1981), 1–32. See also, R. Bruce Elder, *Image and Identity: Reflections on Canadian Film and Culture* (Waterloo, Ont., 1989), 48–72. I am indebted to Elder's work, which introduced me to the idea of "Hegel in Canada."

5 Leslie Armour, *The Idea of Canada and the Crisis of Community* (Ottawa, 1981), 79.

6 Armour and Trott, *The Faces of Reason,* 19.

7 Elizabeth Trott, "Western Mindscapes: A Philosophical Challenge," *American Review of Canadian Studies* 31, no. 4 (2001): 639–41. Trott writes: "Neo-Hegelian traditions influenced the writings of most of the early philosophers across Canada. The Hegelian dialectical method was a tool for making sense of and bringing sense to the young Canada."

8 Peter Emberley and Waller Newell, *Bankrupt Education: The Decline of Liberal Education in Canada* (Toronto, 1994), 159–61. They, too, argue that a "general legacy of Hegelianism" can be found in a variety of Canadian thinkers.

9 Francis Fukuyama, *The End of History and the Last Man* (New York, 1992).

10 Denton Snider, *Modern European Philosophy: The History of Modern Philosophy, Psychologically Speaking* (St Louis: Sigma Publishing, 1904), 737, cited in James A. Good, "A 'World Historical Idea': The St. Louis Hegelians and the Civil War," *Journal of American Studies* 34, no. 3 (2000): 450. See also John E. Smith, "Hegel in St. Louis," in *Hegel's Social and Political Thought,* ed. Donald Phillip Verene (Atlantic Highlands, N.J., 1980), 223.

11 Darby, *The Feast,* xii–xiii.

12 I owe this point to John Burbidge, in conversation, 14 December 1997.

13 This attitude is evident in numerous book titles. A few examples: P.B. Waite, *Arduous Destiny;* Donald Smiley, *Canada in Question;* David Bell, *Roots of Disunity;* Edwin Black, *Divided Loyalties;* J.L. Granatstein, *The Politics of Survival;* J.M.S. Careless, *Canada: A Story of Challenge;* Richard Simeon, *Must Canada Fail?;* Garth Stevenson, *Unfulfilled Union: Canadian Federalism and National Unity;* Clarence Bolt, *Does Canada Matter? Liberalism and the Illusion of Sovereignty*; and, more recently, Andrew Cohen, *The Unfinished Canadian.*

14 J.M.S. Careless, *Canada: A Story of Challenge* (Toronto: Macmillan of Canada, 1970), 3.

15 Goldwin Smith, *Canada and the Canadian Question,* ed. and with an introduction by Carl Berger (1891; reprint, Toronto: University of Toronto Press, 1971).

16 Leslie Armour, "Canadian Ways of Thinking: Logic, Society, and Canadian Philosophy," in *Alternative Frontiers: Voices from the Mountain West*, ed. Allen Seager, Leonard Evenden, Rowland Lorimer, and Robin Mathews (Montreal, 1997), 29.

17 Ibid., 14. Referring to his notion of rational pluralism, Armour suggests that "if there is a 'Canadian way of thinking,' this might well be it." The need for such a way of thinking, he says, "helps to explain the Canadian fascination with Hegel."

18 Ronald Beiner and Wayne Norman, eds, introduction to *Canadian Political Philosophy: Contemporary Reflections* (Toronto, 2001), 3. It is interesting to note that Hegel, too, argued, in Stephen Houlgate's words, that all states need "to maintain an awareness of their own history in order to know what they are and what their deepest aspirations and most valuable endeavours have been." See Houlgate, "World History As Progress of Consciousness: An Interpretation of Hegel's Philosophy of History," *Owl of Minerva* 22, no. 1 (1990): 73.

19 For this consensus view of American history, see Louis Hartz, ed., *The Founding of New Societies* (New York, 1964); and Seymour Lipset, *The First New Nation: The United States in Historical and Comparative Perspective* (New York, 1979).

20 Kenneth McCrae, "The Structure of Canadian History," in *The Founding of New Societies*, ed. Hartz, 219–74; Allan Smith, "Metaphor and Nationality in North America," *Canadian Historical Review* 51, no. 3 (1970): 248–51; and Seymour Lipset, *Continental Divide* (New York, 1990), 1–17, 42–56.

21 Barry Cooper, "Western Political Consciousness," in *Political Thought in Canada: Contemporary Perspectives*, ed. Stephen Brooks (Toronto, 1984), 219.

22 Peter Waite, ed., *The Confederation Debates in the Province of Canada, 1865* (Toronto: McClelland & Stewart, 1963), 50.

23 Trott, "Western Mindscapes," 641.

24 Armour and Trott, *The Faces of Reason*, 4. Elder makes a similar point in *Image and Identity*, 5–7, 55–7.

25 Armour, "Canadian Ways of Thinking," 14–16.

26 Hegel, "The German Constitution," in *Political Writings*, ed. Zibignew Pelczynski and trans. T.M. Knox (Oxford, 1967); and Hegel, *Philosophy of Right*, trans. T.M. Knox (Oxford, 1942), 230–56. On the historical context of Hegel's thought, see Joachim Ritter, *Hegel and the French Revolution*, trans. Richard Dein Winfield (Cambridge, Mass., 1982); Bernard Cullen, Hegel's Social and Political Thought: An Introduction (Dublin, 1979); Shlomo Avineri, "Hegel and Nationalism," in *Hegel's Political Philosophy*, ed. Walter Kaufman (New York, 1970); and Shlomo Avineri, *Hegel's Theory of the Modern State* (Cambridge, U.K., 1971).

27 Avineri, *Hegel's Theory of the Modern State*, 241. As Avineri notes, Hegel's "questions – if not always his answers – point to the direction of understanding that which is, today as much as in his own time."

28 For the etymological roots of *spirit*, see Robert K. Barnhart, ed., *The Barnhart Dictionary of Etymology* (New York: H.W. Wilson Co., 1998); *Bloomsbury Dictionary of Word Origins* (London: Bloomsbury Publishing, 1990); and *The Century Dictionary and Cyclopedia: An Encyclopedic Lexicon*, vol. 7 (New York: Century Co., 1903).

29 It is important to note that for Hegel, Spirit has to be materialized, and even that which seemingly stands in opposition to Spirit, whether nature or matter, is permeated by Spirit. It would be a distortion to understand Hegel as claiming some ontological primacy for the spiritual or mental *over* the material. For Hegel, Spirit or Mind is a barren abstraction unless it is concretely embodied. See Richard Bernstein, "Why Hegel Now?" *Review of Metaphysics* 31, no. 1 (1977): 58.

PART ONE

1 Iris Murdoch, *The Sovereignty of Good* (London, 1967), 72.

2 Scholars offer various interpretations of Hegel's thought on the French Revolution, ranging from the view that he continued to support doctrines of liberation and revolution despite the Terror to the view that he had fundamental metaphysical and theological concerns that were decidedly non-revolutionary. I mention only a few of these interpretations: Darby, *The Feast;* Michael Allen Gillespie, *Hegel, Heidegger and the Ground of History* (Chicago, 1984); Cooper, *The End of History;* Ritter, *Hegel and the French Revolution;* and H.S. Harris, "Hegel and the French Revolution," *Clio* 7 (1977): 5–18.

3 Quoted in Gillespie, *Hegel, Heidegger and the Ground of History*, 38.

4 Hegel, *Phenomenology of Spirit*, trans. A.V. Miller, with analysis and foreword by J.N. Findlay (Oxford, 1977), #11, #12, 6–7. Tradition has it that Hegel finished the *Phenomenology* on the eve of the Battle of Jena on 14 October 1806. In a letter to a friend, Friedrich Niethammer, written on Monday, 13 October, Hegel claimed that at one point he saw Napoleon astride a white horse as he rode through the town. It was, it seems, a revelatory moment despite the upheaval caused by the war: "I saw the Emperor – this world-soul – riding out of the city on reconnaissance. It is indeed a wonderful sensation to see such an individual, who, concentrated here at a single point, astride a horse, reaches out over the world and masters it." See Clark Butler and Christiane Seiler, trans., *Hegel: The Letters* (Bloomington, Ind., 1989), 114.

5 Hegel, *The Difference between Fichte's and Schelling's System of Philosophy*, trans. H.S. Harris and Walter Cerf (Albany, N.Y., 1977), 89. Hegel's emphasis.

6 The phrase *project of reconciliation* is taken from Michael Hardimon's *Hegel's Social Philosophy: The Project of Reconciliation* (Cambridge, 1994). I have made considerable use of Hardimon's comprehensive study.

7 Hardimon, *Hegel's Social Philosophy*, 85–92, 133–4.

8 Bernard Yack makes this point in his review of Hardimon's book in the *American Political Science Review* 89, no. 2 (1995): 486–7. Yack writes that "although Hegel relies on the idea of reconciliation throughout his mature moral and political thought, he never presents a sustained or systematic account of the subject."

9 Daniel Berthold-Bond, *Hegel's Grand Synthesis: A Study of Being, Thought and History* (New York, 1989), 3. This study provides one of the better overviews of Hegel's thought of which I am aware, particularly in its consideration of the metaphysics of his philosophy of history. See also Elliot Jurist, "Hegel's Concept of Recognition," *Owl of Minerva* 19, no. 1 (1987): 5–22; David Duquette, "The Political Significance of Hegel's Concept of Recognition in the *Phenomenology*," *Bulletin of the Hegel Society of Great Britain* 29 (Spring-Summer 1994): 41; and Ivan Soll, *An Introduction to Hegel's Metaphysics* (Chicago, 1989). I have drawn from this material for much of my summary of Hegel's thought.

10 Quoted in Berthold-Bond, *Hegel's Grand Synthesis*, 3.

11 Hardimon, *Hegel's Social Philosophy*, 2–3, 23–4, 85–7. Hardimon also regards reconciliation as the central organizing category in Hegel's thought as a whole and the main goal of his social philosophy. Hegel's concern, he says, is that Spirit, or *Geist*, be reconciled to the world as a whole and, thereby, to itself, and that humans, as those beings in whom Spirit is manifested, be reconciled to the social world in which they have both their subjective and objective being. Another scholar, Eric von der Luft, likewise argues that reconciliation is Hegel's "most fundamental concern." Hegel's phenomenology of the development of consciousness involves the gradual coming-to-consciousness of the essential unity and harmony implicit in the phenomenal world's experience of disjunction and fragmentation. Hegel's dialectical method, his phenomenological analysis of historical development, and his claim for the emergence of an ethical state out of abstract right are all, Luft asserts, "built upon this basic idea of working out a means to reconcile opposing, bifurcated, or inconsistent forces and entities" (Eric v.d. Luft, "Would Hegel Have Liked to Burn Down All the Churches and Replace Them with Philosophical Academies?" *Modern Schoolman* 68 [1990]: 45).

12 Hegel, *Phenomenology*, #27, #28, 15–16. See also Jonathan Rée, *Philosophical Tales* (London: Methuen, 1987), 76–83. Rée offers a literary view of the *Phenomenology*, describing it as "a story of Spirit – or Everyman, 'the universal individual' – travelling the long road leading from the dull realm of 'natural' consciousness to absolute knowledge and 'working its passage' through every possible philosophical system on its way."

13 Hegel, *Phenomenology*, #77, #78, 49–50. Hegel writes: "And in phenomenology, dialectic describes the path of the natural consciousness which presses forward

to true knowledge; of the way of the soul which journeys through the series of its own configurations ... so that it may purify itself for the life of spirit and achieve finally ... the awareness of what it really is in itself."

14 Hardimon, *Hegel's Social Philosophy*, 85–90.

15 Darby, *The Feast*, 96–101, 106–7.

16 Hardimon, *Hegel's Social Philosophy*, 2.

17 Hegel, *Phenomenology*, #671, 409.

18 Hegel, preface to *Philosophy of Right*, trans. T.M. Knox (Oxford, 1967), 12. Hegel's famous statement warrants expansion: "To recognize reason as the rose in the cross of the present and thereby enjoy the present, this is the rational insight which reconciles us to the actual, the reconciliation which philosophy affords to those in whom there has once arisen an inner voice bidding them to comprehend, not only to dwell in what is substantive while still retaining subjective freedom, but also to possess subjective freedom while standing not in anything particular and accidental but in what exists absolutely."

19 Ibid., #257, #258, 155–6.

20 For different perspectives on the concept of Spirit, see Robert Williams, "Hegel's Concept of *Geist*," with commentary by Richard Dien Winfield, in *Hegel's Philosophy of Spirit*, ed. Peter Stillman (Albany, 1987), 1–24; Robert Solomon, "Hegel's Concept of *Geist*," in *Hegel: A Collection of Critical Essays*, ed. Alasdair MacIntyre (New York, 1972), 125–49; and Terry Pinkard, *Hegel's Phenomenology: The Sociality of Reason*, (Cambridge, 1996), 8–9. Pinkard, for example, writes: "[S]pirit is a form of 'social space' reflecting on itself as to whether it is satisfactory with its own terms ... 'Spirit' therefore denotes for Hegel not a metaphysical entity but a fundamental *relation* among persons that mediates their *self-consciousness*, a way in which people reflect on what they have come to take as authoritative for themselves."

21 Hegel, *Phenomenology*, #25, 14.

22 Ibid., #292, #293, 176–7. Hegel writes in #293: "We have a syllogism in which one extreme is the *universal life as a universal* or as genus, the other extreme, however, being the same *universal as a single individual*, or as a universal individual; but the middle term [individuality] is composed of both: the first seems to fit itself into it as a *determinate* universality or as *species*, the other, however, as *individuality proper* or as a single individual [the autonomous self]." On this topic, see Robert M. Wallace, *Hegel's Philosophy of Reality, Freedom and God*, (Cambridge, N.Y., 2005), 287. Wallace writes: "If Self-consciousness is 'determined ... only as a *particular*,' it is not determined as going beyond itself – as free. But as a 'free object' it must be determined as free. To be determined in this way, Hegel proposes, it must be 'present for the other as a free self,' through 'recognition.'"

23 I have also drawn on the essays of Robert Solomon and Robert Williams to explain Hegel's view of the individual. Each of these scholars regards Hegel's philosophy of *Geist* as an instance or descendent of Kant's transcendental philosophy. Solomon argues that Hegel's *Geist* "embodies an important attempt to resolve an important problem in Kant's philosophy" (Solomon, "Hegel's Concept of *Geist*," 131). However, Williams argues that it is "misleading" to stress the similarities between Hegel's *Geist* and Kant's transcendental ego because, in his view, Hegel makes a radical departure from Kant (Williams, "Hegel's Concept of *Geist*," 3). H.S. Harris also points out that much of Hegel's early thought is "largely focused" on Kant's transcendental dialectic, but that while he employs many of Kant's terms, he rejects many of the assumptions on which those terms are based. See Harris's introductory essay in Hegel, *Faith and Knowledge*, trans. H.S. Harris and Walter Cerf (Albany, N.Y., 1977), 17–25.

24 Gillespie, *Hegel, Heidegger and the Ground of History*, 79. Gillespie sees Spirit's two-fold nature as Hegel's "answer to the emptiness of the transcendental unity of apperception." Hegel transforms Kant's placid "eternity of rest" into an eternal struggle of being, of what is, with itself.

25 Ibid. See also Fred Dallmayr, *G.W.F. Hegel: Modernity and Politics* (Newbury, 1993), 4, 23–4.

26 Gillespie, *Hegel, Heidegger and the Ground of History*, 55. On Hegel's philosophy of history, see also Robert S. Hartman, editor's introduction to *Hegel: Reason in History* (New York, 1953), ix–xlii; and John Plamenatz, "History as the realization of freedom," in *Hegel's Political Philosophy: Problems and Perspectives*, ed. Z.A. Pelczynski (Cambridge, 1971), 30–51, and Elder, *Image and Identity*, 58–61.

27 Hegel, *Philosophy of Right*, #4–#7, 20–4. On this topic, see Wallace, *Hegel's Philosophy of Reality, Freedom and God*, 285–93; Allen W. Wood, "Hegel's Ethics," in *The Cambridge Companion to Hegel*, ed. Frederick C. Beiser (Cambridge, 1993): 216–19; and Michael Inwood, *A Hegel Dictionary* (Oxford, 1992), 110–12. Inwood describes Hegel's definition of freedom this way: "Something, especially a person, is free if, and only if, it is independent and self-determining, not determined by or dependent on something other than itself."

28 Ibid., #15, 27. See also, Wood, "Hegel's Ethics," 219. Wood writes: "Hegel explicitly distinguishes his conception of positive freedom from the 'superficial' everyday notion of freedom as the ability to do as you please."

29 Ibid., #27, 32.

30 Johann Fichte, *The Science of Ethics As Based on the Science of Knowledge*, trans. A.E. Kroeger (London: Keegan Paul, 1897), 136.

31 Hegel, *The Difference between Fichte's and Schelling's System*, 144–5. I have drawn my discussion of Hegel's critique of Fichte from Steven B. Smith, Allen W. Wood, Ken Foldes, and Robert Wallace. See Smith, *Hegel's Critique of Liberalism* (Chicago,

1989), 80–5; Wood, "Hegel's Ethics," 212–14; Foldes, "Does the Solution to Our Present Moral and Political Dilemmas Lie in the Theories of the German Idealists?" *www.bu.edu/wcp/Papers/Poli/Pol.Fold.htm*; and Wallace, "How Freedom Requires Community," *www.bu.edu/wcp/Papers/Poli/Pol.Wall.htm*, accessed 20 February 2002.

32 Hegel, *Lectures on the History of Philosophy*, vol. 3, trans. E.S. Haldane and Frances H. Simson (New York, 1955), 504.

33 Foldes, "Does the Solution to Our Present Moral ... Idealists?" 4.

34 Ibid. In addition, see the "Morality" section in Hegel, *Phenomenology*, #599–#602, 365–6. In particular, see #600, which reads in part: "From this determination [the Kantian separation of nature and moral consciousness] is developed a moral view of the world which consists in the relation between the absoluteness of morality and the absoluteness of Nature." See also Wood, "Hegel's Ethics," 223; and Smith, "Hegel's Critique of Liberalism," 80–4.

35 Smith, *Hegel's Critique of Liberalism*, 83. See also Foldes, "Does the Solution to Our Present Moral ... Idealists?" 3–7.

36 Wood, "Hegel's Ethics," 218.

37 Foldes, "Does the Solution to Our Present Moral ... Idealists?" 6. See also Wood, "Hegel's Ethics," 218.

38 Charles Taylor, "Hegel's Ambiguous Legacy for Modern Liberalism," in *Hegel and Legal Theory*, ed. Drucilla Cornell, Michel Rosenfeld, and David Gray Carlson (New York, 1991), 75. Taylor writes: "A Hegelian model, as a model of critical society, is flawed by its Fichtean roots."

39 Hegel, *Phenomenology*, #174, 109. I have drawn my summary of the development of self-consciousness from various sources: Tom Darby, *The Feast*, 94–101; Judith Butler, *Subjects of Desire: Hegelian Reflections in Twentieth-Century France* (New York, 1987), 40–59; Robert Wallace, *Hegel's Philosophy of Reality, Freedom and God*, 288–9; and Adam Krob, "Hegel's Community: Synthesizing the Romantic and the Liberal" (PhD diss., Duke University, 1997), 5–7. However, perhaps the best known analysis of Spirit's dialectical development is Alexandre Kojève's *Introduction to the Reading of Hegel*, ed. Allan Bloom and trans. James Nichols, Jr (New York, 1969).

40 Wood, "Hegel's Ethics," 219.

41 Hegel, *Philosophy of Right*, #149, 107.

42 I owe this summary to Darby, *The Feast*, 97–100.

43 Butler, *Subjects of Desire*, 44; and Dallmayr, *G.W.F. Hegel*, 67.

44 Kojève, *Introduction to the Reading of Hegel*, 7–9.

45 Quoted in Patrick Riley, "Introduction to the Reading of Alexandre Kojève," *Political Theory* 9, no. 1 (1981), 8. Riley cites Kojeve's book *Introduction à la lecture Hegel: Leçons sur la Phenomenologie de l'esprit* (Paris: Gallimard, 1947):184–5.

46 Wallace, "How Freedom Requires Community," 4. See also Wallace, *Hegel's Philosophy of Reason, Freedom, and God* (New York, 2005), 302–7.

47 On this point, see Darby, "The Feast," 96–101; Butler, "Subjects of Desire," 51–7; and Dallmayr, *G.W.F. Hegel*, 66–8, 219.

48 Hegel, *Philosophy of Right*, #41–#53, 40–6. By property, or *Eigentum*, Hegel has in mind everything that a person possesses, including mind and body. He held that in developing your mind and body, you took possession of yourself and became your own property. See #57, 47–8.

49 Wood, "Hegel's Ethics," 222. Wood writes: "It is crucial to Hegel's conception of morality that we deserve credit or blame only for real acts and accomplishments, not for mere inner intentions and dispositions."

50 Hegel, *Philosophy of Right*, #142, 105.

51 Wallace, *Hegel's Philosophy of Reality, Freedom, and God*, 306. See also Wallace, "How Freedom Requires Community," n.p.; and Wood, "Hegel's Ethics," 229–31.

52 Hegel, *Philosophy of Right*, #257, #258, 155–6.

53 Vasanthi Srinivasan, "Freedom, Community and Transcendence: A Comparison of Select Western and Indian Thinkers" (PhD diss., Carleton University, 1997), 120–1, 135–8. I am greatly indebted to Ms Srinivasan. A former colleague, she helped me to get a handle on Hegelian thought, and I have greatly benefited from her work. It is no exaggeration to say our coffee sessions allowed me to go forward with this essay.

54 Hegel, *Reason in History*, 51–2. See also Wood, "Hegel's Ethics," 231. Wood acknowledges that Hegel's notion of the modern state being able to reconcile the individual good of its members and the state's collective ends is not an idea that most moderns share. "For us, modern society remains a battlefield of interests and the state is simply an enforcer, either of some interests over others, or else of the rules of their combat."

55 On this argument, see Leo Strauss, *The Political Philosophy of Thomas Hobbes: Its Basis and Genesis*, trans. Elsa M. Sinclair (Chicago, 1936), 57–8. See also Gillespie, *Hegel, Heidegger, and the Ground of History*, 39–43; and Wood, "Hegel's Ethics," 230–1.

56 Hegel, *Philosophy of Right*, #75, 59.

57 Roger Scruton, "Hegel As a Conservative Thinker," in *The Philosopher on Dover Beach* (Manchester, 1990), 51.

58 Hegel, *Philosophy of Right*, #257, 155. For a succinct analysis on Hegel's view of the state, see Dante Germino, "Hegel As a Political Theorist," *Journal of Politics* 31, no. 4 (1969): 892–6; and Dallmayr, *G.W.F. Hegel*, 135–45.

59 Ibid., #258, 156. Given the concerns of my essay, particularly regarding John Watson's thought, it is worth expanding on how Hegel regards the state's relation to the individual: "Since the state is mind [Spirit] objectified, it is only as one of

its members that the individual himself has objectivity, genuine individuality, and an ethical life. Unification pure and simple is the true content and aim of the individual, and the individual's destiny is the living of a universal life [that is, 'living' as a citizen]." However, Hegel is also careful to point out that the state is rational (that is to say, freedom actualized) only insofar as it manifests "the unity of objective freedom (i.e. freedom of the universal or substantial will) and subjective freedom (i.e. freedom of everyone in his knowing and in his volition of particular ends); and, consequently, so far as its form is concerned, in self-determining action on laws and principles which are thoughts and so universal." In other words, the individual and the state are reconciled insofar as each manifests the freedom and rational development of the other. Watson, as I shall show, gives this idea considerable attention.

60 Scruton, "Hegel As a Conservative Thinker," 51–2.

61 Patchen Markell, "Bound by Recognition: The Politics of Identity after Hegel" (PHD diss., Harvard University, 1999), 106–9. Markell's excellent dissertation was published as a book after I had completed this section of my essay. While I have continued to cite the dissertation in the references that follow, I thought it worthwhile in this instance to note that the corresponding page references in the book *Bound by Recognition* (Princeton: Princeton University Press, 2003) are 103–7.

62 Robert Williams, *Recognition: Fichte and Hegel on the Other* (Albany, N.Y., 1992), 142.

63 Srinivasan, "Freedom, Community and Transcendence," 169–72.

64 Krob, *Hegel's Community*, 175–7.

65 According to the *Cambridge Dictionary of Philosophy* (355–7), *Idealism* is "the philosophical doctrine that reality is somehow mind-correlative or mind-coordinated – that the real objects constituting the 'external world' are not independent of cognizing minds, but exist only as in some way correlative to mental operations. The doctrine centres on the conception that reality as we understand it reflects the workings of mind." I draw this definition to the reader's attention because, throughout my essay, I have deliberately capitalized Idealism on the assumption than there may be some confusion between the philosophic concept and the common usage of the word *idealism* in reference to some kind of sentimental high-mindedness or utopianism. An Idealist is not necessarily an idealist.

66 Hegel, *Philosophy of Right*, #260, 160–1. My emphasis.

67 Ibid., #4, 20.

68 H. Tristram Engelhardt, "*Sittlichkeit* and Post-Modernity: An Hegelian Reconsideration of the State," in *Hegel Reconsidered: Beyond Metaphysics and the Authoritarian State,* ed. H. Tristram Engelhardt and Terry Pinkard (Boston, 1994), 221. See also Stephen Houlgate, *Freedom, Truth and History: An Introduction to Hegel's*

Philosophy (London, 1991), 89. Houlgate writes: "A rational state, for Hegel, is thus one which fosters this sense of freedom in its citizens and which so ensures that the rights which it enshrines in law are also laid claim to by the people themselves."

69 Srinivasan, "Freedom, Community and Transcendence," 118.

70 On this topic, see Francis Fukuyama, *Trust: The Social Virtues and the Creation of Prosperity* (New York, 1995).

71 Srinivasan, "Freedom, Community and Transcendence," 152–4. See also Smith, *Hegel's Critique of Liberalism,* 140–4.

72 Hegel, *Philosophy of Right,* #268, 163–4. Hegel's emphasis.

73 Srinivasan, "Freedom, Community and Transcendence," 130–1. See also Houlgate, *Freedom, Rights and Civility,* 118–21.

74 Hegel, *Philosophy of Right,* #153, 109. See also Houlgate, *Freedom, Truth and History,* 120. He writes: "Ethical freedom is not *fully* realized, therefore, until individuals find freedom in the sense of identity which they share with the whole cultural or geographical community in which they live." His emphasis.

75 Ibid., #258, 155–6.

76 Ibid., #145, 105. In a sense, this is common sense. The community and its institutions exist prior to the individual and will continue to exist after him. Thus, it is not unreasonable (or callous) to say that the community is *per se* indifferent to the individual.

77 Ibid., #105–#107, #141, 75–6, 103–4. See also Krob, "Hegel's Community," 151–2. Krob argues that Hegel's lectures on abstract right "attempt to create a space in which individuals can have a separate existence from the community."

78 Ibid., #138, 92.

79 Ibid., "Additions," #89, 255.

80 Srinivasan, "Freedom, Community and Transcendence," 130–3.

PART TWO

1 John Lukacs, *The End of the Twentieth Century and the End of the Modern Age* (New York, 1993), 174–5.

2 Canada emerged from the conflict between the two largest empires of the eighteenth and nineteenth centuries, the French and English empires. More recently, like it or not, Canadians have had to define themselves as best they could in terms of their perceived relationship to the great imperial power of the twentieth century, the United States. See David Bercuson et al., *Colonies: Canada to 1867* (Toronto, 1992), 480. However, I would also like to speculate about a slight Teutonic tinge to Canada's bloodline. For those who enjoy historical coincidences it is curious to note that in the same year that Bismarck began the uni-

fication of Germany – 1864 – the major push for Confederation began with the Charlottetown Conference. Might it be suggested, then, that Canada's existence as an independent political *state* is linked to the rise of the modern German *state* or, more precisely perhaps, to the British response to the rise of the German Empire? The last British garrison sailed from Quebec in 1871 even as German soldiers continued to occupy French soil. See W.L. Morton, *The Canadian Identity*, 2nd ed. (Toronto: University of Toronto, 1972), 47–8.

3 See George Parkin, "The Reorganization of the British Empire," *Century Illustrated Monthly Magazine* 37 (1888): 187–92. This essay contains the essential elements of Parkin's imperialist thought. It is reprinted in H.D. Forbes, ed., *Canadian Political Thought* (Toronto, 1985), 156–65.

4 G.M. Grant, "Our National Aims and Objects," in *Maple Leaves: Being the Papers Read Before the National Unity Club of Toronto at the "National Evenings" During the Winter of 1890–91* (Toronto: National Club, 1891), 20.

5 George Parkin, "Imperial Federation," *University Magazine* 1, no. 1 (1902): 193.

6 A.B. McKillop, *A Disciplined Intelligence: Critical Inquiry and Canadian Thought in the Victorian Era* (Toronto, 1979), 195–6.

7 McKillop's *A Disciplined Intelligence* remains the most detailed account of the influence of Idealism in Canada, but see also his essay "The Idealist Legacy," in *Contours of Canadian Thought* (Toronto, 1987), 96–110. Other articles that touch on Canada's Idealist heritage include Terry Cook, "George R. Parkin and the Concept of Britannic Idealism," *Journal of Canadian Studies* 10, no. 3 (1975): 15–31; Robert J.D. Page, "Canada and the Imperial Idea in the Boer War Years," *Journal of Canadian Studies* 5, no. 1 (1970): 33–49; D.L. Cole, "Canada's 'Nationalistic' Imperialists," *Journal of Canadian Studies* 5, no. 3 (1970): 44–9; Allan Smith, "Metaphor and Nationality in North America," *Canadian Historical Review* 51, no. 3 (1970): 247–75; and Allan Smith, "Conservatism, Nationalism and Imperialism: The Thought of George Monro Grant," *Canadian Literature* 83 (1979), 90–116. For a sketch of Watson's life and influence, see Christopher Humphrey, "The Sage of Kingston: John Watson and the Ambiguity of Hegelianism" (PhD diss., McGill University, 1992).

8 See Part 1, note 65, for the *Cambridge Dictionary of Philosophy* (355–7) definition of *Idealism*. In the context of Watson's thought it is necessary to expand on the topic. Philosophical Idealism regards reality as an aggregation of experiences that are formed, ordered, and comprehended by Spirit. However, there is a distinction between the philosophies of Objective Idealism and Subjective Idealism. George Berkeley, the eighteenth-century Anglican bishop, exemplifies the latter. Berkeley locates the essence of reality in the individual consciousness and argues that nothing exists except the mind and its states. Objective Idealism, on the other hand, holds that reality is a rational and intelligible order. This order

exists "outside" the individual, but the individual can participate in and come to know this order by means of his rational mind. In describing himself as an Objective Idealist, Watson, like Hegel, holds that reality is, in essence, spiritual. Individuals can know reality for what it is in truth because they, too, participate in reality as fundamentally spiritual beings. Or, put differently, Watson believes that Mind, or Spirit, is fundamental to the constitution of what is, or material reality, and that individuals, in their capacity for reason, participate in Spirit and can thereby comprehend the essential rationality of reality. Watson thus follows Hegel in trying to reconstitute the idea of a cosmic order as the foundation of his political thought.

The antecedents of Watson's Objective Idealism are Hegel's critique of Kant and the subsequent neo-Hegelian thinking of British Idealists such as Benjamin Jowett, T.H. Green, and, in particular, Edward Caird, who was Watson's philosophic mentor. Watson acknowledges the influence of the British Idealists, especially Caird, but his philosophic thought shows some significant departures from their thinking. In the prefaces to the 1895 first edition and the 1898 second edition of *Outline of Philosophy*, Watson says that he is defending the "Idealistic position, as least as held by such writers as the late Professor T.H. Green and the present Master of Balliol [Edward Caird]." In particular, he acknowledges a debt to Green's *Prolegomena to Ethics* and *Philosophical Works* and Caird's *Comte* and *Critical Account of the Philosophy of Kant*. Nevertheless, as one of Watson's students wrote, while Watson "remained faithful to the general principles which they [Green and Caird] expounded, he developed his own original methods of exposition and made significant contributions of his own, particularly in the field of the Philosophy of Religion." See J.M. MacEachern, "John Watson," in *Some Great Men of Queen's*, ed. Robert Charles Wallace (Toronto, 1941), 25–6. Similarly, a more recent student argues that even in his non-religious writings Watson "saw himself not only as an interpreter of Green and Caird, but also as a philosopher who used British Idealism as a basis for his own distinctive philosophical system." See Robert Taylor, "The Darwinian Revolution: The Responses of Four Canadian Scholars" (PhD diss., McMaster University, 1976), 173.

9 John Irving, "One Hundred Years of Canadian Philosophy," in *Philosophy in Canada: A Symposium* (Toronto, 1952), 6.

10 John Irving, "Philosophical Literature to 1910," in *Literary History of Canada*, vol. 1: *Canadian Literature in English*, ed. Carl F. Klinck (Toronto, 1976), 454. Irving writes: "One of the great teachers of philosophy in Canada during the last hundred years, Watson was the first philosopher in this country to achieve an international reputation through his writings. British and American historians of philosophy always list him as one of the leading representatives of the

Idealistic movement in the Anglo-Saxon world." More recently, David Boucher has included Watson as among the best of the British Idealists. See Boucher, ed., *The British Idealists* (Cambridge, 1997). Clifford Williams points out that in the thirty years between 1885 and 1915, one or more of Watson's books were used as texts in at least twelve of the fifteen universities in Canada and certainly in all the larger departments of philosophy. See Clifford J. Williams, "The Epistemology of John Watson" (PhD thesis, University of Toronto, 1966), 6.

11 Leslie Armour and Elizabeth Trott, *The Faces of Reason: An Essay on Philosophy and Culture in English Canada 1850–1950* (Waterloo, 1981), esp. chaps 7 and 8. More recent books have looked at Watson's influence on public educational policy: for example, B. Anne Wood, *Idealism Transformed: The Making of a Progressive Educator* (Kingston and Montreal, 1985); and Peter C. Emberley and Waller R. Newell, *Bankrupt Education: The Decline of Liberal Education in Canada* (Toronto, 1994). Finally, John Burbidge, in an essay that sketches the widespread influence of Hegelian thought in Canada, points out how, after encountering Watson's Idealist teachings at Queen's University, "Presbyterian clergy spread across the country preaching a vision of 'seeing life clearly and seeing it whole'" – offering ideas that, as Burbidge remarks, "molded several generations of Protestant thought, and contributed to the intellectual foundations of the United Church of Canada." See Burbidge, "Hegel in Canada," *Owl of Minerva* 25, no. 2 (1994): 216.

12 McKillop, *A Disciplined Intelligence*, 196, and Bruce Elder, *Image and Identity: Reflections on Canadian Film and Culture* (Waterloo, Ont., 1989), 63–72. Elder offers a concise summary of Watson's "distinctive Canadianness" (64) as a philosopher.

13 Elizabeth Trott, "Experience and the Absolute" (PhD diss., University of Waterloo, 1971), esp. chap. 12; and Williams, "The Epistemology of John Watson," 46. Williams writes that "the ultimate interest Watson has in philosophy is the support it may offer to theology and to a justification of religious belief."

14 Carl Berger, *The Sense of Power: Studies in the Ideas of Canadian Imperialism, 1867–1914* (Toronto, 1970), 259–65. Berger's book remains the single most comprehensive study of the imperialist ideas of Canadian conservatives.

15 Stephen Leacock, "Greater Canada: An Appeal," *University Magazine* 6, no. 1 (1907): 132–41. As late as 1941, Leacock argued that Canada "must be reorganized as the central buttress of imperial power. Wedged, as it were, between Great Britain and the United States, our Dominion becomes the keystone of a new arch of mutual support and common security." See Leacock, *Canada: The Foundations of Its Future* (Montreal: privately printed, 1941), 244. Quoted by James Steele, "Imperial Cosmopolitanism, or the Partly Solved Riddle of Leacock's Multi-National Persona," in *Stephen Leacock: A Reappraisal*, ed. David

Staines (Ottawa: University of Ottawa Press, 1986), 59–68. Interestingly, Leacock's views about Canada's role in the world are very similar to those held by
George Grant in the late 1940s, as I shall discuss in Part 3 of this essay.

16 Carl Berger, *Imperialism and Nationalism, 1884–1914: A Conflict in Canadian
Thought* (Toronto, 1969), 2.

17 Even today there are those who argue that Britain's domination of the world
did not produce an evil empire. Lord Max Beloff argues that on the whole the
British Empire was a force for good in the world: "There's no question in my
mind that Britain, through its colonial administration, brought quite a lot of
benefit to people around the world. There is little doubt that the positive out-
weighed the negative" (quoted in "Three Cheers for the Empire," *Ottawa Citizen*, 29 June 1997, A1). Beloff's argument is presented at greater length in
History Today 46, no. 2 (1996): 13–21. See also Beloff, *Britain's Liberal Empire,
1897–1921*, 2nd ed. (London: Macmillan, 1987). More recently, Deepak Lal
has argued that "[e]mpires have unfairly gotten a bad name." See Lal, *In Defense
of Empires* (Washington, D.C., 2004), 37.

18 Berger, *The Sense of Power*, 217.

19 Donald Creighton, *Canada's First Century* (Toronto, 1970), 91–2.

20 Berger, *The Sense of Power*, 120.

21 James Cappon, "Canada's Relation to the Empire," *Queen's Quarterly* 19, no. 2
(1911): 98. Cappon held the chair of English and was dean of arts during his
long career at Queen's University between 1888 and his retirement in 1919.

22 Arnold Haultain, "A Search for an Ideal," *Canadian Magazine* 22, no. 5 (1904):
427–8. Cited in S.E.D. Shortt, *The Search for an Ideal: Six Canadian Intellectuals
and Their Convictions in an Age of Transition, 1880–1930* (Toronto, 1976), 1.

23 Shortt, *The Search for an Ideal*, 3. Behind the sense of crisis during this "age of
transition" was the destabilizing influence of new ideas. The theories of Darwinian science, the spread of commercialism and social atomization, the philosophical claims of empiricism, and the increasing scepticism toward the
Christian metaphysical claim – all these new modes of thought undermined old
traditions, old certainties, old authorities. Canadians, the intellectuals argued,
were losing their way spiritually and psychologically. Shortt sums up the situation succinctly: "In the quarter century preceding the Great War Canadian intellectuals confronted what they termed a 'Social Crisis.' In common with many
of their articulate contemporaries, they believed that accelerated social change
had swept aside familiar institutions yet left nothing in their place" (137).

24 McKillop, *A Disciplined Intelligence*, 229.

25 Wood, *Idealism Transformed*, xi.

26 Cited in Berger, *The Sense of Power*, 244.

27 John Watson, *The State in Peace and War* (Glasgow, 1919), 271–2. Hereafter
referred to as *State*.

28 Cappon remarked that Watson was "profoundly influenced by the ideas of
   Hegel." See Cappon, "A School of Idealism," in *Philosophical Essays Presented to
   John Watson* (Kingston, 1922), 1. John Irving also points out that shortly after
   his arrival at Queen's University in 1872 Watson "identified himself with the
   St. Louis Hegelians" and was soon contributing to their *Journal of Speculative
   Philosophy*. See Irving, "The Development of Philosophy in Central Canada from
   1850 to 1900," *Canadian Historical Review* 31, no. 3 (1950), 273. See also
   Armour and Trott, *The Faces of Reason*, 291: "Watson's entire metaphysics was,
   throughout his life, determined in part by his interest in Kant and Hegel, especially his interest in Hegel."

29 Clifford J. Williams, "The Political Philosophy of Two Canadians: John Watson
   and Wilfred Currier Keirstead" (MA thesis, University of Western Ontario,
   1952), 1.

30 See, for example, Armour and Trott, *The Faces of Reason*, 233–4.

31 Watson, *State*, 2–3.

32 On this point, see McKillop, *A Disciplined Intelligence*, 229; and Berger, *The Sense
   of Power*, 264. Others who address this issue include Douglas Owram, *The Government Generation: Canadian Intellectuals and the State, 1900–1945* (Toronto, 1991);
   and Barry Ferguson, *Remaking Liberalism: The Intellectual Legacy of Adam Shortt,
   O.D. Skelton, W.C. Clark and W.A. Mackintosh, 1890–1925* (Montreal and Kingston, 1993).

33 Stefan Collini, "Hobhouse, Bosanquet and the State: Philosophical Idealism
   and Political Argument in England, 1880–1918," *Past and Present* 88, no. 72
   (1976): 86; and Sandra den Otter, *British Idealism and Social Explanation: A Study
   in Late Victorian Thought* (Oxford, 1996), 209–13.

34 L.T. Hobhouse, *The Metaphysical Theory of the State* (London, 1918), 6, 18.
   Michael Freeden points out that regardless of whether Hobhouse's view of Idealism was valid, his book was "the most considered, critical and influential examination of Hegelianism to emerge out of the war." See Freeden's *Liberalism
   Divided: A Study in British Political Thought, 1914–1939* (Oxford, 1986), 33.

35 Watson, *State*, 129–30.

36 Karl Popper, *The Open Society and Its Enemies*, vol. 2, 5th ed. (1945; reprint,
   London, 1966), 78.

37 Michael Inwood, *A Hegel Dictionary* (Oxford, 1992), 283–5. As Inwood explains,
   Hegel uses the infinitive *Aufheben*, to sublate, in three main senses that often
   function at the same time, (1) to raise, hold, or lift up; (2) to annul, abolish,
   destroy, or suspend; and (3) to keep, save, or preserve. Hegel also uses other
   words in referring to this notion of sublation, including the noun *Aufhebung*,
   which simultaneously refers to raising up, abolition, and preservation; and
   Aufgehoben, when something is sublated. On this point, see Charles Taylor, *Hegel*

(Cambridge, 1975), 119. Taylor notes that Hegel uses both terms, *Aufheben* and *Aufhebung*, to refer to "the dialectical transition in which a lower stage is both annulled and preserved in a higher one," although *Aufheben* can carry either meaning.

38 Armour and Trott discuss Watson's historical method more thoroughly; see their *The Faces of Reason*, 235–6. See also Frederick Hoffner, "The Moral State in 1919: A Study of John Watson's Idealism and Communitarian Liberalism As Expressed in *The State in Peace and War*" (MA thesis, Queen's University, 1998), 11. I should like to acknowledge my debt to Hoffner's excellent study. I learned a great deal from it and was able to use it to the benefit of this essay.

39 Armour and Trott, *The Faces of Reason*, 234.

40 Watson, *State*, 2–3.

41 Ibid., 10.

42 Ibid., 8–9.

43 Watson, *An Outline of Philosophy*, 2nd ed. (Glasgow, 1898), 232. Hereafter referred to as *Outline*. A first edition was published in 1895 under the title *Comte, Mill and Spencer: An Outline of Philosophy*.

44 McKillop, *A Disciplined Intelligence*, 199. McKillop refers to this passage as "the most revealing and suggestive statement made by a Canadian philosopher in the nineteenth century." He concludes that much of the social philosophy in English Canada in the twentieth century reflected Watson's "moral imperative."

45 Watson, *Outline*, 232.

46 Watson, *State*, viii.

47 Ibid., 120.

48 I am indebted to Hoffner for this idea. See his "The Moral State in 1919," 12–13.

49 Watson, *State*, 1–3. I should like to point out that even in referring to the pre-modern world, Watson uses modern terms such as *individual* when in fact he should be using a pre-modern term like *citizen* when he refers to classical Greece or *subject* when he refers to the medieval period. Strictly speaking, the concept of individual, like that of state, can properly be used only with the arrival of modernity. In this regard, I have retained Watson's terminology when it is used in a direct quotation. Otherwise, for the sake of philosophic consistency, I have substituted words such as *individual* for *citizen* and *state* for *polis* where appropriate.

50 Bernard Bosanquet, *The Philosophical Theory of the State*, 3rd ed. (London, 1920), 50–2. Hoffner, in "The Moral State in 1919" (12), makes this point, too.

51 Watson, *State*, 46.

52 Ibid., 17.

53 Ibid., 4, 47–8.

54 Ibid., 121–2. Hoffner, in "The Moral State in 1919," 14–15, points out that Watson links the ancient sophists and cynics to modern contractarians.

55 Ibid., 48. I refer the reader to note 49 regarding my "correction" of Watson's terminology. Watson uses modern words such as *individual, society,* and *state* when he should be using words such as *citizen, community,* and *polis* in discussing Plato's thought. Plato, after all, was a pre-modern and did not possess the modern historical sense, and therefore could not have conceived of an individual in the sense that we use the word. Thus, where he refers to Plato and Aristotle, Watson should be saying that the freedom of the citizen was shown to be compatible with the authority of the community. Obviously, I cannot repeatedly correct Watson's vocabulary and therefore suggest that readers provide their own substitutions where necessary.

56 For this point, I must thank an academic colleague, Michael Reid, who provided me with a copy of his unpublished 1993 essay "John Watson and Liberal Education." I have benefited from his work.

57 Watson, *State,* 30–2.

58 Ibid., 32.

59 Ibid., 28–9.

60 Ibid., 169–75. Watson's comment on Nietzsche is worth quoting: "The aggressive and ambitious spirit which since 1870 has characterised the German people has been intensified by the writings of Nietzsche. In his later years, it is true, he spoke of nationalism with contempt, advocating a united Europe, and calling for men of rigid austerity and self-discipline; but his worship of power has been eagerly caught up by the new Germany which came to self-consciousness after 1870."

61 Ibid., 167, 172.

62 Ibid., 31.

63 Ibid., 30.

64 Ibid., 47.

65 Ibid., 21.

66 Ibid., 33.

67 Ibid., 48–50.

68 Ibid., vii–viii.

69 Ibid., 54.

70 Ibid., 57.

71 Hegel, *Phenomenology,* #199, 121. Stoicism, says Hegel, "is the freedom which always comes directly out of bondage and returns into the pure universality of thought. As a universal form of the World-Spirit, Stoicism could only appear on the scene in a time of universal fear and bondage, but also a time of universal culture which had raised itself to the level of thought."

72 Watson, *State*, 51.

73 On this point, see Hegel, *Early Theological Writings*, trans. T.M. Knox, with an introduction by R. Kroner (Chicago, 1976), 156–7. It is again worth quoting Hegel to show the close parallel with Watson's thought: "The picture of the State as a product of his own energies disappeared from the citizen's soul [during the Roman Empire]. The care and oversight of the whole rested on the soul of one man or a few … All activity and every purpose now had a bearing on something individual; activity was no longer for the sake of a whole or an ideal … Death, the phenomenon which demolished the whole structure of his purposes and the activity of his entire life, must have become something terrifying, since nothing survived him. But the republican's whole soul was in the republic; the republic survived him, and there hovered before his mind the thought of its immortality."

74 Watson, *State*, 61–3.

75 Ibid., 67.

76 Ibid., 68–9.

77 Hegel, *The Philosophy of History*, trans. J. Sibree, with an introduction by C.J. Friedrich (New York, 1956), 398–400.

78 Watson, *State*, 69.

79 Ibid., 72.

80 Ibid., 73.

81 Ibid., 79. I am indebted to Reid's essay, "John Watson and Liberal Education," for this idea, as well as for that referenced by note 82.

82 Watson, *State*, 81–2.

83 Ibid., 87.

84 Ibid.

85 Ibid., 160.

86 Ibid., 91.

87 Ibid., 99.

88 Ibid., 106. I am indebted to Reid for my comments on Rousseau.

89 Watson, "German Philosophy and Politics," *Queen's Quarterly* 22, no. 4 (1915): 335. My thanks to Michael Reid for drawing this essay to my attention.

90 Watson, *State*, 107.

91 Ibid., 109.

92 Ibid., 105. Hoffner addresses this point in "The Moral State in 1919" (18).

93 Watson, *State*, 118.

94 Ibid., 120.

95 Ibid., 119.

96 Ibid., 124.

97 Watson, "The Problem of Hegel," *Philosophical Review* 3, no. 5 (1894): 549.

98 Watson, *State*, 121–4, 127–9.

99 Ibid., 129.

100 Watson, "German Philosophy and Politics," 341.

101 Watson, *State*, 192. Hoffner notes in "The Moral State in 1919" (48) that Hegel regards the state "as a part of a Kingdom of God. This larger identity imposed moral laws on the conduct of states and therefore provided a check against egoism."

102 Watson, *State*, 195–6.

103 Ibid., 222.

104 Leslie Armour, *The Idea of Canada and the Crisis of Community* (Ottawa, 1981), 84.

105 Hoffner, "The Moral State in 1919," 70–1, 124.

106 Watson, *State*, 122.

107 Watson, *Outline*, 229.

108 Watson, *State*, 222.

109 Ibid., 229.

110 Ibid., 229–30.

111 Ibid., 195.

112 Ibid., 222.

113 Ibid., 160.

114 Watson, *Hedonistic Theories: From Aristippus to Spencer* (Glasgow, 1895), 12.

115 Watson, *State*, 193.

116 Besides his critique of these three in *State*, Watson also examines what he considers to be their influence on German militarism in "German Philosophy and Politics," *Queen's Quarterly* 22 (April–June 1915): 329–44; and "German Philosophy and the War," *Queen's Quarterly* 23 (April–June 1916): 365–79. The basic arguments of these articles are contained in chapter 8 of *The State in Peace and War.*

117 Watson, *State*, 167–8.

118 Ibid., 171.

119 Ibid., 120.

120 Armour, *The Idea of Canada*, 89.

121 Watson, *State*, 196–7. See also Hoffner, "The Moral State in 1919," 60.

122 Watson, *State*, 197. Williams's thesis, "The Political Philosophy of Two Canadians" (14–22), offers a detailed look at Watson's distinction between state and government.

123 Harold Laski, *Studies in the Problem of Sovereignty* (New Haven, 1917), 1, 8, 270. Hoffner's "The Moral State in 1919" (50–1) provides a succinct comparison of Watson and Laski from which I have drawn for my argument. He notes, for instance, that for Watson "Laski's concern that idealism bred monism confused idealist conceptions of sovereignty with absolutism."

124 Watson, *State*, 200–3.

125 Ibid., 208.

126 Ibid., 207. See also Hoffner, "The Moral State in 1919," 59.

127 Hoffner, "The Moral State in 1919," 50–2, 60.

128 The quotation is from T.H. Green, *Principles of Political Obligation*, cited in Bosanquet, *The Philosophical Theory of the State*, 268.

129 Ibid.

130 Ibid., 273.

131 Ibid., 140.

132 Armour and Trott, *The Faces of Reason*, 236.

133 Sandra den Otter places Watson among the second-generation Idealists, such as Bernard Bosanquet, who extend the arguments of first-generation Idealists like T.H. Green and F.H. Bradley. In their political philosophy, she says, all the Idealists stress to one degree or another the importance of the community for individual freedom and identity, the moral role of the state, and various ideas regarding self-development. See den Otter, *British Idealism and Social Explanation*, 6–7.

134 Watson, *State*, 109–11. Watson makes the point that an individual's will in any given situation is not necessarily identical to the will he would have if he truly knew his real nature. Such a claim implies that acting according to the rational will is tied to Watson's epistemological theories and the notion that education should be devoted to the development of an individual's essential rational nature.

135 Ibid., 232. The only situation where Watson seems to grant the state absolute authority, including the right to restrict individual freedom and require the forfeiture of that life, is in a time of war. This is justified, Watson says, because if the state is extinguished, the conditions necessary for the exercise of freedom are lost.

136 Den Otter, *British Idealism and Social Explanation*, 198–9. Den Otter observes that "a recurring criticism of Idealist social philosophy has been that the Idealists dangerously misjudge conflict, discord, and disharmony within modern society." Hobhouse, for example, in *The Metaphysical Theory of the State*, attacks Idealism for not paying sufficient attention to the state's coercive capacities.

137 Watson, *State*, 209. The critique to which Watson refers is in Deslisle Burns, Bertrand Russell, and G.D.H. Cole, "Symposium: The Nature of the *State* in View of Its External Relations," *Proceedings of the Aristotelian Society*, new series, vol. 16, 36th session, 1915–1916. I am indebted to Hoffner for this reference, and his discussion of the topic. See "The Moral State in 1919," 52–5.

138 Watson, *State*, 210.

139 Ibid., 205–10. See also Hoffner, "The Moral State in 1919," 61–2.

140 I have drawn on various scholars for my brief commentary on Bosanquet's
    thought, particularly John Morrow, "British Idealism, German Philosophy and
    the First World War," *Australian Journal of Politics and History* 28, no. 3 (1982):
    380–99; John Morrow, "Liberalism and British Idealist Political Philosophy:
    A Reassessment," *History of Political Thought* 5, no. 1 (1984): 91–108; Peter
    Nicholson, *The Political Philosophy of the British Idealists* (Cambridge, 1990);
    Andrew Vincent and Raymond Plant, *Philosophy, Politics and Citizenship: The Life
    and Thought of the British Idealists* (Oxford, 1984); as well as the previously cited
    material from Stefan Collini, "Hobhouse, Bosanquet and the State," 86–111;
    and den Otter, *British Idealism and Social Explanation*, 98–101.

141 Elizabeth Trott, "Caird, Watson and the Reconciliation of Opposites," in *Anglo-
    American Idealism, 1865–1927*, ed. W.J. Mander (Westport, Conn., 2000), 85.

142 Edward Caird, "The Present State of the Controversy between Individualism
    and Socialism," in *The British Idealists*, ed. Boucher, 185. See also Trott, "Caird
    Watson, and the Reconciliation of Opposites," 83–92.

143 Caird, "Individualism and Socialism," 186.

144 Watson, "The Idealism of Edward Caird," parts 1 and 2, *Philosophical Review* 18,
    nos 2 and 3 (1909): 147–63, 259–80.

145 Ibid., part 1, 159.

146 Ibid., 157.

147 Watson, *State*, 213.

148 Bosanquet, *The Philosophical Theory of the State*, 302. Hoffner addresses this issue
    in "The Moral State in 1919," 63–4.

149 Bosanquet, *The Philosophical Theory of the State*, 304–5.

150 Ibid., 140. See also Nicholson, *The Political Philosophy of the British Idealists*, 219–
    22. He makes the point that Bosanquet never denied that the state was above
    moral criticism, although other theorists thought otherwise.

151 Bosanquet, *The Philosophical Theory of the State*, 141.

152 Watson, *State*, 217–18.

153 Bosanquet, *Philosophical Theory of the State*, 299–301. It is worth quoting
    Bosanquet fully on this point: "The question is complicated by the fact that a
    State has, as its accredited agents, individuals whose acts it must normally
    avow. But it can hardly be saddled with moral responsibility for their per-
    sonal misdoings, except under circumstances which are barely conceivable.
    The State, as such, can have no ends but public ends; and in practice it has
    none but what its organs conceive to be public ends. If an agent, even under
    the order of his executive superior, commits a breach of morality, *bona fide* in
    order to [accomplish] what he conceives to be a public end desired by the
    State, he and his superior are certainly blamable, but the immorality can
    hardly be laid at the door of the public will."

154 Hoffner, "The Moral State in 1919," 65.

155 Watson, *State*, 217.

156 Ibid., 219.

157 Ibid., 219–20.

158 Hoffner, "The Moral State in 1919," 64–5; and den Otter, *British Idealism and Social Explanation*, 175–6. Den Otter observes that many of Bosanquet's contemporaries thought he "did not allow the individual sufficient rights against the state, and that he had placed the state above the morality which constrained individuals."

159 Bosanquet, *The Philosophical Theory of the State*, 142.

160 Armour and Trott, *The Faces of Reason*, 224. See also den Otter, *British Idealism and Social Explanation*, 159. She points out that one of the criticisms levelled against Bosanquet by other social theorists was that his notion of the individual went too far down the path, as one critic put it, of "absorbing and transmuting finite selves" into the state.

161 David Watson, "The Neo-Hegelian Tradition in America," *Journal of American Studies* 14, no. 2 (1980): 220; James A. Good, "'A World-Historical Idea': The St. Louis Hegelians and the Civil War," *Journal of American Studies* 34, no. 3 (2000): 447–64; Henry Pochmann, *New England Transcendentalism and St. Louis Hegelianism* (Philadelphia, 1948), 13–15; and Richard Bernstein, "Why Hegel Now?" *Review of Metaphysics* 31, no. 1 (1977): 29–60. This last essay offers a useful overview of Hegel's influence on American philosophy.

162 William H. Goetzmann, ed., *The American Hegelians: An Intellectual Episode in the History of Western America* (New York, 1973), 15–16. Goetzmann's introductory essay remains the single best summary of Hegel's influence in the United States of which I am aware. Other studies I have drawn upon include Lloyd Easton, *Hegel's First American Followers: The Ohio Hegelians* (Athens, Ohio, 1966); G.A. Kelly, "Hegel's America," *Philosophy and Public Affairs* 2, no. 1 (1972): 3–36; and John E. Smith, "Hegel in St. Louis," in *Hegel's Social and Political Thought*, ed. Donald Phillip Verene (New Jersey, 1980), 215–26.

163 Easton, *Hegel's First American Followers*, 223.

164 I have restricted my discussion of Royce to those aspects of his thought that directly relate to Watson's political concerns. Given this limitation, I have confined myself to Royce's moral philosophy as presented in his 1908 book *The Philosophy of Loyalty* (New York: Macmillan Co., 1908). I have also drawn on only a small portion of the secondary literature, including John Clendenning, *The Life and Thought of Josiah Royce*, rev. ed. (Nashville, Tenn., 1999); Bruce Kuklick, *Josiah Royce: An Intellectual Biography* (New York, 1972); Peter Fuss, *The Moral Philosophy of Josiah Royce* (Cambridge, Mass., 1965); and John Herman Randall, "Josiah Royce and American Idealism," *Journal of Philosophy* 63, no. 3 (1966): 55–83.

165 McKillop, *Contours of Canadian Thought*, 99; and Leslie Armour, "Canadian Ways of Thinking: Logic, Society, and Canadian Philosophy," in *Alternative Frontiers: Voices from the Mountain West*, ed. Allen Seager, Leonard Evenden, Rowland Lorimer, and Robin Mathews (Montreal, 1997), 11–34. Armour notes that at least one American philosopher, George Holmes Howison, supported Watson "in a campaign against ... the choking absolutism of Josiah Royce." It was Howison, says Armour, who set up the Philosophical Union's debate between Watson and Royce.

166 Royce, *The Philosophy of Loyalty*, 3–6.

167 Clendenning, *The Life and Thought of Josiah Royce*, 299.

168 Royce, *The Philosophy of Loyalty*, 9, 44–5. See also on this point Goetzman's introductory essay in *The American Hegelians*, 15.

169 Armour, "Canadian Ways of Thinking," 17.

170 Clendenning, *The Life and Thought of Josiah Royce*, 299; and R. Jackson Wilson, *In Quest of Community: Social Philosophy in the United States, 1860–1920* (New York, 1968), 163–5. Wilson writes that "Royce was most frightened by what he called, in Hegelian language, the 'self-estranged social mind.'"

171 Watson, *State*, 28–30.

172 Royce, *The Philosophy of Loyalty*, 111.

173 Ibid., 254.

174 Fuss, *The Moral Philosophy of Josiah Royce*, 215–16.

175 Royce, *The Philosophy of Loyalty*, 180–1.

176 Fuss, *The Moral Philosophy of Josiah Royce*, 221.

177 Ibid., 222–5.

178 Ibid., 226–8.

179 Watson, *Outline of Philosophy*, 257.

180 Ibid., 211–12.

181 Armour, "Canadian Ways of Thinking," 20.

182 Ibid., 21. See also Trott, "Caird, Watson and the Reconciliation of Opposites," 86. Trott suggests that there is something distinctly Canadian about this, that Watson's desire for reconciliation is rooted in the geographical, political, and cultural realities of his adopted country: "The need to reconcile opposites inspired Watson's agenda as he settled in a country that was not the product of history, tradition, and great minds. Canada, in Watson's time, was just coming into existence as a political entity, and he was not unaware of the need for, and possibility of, new orders."

183 Watson, *State*, 248–9.

184 Ibid., 171–2. Watson cites Hegel in his attack on those theorists such as Treitschke who he says instilled in the minds of young Germans the idea that their longing for unity could be satisfied by completely identifying with the German state. What the theorists forgot, as I noted earlier, was Hegel's

distinction between will and force. Interestingly, Bosanquet says much the same in *The Philosophical Theory of the State*, 274. "What makes and maintains States as States is will and not force, the idea of a common good, and not greed or ambition."

185 Watson, *State*, 249.
186 Ibid., 55.
187 Watson, *Outline of Philosophy*, 227–8.
188 Ibid., 227.
189 Ibid., 228. In Hegelian terms, the "savage" perceives the concept of freedom embodied in the coloniser.
190 Consider this statement from the *Phenomenology*, #194, 117: "In that experience it [the slave's consciousness] has been quite unmanned, has trembled in every fiber of its being, and everything solid and stable has been shaken to its foundation."
191 Watson, *State*, 274.
192 David Boucher, ed., introduction to *The British Idealists*, xxx. Boucher observes that the British Idealists generally agreed that the "only justification for intervention in the affairs of the inferior races was to rule in their interests and, in so far as they have a capacity for participating in the good life, all forms of subjugation were prohibited. The only justification for imperialism, if indeed, it could be justified at all, was the fundamental principle that the superior people saw as its solemn duty to elevate the lower to its own level."
193 Boucher, "British Idealism, the State, and International Relations," *Journal of the History of Ideas* 55 (1994): 682. See also Williams, "The Political Philosophy of Two Canadians," 53–4.
194 Edward Caird, "The Nation As an Ethical Ideal," in *Lay Sermons Delivered in Balliol College* (Glasgow, 1907), quoted in Boucher, "British Idealism, the State, and International Relations," 683.
195 Watson, *State*, 272.
196 Ibid., 248.
197 Ibid., 261.
198 Ibid., 274–5; and Williams, "The Political Philosophy of Two Canadians," 59–60.
199 Watson, *State*, 275.
200 Ibid., 219–21. Also, Hoffner, "The Moral State in 1919," 65.
201 Ibid., 270; and Hoffner, "The Moral State in 1919," 66.
202 Watson, *State*, 222. Watson summarises his understanding of human rights this way: "A man has rights which are recognised by society, but they are not made right by legislation, as Bentham held, but are recognised because they are essential to the development of the common good. The possession of rights and their recognition by society are not two different things, but the organ of the

common good, so the State recognises his rights on the ground that they are required for the realisation of the highest good of all."

203 Ibid., 272–3.

204 Ibid., 273.

205 Ibid., 220–1. See also Williams, "The Political Philosophy of Two Canadians," 57–9.

206 Watson, *State*, 273.

207 Ibid., 2. On this argument, see also Doug Owram's assessment of the influence of Watson's thought on the development of Canadian social institutions in his *The Government Generation*, 90–3. This topic is also addressed in Hoffner, "The Moral State in 1919," 68–70; and Williams, "The Political Philosophy of Two Canadians," 48–51.

208 Watson, "Education and Life. An Address" (Kingston, 1873), quoted in McKillop, *A Disciplined Intelligence*, 199–200.

PART THREE

1 See, for example, Mel Hurtig, "One Last Chance: The Legacy of *Lament for a Nation*," in *By Loving Our Own: George Grant and the Legacy of* Lament for a Nation, ed. Peter Emberley (Ottawa, 1990), 44.

2 George Grant, *Lament for a Nation: The Defeat of Canadian Nationalism* (1965; reprint, Ottawa, 1989), 68; and introduction to the Carleton Library Edition, viii–ix. Hereafter referred to as *Lament*.

3 Clifford Orwin, "Review of Grant's English-Speaking Justice," *University of Toronto Law Journal* 30 (1980): 106.

4 Larry Schmidt, "An Interview with George Grant," *Grail*, no. 1 (March, 1985): 36, cited in William Christian, "George Grant's Lament," *Queen's Quarterly* 100, no. 1 (1993): 211.

5 Grant, *Lament*, 53.

6 George Grant, "Appendix 2, Introduction to the 1966 edition," in *Philosophy in the Mass Age*, ed. William Christian (1959; reprint, Toronto, 1995), 120.

7 Frank Flinn, "George Parkin Grant: A Bibliographical Introduction," in *George Grant in Process*, ed. Larry Schmitt (Toronto, 1978), 197.

8 Grant, "Appendix 2, Introduction to the 1966 edition," in *Philosophy in the Mass Age*, 121–2.

9 Ibid., 120.

10 George Grant, *Technology and Empire* (Toronto, 1969), 104.

11 Arthur Kroker, *Technology and the Canadian Mind* (Montreal, 1984), 51.

12 Abraham Rotstein, "Running from Paradise," *Canadian Forum*, (May, 1969), 26.

13 Larry Schmidt, for example, remarks that despite Grant's acute analysis of historicism, the reader is left asking, "What is a suitable conception of history? Grant does not give us an answer" (Schmidt, "George Grant and the Problem of History," in *George Grant in Process* [Toronto, 1978], 136). Likewise, Ian Box says of Grant that "no constructive alternatives to our present disorder are put forward for consideration" (Box, "George Grant and the Embrace of Technology," *Canadian Journal of Political Science* 15, no. 3 [1982], 504). Larry Lampert states that "in the face of Grant's analysis and hopes one cannot escape a sense of dissatisfaction … What does he stand for? What is his program?" Grant's writings "lack a direct statement of those positive teachings which he alludes to as his own means of survival, and which may seem to be presupposed as the ground of his critique of the modern. Grant gives only the most fragmentary intimations of their content" (Lampert, "The Uses of Philosophy in Grant," in *George Grant in Process*, ed. Schmidt, 190–2).

14 Grant, *Technology and Empire*, 44.

15 Quoted in Charles Taylor, *Radical Tories* (Toronto, 1982), 132. I should perhaps note that the author is Charles Taylor the Canadian journalist, not the philosopher.

16 Dennis Lee, "Grant's Impasse," in *By Loving Our Own*, ed. Emberley, 19.

17 Hegel, *Philosophy of Right* (Oxford, 1942), #260–1, 160–2. Stephen Houlgate observes that Hegel thought that all states need "to maintain an awareness of their own history in order to know what they are and what their deepest aspirations and most valuable endeavours have been." See Houlgate, "World History as Progress of Consciousness: An Interpretation of Hegel's Philosophy of History," *Owl of Minerva* 22, no. 1 (1990): 73.

18 Grant, *Lament*, 68.

19 Ibid., 70.

20 Grant, *Technology and Empire*, 72.

21 Ibid., 73. See also, in the same book, the essay "In Defence of North America," 36.

22 Ibid., 68–9.

23 Ibid., 69.

24 Ian Angus, *A Border Within: National Identity, Cultural Plurality and Wilderness* (Montreal and Kingston, 1997), 78.

25 Grant, *Lament*, 25. In an interview on CBC's *This Country in the Morning* on 10 October 1973, Grant described writing *Lament* after the fall of the Diefenbaker government, saying, "[M]y motive for writing that book was rage, just rage, that they'd brought atomic weapons into Canada." However, in an interview with CBC on 27 June 1965, Grant insisted that his book was "not a defence of Mr. Diefenbaker" and that before the defence crisis he "saw nothing in his favour, just nothing" (Christian, "George Grant's Lament," 205, 207–8).

328 Notes to pages 117–20

26 Peter Emberley, in his introduction to the 1995 Carleton Library edition of *Lament*, writes, "The face of Canada was a microcosm of the confrontation of all peoples with the powerfully transforming forces of the West" (19).

27 Grant, introduction to *Lament* (1989), ix.

28 See William Christian, *George Grant: A Biography* (Toronto, 1993), for a portrait of Grant's intellectual heritage and the influence, direct and indirect, of John Watson on Grant. See also Christian's essay, "Canada's Fate: Principal Grant, Sir George Parkin and George Grant," *Journal of Canadian Studies* 34, no. 4 (Winter 1999/2000): 88–104.

29 Grant, *Lament*, 94. Grant writes: "Those who criticize our age must at the same time contemplate pain, infant mortality, crop failures in isolated areas, and the sixteen-hour day."

30 Hegel, *Philosophy of Right*, #260, 160.

31 Grant, *Lament*, 68. Or, as Grant writes elsewhere in the book, "[m]emory is never enough to guarantee that a nation can articulate itself in the present. There must be a thrust of intention into the future" (12).

32 H.D. Forbes, "The Political Thought of George Grant," *Journal of Canadian Studies* 26, no. 2 (1991): 47. See also Barry Cooper, "A Imperio usque ad Imperium: The Political Thought of George Grant," in *George Grant in Process*, ed. Schmidt, 23–39.

33 Grant, *Lament*, 21.

34 Ibid., 3. Anthony Parel, commenting on Grant's focus on the French-English relationship, remarks how, for Grant, "the principle of Canadian nationalism is the duality and equality of the English and French, and not the concept of the conquest" (A.J. Parel, "Multiculturalism and the Future of Canada," in *George Grant and the Future of Canada,* ed. Yusuf Umar [Calgary, 1992], 143).

35 Grant, "Have We a Canadian Nation?" *Public Affairs* (Institute of Public Affairs, Dalhousie University) 8, no. 3 (1945): 161–6. Hereafter referred to as "Canadian Nation."

36 Grant, *The Empire, Yes or No?* (Toronto, 1945). Hereafter referred to as *Empire*.

37 Grant, "Canadian Nation," 162, 165.

38 Ibid., 162.

39 Ibid., 164–6.

40 Ibid., 163.

41 I have found no indication in the literature, including Grant's notebooks, that Grant had read Hegel before 1945. In his biography of Grant, William Christian seems to suggest that Grant did not study Hegel seriously until he joined the Hegelian scholar James Doull at Dalhousie University in September of 1947, although he knew Doull at Oxford at late 1945. See Christian, *George Grant*, 130.

42 Hegel, *Philosophy of Right*, #260, 160.

43 Grant, "Canadian Nation," 166.

44 For background on the intellectual links between Grant and his forefathers
I refer the reader to William Christian's biography and his previously cited
essay, "Canada's Fate."

45 Brian McKillop, "The Idealist Legacy," in *Contours of Canadian Thought*
(Toronto, 1987), 104.

46 Christian, *George Grant*, 38.

47 McKillop, "The Idealist Legacy," 104. He writes that "'the Queen's spirit' of the
1890s, led by the contemplative Watson and the active Grant, inspired numerous individuals to engage in different forms of social service and to strive in
their secular pursuits to bring about the Kingdom of God on Earth." See also
Leslie Armour and Elizabeth Trott, *The Faces of Reason*, 392. They observe that a
generation after men such as Watson and Wilfrid Keirstead, "a Platonized
Hegelianism is to be found in the writings of George Grant."

48 David Cayley, *George Grant in Conversation* (Toronto, 1995), 46. In a previous interview with Cayley in 1986, Grant, in an obviously heartfelt comment, describes himself as having grown up in "the great sane liberalism" and how his
experiences of the Second World War "just broke that for me" (Cayley, CBC
transcript of an interview with George Grant, "The Moving Image of Eternity,"
Ideas [Toronto, 1986], 4).

49 McKillop, "The Idealist Legacy," 96–110. McKillop suggests that Grant's intellectual heritage can, in part, be traced to his years studying history at Queen's
University, where, as I have previously noted, John Watson's Hegelian Idealism
had such influence.

50 Grant, *Empire*, 9.

51 Ibid., 7.

52 Ibid., 17.

53 Ibid., 31.

54 George Grant, *Selected Letters*, ed. William Christian (Toronto, 1996), 114.

55 Grant, *Lament*, 50.

56 Ibid., 34.

57 Grant, *English-Speaking Justice* (Notre Dame, 1985), 3. Grant writes: "Over the
last centuries, the most influential people in the English-speaking world have
generally taken as their dominant form of self-definition a sustaining faith in a
necessary interdependence between the developments of technological science
and political liberalism." The book was originally published in 1974.

58 Angus, *A Border Within*, 33. Angus observes that Grant saw concrete political
events in symbolic terms: they were not isolated events meaningful only unto
themselves, but rather were condensed signifiers of a significance beyond

themselves, reflecting "the meaning of larger turning points in the way of life of
a people." I would also suggest that, given Grant's Christian faith, he saw
worldly events as partaking of the eternal connection between the city of God
and the city of Man. As Joan O'Donovan comments, "Grant as a thinker (and
not as a man of faith) is impaled on the point of this question concerning the
anchoring of politics or history in eternity." See O'Donovan, "The Battleground
of Liberalism: Politics of Eternity and Politics of Time," *Chesterton Review* 11, no.
2 (1985): 132.

59 Joan O'Donovan, *George Grant and the Twilight of Justice* (Toronto, 1984), 10. She
describes these years as Grant's "Liberal-synthesizing phase," during which
Grant held out hope "for future reconciliation of 'history' and 'eternity'
[because of] his faith in the dialectical progression of reason in time."

60 William Christian, ed., introduction to *Time As History*, by George Grant (1969;
reprint, Toronto, 1995), xi.

61 Christian, introduction to *Philosophy in the Mass Age*, by Grant, xxii. By way of
contrast, H.D. Forbes argues that as strong as Grant's attraction to Hegel may
have been at one time, it ended with Grant's discovery of Leo Strauss's writings.
See Forbes, "George Grant and Leo Strauss," in *George Grant and the Subversion of
Modernity*, ed. Arthur Davis (Toronto, 1996), 190.

62 Cited by Christian, introduction to *Philosophy in the Mass Age*, by Grant, xxii.

63 Grant, *Philosophy in the Mass Age*, 120. I quoted this statement in note 9, but it
bears repeating given its importance to Grant.

64 Grant, *Technology and Empire*, 44.

65 Grant, *Philosophy in the Mass Age*, 3–4.

66 O'Donovan, *George Grant and the Twilight of Justice*, 5.

67 Grant, *Time As History*, 6–7.

68 Grant, *Technology and Empire*, 72.

69 Grant, *English-Speaking Justice*, 17.

70 George Grant, *Technology and Justice* (Toronto, 1986), 79–95.

71 Grant, *Time As History*, 8–10.

72 On this topic, I have greatly benefited from Harris Athanasiadis's study "George
Grant and the Theology of the Cross" (PhD dissertation, McGill University,
1997), which I read while researching my essay. Athanasiadis provides the most
comprehensive study of Grant's religious thought of which I am aware, and
I have relied on it in discussing the linkage between Grant's theology and his
political philosophy. The dissertation was published as a book, *George Grant and
the Theology of the Cross: The Christian Foundations of His Thought* (Toronto, 2001).
I have updated my references to correspond with the book.

73 Grant, *Philosophy in the Mass Age*, 19–21.

74 Grant, *Lament*, 89.

75 Ibid., 88–9.

76 Plato, *The Republic of Plato*, trans. Allan Bloom (New York, 1968), 327a, 376c–383a, 419a–427c. My thanks to Tom Darby for pointing out this aspect of the opening of Plato's *Republic*, although I do not recall whether it was in a conversation or a classroom lecture.

77 Peter Angeles, ed., *Dictionary of Philosophy* (New York, 1981), 292. The word *theology* comes from the Greek word *theos*, or God, and *legein*, meaning "to speak," "to gather together," or, more loosely, "the study of." Negative theology, or *via negativa*, asserts that God's nature cannot be known in any real sense. We can only speak about God or know anything about God by knowing – and speaking – what He is not. Grant's adoption of the *via negativa* was influenced by Simone Weil and should be understood in this light.

78 Grant's most extensive considerations of Protestantism occur in *Philosophy in the Mass Age*, 77–85, and *Technology and Empire*, 19–25.

79 Cayley, *George Grant in Conversation*, 34. Cayley writes: "Much of George Grant's writing followed what was called in theology the *via negativa*, the attempt to reveal what is good not by a positive statement but by the clearing away of obstacles and impostures." See also Christian, *George Grant*, 237. Christian suggests an esoteric purpose to Grant's *via negativa* in pointing out that negative theology "is positive in its effects because, if successful, it leads to the restoration of the possibility of direct contact with the divine." I discuss the esoteric dimension to Grant's writings more fully elsewhere. See Sibley, "The Poetics of Dispossession: A Tracking of George Grant's Speech-Act" (MA thesis, Carleton University, 1991), 100–30.

80 Grant, *Philosophy in the Mass Age*, 94. It is worth noting that Grant thought of himself as writing indirectly, seldom explicitly discussing his religious faith in terms of trying to assert its claims. He says he was forced into this position because the modern discourse gives little credence to serious religious matters. In a conversation with William Christian, Grant says: "I have written indirectly all my life for one reason and one reason alone: I think there has been – I don't think, I'm sure – in the last four centuries in the West, an intense and sustained attack on Christianity from within, and particularly by intellectual people … Therefore, I would see my work as a defence of two figures, Socrates and Christ, for different reasons. And therefore I have always written indirectly because I knew that the intellectual world or the world I inhabited was very hostile to both the figures I chiefly admired. That's why I have written indirectly." Quoted in Barry Cooper, "George Grant and the Revival of Political Philosophy," in *By Loving Our Own*, ed. Emberley, 114.

81 On this point see Edwin and David Heaven, "Some Influences of Simone Weil on George Grant's Silence," in *George Grant in Process*, ed. Schmidt, 68–78. They

argue that no interpretation of Grant's theological thinking can ignore Simone Weil's influence – a subject I shall address later in this essay. While the term *theology of the Cross* may be Martin Luther's, Grant's comprehension of the phrase echoes Weil's. Or so I shall argue.

82 Athanasiadis, *George Grant and the Theology of the Cross*, 4–6.

83 Grant, *Technology and Justice*, 76–77.

84 Quoted in O'Donovan, *George Grant and the Twilight of Justice*, 93ff. See also Athanasiadis, *George Grant and the Theology of the Cross*, 32, 35–42, 48–53. Athanasiadis writes, "The theology of the cross was a great discovery for Grant, a discovery that would shape his thought for the rest of his life." Grant, according to Athanasiadis, was probably first introduced to the concept as he worked on his PhD thesis, "The Concept of Nature and Supernature in the Theology of John Oman." It is beyond the scope of my essay to trace the linkages in Grant's PhD to his later thought. It is perhaps sufficient to summarize Athanasiadis's argument that Oman attempted to articulate Christian theology in philosophical terms, to reconcile reason and revelation. At the core of Oman's thought, according to Grant, is the view that all the circumstances and occurrences in life serve God's providence, although this does not mean that Oman sees God as the author of evil. Oman maintains a theology of the Cross by retaining the ultimate mystery and hiddenness of God's purposes in the world. For Grant, however, Oman does not sufficiently grasp the limits of human freedom and the necessity and mystery of God's grace and thus fails to adequately comprehend the theology of the Cross. As Athanasiadis concludes, Grant thought that Oman remained too much the "liberal optimist" and believer in "historical progress" to truly grasp the concept of the theology of the Cross. I would only add that, in Grant's view, Oman too closely identified the Christian doctrine of providence with the secular or modern doctrine of progress and thereby trivialized the evil in the world. This argument closely parallels Grant's subsequent critique of Hegel's philosophy of history. It would be a worthwhile scholarly project to closely analyse Grant's dissertation with the respect to the roots of his political philosophy.

85 O'Donovan, *George Grant and the Twilight of Justice*, 17. O'Donovan asserts that "Two Theological Languages" is "a microcosm of his [Grant's] work, gathering up the permanent impulses of his thought that will weave themselves into a complete fabric over three decades." According to O'Donovan, "Two Theological Languages" was delivered in 1947 to a group of Reformed Clergy and later revised for presentation to the Maritime Philosophical Association in 1953 before being published that same year in the *United Churchman*. The paper was included in a collection of essays published following a *festschrift* for Grant at McMaster University in 1987. See Wayne Whillier, ed., *Two Theological*

Languages by George Grant and Other Essays in Honour of His Work (Lewiston, N.Y., 1990). It is also included in *Collected Works of George Grant*, vol. 2: *1951–1959*, ed. Arthur Davis (Toronto, 2002), 49–65. See also Athanasiadis, *George Grant and the Theology of the Cross*, 48. Athanasiadis writes that Grant's understanding of Martin Luther, particularly theses 19–21 of the Heidelberg disputation, "serves to orient, structure and guide Grant's thought in its critical, as well as constructive, dimensions." Finally, see Sheila Grant, "George Grant and the Theology of the Cross," in *George Grant and the Subversion of Modernity*, ed. Davis, 249. She writes that Grant's PHD dissertation on Oman and his subsequent study of Luther "marked the beginning of his distrust of rational philosophies of history," including, presumably, Hegelian philosophy.

86 Grant, *Technology and Justice*, 44.
87 Grant, *Lament*, 89.
88 Grant, *Time As History*, 37.
89 Ibid., 46.
90 Grant, "Conversation: Intellectual Background," in *George Grant in Process*, ed. Schmidt, 65–6.
91 On this topic, see Athanasiadis, *George Grant and the Theology of the Cross*, 84–7, 100–9; Schmidt, "George Grant on Simone Weil As a Saint and Thinker," in *George Grant and the Subversion of Modernity*, ed. Davis, 263–81; John Kirby and Louis Greenspan, "Grant, Natural Law and Simone Weil," in *By Loving Our Own*, ed. Emberley, 153–9; O'Donovan, *George Grant and the Twilight of Justice*, 80–4, 176–7; O'Donovan, "Love, Law and the Common Good," in *By Loving Our Own*, ed. Emberley, 135–51; Wayne Sheppard, "The Suffering of Love: George Grant and Simone Weil," in George Grant, *Two Theological Languages by George Grant and Other Essays in Honour of His Work*, ed. Whillier, 20–62; and Edwin Heavens and David Heavens, "Some Influences of Simone Weil on George Grant's Silence," in *George Grant in Process*, ed. Schmidt, 68–78.
92 Grant, "Conversation: Intellectual Background," in *George Grant in Process*, ed. Schmidt, 62.
93 Quoted in Taylor, *Radical Tories*, 132.
94 Grant, "Conversation: Intellectual Background," 63.
95 Ibid., 63.
96 Grant, *Philosophy in the Mass Age*, 71–2.
97 John Dunaway, *Simone Weil* (Boston, 1984), 38–40.
98 Grant, *Lament*, 89.
99 Simone Weil, *The Need for Roots*, trans. Arthur Wills (New York, 1952), 282.
100 Simone Weil, *Intimations of Christianity*, ed. and trans. Elisabeth Geissbuhler (London, 1957), 193.
101 Ibid.

102 O'Donovan discusses this topic in more detail in *George Grant and the Twilight of Justice*, 81–5.

103 Athanasiadis, *George Grant and the Theology of the Cross*, 88, 101. Athanasiadis also points out, however, that Grant was suspicious of Weil's language regarding love of and consent to necessity "as somehow reducing evil and suffering to divine providence, and collapsing the distance between necessity and the good." Nevertheless, Grant continued to admire her understanding of evil and suffering and of how these are embedded in modern technological society.

104 Grant, "Two Theological Languages," 8. See also Athanasiadis, *George Grant and the Theology of the Cross*, 50–1.

105 Grant, "Two Theological Languages," 9. Thirty-five years after writing this, Grant effectively repudiated his own argument about biblical theology, saying that he had basically misunderstood the concept. While such "egregious confusion vitiates the substance of the paper," as he says, it does not undermine the point I am trying to draw out regarding Grant's ambivalent Hegelianism and how he attempted to confront it. See Grant's "Addendum" to "Two Theological Languages," 16–19.

106 Sheila Grant, "George Grant and the Theology of the Cross," 249.

107 Grant, "Two Theological Languages," 13.

108 Ibid., 14; and Athanasiadis, *George Grant and the Theology of the Cross*.

109 Ibid., 18.

110 Sheila Grant, "Grant and the Theology of the Cross," 251. She makes this point, observing that "Hegel is not mentioned in the 1953 address, but the battle lines are already drawn." See also Athanasiadis, *George Grant and the Theology of the Cross*, 48–9, regarding the significance of the theology of the Cross for Grant.

111 Grant, Notebook 4 (1958), 23. I am indebted to William Christian for making photocopies of several of Grant's notebooks available to me. I should note that these photocopies came my way prior to the publication of Grant's collected works. Some of his notebook comments on Hegel were subsequently published in 2002 in the *Collected Works of George Grant*, vol. 2: *1951–1959*, ed. Davis, 520–6.

112 Grant, Notebook 4, 46.

113 Quoted in Sheila Grant, "Grant and the Theology of the Cross," 251.

114 Ibid., 251–2.

115 Grant, Notebook 4, 18.

116 Grant, "Conversation: Intellectual Background," in *George Grant in Process*, ed. Schmidt, 64. Grant adds, "[I]t was Leo Strauss who has taught me to think this through."

117 O'Donovan, *George Grant and the Twilight of Justice*, 45.

118 Grant, *Philosophy in the Mass Age*, 44.

119 Athanasiadis, *George Grant and the Theology of the Cross*, 48–9.

120 Grant, *Philosophy in the Mass Age*, 45.

121 Ibid., 43. Grant refers to Thomas Aquinas's "remarkable synthesis" of Aristotelian natural law and the Christian conception of the God of history.

122 Ibid., 45.

123 Athanasiadis, *George Grant and the Theology of the Cross*, 52, 76. Athanasiadis argues that Grant's interpretation of Luther's theology of the Cross is simplistic in that it associates Luther's rejection of natural theology with his rejection of philosophy and rationality. This prevents Grant from being able to link a theology of the Cross to a more Platonic and mystical philosophy. Athanasiadis's attributes this inadequacy to Grant's dependence on Hegel for his understanding of the Reformation. Hegel regarded the Reformation as the "spiritual version" of the Enlightenment's idea of worldly freedom, which, in our time, has become unrestrained hedonism. Athanasiadis suggests that Grant's reliance on Hegel's interpretation of the Reformation provided "the beginnings of Grant's eventual rejection of Hegel." As he puts it, "[T]he practical, world-reforming understanding of freedom is linked, in Grant's mind, to a Puritan Calvinist brand of Protestantism rather than one influenced by Luther."

124 Grant, "The Uses of Freedom," *Queen's Quarterly* 62, no. 4 (1956): 519.

125 Athanasiadis, *George Grant and the Theology of the Cross*, 136–7.

126 Grant, *Lament*, 89.

127 Grant, "Conversation: Intellectual Background," in *George Grant in Process*, ed. Schmidt, 64.

128 David G. Peddle and Neil G. Robertson, "Lamentation and Speculation: George Grant, James Doull and the Possibility of Canada," *Animus: A Philosophical Journal for Our Time* 7 (2002): 2–3 (PDF version on www.swgc.mun.ca/animus, accessed 29 July 2007). Peddle and Robertson write: "Grant saw in the doctrine of progress, and most fully in the Hegelian expression of it, a confusion between what he referred to as the order of necessity and the order of the good … Grant saw in the Hegelian uniting of progress and providence a radical reduction of all otherness to human historical life, ultimately to human subjectivity and will."

129 Ibid., 7. Peddle and Robertson note that, for Grant, in contrast to Leo Strauss, the origins of modernity are not modern, but traceable to medieval and Augustinian Christianity with its emphasis on will and personality. I am suggesting, however, that Grant traces the progressivist, historicist mindset back even further.

130 Grant, *Philosophy in the Mass Age*, 40.

131 George Grant, "Revolution and Tradition," in *Tradition and Revolution*, ed. Lionel Rubinoff (Toronto, 1971), 93.

132 Hegel, *The Philosophy of History* (New York, 1956), 417.

133 Grant, *Philosophy in the Mass Age*, 39–40.

134 Ibid., 39.

135 Grant, "Revolution and Tradition," 92–3; "The Uses of Freedom," 517–18; and *Philosophy in the Mass Age*, 63–4.

136 Grant, *Philosophy in the Mass Age*, 69.

137 Athanasiadis, *George Grant and the Theology of the Cross*, 112–13. See also Robert Meynell, "Idealism and Identity: George Grant and Charles Taylor Confront the Modern Dilemma" (MA thesis, Acadia University, 1998), 44–5.

138 Grant, *Philosophy in the Mass Age*, 19.

139 Ibid., 24.

140 Meynell, "Idealism and Identity," 45.

141 Christian, *George Grant*, 232.

142 I owe this insight to Ian Angus, *A Border Within*, 86.

143 Grant, *Philosophy in the Mass Age*, 46.

144 Grant, *Time As History*, 29.

145 Grant, *Technology and Justice*, 76.

146 Ibid., 76–7.

147 Cayley, CBC Radio transcript of interview with George Grant (1986), 26.

148 Ibid. See also George Grant, *The George Grant Reader*, ed. William Christian and Sheila Grant, (Toronto, 1998), 218.

149 Christian, *George Grant*, 232–5. Christian writes that after studying Sherrard's book, Grant "thought that he saw a way of accounting for the condition of the modern West without holding Christianity itself responsible." See also Athanasiadis, *George Grant and the Theology of the Cross*, 134–7. Athanasiadis credits Sherrard (along with Weil), more so than Strauss, with helping Grant think through the Western doctrine of providence. But that, I suggest, is tantamount to saying that Sherrard helped Grant breakout of the Hegelian circle.

150 Philip Sherrard, *The Greek East and the Latin West: A Study in the Christian Tradition* (London, 1959), 164. The passage is worth quoting in full because it points up one of the underlying themes of my essay – the question of the relationship between the individual and the community: "Individualism and collectivism are opposite sides of the same coin, and their growth in the West can be traced back to the same rationalising spirit which led to the break-up of the medieval Christian ethos and to the formation of modern western society and culture."

151 Ibid., 6.

152 Athanasiadis, *George Grant and the Theology of the Cross*, 134. I am indebted to Athanasiadis for guiding me through Sherrard's argument.

153 Sherrard, *The Greek East and the Latin West*, 6.

154 Ibid., 7.

155 Ibid., 8.

156 Ibid.

157 Athanasiadis, *George Grant and the Theology of the Cross*, 135.

158 Sherrard, *The Greek East and the Latin West*, 13.

159 Ibid., 47.

160 Ibid., 30–1.

161 Ibid., 61–7. On this point, see also Athanasiadis, *George Grant and the Theology of the Cross*, 136–7.

162 Sherrard, *The Greek East and the Latin West*, 67.

163 Athanasiadis, *George Grant and the Theology of the Cross*, 136.

164 Ibid., 136.

165 Sherrard, *The Greek East and the Latin West*, 155–64.

166 Ibid., 164.

167 Ibid., 166. See also Christian, *George Grant*, 236.

168 Christian, *George Grant*, 234.

169 Athanasiadis, *George Grant and the Theology of the Cross*, 137.

170 O'Donovan, *George Grant and the Twilight of Justice*, 45.

171 Grant, *Philosophy in the Mass Age*, 4–8.

172 Ibid., 8.

173 Christian, "George Grant's Lament," 205, 207–8.

174 Grant, "Introduction," *Lament*, ix.

175 Ibid., 94. As Grant writes, "Has it not been in the age of progress that disease and overwork, hunger and poverty, have been drastically reduced?"

176 Umar, "The Philosophical Context of George Grant's Political Thought," in *George Grant and the Future of Canada*, ed. Umar, 14.

177 Grant, *Lament*, 68.

178 Ibid., 53.

179 Grant, *Technology and Empire*, 35. Grant did not claim that the two primals that shaped the West are completely distinct. Biblical religion was not lacking in thought, nor was Greek rationality without its religious dimensions. Thus, we should not think that the source of Western rationalism is solely Greek philosophy or that Western religion has its only source in Judeo-Christianity. As Grant says in *Time As History*, "both among the Greeks and in the Bible thought and reverence are sustained together" (29).

180 Ibid., 138.

181 Ibid., 20.

182 Ibid. Grant's use of the rather obscure adjective "surd" perhaps needs an explanation. It comes from the medieval Latin *surdus*, meaning speechless

or voiceless. An obscure word, no doubt, but obviously appropriate to the point he makes.

183 Ibid., 23.

184 Christian, *George Grant*, 274. Christian cites as the source of this quotation Grant's essay "Wisdom in the Universities, Part One," *This Magazine Is About Schools* 1, no. 4 (1967): 71.

185 Christian, *George Grant*, 273. Christian writes that Grant "readily acknowledged that the German sociologist Max Weber had taught him much about the Puritanism that was part of his inheritance from his ancestors."

186 Max Weber, *The Protestant Ethic and the Spirit of Capitalism*, trans. Talcott Parsons (New York, 1958), 120.

187 Athanasiadis, *George Grant and the Theology of the Cross*, 61.

188 Grant, "The Uses of Freedom," 519.

189 Ibid., 520.

190 Grant, *Philosophy in the Mass Age*, 7–11.

191 Ibid., 10.

192 Ibid., 34.

193 Grant, *Time As History*, 25–6.

194 Ibid., 22–6. See also Grant, "Knowing and Making," *Transactions of the Royal Society of Canada*, 4th series (1975): 59–61; and Grant, "'The Computer Does Not Impose on Us the Ways It Should Be Used,'" in *Beyond Industrial Growth*, ed. Abraham Rotstein (Toronto: University of Toronto Press, 1976), 117–31.

195 Grant, *Technology and Empire*, 32.

196 Grant, *Time As History*, 44.

197 Grant, "Nationalism and Rationalism," in *Power Corrupted: The October Crisis and the Repression of Quebec*, ed. Abraham Rotstein (Toronto, 1971), 51–6.

198 O'Donovan touches on Weber's influence in *George Grant and the Twilight of Justice*, 45–6. See also Christian, *George Grant*, 273–4, 280–1; and Athanasiadis, *George Grant and the Theology of the Cross*, 59–60. Louis Greenspan makes a similar point in his essay "The Unraveling of Liberalism," in *George Grant and the Subversion of Modernity*, ed. Davis, 207–8.

199 Roger Brubaker, *The Limits of Rationality: An Essay on the Social and Moral Thought of Max Weber* (London, 1984), 35–45. See also Wolfgang Mommsen, *The Age of Bureaucracy: Perspectives on the Political Sociology of Max Weber* (New York, 1974), 56–7, 68–9; Hans Gerth and C. Wright Mills, introduction to *From Max Weber: Essays in Sociology*, ed. C. Wright Mills and trans. Hans Gerth (New York: Oxford University Press, 1946), 51–5; and Gunther Roth and Wolfgang Schluchter, *Max Weber's Vision of History: Ethics and Methods* (Berkeley, 1979), 14–15. Brubaker notes that there are at least sixteen meanings of *rational* in Weber's writings, but he thought that there is a form

of rationalism specific to the Western capitalist consciousness. Generally speaking, Weber regarded rationalisation as the coherent ordering of actions and beliefs aimed at the achievement of a predetermined end, whether by an individual or a group of individuals in some organisation. But what is special about Western rationality is its conception of rationality as a mode of consciousness for the calculation of means and ends. Under this means-ends formulation, what is rational is the calculation of the best available means to achieve a particular end, which itself has already been determined to be rational. Thus, rationality amounts to consistency in creating the logical order of premise to conclusion, of achieving the efficient ordering of means and ends. By this definition, any other mode of thinking that does not follow the logic of the means-ends equation, that does not logically bind premise and conclusion, would be irrational.

200 Mommsen, *The Age of Bureaucracy*, 37; and Brubaker, *The Limits of Rationality*, 41–3.

201 Grant, "Nationalism and Rationalism," 51.

202 Grant, *Lament*, 18. See also Umar, "The Philosophical Context of George Grant's Political Thought," in *George Grant and the Future of Canada*, ed. Umar, 14–15.

203 Grant, *Lament*, 18–19.

204 Ibid., 69.

205 Ibid., 18, 51–2.

206 Ibid., 53.

207 Ramsay Cook, *The Maple Leaf Forever: Essays on Nationalism and Politics in Canada*, 2nd ed. (Toronto, 1977), 10.

208 Ibid., 11.

209 Harald von Riekhoff, "The Impact of Prime Minister Trudeau on Foreign Policy," *International Journal* 33, no. 2 (1978): 268. Von Riekhoff observes, "There is no evidence ... that the concepts of rationality and equilibrium – the former relating to the decision-making process and the latter to political structure – which occupy a central place in Trudeau's thinking on national politics are treated any differently, or assume less significance, when applied to international relations." Trudeau's concern for rationalist decision-making processes is also reflected in the considerable changes he instituted in the federal bureaucracy and the decision-making process, particularly in terms of cabinet proceedings and staff operations in the Prime Minister's Office and the Privy Council Office. On this point, see Peter Aucoin, "Organizational Change in the Machinery of Canadian Government: From Rational Management to Brokerage Politics," *Canadian Journal of Political Science* 19, no. 1 (1986): 3–27. Aucoin argues that Trudeau brought to his office a personal ideology imbued with rationalist aspirations and that this ideology was emulated in his staff.

210 Pierre Trudeau, *Federalism and the French Canadians* (New York, 1968), 195.

211 James Laxer and Robert Laxer, *The Liberal Idea of Canada: Pierre Trudeau and the Question of Canada's Survival* (Toronto: James Lorimer & Co., 1977), 92.

212 Trudeau, *Federalism and the French Canadians*, 203.

213 Ibid., 195–6.

214 Ibid., 154, 179.

215 Max Nemni and Monique Nemni, *Young Trudeau: Son of Quebec, Father of Confederation* (Toronto: McClelland & Stewart, 2006). The book reveals that as youth and young man in the 1930s and early 1940s, Trudeau was no champion of democracy and individual freedoms. He was instead an ardent Quebec nationalist who, during the worst of the war years, admired fascist dictators, regarded reports of Nazi atrocities as British propaganda, plotted treason against the Canadian state, and actively promoted a revolution to establish of an independent Quebec solely for Catholic French Canadians. It seems that Trudeau in his youth was remarkably different from what most Canadians have long assumed. As the Nemnis write in their introduction, "We ourselves could scarcely believe what we discovered." It is interesting to note that the mature Trudeau's hostility to nationalist sentiment has its parallel in Grant's turn away from the liberal assumptions of his youth.

216 Pierre Trudeau, *Memoirs* (Toronto, 1993), 46–7.

217 Quoted in Nemni, *Young Trudeau*, 212.

218 Trudeau, *Memoirs*, 47.

219 George Radwanski, *Trudeau* (Toronto, 1978), 121. Radwanski writes: "In singling out freedom as the distinctively human quality, Trudeau equates it with reason: Man is free because he has the power of reason, the ability to make considered choices, and the only free – and, hence, truly human – actions are those which are rational and intelligent."

220 Trudeau, *Federalism and the French Canadians*, 203.

221 On this point, see Cook's essay "Federalism, Nationalism and the Canadian Nation State," in his *The Maple Leaf Forever*, 11; and Larry Zolf, *Dance of the Dialectic* (Toronto: James Lewis and Samuels, 1973), 4. Zolf describes Trudeau, philosophically speaking, as "Hegelian."

222 Pierre Trudeau et al., "An Appeal for Realism in Politics," *Canadian Forum*, May 1964, 32–3. The essay was published simultaneously in French in *Cité Libre*.

223 Ibid. I am indebted to Barry Cooper for my discussion of Trudeau's manifesto. See his essay "The Political Thought of George Grant," in *George Grant in Process*, ed. Schmitt, 32–3.

224 Grant, *Lament*, 85. It might be noted that Grant's criticism was made before Trudeau entered federal politics.

225 Ibid., 85. See Cooper, "The Political Thought of George Grant," 33.

226 Grant, "Nationalism and Rationality," 53, 55. See also Christian, *George Grant,* 288–9; and Athanasiadis, *George Grant and the Theology of the Cross,* 214.

227 Grant, "Inconsistency Ruled in Canada's 70's," *Globe and Mail,* 31 December 1979, n.p. Cited in William Christian, "Was George Grant a Red Tory," in *Athens and Jerusalem: George Grant's Theology, Philosophy, and Politics,* ed. Ian Angus, Ron Dart, and Randy Peg Peters (Toronto, 2006), 54.

228 Grant, "Nationalism and Rationality," 52. In light of the Nemnis' biography, it is worth noting Grant's suggestion that Trudeau's anti-nationalism betrays the psychological disposition of those who are "recent converts" to a cause. For an interesting study of Trudeau's political psychology, see Paul Nesbitt-Larking, "The Discourse of Aggression: Trudeau in Parliament," *London Journal of Canadian Studies* 18 (2002–3): 63–85.

229 Quoted by Grant in foreword to *The Liberal Idea of Canada,* by Laxer and Laxer, 10.

230 Ibid., 10–11.

231 Grant, *Lament,* 53. It is worth quoting Grant on what he takes Kojève's phrase to mean: "The universal and homogeneous state is the pinnacle of political striving. 'Universal' implies a world-wide state, which would eliminate the curse of war among nations; 'homogeneous' means that all men would be equal, and war among classes would be eliminated."

232 Max Weber, "Science As a Vocation," in *From Max Weber: Essays in Sociology,* ed. Mills and trans. Gerth 155. The quotation is as follows: "The fate of our times is characterized by rationalisation and intellectualization and, above all, by the 'disenchantment of the world.'"

233 George Grant, "Remarks at the 35th Couchiching Conference, 1966," in *Great Societies and Quiet Revolutions,* ed. John Lewin (Toronto, 1967), 74.

234 Grant, "Nationalism and Rationalism," 52. In a 2 July 1964 letter to his friend Derek Bedson, Grant described Trudeau "as a kind of Canadian Kennedy – a shallow politician who makes people think this vulgar society has a slick patina to it." Quoted in Christian, "Was George Grant a Red Tory?" 54.

235 Grant, *Lament,* 54.

236 George Grant, "Ideology in Modern Empires," in *Perspectives of Empire: Essays Presented to Gerald S. Graham,* ed. John E. Flint and Glyndwr Williams (London, 1973), 19–1.

237 Cayley, *George Grant in Conversation,* 101–2. Grant was asked: "So you're saying that your lament was as much a lament for the loss of politics as a practical activity as it was for the loss of Canada – or perhaps that the two are the same?" He replied: "The same, yes. The possibility of building in the northern half of this continent something different from the great empire we share it with is gone."

238 Creighton's statement deserves to be quoted in full: "Well, it's still a good place to live, but that's all Canada is now – just a good place to live." Quoted in Taylor, *Radical Tories*, 23. Canada, in short, is a consumer comfort zone.

239 Grant, *Lament*, 86. One might wonder whether Grant would see Islamist terrorism as the "catastrophe" that leads to Canada's complete integration into the American empire, or, perhaps, he would see the end of the Cold War as the precipitous "great shift of power" that puts an end to Canada's independence.

240 Grant, with Monica Hall, "Lament for a Nation Revisited: An Interview with George Grant," *Insights: A Dalhousie Journal on International Affairs* 4, no. 1 (1988), 7. See also Tim Thomas, "George Grant, the Free Trade Agreement and Contemporary Quebec," *Journal of Canadian Studies*, 27, no. 4 (1992–93): 180–96. One cannot help but wonder what Grant would say about the 2005 report from the Council on Foreign Relations, "Building a North American Community," which recommends, among other measures, "a security and economic community for North America." At least one newspaper columnist, Margret Kopala, has recognized that what prompts this further move toward continental integration is, as Grant foresaw, a crisis, which, in this case, is global terrorism. See Margret Kopala, "The Challenge of a United North America," *Ottawa Citizen*, 15 July 2006, B7.

241 Grant, *Lament*, ix.

242 Ibid., 53.

243 O'Donovan, "The Battle Ground of Liberalism: Politics of Eternity and Time," 443. See also Christian, editor's introduction to *Philosophy in the Mass Age*, by Grant, xxi. He argues that Grant's reading of Strauss showed him "that he had been wrong in holding out any hope that the tensions of modernity might be resolved as freedom became more fully developed in the world."

244 Allan Bloom, "Leo Strauss," in *Giants and Dwarfs* (New York, 1991), 241.

245 Leo Strauss, *Thoughts on Machiavelli* (Chicago, 1958), 298. Strauss writes: "Modern man as little as pre-modern man can escape imitating nature as he understands nature. Imitating an expanding universe, modern man has ever more expanded and thus become evermore shallow."

246 Leo Strauss, *What Is Political Philosophy?* (Chicago, 1959), 21–5.

247 Leo Strauss, "The Three Waves of Modernity," in *An Introduction to Political Philosophy: Ten Essays by Leo Straus*, ed. Hilail Gildin (Detroit, 1989), 81–98. See also Stanley Rosen, "Post-modernism and the End of Philosophy," *Canadian Journal of Political and Social Theory* 9, no. 3 (1985): 92. Rosen remarks: "Modernity arises as a 'project,' namely, as the conscious rejection (by a few remarkable individuals) of antiquity."

248 Strauss, *Thoughts on Machiavelli*, 295. On Grant's relationship to Strauss, I have drawn from H.D. Forbes, "George Grant and Leo Strauss," in *George Grant and the Subversion of Modernity*, ed. Davis, 169–98; and Athanasiadis, *George Grant and the Theology of the Cross*, 126–34.

249 Strauss, "Three Waves of Modernity," 89–92.

250 Leo Strauss, *On Tyranny: An Interpretation of Xenophon's "Hiero,"* rev. ed. (Ithaca, N.Y., 1963), 205. See also Athanasiadis, *George Grant and the Theology of the Cross*, 128.

251 Strauss, *Thoughts on Machiavelli*, 297.

252 Strauss, "Three Waves of Modernity," 96–7; and *Thoughts on Machiavelli*, 297–8. See also Forbes, "George Grant and Leo Strauss," 182–3.

253 Bloom, "Leo Strauss," 251.

254 In Grant, *Technology and Empire*, 81–109.

255 Ibid., 81.

256 Grant, *Lament*, 53–4.

257 Ibid., 96. See also Forbes, "George Grant and Leo Strauss," 184–5.

258 Grant, *Technology and Empire*, 84.

259 Michael S. Roth, *Knowing and History: Appropriations of Hegel in Twentieth-Century France* (Ithaca, 1988), 96.

260 Patrick Riley, "Introduction to the Reading of Alexandre Kojève," *Political Theory* 9, no. 1 (1981): 8. Riley cites Kojève's book *Introduction à la lecture Hegel: Leçons sur la Phénoménologie de l'esprit* (Paris: Gallimard, 1947).

261 Alexandre Kojève, *Introduction to the Reading of Hegel*, ed. Allan Bloom and trans. James Nichols, Jr (New York, 1969), 7.

262 Umar, "The Philosophical Context of George Grant's Political Thought," 5. My emphasis.

263 Kojève, "Hegel, Marx and Christianity," *Interpretation* 1 (1970): 29–30. See also Roth, *Knowing and History*, 115–17; and Riley, "Introduction to the Reading of Alexandre Kojève," 6–9.

264 Hegel, *Philosophy of Right*, #260, 160.

265 Kojève, "The Idea of Death in the Philosophy of Hegel," *interpretation: a journal of political philosophy* 8 (Winter 1973): 123. This essay was not included in the 1969 English translation of Kojève's *Introduction to the Reading of Hegel*, although it was included in the original French version of 1947. Kojève states Hegel's God-is-dead claim this way: "Hegel does not accept the Judeo-Christian anthropological tradition except in a radically secularised or atheistic form. The Spirit-Absolute of the Subject-Substance, of which Hegel speaks, is not God. The Hegelian Spirit is the spatio-temporal totality of the natural World and implies human Discourse revealing this World and itself. Or better, and what is the same thing, Spirit is Man-in-the-World: the mortal

Man who lives in a World without God and who speaks of all that exists in it and of all that he creates in it, including himself."

266 Kojève, *Introduction to the Reading of Hegel*, 159.

267 I first encountered this idea many years ago as a master's student and would like to acknowledge its source: David Venour, "The Political Thought of George Grant" (MA thesis, University of Calgary, 1986), 21–5.

268 Kojève, "Tyranny and Wisdom," in Leo Strauss, *On Tyranny*, 181–2. See also Grant, *Technology and Empire*, 87–8; and O'Donovan, *George Grant and the Twilight of Justice*, 70–1.

269 Grant, *Technology and Empire*, 87. Grant's emphasis.

270 Kojève, "Tyranny and Wisdom," 183–4.

271 Ibid. See Kojève, "The Idea of Death in the Philosophy of Hegel," 154. Kojève writes: "Everything said by Christian theology is absolutely true, provided it is applied not to an imaginary transcendent God, but to real Man, living in the World."

272 Grant, *Technology and Empire*, 90.

273 Grant, *Lament*, 89.

274 Grant is following Strauss in this argument. See Leo Strauss, *Natural Right and History* (Chicago, 1950), 274. Strauss writes: "To the extent to which the historical process is accidental, it cannot supply man with a standard, and … if that process has a hidden purpose, its purposefulness cannot be recognized except if there are transhistorical standards. The historical process cannot be recognized as progressive without previous knowledge of the end or purpose of the process."

275 Strauss, *Natural Right and History*, 25. Strauss writes: "Historicism asserts that all human thoughts or beliefs are historical; and hence deservedly destined to perish; but historicism itself is a human thought; hence historicism can be of only temporary validity, or it cannot be simply true. To assert the historicist thesis means to doubt it and thus to transcend it … Historicism thrives on the fact that it inconsistently exempts itself from its own verdict about all human thought."

276 Grant, *Technology and Empire*, 92–3.

277 Ibid., 98.

PART FOUR

1 Mark Redhead, *Charles Taylor: Thinking and Living Deep Diversity* (Lanham, Md, 2002), 88–9. Redhead writes: "Modern forms of procedural liberalism, such as the Charter and English Canadian Charter consciousness … are problematic to Taylor because they invert the proper relationship of *Moralität* to *Sittlichkeit*."

2 Charles Taylor, *Hegel* (Cambridge, 1975), 377.

3 Redhead, *Charles Taylor*, 87. Redhead notes that Taylor dislikes the communitarian label. Perhaps so, but Taylor's works share much with communitarians such as Alistair MacIntyre, Michael Sandel, and Michael Walzer, all of whom have criticised procedural liberalism.

4 Charles Taylor, *The Malaise of Modernity* (Toronto, 1991), 4. On this topic, see also Norman Barry, "Charles Taylor on Multiculturalism and the Politics of Recognition," in *Community and Tradition: Conservative Perspectives on the American Experience*, ed. George W. Carey and Bruce Frohnen (Lanham, Md, 1998), 105. Barry argues that Taylor's individualism is holistic in that it "identifies the person by reference to his involvement in shared values and is resistant to the economic (or classical) liberal's conception of the individual as an anonymous choosing agent."

5 Charles Taylor, *Modern Social Imaginaries* (Durham, N.C., 2004), 18.

6 Norman Barry, "Charles Taylor on Multiculturalism and the Politics of Recognition," 104.

7 Nicholas H. Smith, *Charles Taylor: Meaning, Morals and Modernity* (Cambridge, 2002), 216. Smith observes that unlike other critics of modernity, Taylor does not ignore "the moral motivation behind the Enlightenment." "The crux of Taylor's argument is that the rise of Enlightenment rationalism and the consolidation of the modern moral order catalysed a counter-current aimed at realizing a 'heightened, more vibrant quality of life.'" Hence Taylor's belief in the value of recovery.

8 Charles Taylor, *Sources of the Self: The Making of the Modern Identity* (Cambridge, Mass., 1991), 520.

9 John Dunn, *Interpreting Political Responsibility* (Princeton, 1990), 186.

10 Amelie Rorty, "The Hidden Politics of Cultural Identification," *Political Theory* 22, no. 1 (1994): 163. Rorty writes: "Taylor's defence of multiculturalism remains rooted in the premises of Hegelian idealism."

11 Janet Ajzenstat, "Decline of Procedural Liberalism: The Slippery Slope to Succession," in *Is Quebec Nationalism Just? Perspectives from Anglophone Canada*, ed. Joseph H. Carens (Montreal and Kingston, 1995), 122.

12 Nancy Fraser, *Justice Interruptus: Critical Reflections on the "Postsocialist" Condition* (New York, 1997), 11.

13 Charles Taylor, *Multiculturalism and "The Politics of Recognition,"* ed. Amy Gutmann (Princeton, N.J., 1992), 25. Taylor's emphasis. Besides Taylor's essay "The Politics of Recognition," this book contains four commentaries on the essay, including ones by Gutmann, Steven Rockefeller, Michael Walzer, and Susan Wolf.

14 Ibid., 50.

15 Charles Taylor, *Reconciling the Solitudes: Essays on Canadian Federalism and Nationalism* (Montreal, 1993), 188.
16 Andy Lamey offers a succinct overview of Taylor's politics of recognition in "Francophonia Forever: The Contradictions in Charles Taylor's 'Politics of Recognition,'" *Times Literary Supplement*, 23 July 1999, 12–15.
17 Taylor, *Multiculturalism and "The Politics of Recognition,"* 26.
18 Patchen Markell, "Bound by Recognition: The Politics of Identity after Hegel" (PHD diss., Harvard University, 1999), 15–16.
19 Anthony Appiah, "Identity, Authenticity, Survival," in Charles Taylor et al., *Multiculturalism: Examining "The Politics of Recognition,"* ed. and with an introduction by Amy Gutmann (Princeton, N.J., 1994), 149. This book is an expansion of the 1992 edition, *Multiculturalism and "The Politics of Recognition,"* and includes additional commentaries by Appiah and Jürgen Habermas.
20 Taylor, *Multiculturalism and "The Politics of Recognition,"* 25.
21 My questions are prompted by observations in Ruth Abbey, *Charles Taylor* (Princeton, 2000), 67–8; and Lamey, "Francophonia Forever," 12–13.
22 Taylor, *Multiculturalism and "The Politics of Recognition,"* 34.
23 Ibid., 32–4. See also Taylor, *Sources of the Self,* 35–6.
24 Taylor, *Multiculturalism and "The Politics of Recognition,"* 36.
25 Ibid., 35. See also Taylor, *Sources of the Self,* 36.
26 Taylor, *Multiculturalism and "The Politics of Recognition,"* 38.
27 Norman Barry, "Charles Taylor on Multiculturalism and the Politics of Recognition," 107.
28 Taylor, *Multiculturalism and "The Politics of Recognition,"* 27.
29 Ibid., 30. Taylor's emphasis.
30 Ibid., 36.
31 Norman Barry, "Charles Taylor on Multiculturalism and the Politics of Recognition," 108.
32 Taylor, *Multiculturalism and "The Politics of Recognition,"* 38.
33 Ibid., 39.
34 Ibid., 62.
35 Lamey, "Francophonia Forever," 13.
36 Linda Nicholson, "To Be or Not to Be: Charles Taylor and the Politics of Recognition," *Constellations* 3, no. 1 (1996): 7–8.
37 Taylor, *Multiculturalism and "The Politics of Recognition,"* 43. On this point, Taylor's argument goes beyond the matter with which I am concerned. However, elsewhere in this essay he argues that debates about multiculturalism involve not just the recognition of different cultures, but also the recognition that all cultures are of equal worth. I would suggest that Taylor reveals the problematic nature of the equal-worth argument, no doubt inadvertently, when he defends the *fatwa* against Salman Rushdie, which I discuss later in this section.

See Charles Taylor, "The Rushdie Controversy," *Public Culture* 2, no. 1 (1989): 118–22.

38 Taylor, *Multiculturalism and "The Politics of Recognition,"* 61.

39 Ibid.

40 Taylor, *Sources of the Self,* 111, 185–6; and *The Malaise of Modernity,* 26.

41 Taylor *Multiculturalism and "The Politics of Recognition,"* 29.

42 In tracing Taylor's philosophical history of this "new form of inwardness," I have been guided by two essays in particular: Gary Gutting, "Charles Taylor: An Augustinian Modern," in *Pragmatic Liberalism and the Critique of Modernity* (Cambridge, U.K., 1999), 113–61; and Craig Calhoun, "Morality, Identity and Historical Explanation: Charles Taylor on the Sources of the Self," *Sociological Theory* 9, no. 2, (1991): 232–63.

43 Taylor, *Sources of the Self,* 121. See also Gutting, "Charles Taylor," 114–15.

44 Calhoun, "Morality, Identity and Historical Explanation," 243–4.

45 Taylor, *Sources of the Self,* 127–8.

46 Calhoun, "Morality, Identity and Historical Explanation," 244.

47 Taylor, *Sources of the Self,* 129–32. See also Gutting, "Charles Taylor," 115.

48 Taylor, *Sources of the Self,* 141; Calhoun, "Morality, Identity and Historical Explanation," 244.

49 Taylor, *Sources of the Self,* 143.

50 Ibid., 157; Calhoun, "Morality, Identity and Historical Explanation," 245; and Gutting, "Charles Taylor," 116.

51 Gutting, "Charles Taylor," 116.

52 Taylor, *Sources of the Self,* 146.

53 Gutting, "Charles Taylor," 117; Calhoun, "Morality, Identity and Historical Explanation," 245.

54 Taylor, *Sources of the Self,* 158. Taylor's emphasis.

55 Calhoun, "Morality, Identity and Historical Explanation," 245–6; and Gutting, "Charles Taylor," 118–20.

56 Taylor, *Sources of the Self,* 166–7.

57 Ibid., 167. See also Gutting, "Charles Taylor," 120.

58 Taylor, *Sources of the Self,* 171.

59 Ibid., 176. See also Calhoun, "Morality, Identity and Historical Explanation," 246.

60 Taylor, *Sources of the Self,* 218.

61 Ibid., 213; Gutting ("Charles Taylor," 124–7) provides a detailed discussion of Taylor's arguments regarding ordinary life.

62 Ibid., 232. Taylor's emphasis. Calhoun ("Morality, Identity and Historical Explanation," 248–9) addresses Taylor's analysis of the Protestant rejection of Catholicism's hierarchical structure.

63 Taylor, *Modern Social Imaginaries,* 19.

64 Lawrence Vogel, "Critical Notices: Taylor's *The Ethics of Authenticity and Multicul-turalism and the Politics of Recognition*," *International Journal of Philosophical Studies* 1, no. 2 (1993): 326.

65 Taylor, *Modern Social Imaginaries*, 18. He writes: "Individualism and mutual benefit are the evident residual ideas that remain after you have sloughed off the older religions and metaphysics."

66 Taylor, *The Malaise of Modernity*, 72–3. Taylor's emphasis.

67 Charles Taylor, "Language and Human Nature," in *Human Agency and Language: Philosophical Papers* (Cambridge, 1985), 1:219. Taylor applies the term *expressivism* for the constitutive basis of any human action: "Something is expressed when it is embodied in such a way as to be made manifest ... Something is manifest when it is directly available for all to see."

68 Robert Meynell, "Idealism and Identity: George Grant and Charles Taylor Confront the Modern Dilemma" (MA thesis, Dalhousie University, 1998), 105. Meynell neatly encapsulates Taylor's expressivism, saying that it provides him with the means to reconcile Rousseau's substantive community and Kant's radical freedom by drawing on Herder's expressivist theory and Hegel's concept of recognition. It might also be argued that the Quebec crisis and the problem of Canada reflect concrete manifestations of the theoretical tension between Kant and Rousseau and Hegel and Herder.

69 For a summary of Taylor's understanding of expressivism, see Charles Taylor, *Hegel* (Cambridge, 1975), chap. 1; and Taylor, *Sources of the Self*, chap. 21.

70 Taylor, *Sources of the Self*, 357–8.

71 Ibid., 359.

72 Ibid., 360.

73 Ibid., 358–60; and Calhoun, "Morality, Identity and Historical Explanation," 254.

74 Taylor, *Multiculturalism and "The Politics of Recognition*," 46–50.

75 Ibid., 34–5.

76 Ibid., 49; and Calhoun, "Morality, Identity and Historical Explanation," 254.

77 Taylor, *Multiculturalism and "The Politics of Recognition*," 51.

78 Ibid. Taylor clearly follows Hegel when he writes that Rousseau's general will "has been the formula for the most terrible forms of homogenizing tyranny, starting with the Jacobins and extending to the totalitarian regimes of our century."

79 Hegel, *Philosophy of Right*, #258, 156–7. Hegel states that Rousseau "takes the will only in a determinate form as the individual will, and he regards the universal will not as the absolutely rational element of the will, but only as a 'general' will which proceeds out of this individual will as out of a conscious will. The result is that he reduces the union of the individuals in the state to a contract and

therefore to something based on their arbitrary wills, their opinion, and their capriciously given express consent; and abstract reasoning proceeds to draw the logical inferences which destroy the absolutely divine principle of the state ... The will of its refounders was to give it what they alleged was a purely rational basis, but it was only abstractions that were being used; the Idea was lacking; and the experiment ended in the maximum of frightfulness and terror."

80 Taylor, *Multiculturalism and "The Politics of Recognition,"* 50.
81 Ibid., 39–44; and Barry, "Charles Taylor on Multiculturalism and the Politics of Recognition," 108.
82 Taylor, *Multiculturalism and "The Politics of Recognition,"* 56–7.
83 Ibid., 43; and Barry, "Charles Taylor on Multiculturalism and the Politics of Recognition," 107–9.
84 Taylor, *Multiculturalism and "The Politics of Recognition,"* 51–2. See also Meynell, "Idealism and Identity," 105.
85 Taylor, *Multiculturalism and "The Politics of Recognition,"* 61.
86 Ibid., 30.
87 Vasanthi Srinivasan, "Freedom, Community and Transcendence: A Comparison of Select Western and Indian Thinkers" (PhD dissertation, Carleton University, 1997), 54.
88 Taylor, *Multiculturalism and "The Politics of Recognition,"* 25.
89 Alan Wolfe, *Whose Keeper? Social Science and Moral Obligation* (Berkeley, 1989), 2; and Markell, "Bound by Recognition," 17–20.
90 Taylor, *Multiculturalism and "The Politics of Recognition,"* 31.
91 Srinivasan, "Freedom, Community and Transcendence," 55. She states the matter succinctly: "In other words, we do not think first and then express it but our expression constitutes and clarifies our thoughts."
92 Taylor, *Sources of the Self*, 35.
93 Taylor, *Multiculturalism and "The Politics of Recognition,"* 32.
94 Charles Taylor, introduction to *Human Agency and Language* (Cambridge, 1985), 1.
95 Markell, "Bound by Recognition," 20–7.
96 Taylor, introduction to *Human Agency and Language*, 5.
97 Charles Taylor, "Overcoming Epistemology," in *Philosophical Arguments* (Cambridge, 1995), 8.
98 Ibid., 7–8. See also Taylor, *Sources of the Self*, 23–4.
99 Taylor, introduction to *Human Agency and Language*, 8.
100 Charles Taylor, "Irreducibly Social Goods" and "Cross-Purposes: The Liberal-Communitarian Debate," in *Philosophical Arguments*, 128–30 and 194–5.
101 Taylor, "Language and Human Nature," 223–6; and Taylor, "The Importance of Herder," in *Philosophical Arguments*, 81–8. Markell and Meynell also make

this point. See, respectively, "Bound by Recognition," 25–6, and "Idealism and Identity," 106–8.

102 Markell, "Bound by Recognition," 24–7. Markell writes: "[S]ince the correlation between word and thing is an observable external relationship, designative theories of language account for meaning in ways that remain entirely indifferent to the first-person perspective of language-users, and which therefore threaten to reduce meaning and understanding to matters of behaviour, of the effective production of and response to signals" (24).

103 Taylor, "The Importance of Herder," 96.

104 Taylor "Language and Human Nature," 226.

105 Taylor, "The Importance of Herder," 96.

106 Ibid., 84. See also Srinivasan, "Freedom, Community and Transcendence," 55.

107 Richard Nutbrown, "The Self, Language and Community: Taylor's Hermeneutic Project," *Eidos* 5, no. 1 (1986): 19; and Meynell, "Idealism and Identity," 106.

108 Taylor, "The Importance of Herder," 97.

109 Taylor, "Language and Human Nature," 230.

110 Ibid., 234. Taylor's emphasis.

111 Charles Taylor, *Hegel and Modern Society* (Cambridge, 1979), 18. Taylor writes: "Language is seen not just as a set of signs, but as the medium of expression of a certain way of seeing and experiencing; as such it is continuous with art. Hence there can be no thought without language; and indeed the languages of different peoples reflect their different visions of things."

112 Taylor, *Modern Social Imaginaries*, 26. Taylor writes: "[F]or most of human history and for most of social life, we function through the grasp we have on the common repertory, without benefit of theoretical overview. Humans operated with a social imaginary well before they ever got into the business of theorizing about themselves."

113 Srinivasan, "Freedom, Community and Transcendence," 56. Srinivasan writes: "The expressivist account of language anchors our reason and humanity in a larger order and thus, clears the way for a communitarian politics."

114 Ibid., 57.

115 Taylor, *Hegel and Modern Society*, 2.

116 Taylor, *Sources of the Self*, 415. See also Srinivasan, "Freedom, Community and Transcendence," 59. Srinivasan makes the telling point that for Taylor national identity is not something established once and for all, but is continually "contested and negotiated in history and politics."

117 Taylor, *Multiculturalism and "The Politics of Recognition,"* 31.

118 Taylor, *Sources of the Self*, 415.

119 Ibid.

120 Charles Taylor, "Hegel's Ambiguous Legacy for Modern Liberalism," in *Hegel and Legal Theory*, ed. Drucilla Cornell, Michel Rosenfeld, and David Gray Carlson (New York, 1991), 64.

121 Hegel, *Philosophy of Right*, #141, 103–4. Hegel defines *Sittlichkeit*, or ethical life, as "the identity of the good with the subjective will," while *Moralität* refers to an abstract, formal notion of moral obligation. In effect, ethical life is the concrete morality of a rational social order as reflected in and embodied through the rational institutions of a society. See also Taylor, *Hegel*, 376–7. Taylor says that *Sittlichkeit* refers to the moral obligations that an individual has to a preexisting and ongoing community of which he is a part. In short, morality becomes ethical life to the degree that it has its completion in a community.

122 Taylor, "Hegel's Ambiguous Legacy for Modern Liberalism," 71.

123 Ibid., 70.

124 Ibid., 72.

125 Ibid.

126 Ibid., 72–3.

127 Taylor, *Hegel*, 571.

128 Taylor, "Hegel's Ambiguous Legacy for Modern Liberalism," 75–6.

129 Taylor, *Multiculturalism and "The Politics of Recognition,"* 35.

130 Ibid.

131 Srinivasan, "Freedom, Community and Transcendence," 184.

132 Ibid., 68–9.

133 Taylor, "Hegel's Ambiguous Legacy for Modern Liberalism," 75.

134 Srinivasan, "Freedom, Community and Transcendence," 182–3.

135 Taylor, *Multiculturalism and "The Politics of Recognition,"* 50.

136 Taylor, *Hegel*, 154.

137 Ibid., 539.

138 Ibid., 153.

139 David Duquette, "The Political Significance of Hegel's Concept of Recognition in the *Phenomenology*," *Bulletin of the Hegel Society of Great Britain* 29 (Spring-Summer 1994): 41.

140 Ibid., 48; and Srinivasan, "Freedom, Community, and Transcendence," 186. Srinivasan notes that Hegel's ethical order "is based on freedom rather than identity."

141 Hegel, *Philosophy of Right*, #258, 156. See note 88 in Part 1.

142 Taylor, *Reconciling the Solitudes*, 188.

143 I owe this point to Adam Krob, "Hegel's Community: Synthesizing the Romantic and the Liberal" (PhD diss., Duke University,1997), 254–5.

144 Taylor, *Multiculturalism and "The Politics of Recognition,"* 57–61. This point is also made in Krob, "Hegel's Community," 254–6; and Meynell, "Idealism and Identity," 93, 105.

145 Nicholas H. Smith, *Charles Taylor*, 146. Smith observes that Taylor's critique of procedural liberalism has prompted criticism from liberal theorists who worry about "the illegitimate threat to individual freedom posed by Taylor's communitarian line of thinking."

146 Charles Taylor, *Philosophical Papers*, vol. 2: *Philosophy and the Human Sciences* (Cambridge, 1985), 2:206.

147 Taylor, *Hegel and Modern Society*, 160.

148 Nicholas H. Smith, *Charles Taylor*, 150.

149 Taylor, "Shared and Divergent Values," in *Reconciling the Solitudes*, 183.

150 Ibid., 182–4.

151 Charles Taylor, "Alternative Futures: Legitimacy, Identity and Alienation in Late-Twentieth-Century Canada," in *Reconciling the Solitudes*, 102.

152 Charles Taylor, "Can Canada Survive the Charter?" *Alberta Law Review* 30, no. 2 (1992): 432.

153 Arthur Ripstein, "Recognition and Cultural Membership," *Dialogue* 34 (1995): 334. See also Lamey, "Francophonia Forever," 13; and Meynell, "Idealism and Identity," 133.

154 Barry Cooper and David Bercuson, *Deconfederation: Canada without Quebec* (Toronto, 1991).

155 Taylor, *Multiculturalism and "The Politics of Recognition,"* 58.

156 Cooper and Bercuson, *Deconfederation*, 100.

157 Hilliard Aronovitch, "Trudeau or Taylor? The Central Question," *Critical Review of International Social and Political Philosophy* 8, no. 3 (2005): 309–25.

158 Max Nemni, "Trudeau's Canada," *Cité Libre* 28, no. 4 (2000): 16–24.

159 Aronovitch, "Trudeau or Taylor?" 310–13.

160 Taylor, "Shared and Divergent Values," 177.

161 Alan Cairns, *Charter versus Federalism: The Dilemmas of Constitutional Reform* (Montreal and Kingston: McGill-Queen's University Press, 1992), 79. Cairns notes this "Janus-faced" quality to the charter, arguing that it presents "both liberal individualism and a constitutionalization of the linguistic, ethnic, racial, cultural and sexual identities of Canadians."

162 Trudeau, *Memoirs* (Toronto, 1993), 323.

163 Rainer Knopf and F.L. Morton, "Nation-Building and the Charter of Rights and Freedoms," in *Constitutionalism, Citizenship and Society in Canada*, ed. Alan Cairns and Cynthia Williams, research report of the Royal Commission on the Economic Union and Development Prospects for Canada (Ottawa: Supply and Services Canada, 1985), 136.

164 Trudeau, *Memoirs*, 322–3.

165 H.D. Forbes, "Trudeau Haunts Us Still," *Books in Canada* 28, no. 1 (1999): 12. Forbes is puzzled by the paradox of Trudeau's legacy: "The threatening

problem he had been expected to solve 30 years ago, the Quebec problem, had grown rather than diminished ... Canada had come within a hair's breadth of splitting apart and possibly plunging into civil war. Yet this did not seem to diminish Trudeau's stature and authority. He had become a legendary figure, a symbol of mature wisdom and steadfast dedication to principle."

166 Kenneth McRoberts, *Misconceiving Canada: The Struggle for National Unity* (Toronto, 1997), 276.

167 Ibid., xii.

168 Robert Martin, "A Lament for British North America," in *Rethinking the Constitution: Perspectives on Canadian Constitutional Reform, Interpretation, and Theory,* ed. Anthony Peacock (Toronto, 1996), 3–16.

169 Louis Balthazar, "Quebec and the Ideal of Federalism," *Annals of the American Academy of Political and Social Science* 538 (March 1995): 40–53.

170 Trudeau, *Memoirs*, 47. Trudeau's admiration for T.H. Green's thought is well known.

171 Pierre Trudeau, *Against the Current: Selected Writings, 1939–1996* (Toronto, 1996), 68. The essay was first published in 1958 in the magazine *Vrai* with the title "Les cheminements de la politique."

172 Taylor, *Reconciling the Solitudes*, 177–8.

173 Pierre Trudeau, *The Essential Trudeau*, ed. Ron Graham (Toronto, 1998), 80.

174 Quoted in Nemni, "Trudeau's Canada," 20.

175 Ibid., 22.

176 Quoted in ibid., 22.

177 Trudeau, *The Essential Trudeau*, 165.

178 Russell Hardin, *One for All: The Logic of Group Conflict* (Princeton: Princeton University Press, 1995), 220, cited in Redhead, *Charles Taylor*, 123.

179 Jürgen Habermas, "Struggles for Recognition in the Democratic Constitutional State," in Taylor et al., *Multiculturalism: Examining "The Politics of Recognition,"* 132.

180 Redhead, *Charles Taylor*, 124–5.

181 Lamey, "Francophonia Forever," 14.

182 Steven C. Rockefeller, "Comment," in Taylor, *Multiculturalism and "The Politics of Recognition,"* 92–3.

183 Pierre Trudeau, "Say Goodbye to the Dream of One Canada," in *With a Bang, Not a Whimper*, ed. Donald Johnston (Toronto, 1988), 10. The article was originally published simultaneously in the *Toronto Star* and *La Presse* on 27 May 1987.

184 Guy Laforest, *Trudeau and the End of the Canadian Dream*, trans. Paul Leduc Brown and Michelle Weinroth (Montreal, 1995), 107–9. Laforest says that Trudeau took advantage of the weaknesses in the ratification process "and

thereby played a key role in the dismantling of the accord ... Within the context of a study of Mr. Trudeau's political commitment, the Meech Lake saga takes on the form of a classic ancient tragedy."

185 Charles Taylor, "The Stakes of Constitutional Reform," in *Reconciling the Solitudes*, 140–54. Taylor appeared before the committee on 19 December 1990. While his presentation does not renounce his federalist outlook or claim that Quebec's desire for distinct society status should be accommodated *within* Canada, Taylor seems to demonstrate by his use of language – he refers to "our" situation or "our" borders – that he regards himself first as a Quebecer and secondly as a Canadian. For an analysis of Taylor's role in Canada's constitutional debates, see Guy LaForest, "Philosophy and Political Judgement in a Multinational Federation," in *Philosophy in an Age of Pluralism: The Philosophy of Charles Taylor in Question*, ed. James Tully (Cambridge, 1994), 194–9.

186 Taylor, *Multiculturalism and "The Politics of Recognition*," 60–1.

187 Ibid., 56. To clarify Taylor's distinction, it is worth quoting him more fully. Citing Ronald Dworkin's distinction between two kinds of moral commitment, Taylor writes: "We all have views about the ends of life, about what constitutes a good life, which we and others ought to strive for. But we also acknowledge a commitment to deal fairly and equally with each other, regardless of how we conceive our ends. We might call this latter commitment 'procedural,' while commitments concerning the ends of life are 'substantive.' Dworkin claims that a liberal society is one that as a society adopts no particular substantive view about the ends of life. The society is, rather, united around a strong procedural commitment to treat people with equal respect."

188 Taylor, "Shared and Divergent Values," 175.

189 Ibid., 172–9. See also Taylor, *Multiculturalism and "The Politics of Recognition*," 52–60.

190 Taylor, *Multiculturalism and "The Politics of Recognition*," 58.

191 Ibid., 58–60. See also Taylor, "Shared and Divergent Values," 175–7.

192 For a commentary on this issue, see Barry Cooper, "Political Religions in Quebec and the Constitutional Politics of Identity" (paper presented to the Canadian Political Science Association at the Learned Societies, St John's, Nfld, June 1997).

193 Michael Lusztig, "Canada's Long Road to Nowhere: Why the Circle of Command Liberalism Cannot Be Squared," *Canadian Journal of Political Science* 32, no. 3 (1999): 451–2, 462–3. Lusztig distinguishes command liberals from anti-liberal communitarians. The latter eschew liberalism, subordinating individual rights to a collectively derived conception of the good life. He refers to Taylor as the "quintessential command liberal."

194 Cooper and Bercuson, *Deconfederation*, 135.

195 Habermas, "Struggles for Recognition in the Democratic Constitutional State," in 127–8. See also John Erik Fossum, "Deep Diversity versus Constitutional Patriotism: Taylor, Habermas and the Canadian Constitutional Crisis," *Ethnicities* 1, no. 2 (2001): 179–206. Fossum provides a detailed comparison of the thinking of Taylor and Habermas on this issue.

196 Habermas, "Struggles for Recognition in the Democratic Constitutional State," 109.

197 Ibid., 113.

198 Janet Ajzenstat, *The Once and Future Canadian Democracy* (Montreal and Kingston, 2003), 122. Ajzenstat's emphasis.

199 Cooper, "Political Religions in Quebec and the Constitutional Politics of Identity," 21.

200 Taylor, "Irreducibly Social Goods" and "Cross-Purposes: The Liberal-Communitarian Debate," in *Philosophical Arguments*, 145, 143, 188.

201 Stephen Mulhall and Adam Swift discuss Taylor's elaboration of this relationship between individuality and culture in *Liberals and Communitarians* (Oxford, 1997).

202 Ruth Abbey, *Charles Taylor*, 105. Abbey writes: "Taylor replaces the primacy of the individual with the primacy of the community."

203 Taylor, *Hegel*, 376.

204 Ibid.

205 Abbey, *Charles Taylor*, 106.

206 Srinivasan, "Freedom, Community and Transcendence," 130–1.

207 Ibid., 131.

208 I have taken the phrase *illiberal strand* from Max Nemni, who used it in the title of a paper, "The Illiberal Strand in Taylor's Conception of Quebec's Contemporary Nationalism," cited in Cooper, "Political Religions in Quebec and the Constitutional Politics of Identity," 21.

209 Hegel, *Philosophy of Right*, #138, #139, 92, and "Additions," #89, 254–5. It should be noted that Hegel realizes that to have a conscience, if conscience is only a formal subjectivity (that is to say, lacking a sense of community), "is to be on the verge of slipping into evil; in independent self-certainty, with its independence of knowledge and decision, both morality and evil have their common root. The origin of evil in general is to be found in the mystery of freedom."

210 Will Kymlicka, *Liberalism, Community and Culture* (New York: Oxford University Press, 1989), 50. See also Krob, "Hegel's Community," 151–3.

211 Brian Barry, *Culture and Equality: An Egalitarian Critique of Multiculturalism* (Cambridge, Mass., 2001), 65.

212 Ibid., 65.

213 Taylor, "The Rushdie Controversy," 118–22.

214 Ibid., 122.

215 Ibid., 120.

216 Ibid., 122.

217 In considering Taylor's essay "The Rushdie Controversy," I have benefited from three main sources: Daniel O'Neill, "Multicultural Liberals and the Rushdie Affair: A Critique of Kymlicka, Taylor and Walzer," *Review of Politics* 61, no. 2 (1999): 219–51; Ronald Beiner, *Philosophy in a Time of Lost Spirit: Essays on Contemporary Theory* (Toronto, 1997), 159–60; and Brian Barry, *Culture and Equality*, 294–5.

218 Taylor, *Multiculturalism and "The Politics of Recognition,"* 63.

219 Brian Barry, *Culture and Equality*, 280. See also Beiner, *"Philosophy in a Time of Lost Spirit,* 159. Beiner writes: "[T]he onus of understanding falls predominantly on one side in this cultural struggle. For myself, I have trouble seeing why Rushdie is obliged to be fully understanding of how the faithful see the world, but the faithful are not obliged to understand how Rushdie sees the world."

220 Ibid., 283.

221 Taylor, *Multiculturalism and "The Politics of Recognition,"* 62.

222 Ibid., 59.

223 O'Neill, "Multicultural Liberals and the Rushdie Affair," 239–41.

224 Taylor, "The Rushdie Controversy," 118.

225 Ibid., 120.

226 Ibid., 121.

227 Taylor, *Multiculturalism and "The Politics of Recognition,"* 64.

228 O'Neill, "Multicultural Liberals and the Rushdie Affair," 238–9.

229 Ibid., 239.

230 Ibid., 219.

231 Taylor, *Multiculturalism and "The Politics of Recognition,"* 42.

232 Lamey, "Francophonia Forever," 14–15. Lamey cites Bellow's article in the *New York Times*, 10 March 1994.

233 Brian Barry, *Culture and Equality*, 267.

234 Dunn, *Interpreting Political Responsibility*, 186.

235 John Dunn, "Pursuing the Personal by Way of the Communal," *Times Higher Education Supplement*, 22 January 1993, 20.

236 Beiner, *Philosophy in a Time of Lost Spirit*, 155.

237 Ibid., 156–7. Beiner's emphasis. It is worth quoting Beiner in full on this point because he succinctly summarizes the source of tension in Taylor's thought: "Taylor indeed seems inspired by the Hegelian impulse to combine somehow these two distinct endeavours (the validity of the modern self and the notion

of a larger moral order beyond the self); yet in the absence of Hegel's own philosophical commitment to a necessary coincidence of the larger rational order and the historically evolved articulation of selfhood, the tension persists."

238 Brian Barry, "Statism and Nationalism: A Cosmopolitan Critique," in *Nomos*, vol. 41: *Global Justice*, ed. I. Shapiro and L. Brilmayer (New York: New York University Press, 1999), cited in Redhead, *Charles Taylor*, 139.

239 Charles Taylor, "Reply and Re-articulation," in *Philosophy in an Age of Pluralism*, ed. James Tully, 254.

240 Ripstein, "Recognition and Cultural Membership," 334.

241 Rockefeller, "Comment," in *Multiculturalism and "The Politics of Recognition,"* 88.

242 Ibid., 89.

243 Mark Redhead, "Charles Taylor's Deeply Diverse Response to Canadian Fragmentation: A Project Often Commented On but Seldom Explored," *Canadian Journal of Political Science* 36, no. 1 (2003): 75.

PART FIVE

1 David Taras and Beverly Rasporich, eds, introduction to *A Passion for Identity: Introduction to Canadian Studies* (Toronto, 1997), 10.

2 Charles Taylor, *Reconciling the Solitudes: Essays on Canadian Federalism and Nationalism* (Montreal and Kingston, 1993), 59.

3 Charles Taylor, *Hegel* (Cambridge, 1975), 570.

4 Taylor, *Reconciling the Solitudes*, 183.

5 Charles Taylor, *Multiculturalism and "The Politics of Recognition,"* ed. Amy Gutmann (Princeton, 1992), 43.

6 Taylor, *Reconciling the Solitudes*, 183.

7 Vasanthi Srinivasan, "Freedom, Community and Transcendence: A Comparison of Select Western and Indian Thinkers" (PhD diss., Carleton University, 1997), 70.

8 Taylor, *Multiculturalism and "The Politics of Recognition,"* 64.

9 Quoted in Patchen Markell, "Bound by Recognition: The Politics of Identity after Hegel" (PhD diss., Harvard University, 1999), 171. I owe my questions to a reading of Amelie Rorty, "The Hidden Politics of Cultural Identification," *Political Theory* 22, no. 1 (1994): 152–66; and Arthur Ripstein, "Recognition and Cultural Membership," *Dialogue* 34 (1995): 332–4.

10 Elizabeth Trott, "Multiculturalism, Charles Taylor, and the Idea of Canada," in *Alternative Frontiers: Voices from the Mountain West*, ed. Allen Seager, Leonard Evenden, Rowland Lorimer, and Robin Mathews (Montreal, 1997), 45.

11 Ibid.

12 Michael Lusztig, "Canada's Long Road to Nowhere: Why the Circle of Command Liberalism Cannot be Squared," *Canadian Journal of Political Science* 32, no. 3 (1999): 465.

13 Iris Marion Young, "Difference As a Resource for Democratic Deliberation," in *Deliberative Democracy: Essays on Reason and Politics*, ed. J. Bohman and W. Rehg (Cambridge, Mass.: MIT Press, 1997), 387–8, cited in Andrew Schaap, "Political Reconciliation through a Struggle for Recognition?" *Social and Legal Studies* 13, no. 4 (2004): 535.

14 Norman Barry, "Charles Taylor on Multiculturalism and the Politics of Recognition," in *Community and Tradition: Conservative Perspectives on the American Experience*, ed. George W. Carey and Bruce Frohnen (Lanham, Md, 1998), 123.

15 Jurgen Habermas, "Struggles for Recognition in the Democratic Constitutional State," in Charles Taylor, *Multiculturalism: Examining the Politics of Recognition*, ed. Amy Gutmann (Princeton, 1994), 131.

16 Schaap, "Political Reconciliation through a Struggle for Recognition?" 535.

17 Ibid., 523.

18 Ibid., 531. Schaap quotes Majid Yar, "Recognition and the Politics of Human(e) Desire," *Theory, Culture and Society* 18, nos 2–3 (2001): 62.

19 Schaap, "Political Reconciliation through a Struggle for Recognition?" 532. Schaap quotes Albert Memmi, *The Coloniser and the Colonised* (1965; reprint, London: Earthscan Publications, 1990), 201, 205.

20 Schaap, "Political Reconciliation through a Struggle for Recognition?" 533. Schaap quotes Franz Fanon, *Black Skin, White Masks* (1952; reprint, London: Pluto Press, 1986), 220; and Fanon, *The Wretched of the Earth* (London: Macgibbon & Kee, 1963), 31–2.

21 Schaap, "Political Reconciliation through a Struggle for Recognition?" 531.

22 Ibid., 524–5.

23 Ibid., 534–5.

24 Ibid., 538.

25 Janet Ajzenstat, "Decline of Procedural Liberalism: The Slippery Slope to Succession," in *Is Quebec Nationalism Just? Perspectives from Anglophone Canada*, ed. Joseph H. Carens (Montreal and Kingston, 1995), 120–2, 132. Ajzenstat quotes Taylor's essay "Shared and Divergent Values."

26 Leslie Armour, "Canadian Ways of Thinking: Logic, Society, and Canadian Philosophy," in *Alternative Frontiers: Voices from the Mountain West*, ed. Allen Seager, Leonard Evenden, Rowland Lorimer, and Robin Mathews (Montreal, 1997) 29, 14. In the latter reference, Armour writes that Canadians have needed "new ways of thinking because they recognized that certain kinds of pluralism were

inevitable," which required "the kind of openness a society needs when its future cannot be wholly predicted. But they also recognized that such a system could only work in the context of some kind of general agreement about reason and how it should be applied."

27 Ajzenstat, "Decline of Procedural Liberalism," 132.

28 John Dunn, *Interpreting Political Responsibility* (Princeton, 1990), 184. Dunn refers to one of Taylor's most "ambitious and fruitful themes" as "the conception of the self-interpreting individual as metaphysically dependent upon rather than independent of society."

29 Ibid., 184.

30 Adam Krob, "Hegel's Community: Synthesizing the Romantic and the Liberal" (PhD diss., Duke University, 1997), 253, 261.

31 Norman Barry, "Charles Taylor on Multiculturalism and the Politics of Recognition," 113.

32 Ibid., 112.

33 Janet Ajzenstat, *The Once and Future Canadian Democracy: An Essay in Political Thought* (Montreal and Kingston, 2003), 122. Ajzenstat writes: Taylor "supports the building of a Québécois way of life to distinguish the citizens of Quebec from other populations on the North American continent but hopes at the same time that Quebec will not differ from other jurisdictions in its adherence to broad principles of liberal-democratic justice. In all his writings on Quebec, Taylor is looking for the halfway house."

34 Clifford Orwin, "Charles Taylor's Pedagogy of Recognition," in *Canadian Political Philosophy: Contemporary Reflections*, ed. Ronald Beiner and Wayne Norman (Toronto, 2001), 239.

35 Leslie Armour and Elizabeth Trott, *The Faces of Reason: An Essay on Philosophy and Culture in English Canada 1850–1950* (Waterloo, Ont., 1981), 14–15.

36 George Grant, *Selected Letters*, ed. William Christian (Toronto, 1996), 194–5. It is worth quoting the letter more fully because it reinforces the influence Hegel had on Grant: "I think one has to admit that Hegel is onto something prodigious when he says that history is the unfolding of freedom in the world. To say it is prodigious is not here to discuss its truth or falsity, but to say that it is what the modern consciousness is."

37 George Grant, "Appendix 2, Introduction to the 1966 Edition," in *Philosophy in the Mass Age*, ed. William Christian (1959; reprint, Toronto, 1995), 118. Grant writes: "I mean by liberalism the belief that man's essence is his freedom." See also David Cayley, *George Grant in Conversation* (Toronto, 1995), 47.

38 Harris Athanasiadis. *George Grant and the Theology of the Cross: The Christian Foundations of His Thought* (Toronto, 2001). Athanasiadis sums up the issue rather succinctly: "The whole movement of freedom from and rejection of

transcendent standards above the human intellect or will, is simply the continuation of the theology of glory."

39 Joan O'Donovan, *George Grant and the Twilight of Justice* (Toronto, 1984), 76–7. O'Donovan sums up this aspect of Strauss's thought with this statement: "For Strauss, as for Plato and Aristotle, neither the phenomenal world, the givens of experience, nor the eternal things, as objects of contemplation, change or evolve. Being and truth are unchanging and self-identical. They do not dialectically complete themselves through successive 'historical' stages so that the structure and content of experience and thought change from stage to stage. The situation of thought is a permanent one; it is not fundamentally transformed by political action or religious 'revelations.'"

40 Leo Strauss, *Natural Right and History* (Chicago, 1950), 22–3.

41 Leo Strauss, *What Is Political Philosophy? and Other Studies* (Chicago, 1959), 26.

42 Strauss, *Natural Right and History*, 25.

43 George Grant, *Time As History*, ed. William Christian (1969; reprint, Toronto, 1995), 11–13.

44 Grant, *Philosophy in the Mass Age*, 102–3.

45 George Grant, *Technology and Empire* (Toronto, 1969), 105.

46 Ibid., 103.

47 H.D. Forbes, "George Grant and Leo Strauss," in *George Grant and the Subversion of Modernity*, ed. Davis, 185–6. Forbes writes: "Grant observes that Strauss says little about the relationship between the history of philosophy and biblical religion." See also Wayne Whillier, "George Grant and Leo Strauss: A Parting of the Ways," in George Grant, *Two Theological Languages by George Grant and Other Essays in Honour of His Work*, ed. Wayne Whillier (Lewiston, N.Y., 1990), 69–73.

48 Grant, *Technology and Empire*, 108.

49 Yusuf Umar, "The Philosophical Context of George Grant's Political Philosophy," in *George Grant and the Future of Canada* (Calgary, 1992), 13.

50 Forbes, "George Grant and Leo Strauss," 182.

51 Strauss, "Interpretations of Genesis" (lecture in the *Works of the Mind* series, University of Chicago, 25 January 1957), 14, cited in Whillier, "George Grant and Leo Strauss," 67.

52 Forbes, "George Grant and Leo Strauss," 187. Forbes writes: "In his interpretations of ancient authors, Strauss implicitly elevated intellectual above moral virtue ... In contrasting ancients and moderns, he was always silent about Christianity."

53 Leo Strauss, *Persecution and the Art of Writing* (Glencoe, Ill., 1952), 21. The full statement is as follows: "The precarious status of philosophy in Judaism as well as in Islam was not in every respect a misfortune for philosophy. The official recognition of philosophy in the Christian world made philosophy subject to

ecclesiastical supervision. The precarious position of philosophy in the Islamic-Jewish world guaranteed its private character and therein its inner freedom from supervision."

54 Grant, *Two Theological Languages*, 12.

55 George Grant, "Conversation: Intellectual Background," in *George Grant in Process*, ed. Schmidt (Toronto, 1978), 65. See also Forbes, "George Grant and Leo Strauss," 190–1; and Whillier, "George Grant and Leo Strauss," 69.

56 Quoted in Larry Schmidt, "An Interview with George Grant," *Grail: An Ecumenical Journal* 1, no. 1 (1985): 44.

57 Grant, "Conversation," 65.

58 Grant, *Technology and Empire*, 139.

59 George Grant, *Lament for a Nation: The Defeat of Canadian Nationalism* (1965; reprint, Ottawa, 1989), 96.

60 Ibid., 68.

61 Ibid., 21–2. Grant writes: "[Diefenbaker's] failure to recognize the rights of French Canadians, *qua* community, was inconsistent with the roots of Canadian nationalism."

62 George Grant, "Nationalism and Rationalism," in *Power Corrupted: The October Crisis and the Repression of Quebec*, ed. Abraham Rotstein (Toronto, 1971), 51.

63 Janet Ajzenstat says that the country that Grant loved as his own "was almost entirely fabricated from his imagination and his personal preferences." See Ajzenstat, *The Once and Future Canadian Democracy*, 110.

64 Michael Allen Gillespie, "George Grant and the Tradition of Political Philosophy," in *By Loving Our Own: George Grant and the Legacy of Lament for a Nation*, ed. Peter Emberley (Ottawa, 1990), 125.

65 Grant, *Selected Letters*, 221.

66 Quoted in Charles Taylor, *Radical Tories: The Conservative Tradition in Canada* (Toronto, 1982), 23. The full quotation is in note 239, Part 3.

67 Cited in Michael Bliss, "The Multicultural North American Hotel," *National Post*, 15 January 2003, A16.

68 Hans Hauge, "George Grant's Critique of Modernity: Canadian Refractions of Continental Ideas," *Canadian Issues* 12 (1990): 109–23.

69 Grant, *Time As History*, 40.

70 Ibid., 40.

71 Zdravko Planinc, "Paradox and Polyphony in Grant's Critique of Modernity," in *George Grant and the Future of Canada*, ed. Yusuf Umar (Calgary, 1992), 31.

72 R.W. Crook, "Modernization and Nostalgia: A Note on the Sociology of Pessimism," *Queen's Quarterly* 73 (Summer 1966): 269–83; Robert Blumstock, "Anglo-Saxon Lament," *Canadian Review of Sociology and Anthropology* 3 (May 1966): 98–105; Abraham Rotstein, "Running from Paradise," *Canadian Forum*, May

1969, 26–8; and Dennis Duffy, "The Ancestral Journeys: Travels with George Grant," *Journal of Canadian Studies* 22, no. 3 (1987): 90–103.

73 Grant, "Conversation: Intellectual Background," 63.

74 Grant, *Lament*, xi.

75 Vergil, *The Aeneid*, trans. Frank Copley (New York: Bobbs-Merrill Co., 1965), lines 305–29, 125. Arguably, the resonance of Grant's mythic allusion reaches even deeper when you consider that Vergil's poem was commissioned by Caesar Augustus to unite Romans during the transition from republic to empire. Vergil's poem was intended to provide a diverse people a myth of their origins that would help them understand the newly emergent empire. Is *Lament* the *Aeneid* for lost and wandering post-Canadians? Is Grant Canada's Vergil, providing the consolations of philosophy to help us cope with our loss and reconcile ourselves to the new world order? If so, then he is being rather Hegelian to the extent that he fulfils Hegel's metaphoric explanation of philosophy's purposes: the Owl of Minerva flies only at dusk. That said, there is another possible layer of allusion: in casting Diefenbaker as the tragic hero of his tale, Grant reminds the reader of another tragic figure, King Lear, who eventually lamented his foolishness in dividing his kingdom. In act 5, scene 3, Lear carries the dead Cordelia in his arms, shouting, "Howl, howl, howl … Thou'll come no more, never, never, never …" Interestingly, the word *howl* refers us back to *lament*, with its etymological roots in the Latin word *latrare*, meaning to bark or cry. For these insights – and the pleasure of our conversation – I thank Professor Tom Darby.

76 The only substantive comparison of Watson and Grant of which I am aware is that in Bruce Elder, *Image and Identity: Reflections on Canadian Film and Culture* (Waterloo, Ont., 1989), chap. 2. Elder's essay provided me with the seed of my essay, and I thank Professor Brian McKillop at Carleton University for drawing it to my attention.

77 John Watson, *The State in Peace and War* (Glasgow, 1919), 55.

78 Ibid.

79 Ibid., 213.

80 Ibid., 248.

81 Ibid., 214.

82 Ibid., 275.

83 Ibid., 274.

84 Ibid., 272.

85 Taylor, *Multiculturalism and "The Politics of Recognition,"* 72.

86 Charles Taylor, "Globalization and the Future of Canada," *Queen's Quarterly* 105, no. 3 (1998): 340–1.

87 Bliss, "The Multicultural North American Hotel," A16.

88 Watson, *The State in Peace and War*, 181.

89 Ibid., 275. See also Robert Conquest, *Reflections on a Ravaged Century* (New York, 1999), 246. Even Indians acknowledge the general beneficence of British rule. Nirad Chaudhuri dedicates his book *The Autobiography of an Unknown Indian* "to the memory of the British Empire in India which conferred subjecthood on us but withheld citizenship; to which yet every one of us threw out the challenge: *Civis Brittanicus Sum* because all that was good and living within us was made, shaped, and quickened by the same British rule." The quotation is from Conquest's book.

90 Michael Hardt and Antonio Negri, *Empire* (Cambridge, Mass., 2000).

91 Michael Ignatieff, "Nation-Building Lite," *New York Times Magazine,* 28 July 2002, n.p.

92 Ignatieff, "Who Are Americans to Think That Freedom Is Theirs to Spread?" *New York Times Magazine,* 26 June 2005, n.p.

93 Ignatieff, "Canada in the Age of Terror – Multilateralism Meets a Moment of Truth," *Policy Options* 24, no. 2 (2003): 14–15.

94 Hardt and Negri, *Empire*, xi–xvii.

95 Ibid., xv, 397.

96 Ian Angus, *Empire, Borders, Place: A Critique of Hardt and Negri's Concept of Empire.* This article can be accessed at http://muse.jhu.edu/journals/ theory_and_event/v007/7.3angus.html.

97 Hardt and Negri, *Empire*, chap. 4.3.

98 Hardt and Negri's vision of empire has all the trappings of a manifestation of the kind of spiritual disorder that Eric Voegelin describes in his 1938 study of Nazism, *Die Politischen Religionen,* as symptomatic of pneumopathology – the projection of a daydream, or second-order reality, as a way to understand the world. The book was reprinted as *The Political Religions* (Lewiston, N.Y.: E. Mellen Press, 1986). Barry Cooper examines this intellectual phenomenon in more contemporary terms in *New Political Religions, or An Analysis of Modern Terrorism* (Columbia, Mo.: University of Missouri Press, 2004).

99 Deepak Lal, *In Defense of Empires* (Washington, D.C., 2004), 37.

100 Lewis Feuer, *Imperialism and the Anti-Imperialist Mind* (New York: Prometheus Books, 1986), esp. chaps 2, 4, and 5. Lewis points out that the end of imperialism brought a resurgence of tribal killings in many now independent African states. He notes, for example, that Tutsi and Hutu tribesmen first began killing each other by the thousands in Rwanda and Burundi in the 1960s and 1970s, at the height of the anti-colonial movement.

101 Ibid., 1, 20. Feuer defends his ideas about empire, arguing that "anti-imperialist literature has perhaps beclouded the great fact that the world's advances have been associated with the eras of progressive imperialism ... A progressive imperialism is one in which energies are liberated for the advancement of civili-

zation and creative activity … A rising, progressive people will be a correspond-
ingly commercial, scientific, and imperialist people; such imperialism is not
atavistic but creative. Decay comes when those energies have become effete."

102 Ibid., 104. Feuer writes: "Between the years 1860 to 1876 at least four hundred thousand natives, it has been estimated, were enslaved for use in the Middle East and North Africa." He also notes that thousands of African boys were
castrated by Arab slave traders, and questions why "the writings of Arab and
black ideologists alike evince no trace of an Arab-Muslim guilt" comparable to
the guilt Westerners are supposed to feel about their imperial past. He goes on
to observe, borrowing an argument from Bernard Lewis, that somehow the
idea of the "white man's burden" has transmuted into a burden not of power
but of guilt that was enthusiastically taken up by leftist intellectuals after the
First World War.

103 Ibid., 105.

104 The idea of empire is, indeed, intellectually respectable again, even in the
popular press. See, for example, Max Boot, "The Case for American Empire,"
Weekly Standard 7, no. 5 (2001); Philip Hensher, "Let's Be Honest: We Need to
Impose Our Imperial Rule on Afghanistan," *Independent*, 17 October 2001;
Emily Eakin, "'It Takes an Empire, Say Several U.S. Thinkers," *International
Herald Tribune*, 2 April 2002; and Robert Cooper, "Why We Still Need Em-
pires," *Sunday Observer*, 7 April 2002.

105 Tom Darby, "On Spiritual Crisis, Globalization, and Planetary Rule," in *Faith,
Reason and Political Life Today,* ed. Peter Augustine Lawler and Dale McConkey
(Lanham, Md, 2001), 58–9.

106 Robert Cooper, *The Postmodern State and the World Order* (London, 1996),
11–12.

107 Robert Cooper, "The Next Empire," *Prospect Magazine*, October 2001, n.p.
Interestingly, even some Africans feel this way. On 1 July 2007, the Catholic
archbishop of Zimbabwe's second-largest city, Bulawayo, called for the return
of British rule. He was quoted in the London *Sunday Times* as saying, "I think it
is justified for Britain to raid Zimbabwe and remove Mugabe. We should do
it ourselves but there's too much fear." Cited in James Kirchik, "The Case for
Invading Zimbabwe," *National Post*, 27 July 2007, A-11.

108 Robert Cooper, *The Breaking of Nations: Order and Chaos in the Twenty-first
Century* (Toronto, 2005), 71, 78–9. See also Cooper, "Imperial Liberalism,"
National Interest 79 (Spring 2005): 25–34. Cooper writes: "Liberal
imperialism may be an oxymoron, but imperial liberalism may be the reality
of today."

109 Conquest, *Reflections on a Ravaged Century,* 281.

110 Lal, *In Defense of Empires*, 2.

111 Ibid., 37.
112 Ibid., 26–7.
113 Ibid., 27, 37.
114 Quoted in Cooper, "The Next Empire," n.p.
115 Quoted in John Ibbitson, "Empire Strikes Back in Harper's Rhetoric," *Globe and Mail*, 27 July 2006, A10. As Ibbitson observes, it was an extraordinary thing for a Canadian prime minister to acknowledge Canada's British heritage and colonial legacy after four decades in which successive federal governments "have portrayed the French and English heritage as equivalent, and multiculturalism as transcendent."
116 Ignatieff, "Canada in the Age of Terror," 14.
117 Conquest, *Reflections on a Ravaged Century*, 276–8.
118 Alexandre Kojève, "Outline of a Doctrine of French Policy (August 27, 1945)," *Policy Review*, no. 126 (August 2004): 2. See also Robert Howse's commentary, "Kojève's Latin Empire," in the same issue. Both articles can be accessed at *www.policyreview.org/aug04/kojeve*. For a comprehensive discussion of Kojève's essay, see Erik de Vries, "A Kojèvean Citizenship Model for the European Union" (PhD diss., Carleton University, 2004), 208–20.
119 Kojève, "Outline of a Doctrine of French Policy," 9. Kojève's emphasis.
120 Ibid., 7.
121 Howse, "Kojève's Latin Empire," 4; and de Vries, "A Kojèvean Citizenship Model for the European Union," 209.
122 Kojève, "Outline of a Doctrine of French Policy," 7.
123 Ibid., 20.
124 Michael Ignatieff, *Empire Lite: Nation-Building in Bosnia, Kosovo and Afghanistan* (Toronto, 2003), 124.
125 Ignatieff, "Canada in the Age of Terror," 14–18.
126 Jennifer Welsh, *At Home in the World: Canada's Global Vision for the 21st Century* (Toronto, 2004). Welsh argues that Canada should be an example to the world by promoting multilateralism, human rights, pluralism, and basic decency. Some commentators dismiss such notions as dangerously naive, the kind of soft-power thinking that makes Canada increasingly irrelevant on the international stage. For example, former Canadian ambassador to the United States Derek Burney says that a foreign policy based on values and model citizenship will relegate Canada "more permanently to the periphery as a dilettante, not to be taken seriously" (quoted in "Still Waiting," *Ottawa Citizen*, 28 March 2005, A12).
127 Ignatieff, *Empire Lite*, 125.
128 Ibid., 23.
129 Watson, *The State in Peace and War*, 274. See also Lal, *In Defense of Empires*, 1.

Lal cites an 1881 letter to British prime minister William Gladstone from
King Bell and King Acqua of the Cameroons River, West Africa. The kings
write: "We want to be under Her Majesty's control. We want our country to
be governed by British Government. We are tired of governing this country
ourselves, every dispute leads to war, and often to great loss of lives, so we
think it is best thing to give up the country to you British men who no doubt
will bring peace, civilization, and Christianity in the country ... We are quite
willing to abolish all our heathen customs ... No doubt God will bless you for
putting a light in our country" (Kings Bell and Acqua to William Gladstone,
6 November 1881, Foreign Office 403/18, Public Record Office, Kew, in
M.W. Doyle, *Empires* [Ithaca: Cornell University Press, 1986], 162). No
doubt, some will dismiss the letter as reflecting a sentiment born out of ignorance of imperialism – the kings did not know what they were doing. But
such a response is implicitly condescending and patronizing in that it assumes the "savages" know less about the needs of their people than the anti-
imperialist liberal who supposedly has the natives' best interests at heart in
insisting on their right to self-determination. In any case, were the kings not
asking for the kind of help that soft-power enthusiasts say the West should be
providing to the Third World?

130 Ignatieff, *Empire Lite*, 25.

131 Ibid., 21.

132 Roald Nasgaard, *The Mystic North: Symbolist Landscape Painting in Northern
Europe and North America, 1890–1940* (Toronto: University of Toronto Press,
1984), 169ff; and David Burnett, *Masterpieces of Canadian Art from the National
Gallery of Canada* (Edmonton: Hurtig Publishers, 1990), 92. Nasgaard argues
that Harris's painting is a metaphoric response to the problematic nature of
living in the geographic vastness of Canada and, as such, a symbolic exploration of Canadian identity. See also Northrop Frye, *The Bush Garden: Essays on
the Canadian Imagination* (Toronto: House of Anansi Press, 1971), 209.
Frye remarked that Harris's paintings of Lake Superior and the Rocky Moun-
tains are "as much an exploration as the literal or physical explorations of
La Vérendrye or Mackenzie."

133 Richard Gwyn, *Nationalism without Walls: The Unbearable Lightness of Being Canadian* (Toronto: McClelland & Stewart, 1995).

134 Michael Bliss, "A Working Non-Nation?" *National Post*, 24 March 2006, A22.
This essay is a shorter version of one that appeared in the March 2006 edition
of the *Literary Review of Canada*. Again, Bliss is worth quoting more extensively
to illustrate my point: "It may even be possible that Canada is evolving beyond
the traditional nation-state ... and becoming one of the world's first working
non-nations ... Economically our destiny appears to be wary, friction-fraught

continental integration rather than northern sufficiency."

135 Bliss, "The Multicultural North American Hotel," A16. Bliss's words are again worth quoting more fully as an example of the sentiment to which I am referring: "Canada became Americanized in the 20th century. The process was not merely the effect of penetration by American popular culture, significant and complete as that has been. 'Americanization' went directly to the core of how Canadians wanted their own society to evolve. Drifting away from failed identity experiments (anglophilism, northernness, socialism, biculturalism), Canadians opted to mirror the United States as another pluralistic, human rights–based North American democracy. They also decided to complete the integration of their economy on a continental basis. The Canada-U.S. border became not so much a fence as a lawn marker. The difference was no longer between 'us' and 'them,' but rather between 'us' and 'us'– except on the issue of global military responsibility."

136 Michael Bliss, "Is Canada a Country in Decline?" *National Post*, 30 November 2001, A18; and Bliss, "A Country Going to Pieces," *National Post*, 22 October 2004, A18. See also Drew Fagan, "Has Canada Become the 51st State? *Globe and Mail*, 16 March 2002, F1; and Brian Kappler, "It's Time for Canadians to Ask: Do We Unite with the U.S. or Not?" *Ottawa Citizen*, 6 February 2002, A14. And then there is this headline for a newspaper article on "Canadians' Fear of a U.S. Takeover": "It's the Year 2025. There is no U.S. border. Has Canada become the 51st State?" *Globe and Mail*, 16 March 2002, F1.

137 Michael Ignatieff, "The Coming Constitutional Crisis," *National Post*, 16 April 2005, A19. See also Leslie Armour, *The Idea of Canada and the Crisis of Community* (Ottawa, 1981), 15. In a remark that is practically a corollary of Ignatieff's, Armour says that "a community shows itself in the institutions it legitimizes – or tries to legitimize." Is this another example, perhaps, of rational pluralism at work?

Bibliography

PRIMARY SOURCES

Georg Wilhelm Friedrich Hegel

Hegel: Reason in History. Translated by Robert S. Hartman. New York: Macmillan Publishing, 1953.

Lectures on the History of Philosophy. Vol. 3. Translated by H.S. Haldane and Frances H. Simson. New York: Humanities Press, 1955.

The Philosophy of History. Translated by J. Sibree, with an introduction by C.J. Friedrich. New York: Dover Publications, 1956.

Political Writings. Translated by T.M. Knox, with introduction by Z.A. Pelczynski. Oxford: Clarendon Press, 1965.

Philosophy of Right. Edited and translated by T.M. Knox. Oxford: Clarendon Press, 1967.

Hegel's Logic: Being Part One of the Encyclopedia of the Philosophical Sciences (1830). Translated by William Wallace. Oxford: University of Oxford Press, 1975. Also, Parts 2 and 3.

Lectures on the Philosophy of World History: Introduction. Translated by H.B. Nisbet, with an introduction by Duncan Forbes. Cambridge: Cambridge University Press, 1975.

Early Theological Writings. Translated by T.M. Knox, with an introduction by R. Kroner. Chicago: Chicago University Press, 1976.

The Difference between Fichte's and Schelling's System of Philosophy. Translated by H.S. Harris and Walter Cerf. Albany: State University of New York Press, 1977.

Faith and Knowledge. Translated by H.S. Harris and Walter Cerf. Albany: State University of New York Press, 1977.

Phenomenology of Spirit. Translated by A.V. Miller, with analysis and foreword by J.N. Findlay. Oxford: Oxford University Press, 1977.

Hegel Lectures on the Philosophy of Religion. One-volume edition. Edited by Peter Hodgson. Berkeley: University of California Press, 1988.

John Watson

"The Problem of Hegel." *Philosophical Review* 3 (1894): 546–67.

"The Absolute and the Time Process." *Philosophical Review* 4 (1895): 353–72, 486–505.

Comte, Mill and Spencer: An Outline of Philosophy. Glasgow: James Maclehose and Sons, 1895.

Hedonistic Theories from Aristippus to Spencer. Glasgow: James Maclehose and Sons, 1895.

Christianity and Idealism. New York: Macmillan, 1896.

"Art, Morality and Religion." Parts 1 and 2. *Queen's Quarterly* 5 (1897): 287–96; and 6 (1898): 132–53.

An Outline of Philosophy. 2nd ed. Glasgow: James Maclehose and Sons, 1898.

"The Outlook in Philosophy." *Queen's Quarterly* 8 (1901): 241–56.

The Philosophical Basis of Religion. Glasgow: James Maclehose and Sons, 1907.

"Christianity and History." *Queen's Quarterly* 15 (1908): 163–75.

The Philosophy of Kant Explained. Glasgow: James Maclehose and Sons, 1908.

"Idealism of Edward Caird." Parts 1 and 2. *Philosophical Review* 28, nos 2 and 3 (1909): 147–63, 259–80.

The Interpretation of Religious Experience. 2 vols. Glasgow: James Maclehose and Sons, 1912.

"Pragmatism and Idealism." *Queen's Quarterly* 21 (1914): 465–72.

"German Philosophy and Politics." *Queen's Quarterly* 22 (April–June 1915): 329–44.

"German Philosophy and the War." *Queen's Quarterly* 23 (April–June 1916): 365–79.

The State in Peace and War. Glasgow: James Maclehose and Sons, 1919.

"The Conflict of Absolutism and Realism." *Philosophical Review* 33 (1924): 229–44.

"The Conflict of Idealism with Realism." Parts 1 and 2. *Philosophical Review* 31 (1924): 14–42, 105–18.

"Bosanquet on Mind and the Absolute." *Philosophical Review* 34 (1925): 427–42.

John Watson Papers, Queen's University Archives.

George Grant

The Empire, Yes or No? Toronto: Ryerson Press, 1945.

"Have We a Canadian Nation?" *Public Affairs* (Institute of Public Affairs, Dalhousie University) 8, no. 3 (1945): 161–6.

"Philosophy in Canada." In *Royal Commission on National Development, Royal Commission Studies: The Massey Report*. Ottawa: King's Printer, 1951.

"Plato and Popper." *Canadian Journal of Economics and Political Science* 20 (September–October 1954): 185–94.

"The Uses of Freedom – A Word and Our World." *Queen's Quarterly* 62, no. 4 (1956): 515–27.

Philosophy in the Mass Age. Edited by William Christian. 1959; reprint, Toronto: University of Toronto Press, 1995.

"An Ethic of Community." In *Social Purpose for Canada*, edited by Michael Oliver, 3–26. Toronto: University of Toronto Press, 1961.

Lament for a Nation: The Defeat of Canadian Nationalism. 1965; reprint, Ottawa: Carleton University Press, 1989.

"Comments on the Great Society from the 35th Couchiching Conference, 1966." In *Great Societies and Quiet Revolutions*, edited by John Irwin, 71–6. Toronto: Canadian Broadcasting Corporation, 1967.

Technology and Empire. Toronto: House of Anansi Press, 1969.

Time As History. Edited by William Christian. 1969; reprint, Toronto: University of Toronto Press, 1995.

"Nationalism and Rationalism." In *Power Corrupted: The October Crisis and the Repression of Quebec*, ed. Abraham Rotstein, 51–6. Toronto: New Press, 1971.

"Revolution and Tradition." In *Tradition and Revolution*, edited by Lionel Rubinoff, 81–95. Toronto: Macmillan Publishing Co., 1971.

"Ideology in Modern Empires." In *Perspectives of Empire: Essays Presented to Gerald S. Graham*, edited by John E. Flint and Glyndwr Williams, 189–97. London: Longman, 1973.

"Knowing and Making." *Transactions of the Royal Society of Canada*. 4th series, 1975.

Foreword to *The Liberal Idea of Canada: Pierre Trudeau and the Question of Canada's Survival*, by James and Robert Laxer, 9–12. Toronto: James Lorimer & Co., 1977.

"Celine: Art and Politics." *Queen's Quarterly* 90 (1983): 801–13.

English-Speaking Justice. Notre Dame: University of Notre Dame, 1985.

Technology and Justice. Toronto: House of Anansi Press, 1986.

With Monica Hall. "Lament for a Nation Revisited: An Interview with George Grant." *International Insights: A Dalhousie Journal on International Affairs* 4, no. 1 (1988): 5–9.

"Obedience." *Idler Magazine* 29 (August 1990): 23–8.

Two Theological Languages by George Grant and Other Essays in Honour of His Work. Edited by Wayne Whillier. Lewiston, N.Y.: Edwin Mellon Press, 1990.

Selected Letters. Edited by William Christian. Toronto: University of Toronto Press, 1996.

The George Grant Reader. Edited by William Christian and Sheila Grant. Toronto: University of Toronto Press, 1998.

Collected Works of George Grant. Vol. 2. Edited by Arthur Davis. Toronto: University of
    Toronto Press, 2002

                                Charles Taylor

The Explanation of Behaviour. London: Routledge and Kegan Paul, 1964.
"Interpretation and the Sciences of Man." *Review of Metaphysics* 35, no. 1 (1971): 3–51.
"The Opening Arguments of the Phenomenology." In *Hegel: A Collection of Critical
    Essays,* edited by A. MacIntyre. New York: Doubleday Anchor, 1972.
Hegel. Cambridge: Cambridge University Press, 1975.
Hegel and Modern Society. Cambridge: Cambridge University Press, 1979.
Philosophical Papers. Vol. 1: *Human Agency and Language.* Cambridge: Cambridge
    University Press, 1985.
Philosophical Papers. Vol. 2: *Philosophy and the Human Sciences.* Cambridge: Cam-
    bridge University Press, 1985.
"Balancing the Humours: Modernity with a Twist." *Idler* 26 (November–December
    1989): 21–9.
"Cross-Purposes: The Liberal-Communitarian Debate." In *Liberalism and the Moral Life,*
    edited by Nancy Rosenblum. Cambridge, Mass.: Harvard University Press, 1989.
"The Rushdie Controversy." *Public Culture* 2, no. 1 (1989): 118–22.
Sources of the Self: The Making of the Modern Identity. Cambridge, U.K.: Cambridge
    University, 1989.
"Hegel's Ambiguous Legacy for Modern Liberalism." In *Hegel and Legal Theory,* ed-
    ited by Drucilla Cornell, Michel Rosenfeld, and David Gray Carlson, 64–77. New
    York: Routledge, 1991.
The Malaise of Modernity. Toronto: Anansi Press, 1991.
"Can Canada Survive the Charter?" *Alberta Law Review* 30, no. 2 (1992): 427–47.
Multiculturalism and "The Politics of Recognition." Edited and with commentary by
    Amy Gutmann. Princeton, N.J.: Princeton University Press, 1992.
"The Motivation behind Procedural Ethics." In *Kant and Political Philosophy: The
    Contemporary Legacy,* edited by Ronald Beiner and William James Booth, 337–60.
    New Haven, Conn.: Yale University Press, 1993.
Reconciling the Solitudes: Essays on Canadian Federalism and Nationalism. Montreal and
    Kingston: McGill-Queen's University Press, 1993.
Multiculturalism: Examining "The Politics of Recognition." Edited and with an introduc-
    tion by Amy Gutmann. Princeton, N.J.: Princeton University Press, 1994.
Philosophical Arguments. Cambridge, Mass.: Harvard University Press, 1995.
"Globalization and the Future of Canada." *Queen's Quarterly* 105, no. 3 (1998):
    331–42.
Modern Social Imaginaries. Durham, N.C.: Duke University Press, 2004.

SECONDARY SOURCES

Abbey, Ruth. *Charles Taylor.* Princeton: Princeton University Press, 2000.

– "Humanism and Enchantment." *Literary Review of Canada,* March 2000, 9–12.

Ajzenstat, Janet. *The Once and Future Canadian Democracy: An Essay in Political Thought.* Montreal and Kingston: McGill-Queen's University Press, 2003.

Andrew, Edward. "George Grant on the Political Economy of Technology." *Bulletin of Science, Technology and Society* 23, no. 6 (December 2003): 479–85.

Angeles, Peter, ed. *Dictionary of Philosophy.* New York: Barnes & Noble Books, 1981.

Angus, Ian. *George Grant's Platonic Rejoinder to Heidegger.* Lewiston and Queenston: Edwin Mellon Press, 1987.

– "For a Canadian Philosophy: George Grant." *Canadian Journal of Political and Social Theory* 13, no. 1 (1989): 140–3.

– *A Border Within: National Identity, Cultural Plurality and Wilderness.* Montreal and Kingston: McGill-Queen's University Press, 1997.

– *Empire, Borders, Place: A Critique of Hardt and Negri's Concept of Empire,* http:// muse.jhu.edu/journals.theory_and_event/vo07/7.3angus.html.

Armour, Leslie. *The Idea of Canada and the Crisis of Community.* Ottawa: Steel Rail Publishing, 1981.

– "Canadian Ways of Thinking: Logic, Society, and Canadian Philosophy." In *Alternative Frontiers: Voices from the Mountain West,* edited by Allen Seager, Leonard Evenden, Rowland Lorimer, and Robin Mathews, 11–34. Montreal: Institute of Canadian Studies, 1997.

Armour, Leslie, and Elizabeth Trott. *The Faces of Reason: An Essay on Philosophy and Culture in English Canada 1850–1950.* Waterloo, Ont.: Wilfrid Laurier University Press, 1981.

Aronovitch, Hilliard. "Trudeau or Taylor? The Central Question." *Critical Review of International Social and Political Philosophy* 8, no. 3 (2005): 309–25.

Athanasiadis, Harris. "George Grant and the Theology of the Cross: The Christian Foundations of His Thought." PhD dissertation, McGill University, 1997.

– *George Grant and the Theology of the Cross.* Toronto: University of Toronto Press, 2001.

Aucion, Peter. "Organizational Change in the Machinery of Canadian Government." *Canadian Journal of Political Science* 19, no. 1 (1986): 3–27.

Avineri, Shlomo. *Hegel's Theory of the Modern State.* Cambridge: Cambridge University Press, 1972.

Avineri, Shlomo, and Avner de-Shalit, eds. *Communitarianism and Individualism.* Oxford: Oxford University Press, 1992.

Badertscher, John. "The Prophecy of George Grant." *Canadian Journal of Political and Social Theory* 4, no. 1 (1980): 183–9.

Barry, Brian. *Culture and Equality: An Egalitarian Critique of Multiculturalism.* Cambridge, Mass.: Harvard University Press, 2001.

Barry, Norman. "Charles Taylor on Multiculturalism and the Politics of Recognition." In *Community and Tradition: Conservative Perspectives on the American Experience*, edited by George W. Carey and Bruce Frohnen, 103–24. Lanham, Md: Rowman and Littlefield Publishing, 1998.

Beiner, Ronald. *Philosophy in a Time of Lost Spirit: Essays on Contemporary Theory.* Toronto: University of Toronto Press, 1997.

Beiner, Ronald, and Wayne Norman, eds. *Canadian Political Philosophy: Contemporary Reflections.* Toronto: University of Toronto Press, 2001.

Beiser, Frederick C., ed. *The Cambridge Companion to Hegel.* Cambridge, U.K.: Cambridge University Press, 1993.

Bellah, Robert N., et al. *Habits of the Heart: Individualism and Commitment in American Life.* Berkeley: University of California Press, 1985.

Bercuson, David, et al. *Colonies: Canada to 1867.* Toronto: McGraw-Hill Ryerson, 1992.

Berger, Carl. *The Sense of Power: Studies in the Ideas of Canadian Imperialism, 1867–1914.* Toronto: University of Toronto Press, 1970.

– ed. *Imperialism and Nationalism, 1884–1914: A Conflict in Canadian Thought.* Toronto: Copp Clark Publishing, 1969.

Bernstein, Richard. *Praxis and Action.* Philadelphia: University of Pennsylvania Press, 1971.

– "Why Hegel Now?" *Review of Metaphysics* 31, no. 1 (1977): 29–60.

Berthold-Bond, Daniel. *Hegel's Grand Synthesis: A Study of Being, Thought and History.* New York: Columbia University Press, 1989.

Bickerton, James, Stephen Brooks, and Alain-G. Gagnon. *Freedom, Equality and Community: The Political Philosophy of Six Influential Canadians.* Montreal and Kingston: McGill-Queen's University Press, 2006.

Blodgett. E.D. "George Grant, the Uncertain Nation and Diversity of Being." *Canadian Literature* 152–3 (Spring-Summer 1997): 107–23.

Bloom, Allan. *Giants and Dwarfs.* New York: Free Press, 1991.

Blumstock, Robert. "Anglo-Saxon Lament." *Canadian Review of Sociology and Anthropology* 3 (May 1966): 98–105.

Bosanquet, Bernard. *The Philosophical Theory of the State.* 3rd ed. London: Macmillan and Co., 1920.

Boucher, David. "British Idealism, the State, and International Relations." *Journal of the History of Ideas* 55 (1994): 671–94.

– "British Idealism and the Human Rights Culture." *History of European Ideas* 27 (2001): 61–78.

– ed. *The British Idealists.* Cambridge: Cambridge University Press, 1997.

Boucher, David, et al. "British Idealism and the Political Philosophy of T.H. Green, Bernard Bosanquet, R.G. Collingwood and Michael Oakeshott." *British Journal of Politics and International Relations* 7 (2005): 97–123.

Box, Ian. "George Grant and the Embrace of Technology." *Canadian Journal of Political Science* 15, no. 3 (1982): 503–15.

Braybrooke, David. "Inward and Outward with the Modern Self." *Dialogue* 33 (1994): 101–8.

Brod, Harry. *Hegel's Philosophy of Politics: Idealism, Identity and Modernity.* Boulder, Colo.: Westview Press, 1992.

Brubaker, Roger. *The Limits of Rationality: An Essay on the Social and Moral Thought of Max Weber.* London: Cambridge University Press, 1984.

Burbidge, John. *Hegel on Logic and Religion: The Reasonableness of Christianity.* Albany: State University of New York Press, 1992.

– "Hegel in Canada." *Owl of Minerva* 25, no. 2 (1994): 215–19.

Butler, Clark, and Christiane Seiler, trans. *Hegel: The Letters.* With commentary by Clark Butler. Bloomington: University of Indiana Press, 1989.

Butler, Judith. *Subjects of Desire: Hegelian Reflections in Twentieth-Century France.* New York: Columbia University Press, 1987.

Cairns, Alan. *Disruptions: Constitutional Struggles from the Charter to Meech Lake.* Edited by Douglas Williams. Toronto: McClelland & Stewart, 1991.

Calhoun, Craig. "Morality, Identity and Historical Explanation: Charles Taylor on the Sources of the Self." *Sociological Theory* 9, no. 2 (1991): 232–63.

Cappon, James. "Canada's Relation to the Empire." *Queen's Quarterly* 19, no. 2 (1911): 98–9.

Carens, Joseph H., ed. *Is Quebec Nationalism Just? Perspectives from Anglophone Canada.* Montreal and Kingston: McGill-Queen's University Press, 1995.

Cave, Terence. *Recognitions: A Study in Poetics.* Oxford: Clarendon Press, 1990.

Cayley, David. "The Moving Image of Eternity." Transcript of interview with George Grant. *Ideas.* Toronto: Canadian Broadcasting Corporation, 1986.

– *George Grant in Conversation.* Toronto: House of Anansi Press, 1995.

Christian, William. "George Grant and the Twilight of Our Justice." *Queen's Quarterly* 85 (1978): 485–91.

– "George Grant and Love: A Comment on Ian Box's 'George Grant and the Embrace of Technology.' With Box's 'Reply: Thinking Through Technology.'" *Canadian Journal of Political Science* 16, no. 2 (June 1983): 347–59.

– "George Grant and Religion: A Conversation Prepared and Edited by William Christian." *Journal of Canadian Studies* 26, no. 1 (1991): 42–6.

– "Religion, Faith and Love." *Studies in Political Theory* 1, no. 1 (1992): 61–73.

– *George Grant: A Biography.* Toronto: University of Toronto Press, 1993.
– "Canada's Fate: Principal Grant, Sir George Parkin and George Grant." *Journal of Canadian Studies* 34, no. 4 (1999/2000): 88–104.
– "Was George Grant a Red Tory?" In *Athens and Jerusalem: George Grant's Theology, Philosophy, and Politics,* edited by Ian Angus, Ron Dart, and Randy Peg Peters, 39–61. Toronto: University of Toronto Press, 2006.
Clendenning, John. *The Life and Thought of Josiah Royce.* Rev. ed. Nashville: Vanderbilt University Press, 1999.
Cole, D.L. "Canada's 'Nationalistic' Imperialists." *Journal of Canadian Studies* 5, no. 3 (1970): 44–9.
Collini, Stefan. "Hobhouse, Bosanquet and the State: Philosophical Idealism and Political Argument in England, 1880–1918." *Past and Present* 88, no. 72 (1976): 86–111.
Conquest, Robert. *Reflections on a Ravaged Century.* New York: W.W. Norton & Co., 1999.
Cook, Ramsay. "Loyalism, Technology and Canada's Fate." *Journal of Canadian Studies* 5 (1970): 50–60.
– *The Maple Leaf Forever: Essays on Nationalism and Politics in Canada.* 2nd ed. Toronto: Macmillan of Canada, 1977.
Cook, Terry. "George R. Parkin and the Concept of Britannic Idealism." *Journal of Canadian Studies* 10, no. 3 (1975): 15–31.
Cooper, Barry. *The End of History: An Essay on Modern Hegelianism.* Toronto: University of Toronto Press, 1984.
– "Western Political Consciousness." In *Political Thought in Canada: Contemporary Perspectives,* edited by Stephen Brooks, 213–39. Toronto: Irwin, 1984.
– "Taylor-made Canada." *Literary Review of Canada,* February 1996, 19–22.
– "Political Religions in Quebec and the Constitutional Politics of Identity." Paper presented to the Canadian Political Science Association at the Learned Societies, St John's, Nfld, June 1997.
Cooper, Barry, and David Bercuson. *Deconfederation: Canada without Quebec.* Toronto: Key Porter, 1991.
Cooper, Robert. *The Postmodern State and the World Order.* London: Demos, 1996.
– "The Next Empire." *Prospect Magazine,* October 2001.
– *The Breaking of Nations: Order and Chaos in the Twenty-first Century.* Toronto: McClelland & Stewart, 2005.
– "Imperial Liberalism." *National Interest* 79 (Spring 2005): 25–34.
Creighton, Donald. *Canada's First Century.* Toronto: Macmillan of Canada, 1970.
Crook, R.W. "Modernization and Nostalgia: A Note on the Sociology of Pessimism." *Queen's Quarterly* 73 (Summer 1966): 269–83.

Cullen, Bernard. *Hegel's Political and Social Thought.* Dublin: Gill and Macmillan, 1979.

Dahlstrom, Daniel. "The Dialectic of Conscience and the Necessity of Morality in Hegel's *Philosophy of Right.*" *Owl of Minerva* 24, no. 2 (1993): 181–9.

Dallmayr, Fred. *G.W.F. Hegel: Modernity and Politics.* Newbury Park, Calif.: SAGE Publications, 1993.

Darby, Tom. *The Feast: Meditations on Politics and Time.* 2nd ed. Toronto: University of Toronto Press, 1990.

– "On Spiritual Crisis, Globalization, and Planetary Rule." In *Faith, Reason and Political Life Today,* edited by Peter Augustine Lawler and Dale McConkey, 35–65. Lanham, Md: Lexington Books, 2001.

Davis, Arthur, ed. *George Grant and the Subversion of Modernity: Art, Philosophy, Politics, Religion and Education.* Toronto: University of Toronto Press, 1996.

Davis, Steven. "Charles Taylor on Expression and Subject-Related Properties." *Canadian Journal of Philosophy* 18, no. 3 (1988): 433–47.

den Otter, Sandra. *British Idealism and Social Explanation: A Study in Late Victorian Thought.* Oxford: Oxford University Press, 1996.

De Sousa, Ronald. "Seizing the Hedgehog by the Tail: Taylor on the Self and Agency." *Canadian Journal of Philosophy* 18, no. 3 (1988): 421–32.

– "Bashing the Enlightenment: A Discussion of Charles Taylor's *Sources of the Self.*" *Dialogue* 33 (1994): 109–23.

de Vries, Erik. "A Kojèvean Citizenship Model for the European Union." PhD diss., Carleton University, 2002.

Doull, James. "Would Hegel today be a Hegelian? *Dialogue* 9 (1970): 226–35.

Duffy, Dennis. "The Ancestral Journeys: Travels with George Grant." *Journal of Canadian Studies* 22, no. 3 (1987): 90–103.

Dunaway, John. *Simone Weil.* Boston: Twayne Publishing, 1984.

Dunn, John. *Interpreting Political Responsibility.* Princeton: Princeton University Press, 1990.

– "Pursuing the Personal by Way of the Communal." *Times Higher Education Supplement,* 22 January 1993.

Duquette, David. "The Political Significance of Hegel's Concept of Recognition in the *Phenomenology.*" *Bulletin of the Hegel Society of Great Britain* 29 (Spring–Summer 1994): 41.

Easton, Lloyd. *Hegel's First American Followers: The Ohio Hegelians.* Athens, Ohio: Ohio University Press, 1966.

Elder, R. Bruce. *Image and Identity: Reflections on Canadian Film and Culture.* Waterloo, Ont.: Wilfrid Laurier University Press, 1989.

– "The Incurable Optimist." *Literary Review of Canada* 3, no. 1 (1994): 10–14.

Emberley, Peter. "Values and Technology: George Grant and Our Present Possibilities." *Canadian Journal of Political Science* 11, no. 3 (1988): 465–94.

– ed. *By Loving Our Own: George Grant and the Legacy of Lament for a Nation.* Ottawa:
Carleton University Press, 1990.

Emberley, Peter C., and Waller R. Newell. *Bankrupt Education: The Decline of Liberal
Education in Canada.* Toronto: University of Toronto Press, 1994.

Engelhardt, H. Tristram, and Terry Pinkard, eds. *Hegel Reconsidered: Beyond Metaphysics and the Authoritarian State.* Boston: Kluwer Academic Publishers, 1994.

Fackenheim, Emil. *The Religious Dimension in Hegel's Thought.* Bloomington: Indiana
University Press, 1967.

Ferguson, Barry. *Remaking Liberalism: The Intellectual Legacy of Adam Shortt, O.D.
Skelton, W.C. Clark and W.A. Mackintosh, 1890–1925.* Montreal and Kingston:
McGill-Queen's University Press, 1993.

Feuer, Lewis. *Imperialism and the Anti-Imperialist Mind.* New York: Prometheus Books,
1986.

Findlay, John. *Hegel: A Re-examination.* Oxford: Oxford University Press, 1976.

Foldes, Ken. "Does the Solution to Our Present Moral and Political Dilemmas Lie
in the Theories of the German Idealists?" www.bu.edu/wcp/Papers/Poli/
Pol.Fold.htm.

Forbes, H.D. "Trudeau Haunts Us Still." *Books in Canada* 28, no. 1 (1999): 12–
14.

– "The Political Thought of George Grant." *Journal of Canadian Studies* 26, no. 2
(1991): 46–68.

– ed. *Canadian Political Thought.* Toronto: Oxford University Press, 1985.

Fossum, John Erik. "Deep Diversity versus Constitutional Patriotism." *Ethnicities* 1,
no. 2 (2001): 179–206.

Fraser, Nancy. *Justice Interruptus: Critical Reflections on the "Postsocialist" Condition.*
New York: Routledge, 1997.

Freeden, Michael. *Liberalism Divided: A Study in British Political Thought, 1914–1939.*
Oxford: Clarendon Press, 1986.

Fukuyama, Francis. *The End of History and the Last Man.* New York: Free Press, 1992.

– *Trust: The Social Virtues and the Creation of Prosperity.* New York: Free Press, 1995.

Fulford, Robert. "Keeping the Hegelian Spirit Alive." *Globe and Mail,* 1 February
1995, A9.

– "Review of *Hegel: A Biography* by Terry Pinkard." *National Post,* 29 July 2000, B7.

Fuss, Peter. *The Moral Philosophy of Josiah Royce.* Cambridge, Mass.: Harvard University Press, 1965.

Gauthier, David. "George Grant's Justice." *Dialogue* 27 (Spring 1988): 121–31.

Germino, Dante. "Hegel As a Political Theorist." *Journal of Politics* 31 (1969): 885–
912.

Gerth, Hans, and C. Wright Mills. *Max Weber: Essays in Sociology.* New York: Harper and Row, 1946.

Gillespie, Michael Allan. *Hegel, Heidegger and the Ground of History.* Chicago: University of Chicago Press, 1984.

Gillis, Hugh. "Latecomers to the End of History. A review of Shadia Drury's *Alexandre Kojève: The Roots of Political Postmodernism.*" *Literary Review of Canada,* March 1995, 17–19.

– "Review: Intimations of Deprival." *Literary Review of Canada,* July–August 1996, 16–18.

Goetzmann, William, ed. *The American Hegelians: An Intellectual Episode in the History of Western America.* New York: Alfred A. Knopf, 1973.

Good, James A. "A World Historical Idea: The St. Louis Hegelians and the Civil War." *Journal of American Studies* 34, no. 3 (2000): 447–64.

Goudge, T.A. "A Century of Philosophy in English-Speaking Canada." *Dalhousie Review* 47, no. 4 (1967–68): 537–49.

Grant, G.M. "Our National Aims and Objects." In *Maple Leaves: Being the Papers Read Before the National Unity Club of Toronto at the "National Evenings" during the Winter of 1890–91.* Toronto: National Club, 1891.

Green, T.H. *Lectures on the Principles of Political Obligation.* London: Longmans, Green and Co., 1895.

Gutmann, Amy. "Communitarian Critics of Liberalism." *Philosophy and Public Affairs* 14 (1985): 308–22.

Gutting, Gary. *Pragmatic Liberalism and the Critique of Modernity.* Cambridge: Cambridge University Press, 1999.

Hanson, Philip. "George Grant: A Negative Theologian on Technology." In *Research in Philosophy and Technology.* Edited by Carl Mitcham, 1:307–11. Greenwich, Conn.: JAI Press, 1978.

Hardimon, Michael. *Hegel's Social Philosophy: The Project of Reconciliation.* Cambridge, U.K.: Cambridge University Press, 1994.

Hardt, Michael, and Antonio Negri. *Empire.* Cambridge, Mass.: Harvard University Press, 2000.

Harris, H.S. *Hegel's Development.* Vols 1 and 2. Oxford: Clarendon Press, 1972 and 1983.

– "Hegel and the French Revolution." *Clio* 7 (1977): 5–18.

– "Hegel for Today?" *Philosophy of Social Sciences* 7 (1977): 303–10.

– "'And the darkness comprehended it not': The Origin and Significance of Hegel's Concept of Absolute Spirit." *University of Ottawa Quarterly* 52, no. 4 (1982): 444–66.

– "The Hegel Renaissance in the Anglo-Saxon World since 1945." *Owl of Minerva* 15, no. 1 (1983): 77–106.

Hartz, Louis, ed. *The Founding of New Societies*. New York: Harcourt, Brace and World, 1964.

Hauge, Hans. "George Grant's Critique of Modernity: Canadian Refractions of Continental Ideas." *Canadian Issues* 12 (1990): 109–23.

Hobhouse, L.T. *The Metaphysical Theory of the State*. London: Macmillan and Co., 1918.

Hoffner, Frederick. "The Moral State in 1919: A Study of John Watson's Idealism and Communitarian Liberalism As Expressed in *The State in Peace and* War." MA thesis, Queen's University, 1998.

Holmes, Stephen. *The Anatomy of Anti-liberalism*. Cambridge, Mass.: Harvard University Press, 1993.

Houlgate, Stephen. "World History As the Progress of Consciousness: An Interpretation of Hegel's Philosophy of History." *Owl of Minerva* 22, no. 1 (1990): 69–80.

– *Freedom, Truth and History: An Introduction to Hegel's Philosophy*. London: Routledge, 1991.

Howse, Robert. "Kojève's Latin Empire." *Policy Review*, no. 126 (August 2004): 2, www.policyreview.org/aug04/howse.

Hoy, David Couzens. "Hegel, Taylor-made." *Dialogue* 16, no. 4 (1977): 715–31.

Humphrey, Christopher. "The Sage of Kingston: John Watson and the Ambiguity of Hegelianism." PhD diss., McGill University, 1992.

Huntington, Samuel. *The Clash of Civilizations and the Remaking of the World*. New York: Simon and Schuster, 1996.

Hyppolite, Jean. *Genesis and Structure of Hegel's Phenomenology of Spirit*. Translated by S. Cherniak and J. Heckman. Evanston, Ill.: Northwestern University Press, 1974.

Ignatieff, Michael. "Nation-Building Lite." *New York Times Magazine*, 28 July 2002.

– "Canada in the Age of Terror – Multilateralism Meets a Moment of Truth." *Policy Options* 24, no. 2 (2003): 14–18.

– *Empire Lite: Nation-Building in Bosnia, Kosovo and Afghanistan*. Toronto: Penguin Canada, 2003.

– "The Coming Constitutional Crisis." *National Post*, 16 April 2004, A19.

– "Who Are Americans to Think That Freedom Is Theirs to Spread." *New York Times Magazine*, 26 June 2005.

Inwood, Michael. *A Hegel Dictionary*. London: Blackwell, 1992.

Irving, John. "The Development of Philosophy in Central Canada from 1850 to 1900." *Canadian Historical Review* 31, no. 3 (1950): 252–87.

– ed. *Philosophy in Canada: A Symposium*. Toronto: University of Toronto Press, 1952.

Johnston, Donald, ed. *With a Bang, Not a Whimper*. Toronto: Stoddart, 1988.

Jurist, Elliot. "Hegel's Concept of Recognition." *Owl of Minerva* 19, no. 1 (1987): 5–22.

Karmis, Dimitrios. "Cultures autochtones et liberalisme au Canada: les vertus mediatrices du communautarisme liberal de Charles Taylor." *Canadian Journal of Political Science* 26, no. 1 (1993): 69–96.

Kaufman, Walter, ed. *Hegel's Political Philosophy*. New York: Atherton Press, 1970.
– "Coming to terms with Hegel: A Review of Charles Taylor's *Hegel*." *Times Literary Supplement*, 2 January 1976, 13–14.
Kautz, Steven. *Liberalism and Community*. Ithaca and Cornell: Cornell University Press, 1995.
Kelly, G.A. "Hegel's America." *Philosophy and Public Affairs* 2, no. 1 (1972): 3–36.
Kitchen, Gary. "Charles Taylor: The Malaises of Modernity and the Moral Sources of the Self." *Philosophy and Social Criticism* 25, no. 3 (1999): 29–55.
Klinck, Carl F., ed. *Literary History of Canada*. Vol. 1: *Canadian Literature in English*. Toronto: University of Toronto Press, 1976.
Kojève, Alexandre. *Introduction to the Reading of Hegel*. Edited by Allan Bloom and translated by James Nichols, Jr. New York: Basic Books, 1969.
– "The Idea of Death in the Philosophy of Hegel." *interpretation: a journal of political philosophy* 8 (Winter 1973): 114–56.
– *Outline of a Phenomenology of Right*. Lanham, Md: Rowman and Littlefield Publishing, 2000.
– "Outline of a Doctrine of French Policy." *Policy Review*, no. 126 (2004): www.policyreview.org/aug04/kojeve.
Kolb, David. *The Critique of Pure Modernity: Hegel, Heidegger and After*. Chicago: Chicago University Press, 1986.
Krob, Adam. "Hegel's Community: Synthesizing the Romantic and the Liberal." PhD diss., Duke University,1997.
Kroker, Arthur. *Technology and the Canadian Mind*. Montreal: New World Perspectives, 1984.
Kuklick, Bruce. *Josiah Royce: An Intellectual Biography*. New York: Bobbs-Merrill Co., 1972.
Kymlicka, Will. "Liberalism and Communitarianism." *Canadian Journal of Philosophy* 18, no. 2 (1988): 181–204.
– *Liberalism, Community and Culture*. Oxford: Oxford University Press, 1990.
– "The Rights of Minority Cultures: Reply to Kukathos." *Political Theory* 20, no. 1 (1992): 140–6.
LaForest, Guy. *Trudeau and the End of the Canadian Dream*. Translated by Paul Leduc and Michelle Weinroth. Montreal and Kingston: McGill-Queen's University Press, 1995.
Lal, Deepak. *In Defense of Empires*. Washington, D.C.: AEI Press, 2004.
Lamey, Andy. "Francophonia Forever: The Contradictions in Charles Taylor's 'Politics of Recognition.'" *Times Literary Supplement*, 23 July 1999, 12–15.
LaSelva, Samuel. *The Moral Foundations of Canadian Federalism*. Montreal and Kingston: McGill-Queen's University Press, 1996.

Laski, Harold. *Studies in the Problem of Sovereignty.* New Haven, Conn.: Yale University Press, 1971.

Leacock, Stephen. "Greater Canada: An Appeal." *University Magazine* 6, no. 1 (1907): 132–41.

Lee, Dennis. "Cadence, Country, Silence: Writing in Colonial Space." *Boundary* 2–3, no. 1 (1974): 151–68.

Lenihan, Donald. *Freedom and Belonging: An Essay on Liberal Moral Identity.* PhD diss., University of Ottawa, 1993.

Lipset, Seymour. *The First New Nation: The United States in Historical and Comparative Perspective.* New York: Norton, 1979.

– *Continental Divide.* New York: Routledge, 1990.

Luft, Eric v.d. "Would Hegel Have Liked to Burn Down All the Churches and Replace Them with Philosophical Academies?" *Modern Schoolman* 68 (November 1990): 41–56.

Lukacs, John. *The End of the Twentieth Century and the End of the Modern Age.* New York: Free Press, 1993.

Lusztig, Michael. "Canada's Long Road to Nowhere: Why the Circle of Command Liberalism Cannot be Squared." *Canadian Journal of Political Science* 32, no. 3 (1999): 451–63.

Lynch, Richard A. "Mutual Recognition and the Dialectic of Master and Slave: Reading Hegel against Kojève." *International Philosophical Quarterly* 41, no. 1 (2001): 33–48.

MacDonald, R.D. "The Persuasiveness of Grant's *Lament for a Nation.*" *Studies in Canadian Literature* 2 (Summer 1977): 239–51.

MacEachran, J.M. "John Watson." In *Some Great Men of Queen's,* edited by Robert Charles Wallace. Toronto: Ryerson Press, 1941.

MacGregor, David. *Hegel, Marx and the English State.* Boulder, Colo: Westview Press, 1992.

– "Canada's Hegel." *Literary Review of Canada,* February 1994, 18–19.

MacIntosh, D.C. *The Problem of Knowledge.* New York: Macmillan, 1915.

MacIntyre, Alasdair, ed. *Hegel: A Collection of Critical Essays.* Garden City, N.Y.: Anchor Books, 1972.

McKillop, A.B. *A Disciplined Intelligence: Critical Inquiry and Canadian Thought in the Victorian Era.* Toronto: University of Toronto Press, 1979.

– "John Watson and the Idealist Legacy." *Canadian Literature* 83 (1979): 72–88.

– *Contours of Canadian Thought.* Toronto: University of Toronto Press, 1987.

McNeill, W.E. "John Watson, 1847–1939." *Proceedings and Transactions of the Royal Society of Canada,* Appendix B, 3rd series, 30 (1939): 159–61.

McRoberts, Kenneth. *Misconceiving Canada: The Struggle for National Unity.* Toronto: Oxford University Press, 1997.

Mandel, Eli. "George Grant: Language, Nation, the Silence of God." *Canadian Literature* 83 (1979): 163–75.

Markell, Patchen. "Bound by Recognition: The Politics of Identity after Hegel." PhD diss., Harvard University, 1999.

Marks, Jonathan. "Misreading One's Sources: Charles Taylor's Rousseau." *American Journal of Political Science* 49, no. 1 (2005): 119–39.

Martin, Geoffrey. "Justice in the Thought of George Grant." *Canadian Journal of Political and Social Theory* 13, nos 1–2 (1989): 144–61.

Meynell, Robert. "Idealism and Identity: George Grant and Charles Taylor Confront the Modern Dilemma." MA thesis, Dalhousie University, 1998.

Min, Anselm. "Hegel's Absolute: Transcendent or Immanent." *Journal of Religion* 56 (1978): 61–87.

Mommsen, Wolfgang. *The Age of Bureaucracy: Perspectives on the Political Thought of Max Weber.* New York: Harper and Row, 1974.

Morrow, John. "British Idealism, German Philosophy and the First World War." *Australian Journal of Politics and History* 28, no. 3 (1982): 380–99.

– "Liberalism and British Idealist Political Philosophy: A Reassessment." *History of Political Thought* 5, no. 1 (1984): 91–108.

Mulhall, Stephen, and Adam Swift. *Liberals and Communitarians.* Oxford: Blackwell, 1997.

Murdoch, Iris. *The Sovereignty of Good.* London: Cambridge University Press, 1967.

Nemni, Max. "Trudeau's Canada." *Cité Libre* 28, no. 4 (2000): 16–24.

Nicholson, Linda. "To Be or Not to Be: Charles Taylor and the Politics of Recognition." *Constellations* 3, no. 1 (1996): 1–16.

Nicholson, Linda, and Steven Seidman, eds. *Social Postmodernism.* New York: Cambridge University Press, 1995.

Nicholson, Peter. *The Political Philosophy of the British Idealists.* Cambridge: Cambridge University Press, 1990.

Noel, S.J.R. "Domination and Myth in the Works of George Grant and C.B. MacPherson." *Dalhousie Review* 59 (1978): 534–51.

O'Donovan, Joan. *George Grant and the Twilight of Justice.* Toronto: University of Toronto Press, 1984.

– ed. "George Grant Special Edition." *Chesterton Review* 11, no. 2 (1985).

O'Neill, Daniel. "Multicultural Liberals and the Rushdie Affair: A Critique of Kymlicka, Taylor and Walzer." *Review of Politics* 61, no. 2 (1999): 219–55.

Owram, Doug. *The Government Generation: Canadian Intellectuals and the State, 1900–1945.* Toronto: University of Toronto Press, 1991.

Page, Robert J.D. "Canada and the Imperial Idea in the Boer War Years." *Journal of Canadian Studies* 5, no. 1 (1970): 33–49.

Peacock, Anthony, ed. *Rethinking the Constitution: Perspectives on Canadian Constitutional Reform, Interpretation, and Theory.* Toronto: Oxford University Press, 1996.

Peddle, David G., and Neil G. Robertson. "Lamentation and Speculation: George Grant, James Doull and the Possibility of Canada." *Animus: A Philosophical Journal of Our Time* 7 (2002): www.swgc.mun.ca/animus.

Pelczynski, Z.A. *Hegel's Political Philosophy: Problems and Perspectives.* Cambridge: Cambridge University Press, 1971.

– ed. *The State and Civil Society: Studies in Hegel's Political Philosophy.* Cambridge: Cambridge University Press, 1984.

Philosophical Essays Presented to John Watson. Kingston, Ont.: Queen's University, 1922.

Pinkard, Terry. *Hegel's Phenomenology: The Sociality of Reason.* Cambridge: Cambridge University Press, 1996.

Pippin, Robert. *Modernism As a Philosophical Problem: On the Dissatisfactions of European High Culture.* Cambridge: Basil Blackwell, 1991.

– *Idealism As Modernism: Hegelian Variations.* Cambridge: Cambridge University Press, 1997.

Plant, Raymond. *Hegel: An Introduction.* 2nd ed. Oxford: Basil Blackwell, 1983.

Plato. *The Republic of Plato.* Translated by Allan Bloom. New York: Basic Books, 1968.

Pochmann, Henry. *New England Transcendentalism and St. Louis Hegelianism.* Philadelphia: Carl Schurz Memorial Foundation, 1948.

Popper, Karl. *The Open Society and Its Enemies.* Vol. 2, 5th ed. London: Routledge and Kegan Paul, 1966.

Radwanski, George. *Trudeau.* Toronto: Macmillan of Canada, 1978.

Randall, John Herman. "Josiah Royce and American Idealism." *Journal of Philosophy* 63, no. 3 (1966): 57–83.

Rayner, Jeremy. "Therapy for an Imaginary Invalid: Charles Taylor and the Malaise of Modernity." *History of the Human Sciences* 5, no. 3 (1992): 145–55.

Redhead, Mark. *Charles Taylor: Thinking and Living Deep Diversity.* Lanham, Md: Rowman and Littlefield Publishing, 2002.

– "Charles Taylor's Deeply Diverse Response to Canadian Fragmentation: A Project Often Commented On but Seldom Explored." *Canadian Journal of Political Science* 36, no. 1 (2003): 61–83.

Resnick, Philip. *The Masks of Proteus: Canadian Reflections on the State.* Montreal and Kingston: McGill-Queen's University Press, 1990.

Riedel, Manfred. *Between Tradition and Revolution: The Hegelian Transformation of Political Philosophy.* Translated by Walter Wright. Cambridge: Cambridge University Press, 1984.

Riley, Patrick. "Introduction to the Reading of Alexandre Kojève." *Political Theory* 9, no. 1 (1981): 5–48.

Ripstein, Arthur. "Recognition and Cultural Membership." *Dialogue* 34 (1995): 331–41.

– "What Can Philosophy Teach Us about Multiculturalism?" *Dialogue* 36 (1997): 607–14.

Ritter, Joachim. *Hegel in the French Revolution.* Translated by Richard Dein Winfield. Cambridge: MIT Press, 1982.

Rorty, Amelie Oksenberg. "The Hidden Politics of Cultural Identification." *Political Theory* 22, no.1 (1994): 152–66.

Roth, Gunther, and Wolfgang Schluchter. *Max Weber's Vision of History: Ethics and Methods.* Berkeley: University of California Press, 1979.

Roth, Michael S. *Knowing and History: Appropriations of Hegel in Twentieth-Century France.* Ithaca: Cornell University Press, 1988.

Rotstein, Abraham. "Running from Paradise." *Canadian Forum* (May 1969): 26–8.

Rosen, Stanley. "Post-modernism and the End of Philosophy." *Canadian Journal of Political and Social Theory* 9, no. 3 (1985): 90–101.

Schaap, Andrew. "Political Recognition through a Struggle for Recognition?" *Social and Legal Studies* 13, no. 14 (2004): 523–40.

Schmidt, Larry, ed. *George Grant in Process.* Toronto: House of Anansi Press, 1978.

Schmitz, Kenneth. "Embodiment and Situation: Charles Taylor's *Hegel.*" *Journal of Philosophy* 73, no. 19 (1976): 697–723.

Scruton, Roger. *The Philosopher on Dover Beach.* Manchester: Carcanet Press, 1990.

Seeberger, Wilhelm. "The Political Significance of Hegel's Concept of History." *Monist* 48 (1964): 77–96.

Sherrard, Philip. *The Greek East and the Latin West: A Study in the Christian Tradition.* London: Oxford University Press, 1959.

Shortt, S.E.D. *The Search for an Ideal: Six Canadian Intellectuals and Their Convictions in an Age of Transition.* Toronto: University of Toronto Press, 1976.

Sibley, Robert. "The Poetics of Dispossession: Tracking George Grant's Speech-Act." MA thesis, Carleton University, 1991.

Smith, Allan. "Metaphor and Nationality in North America." *Canadian Historical Review* 51, no. 3 (1970): 247–75.

– "Conservatism, Nationalism and Imperialism: The Thought of George Monro Grant." *Canadian Literature* 83 (1979): 90–116.

Smith, Nicholas H. *Charles Taylor: Meaning, Morals and Modernity.* Cambridge, U.K.: Polity Press, 2002.

Smith, Steven B. *Hegel's Critique of Liberalism.* Chicago: University of Chicago Press, 1989.

Soll, Ivan. *An Introduction to Hegel's Metaphysics.* Chicago: University of Chicago Press, 1969.

Srinivasan, Vasanthi. "Freedom, Community and Transcendence: A Comparison of Select Western and Indian Thinkers." PhD dissertation, Carleton University, 1997.

Stillman, Peter, ed. *Hegel's Philosophy of Spirit.* Albany: State University of New York Press, 1987.

Strauss, Leo. *The Political Philosophy of Thomas Hobbes: Its Basis and Genesis.* Translated by Elsa M. Sinclair. Chicago: University of Chicago, 1936.

– *Natural Right and History.* Chicago: University of Chicago Press, 1950.

– *Persecution and the Art of Writing.* Glencoe, Ill.: Free Press, 1952.

– *Thoughts on Machiavelli.* Chicago: University of Chicago Press, 1958.

– *What Is Political Philosophy? and Other Studies.* Chicago: University of Chicago Press, 1959.

– *On Tyranny: An Interpretation of Xenophon's "Hiero."* Rev. ed. Ithaca, N.Y.: Cornell University Press, 1963.

– *An Introduction to Political Philosophy: Ten Essays by Leo Strauss.* Edited by Hilail Gildin. Detroit: Wayne State University Press, 1989.

Taras, David, and Beverley Rasporich, eds. *A Passion for Identity: Introduction to Canadian Studies.* Toronto: ITP Nelson, 1997.

Taylor, Charles. *Radical Tories: The Conservative Tradition in Canada.* Toronto: House of Anansi Press, 1982.

Taylor, Robert. "The Darwinian Revolution: The Responses of Four Canadian Scholars." PhD diss., McMaster University, 1976.

Thomas, Tim. "George Grant, the Free Trade Agreement and Contemporary Quebec." *Journal of Canadian Studies* 27, no. 4 (1992–93): 180–95.

Trott, Elizabeth. "Experience and the Absolute." PhD diss., University of Waterloo, 1971.

– "Multiculturalism, Charles Taylor, and the Idea of Canada." In *Alternative Frontiers: Voices from the Mountain West,* edited by Allen Seager, Leonard Evenden, Rowland Lorimer, and Robin Mathews, 35–50. Montreal: Association for Canadian Studies, 1997.

– "Caird, Watson and the Reconciliation of Opposites." In *Anglo-American Idealism, 1865–1927.* Edited by W.J. Mander. Westport, Conn.: Greenwood Press, 2000: 81–92.

– "Western Mindscapes: A Philosophical Challenge." *American Review of Canadian Studies* 31, no. 4 (2001): 630–45.

Trudeau, Pierre, et al. "An Appeal for Realism in Politics." *Canadian Forum,* May 1964, 29–33.

– *Federalism and the French Canadians.* New York: St Martin's Press, 1968.

– *Approaches to Politics.* Toronto: Oxford University Press, 1970.

– *Memoirs.* Toronto: McClelland & Stewart, 1993.

– *Against the Current: Selected Writings, 1939–1996.* Toronto: McClelland & Stewart, 1996.

– *The Essential Trudeau.* Edited by Ron Graham. Toronto: McClelland & Stewart, 1998.

Tully, James, ed. *Philosophy in an Age of Pluralism: The Philosophy of Charles Taylor in Question.* Cambridge: Cambridge University Press, 1994.

Umar, Yusuf, ed. *George Grant and the Future of Canada.* Calgary: University of Calgary Press, 1992.

Venour, David. "The Political Thought of George Grant." MA thesis, University of Calgary, 1986.

Verene, Donald Phillip, ed. *Hegel's Social and Political Thought.* Atlantic Highlands, N.J.: Humanities Press, 1980.

Vincent, Andrew, ed. *The Philosophy of T.H. Green.* Aldershot, U.K.: Gower Publishing, 1986.

Vincent, Andrew, and Raymond Plant. *Philosophy, Politics and Citizenship: The Life and Thought of the British Idealists.* Oxford: Basil Blackwell, 1984.

Voegelin, Eric. "On Hegel – A Study in Sorcery." *Studium Generale* 24 (1971): 335–68.

Vogel, Lawrence. "Critical Notices: Taylor's *The Ethics of Authenticity and Multiculturalism and the Politics of Recognition.*" *International Journal of Philosophical Studies* 1, no. 2 (1993): 325–35.

Von Riekhoff, Harald. "The Impact of Prime Minister Trudeau on Foreign Policy." *International Journal* 33, no. 2 (1978): 267–86.

Wallace, Robert. "Mutual Recognition and Ethics: A Hegelian Reconstruction of the Kantian Argument for the Rationality of Morality." *American Philosophical Quarterly* 32, no. 3 (1995): 263–70.

– *Hegel's Philosophy of Reality, Freedom, and God.* New York: Cambridge University Press, 2005.

– "How Freedom Requires Community": www.bu.edu/wcp/Papers/Poli/Pol. Wall.htm.

Watson, David. "The Neo-Hegelians in America." *Journal of American Studies* 14, no. 2 (1980): 219–34.

Weber, Max. *The Protestant Ethic and the Spirit of Capitalism.* Translated by Talcott Parsons. New York: Charles Scribner's, 1958.

Weil, Simone. *The Need for Roots.* Translated by Arthur Wills. New York: Routledge, 1952.

– *Intimations of Christianity.* Edited and translated by Elisabeth Geissbuhler. London: Routledge and Kegan Paul, 1957.

Welsh, Jennifer. *At Home in the World: Canada's Global Vision for the 21st Century.* Toronto: HarperCollins Publishers, 2004.

Williams, Clifford J. "The Political Philosophy of Two Canadians: John Watson and Wilfred Currier Keirstead." MA thesis, University of Western Ontario, 1952.
– "The Epistemology of John Watson." PHD diss., University of Toronto, 1966.
Williams, Robert. *Recognition: Fichte and Hegel on the Other.* Albany: State University of New York Press, 1992.
– *Hegel's Ethics of Recognition.* Berkeley: University of California Press, 1997.
Willis, Kirk. "The Introduction and Critical Reception of Hegelian Thought in Britain, 1830–1900." *Victorian Studies* 31 (1988): 85–111.
Wilson, R. Jackson. *In Quest of Community: Social Philosophy in the United States, 1860–1920.* New York: John Wiley and Sons, 1968.
Winfield, Richard. *Reason and Justice.* Albany: State University of New York Press, 1988.
Wolfe, Alan. *Whose Keeper? Social Science and Moral Obligation.* Berkeley: University of California Press, 1989.
Wood, B. Anne. *Idealism Transformed: The Making of a Progressive Educator.* Kingston and Montreal: McGill-Queen's University Press, 1985.
Yack, Bernard. Review of Michael Hardimon's *Hegel's Social Philosophy. American Political Science Review* 89, no. 2 (1995): 486–7.
Zolf, Larry. *Dance of the Dialectic.* Toronto: James Lewis and Samuels Publishing, 1973.

Index